Invoking the Spirits

Invoking the Spirits

Fieldwork on the material and spiritual life of the
hunter-gatherers Mlabri in Northern Thailand

By Jesper Trier

with contribution by Verner Alexandersen

Jutland Archaeological Society

Content

Preface

The interest in foreign cultures and especially the early explorers of Central Asia goes back to my childhood. The desire to follow in their footsteps began to materialise when I visited India and Northern Nepal in 1961. My father was not particularly happy with this interest, but said that it was hardly surprising, since his own father, Gerson Trier, had also studied anthropology. Just like several other political writers around 1900, who had witnessed the appalling conditions of the working class in, for example, England, he thought that the development from 'primitive' societies into world-wide industrial mass production would inevitably lead to capitalism and disaster, only to be avoided by promoting radical socialist ideas. But neither of these two opposite extremes seems to have brought much happiness to the world! Anyway, we know now that even the smallest human societies do not comply with simple rules enabling anyone to predict with certainty future developments, and even less so with those of complex cultures. However, as man has been a hunter-gatherer during more than 97% of his existence, it is still of paramount interest to study these vanishing peoples to catch glimpses of our deeply embedded common heritage, despite the fact that most hunter-gatherers, like ourselves, have adapted to specific environments and conditions.

After a Master of Science in electrical engineering at the Polytechnic University and two years of national service in the Royal Danish Navy, I had saved enough money to undertake an expedition to Northern Nepal in 1964 and again in 1967, resulting in a doctorate in 1972 ("Ancient Paper of Nepal" with the primary aim of determining the provenience of ancient manuscripts from Central Asia). Incidentally, it was while trekking into eastern Nepal that my interest for hunter-gatherers was initiated when staying overnight with a family who kept a 17-year-old young man as their slave. The sad-looking fellow had the unusual combination of Mongoloid eyes but a dark brown skin. Allegedly, he was the only surviving member of a tribe deriving from the inaccessible, jungle-clad and malaria-infested ravines south thereof.

During subsequent appointments, first at the Royal Library and the National Museum in Copenhagen and finally at Moesgaard Museum in Århus, I became personally acquainted with several anthropologists, among others Johannes Nicolaisen, Klaus Ferdinand and Professor Halfdan Siiger, all of whom had performed distinguished fieldwork in Asia. My interest in hunter-gatherers was reactivated during seven months' fieldwork in Northern Thailand in 1970, when my wife and I traced the very shy and elusive Mlabri, after months of stubborn searching in the mountain jungles in the border areas towards Laos. When we finally encountered the Mlabri, after three months of arduous search in many inaccessible mountain tracts, it was a thrilling experience, although communicating with the jungle dwellers was indeed problematic.

The main difficulties turned out to be of two related kinds – language and that the Mlabri were totally unfamiliar with our way of questioning. Eventually it was this challenge, together with their extraordinary life in the jungle and an unspoiled charm, which appealed to us. The spiritual world of the Mlabri is closely related to the secluded jungle, but is rather more complicated than one might think at first. It gradually emerged that they have borrowed many ideas, not only from their present neighbours, but from others far back in time and space. Some of the answers to our repeated questions, such as about an afterlife, may diverge or even reveal contradictions, but on the whole all Mlabri share the same beliefs.

Originally it was the intention, besides giving a general description of their material and social life, to concentrate on translating and explaining their prayers. The manuscript for this was almost ready for printing in 1997, but with much other material having been left aside, it was tempting to incorporate it somehow in the book. However, general obligations and other work only permitted us to return to the material now and then until 2002, when I decided to include the material on the tracing of the other Mlabri groups as well as their migrations during the 20th century; information which otherwise might have been lost for ever (Appendix 1). Furthermore, I wished to add our investigations of their camps (2), tools (3), useful plants (4) and animals (5), the psychotechnical investigations (6) and investigations of their teeth (7). What remains by and large unpublished are our anthropological measurements including weight, fingerprints, blood samples, etc., not only of the Mlabri but for comparison also those of their immediate neighbours the Khon Muang, the T'in and the Hmong, but the main results of these studies have been mentioned in Chapter 1.

Acknowledgements

Many institutions and individuals have been of help to us. First and foremost I would like to thank the Ministry of Science, Technology and Innovation, which has supported most of our stays with the Mlabri, as well as Kronprins Frederiks Fond, Knud Højgaard's Foundation and the Velux Foundation, the Ministry of Foreign Affairs and my own institution, Moesgaard Museum, including its present director Jan Skamby Madsen, who has granted me leave of absence for several months and supported my work in other ways.

A special debt of gratitude is directed to Fellow Researcher, Vicechair UNPFII Ida Nicolaisen, former Rigsantikvar, Professor dr.phil. Olaf Olsen and Professor Anthony Walker, Ohio State University, for their personal assistance and advice, dental surgeon Verner Alexandersen for his contribution on various aspects of the anthropometrical issues, dental surgeon Carl Erik Andersen and Dr. Ryon Sørensen who, with their wives, have helped us in our fieldwork. Other valuable contributions came from the late Charles Vogelius Andersen, a specialist on genetics, who meticulously studied the many Mlabri fingerprints, as well as linguist Uffe Bergeson Larsen, University of Los Angeles, who has made valuable corrections to my own short presentation of the Mlabri language, and Assistant Professor Poul Petersen, publisher Jesper Laursen as well as graphic designer Louise Hilmar for their thorough work and finally Peter Crabb and Anne and David Robinson, who corrected the English manuscript.

However without the generous support from Dronning Margrethes og Prins Henriks Fond, Bodil Pedersen Fonden, Ministry of Science, Technology and Innovation, Højesteretssagfører C.L. Davids Legat for Slægt og Venner, Lillian og Dan Finks Fond, Velux Fonden as well as ØK's Almennyttige Fond it would probably not have been possible to print the book.

In Thailand, many people have assisted us. During the first stay in 1970 we received much help from the East Asiatic Company Assistant Professor Per Sørensen at the former CINA field station in Lampang, and during all the subsequent expeditions from the late ambassador Frantz Howitz and his wife Dr. Pensak Howitz, in Bangkok. In addition to a number of Thai interpreters who endured hardships on our tours, we feel much obliged to the Thai border police as well as Thai farmers and various hill tribes who have joined us and from whom we have received a great deal of help and hospitality, not forgetting the Mlabri themselves whom we feel so strongly about. Last, but not least, I wish to thank my wife, anaesthetic nurse, Birgit Trier, who has taken her turn during all our travels in Thailand – among other things driving our jeep on impossible roads and performing many of the anthropometrical measurements, in addition to taking care of everyone around, not forgetting her help in preparing the manuscript for printing.

Introduction

During a seven month field study in 1970 among the hill tribes of Northern Thailand, my wife and I repeatedly heard rumours of secluded and very shy jungle dwellers, called Phi Thong Leuang ("Spirits of the Yellow Leaves") or Khon Pa (lit.: "people forest") by the Thai, but who call themselves Mlabri (lit. also "people forest"). They had appeared in many widespread localities previously (figs. 5-7), when the jungles were still extensive, but it was only after four months of arduous searching in remote places that we found them in the mountain jungles between the Phrae and Nan provinces (figs. 4-9). At this point, our knowledge of these people was confined to the first descriptions by E. Seidenfaden in 1919 and 1926 and the famous encounter by H. Bernatzik in 1936, but we knew nothing about the two brief visits of the team led by Kraisri Nimmanahaeminda in 1962-63 (see bibliography: Kraisri Nimmanahaeminda and J. Hartland-Swann 1962, and J.J. Boeles et al. 1962-63).

There are different groups of Mlabri in Thailand which, though they may have originated from the same area at some point in time, are now scattered in tiny groups in remote parts of Northern and Northeastern Thailand. We have traced four such groups, in addition to the larger one in the Phrae and Nan provinces. Most of the prayers in this book come from this larger group (abbreviated: Ml) comprising about 140 individuals, whereas the remainder derive from a small refugee group (M3) of 15 individuals, who came from the border area between the Sayabouri province of Laos and the Nan province in 1975. The speech of the two groups is so similar as to be merely two dialects of the same language. However, quite a number of glosses are different, and in describing the Mlabri language (see Chapter 3) I have elected to take my examples primarily from the larger group (M1), also because the prayers mainly derive from that group.

Since January 1977 we have visited both groups regularly and stayed with them in their shelters. Language has been an ever-present problem, especially at the outset, when only a few Mlabri spoke Thai well enough to allow communication through our Northern Thai (Khon Muang) interpreters. There have, of course, been other difficulties to cope with, such as security, owing to the fighting between the Communist insurgents and the Thai border police.

There are only a few detailed descriptions of the ceremonies in the literature, and even less about the prayers themselves. This is also true with regard to the material collected by H.A. Bernatzik and published in his famous but somewhat controversial book from 1938. However, as he met a group of Mlabri near the border between Laos and Thailand with close affiliations to both our Ml and M3 groups, but especially the larger one, some comparisons with our material will be made.

The Field Studies

During our first longer stays with the Mlabri (Ml and M3) in 1976-77, 1978 and 1980 we were eager to collect as much ethnographical data as possible on their traditional life. This was disappearing before our eyes as a result of the transition from a dependence on jungle products to one based on rice, pigs, salt, clothing, iron and tobacco acquired from their Thai or Hmong employers. We also recorded their physical characteristics and took fingerprints, tooth impressions, blood samples, etc. The results of our colour tests, the psycho-technical and the Rorschack tests are no less interesting, for they furnish information which is difficult or impossible to obtain in other ways. Similar data were obtained from the other, though very small, Mlabri-like splinter groups in Northeastern Thailand, as well as from neighbouring hill tribes. *However, the primary aim for our studies has been to record, as carefully as possible, the Mlabri's own oral traditions, while this was still possible.*

Ethical Issues

Some of the various tests performed on the Mlabri were also repeated on the other ethnic groups, such as the blood tests on 10 Hmong, 10 T'in and 10 Northern Thai (Khon Muang). First, we explained the purpose of each particular test to those who wanted to participate, and then they were demonstrated. For example, when taking 5 ml blood samples, medical doctor Ryon Sørensen or my wife first took samples from ourselves. All participants were paid the same – also those who decided not to participate. The Mlabri said afterwards that our needles did not hurt them, as they were so accustomed to all kinds of stings in the jungle.

Already during our expedition 1976 we were advised to give all members of each band visited the same amounts of gifts bought at the local market and following the immediate needs of the Mlabri such as: blankets, clothes, iron bars, tools, rice, tobacco and candles to be distributed by their band leader, including the Hmong pig to be shared by all the members of the band at our departure.

We also told them the purpose of our studies, namely to document both their material culture and their oral traditions in writing, photographs, tape recordings of their speech, the prayers and songs as well as their tools to be exhibited in a big house (Moesgaard Museum) together with similar items from other tribes of the world in honour of their forefathers – an idea they approved of. Actually, they said that as long as our small family was around they themselves would not be harassed by anybody!

During the later stays we also asked several groups of two or three Mlabri to stay with us at our hotel in Nan to improve the tape recordings, especially of the prayers. It was an experience for all of us and may have made way for the Mlabri's dealings with city people subsequently.

Working with the Language

Although word lists were compiled already during our second visit in 1977 and onwards, our primary objective was to concentrate on traditional anthropological aspects of the Mlabri and their culture, while trying to persuade others to work on the language. But for various reasons this did not work out very well. Somewhat earlier we should have realised that without an intimate knowledge of the language, no real understanding of the more intricate aspects of their culture, such as religion, is at all possible. Therefore, during the field studies in 1982,

1987, 1989 and 1994, increasing emphasis was placed on the language, with a view to translating and understanding the prayers in particular.

Usually, we endeavoured to find the most suitable interpreter available in Chieng Mai and then travelled to the Nan province, whence we traced the various bands of Mlabri staying in 4-5 different localities on the edge of the deep jungle, up to 40 miles apart as the crow flies.

Before 1980, only a few Mlabri men were able to communicate satisfactorily in Northern Thai. Our guides often complained that they were difficult to understand, and some even laughed at the Mlabri way of twisting the Thai language. But through the eighties more Mlabri learned to speak Thai, because now they were compelled to work for the other hill tribes in swidden farming, as first the animals in the jungle vanished and then much of the jungle itself.

By 1982 we had obtained a reasonable number of prayers to start with, together with the first tentative translations. Now the Mlabri were asked to listen to the recordings themselves, while the interpreter and I asked them about difficult words and phrases. Usually, I played each prayer twice before running it sentence by sentence and word by word. In order to check the results, to obtain more information as well as not to tire the Mlabri, these sessions were interrupted with a discussion of the content of the prayer. Every two or three hours we had something to eat, smoked, or had a short rest. Just as Kraisri Nimmanahaeminda had been ten years before, we were impressed by the Mlabri's ability to continue hour after hour – young and old alike.

The first translations were not at all satisfactory, although their main content was not too far off, thanks to the many supplementary data obtained in other ways. But by re-transcribing the prayers and asking other Mlabri to explain them again and again, we made some improvements. The tiresome process of correcting the transcripts has been repeated during the last three stays in Thailand, including the rewriting of the short chapter of introduction to the Mlabri language. At least the prayers have now been recorded, and many questions were answered at a time when the Mlabri were still remembering former times and had feelings for their spirits, about whom the great majority are now having serious doubts. Already at the end of the 1980s, the younger Mlabri said that they had never learned the prayers, while more and more of the older men complained that they knew the words but have forgotten their precise meaning.

Staying with the Mlabri, the Larger Group Ml

Before entering into a more detailed description of the Mlabri material and spiritual world, I would like to render a few of our personal impressions when meeting and staying with these remarkable people. Our first brief visit to the forest dwellers in 1970 was one of surprise, because from the tales of the mountain Thai and the Hmong we had expected them to be quite different. However, we could acknowledge many of Bernatzik's observations, but not all his far-reaching statements, and soon we realised that the Mlabri presented a number of intriguing enigmas. Above all, where did these people originate – were they refugees from culture or rather autochthonous, i.e. descendants of some early inhabitants of this corner of the world?

We had traced an old Thai farmer who had occasional contacts with the Mlabri half a day's walk from his village Ban Nagar, Nan province, where the other villagers had only very rarely seen anything of the Mlabri. In an abandoned field in the jungle we met them, four men and two boys of the main group (Ml). At first, I thought they had run away again, but there, just a few steps ahead, they were sitting and waiting for us in the deep grass. My wife and I had been asked to put on local Thai farmer's dress, and in the twilight they did not conceive us to be so different from our Khon Muang interpreter and porters. Still they were very timid, and only after having assuring themselves that we carried no weapons did they relax, as a matter of fact we ourselves have never carried weapons.

The gifts agreed upon with the old Thai twelve days earlier were handed over, and I started to ask a number of questions. But when their spirits were referred to, the leader of the group, Paeng became so upset that he was ready to leave. Fortunately, they stayed on until late afternoon the next day, after having demonstrated some of their skills, such as how they use their spears or build a windscreen. They were smaller and more light-skinned than we had expected, and the triangular, flat face with broad cheekbones fascinated us. They were gentle, softly spoken and good-humoured people, but they did not ask us any questions or show any interest in our cameras or camping utensils, apart from enjoying hearing their own voices from the tape recorder. They seemed to be honest and completely unpretentious.

The next time we visited them was during the winter of 1976-77, and now we were allowed into their camp, where we met also their womenfolk. Some Hmong, who lived nearby and who accompanied us, said that this was also their very first visit to an inhabited camp! The women were sitting two or three close together with their children. Even though it was quite warm, the women shivered from fear. They were dressed in dirty old rags and looked utterly pitiful and solemn. Except for one of the young women, it was impossible to exchange a smile, and when they were addressed they looked away. We learned later that they had feared I would abduct one of the girls.

Only little by little did we gain their confidence, and it turned out to be of great help that we had our daughter Xenia with us, then only four years old, because being a family we did not constitute a threat to them. When my wife really gained access to the women, I still regret that I was too preoccupied, talking with the men, to photograph the women's first encounter with, for example, needle and thread, a mirror or a piece of soap. Their astonishment when weeks of old soot and dirt was removed from their faces was really a thrill, bringing smiles and eager discussion in their characteristic high-pitched way.

After the first two or three stays with the Mlabri we still found it difficult to discuss any abstract matter with them, partly because it was so hard to communicate through our interpreters. Our interpreter had sometimes difficulty understanding the Mlabri way of twisting the Thai language, and again and again I had to ask our helpers not to laugh at the replies, since it evidently hurt the Mlabri.

Naturally, many obstacles come into play when three very different cultures come into close contact with one another, one being that the Mlabri often found our questions odd and perhaps sometimes also impolite. Gradually, we became aware of the fact that they have no need of many of the concepts we consider important. When, for example, we asked them about the terms for "right" and "left" or the numbers above five or six, it turned out after hour-long discussions that many did not know the words. Only later have we come to realize fully that they on their part, have many skills we cannot even grasp, for instance how they 'read' the jungle as they move through it. Precisely here, they may disclose what they themselves claim to be – the people of the forest. When an animal is located they approach it very, very carefully, and suddenly they move extremely fast to kill it within a couple of seconds. But their abilities in the forest are demonstrated in even more spectacular ways, *viz.*

when climbing trees, which they do when hunting, collecting honey, picking fruit or evading danger. On several occasions young lads have demonstrated their extraordinary skills in ascending tall trees in no time, balancing on a branch 30 m up or jumping from one tree top to another, until we have pleaded with them to come down.

However, one important circumstance remains to be mentioned, which I think may present a real handicap, being cultural rather than innate. Children up to 5-6 years of age are almost never instructed by their parents – they learn primarily by imitation. Therefore they have lacked stimulation during the most crucial years of mental development, i.e. those of early childhood. The younger generation actually blames their parents for not having taught them some of the basic skills they need now, after the Mlabri have obtained more contact with the other hill peoples. It should be added that this contact has resulted in a substantial change in the mentality of the younger generation towards much greater interest in the outside world.

Since the eighties, we have stayed in Mlabri camps for several weeks during each visit. We have also joined them in the jungle, while they have been collecting all kinds of roots, herbs, crabs, etc., and they have indeed earned our increasing respect. Their life has all too often been a hard struggle merely to survive. For the few months during which they work for the Hmong each year by felling trees and clearing the land for planting rice, they are grossly underpaid. The rest of the year they drift from one place to another in a sort of half-forest, of which most turned into scrub since the 1990s – all that remains of their former magnificent jungles. During such periods they mainly live on wild tubers and small animals, by doing a few days of work for a farmer or from begging rice. Sometimes they go hungry for several days at a time. This has taken its toll on the infants, in particular.

Right from the outset we liked the Mlabri, as so many others do, the Thai and even some of the Hmong included. Generally speaking, they are not only honest, great individualists, but also good-natured people, being in excellent spirits as long as they have enough to eat. Their favourite food is the fatty parts of pigs. They also like to drink the local whisky, on the few occasions when they can afford it, and most of them are inveterate pipe-smokers, some of the women included. Above all, they openly cherish the opposite sex and marry on average three times in the course of a lifetime. Once, when asking the good-looking wife of a band leader why they do not stick to one partner all through life like my wife and me, she answered with a shy, but very charming smile, that that would really be too dull!

In addition they like a good joke. Two Mlabri men told us during our last visit how they had recently been hunting a big monkey called kwar (stump-tailed macaque), using a wooden stick. However, the beast had suddenly grasped the stick and started beating and chasing the two unfortunate hunters. Even though the Mlabri acknowledged the similarities between man and ape, they were not quite happy with my tale of a kinship. But when I enquired whether kwar is related somehow to the similar word kwʌr "stranger, townsman", they said "perhaps" and could not help laughing.

During later years most of the Mlabri men have visited Nan city briefly, but seldom stay overnight. However, we took a few of them down for a couple of days to improve the tape recordings as early as in 1982. It was interesting to see how easily they adapted to our very different world. They were happy with the abundance of food and all kinds of articles in the market as well as the beds in the hotel, so they could sleep without being troubled by insects. They were also somewhat impressed by the television in their room which they commented on by saying: "Too many people in a small box". Meanwhile, when our interpreter took them to see a Thai film, they said afterwards that they were fascinated by their new experience but they disliked the scenes with sex and bloodshed! Coming down to 'civilisation' after many days with the Mlabri we ourselves often had a strange feeling of being in some kind of madhouse!

The M3 Mlabri

While staying with the larger group in 1976-77 we heard rumours about some Mlabri being kept in a refugee camp somewhere in the Nan or the Chieng Rai province. After having searched for them in several places we found a group in the overcrowded Nam Yao refugee camp, 13 miles to the southeast of Pua. The group consisted of five men, four women and six children. A T'in man, who had followed them all the way from Laos, was a sort of spokesman for them. They were considerably smaller than those of the main group, looking altogether somewhat different. They were shy and spoke in a very low voice. What made the greatest impression was that they were extremely thin and obviously starving. Our gifts of food and clothing were grasped with a faint smile of approval. The Thai camp leader on his part was quite aware of their critical situation and on our request they were allowed to leave the camp in 1977, provided they stayed in the area.

Actually they settled down near a Hmong village, Ban Uy, to be used as cheap labour in the fields. We met them there in 1978, where they stayed together in one large double windscreen half a kilometre from Ban Uy. They were now in better shape, but already addicted to opium due to their unscrupulous Hmong 'owner', who employed them to grow the plant until he was eventually arrested in 1992 and imprisoned for one year. In 1980 the Mlabri were still one group, but soon after they split. Two of their young women married T'in men, since there were no young Mlabri men available, but without having had surviving children in 1994. Since 1976 four of the older members of their group have died, and in 1994 the 11 remaining persons were divided into three groups (only three members remained in 2006). In a few years time they will cease to exist. But still into the 1990s their members enjoyed going out to stay in the cooler jungle during the hot season, when they did not have to work for the Hmong, who at best treat them in a patronising way.

When we got to know them better we enjoyed their kindness and sensible way of answering our questions, although just as the members of the main group, they would seldom tell us anything on their own initiative. On the other hand, they did not go so easily astray when questioned, because they were more used to others, having stayed with T'in villagers, probably since the 1960s.

Our relationship with the small Mlabri has been somewhat one-sided. When asked all kinds of questions, even some intimate ones, they never hesitated to answer, whereas they on their part seldom asked us about our previous whereabouts. Even then we feel a kind of close friendship. After having gone through the prayers with the aid of our tape recorder with old Oy for some days during our last visit, I woke up at night hearing that he was both praying and talking in Mlabri in his small hut next to ours. When I enquired about the matter in the morning, he told us that he had been praying to and arguing with the spirit of his dead wife, and that he missed her very much.

Mlabri seldom openly show affection for one another, except when in love or towards their children. When they are leaving some of their close family or friends they just say: 'ar jak "go first, leave, have left". Or the departing person is followed for a while, and then left without further remarks or gestures, perhaps except for a smile.

The prospects for the Mlabri are somewhat gloomy. One American missionary Long and his wife have tried to make a group of the Ml Mlabri into planters on their estate in the Phrae province, and other aid organisations have suggested something similar, or that they should be workers or make tourist souvenirs! None of these solutions are in accordance with the Mlabri. They prefer to be free and drift from place to place, though it is not easy to see how this kind of freedom can continue, there being hardly any jungle left. It would indeed be a tragedy for themselves and a loss for the region if they are reduced to underpaid, small farmers, as has been the fate of many former Mlabri-like groups of Indo-China. As regards their situation now in 2006 please see p. 57.

15

Fig. 4. Tracing the Mlabri with the aid of the Hmong, with whom they have had more contact than with any of the other hill tribes. However, regular work for the Hmong only began about 1980.

Fig. 5. Mlabri were previously seen in many remote spots of Northern Thailand. This Akha headman shows a spear bought from the Mlabri north of Wieng Pa Pao, Chieng Rai province, around 1950.

Fig. 7. A Khon Muang hunter shows a pointed iron lancehead, which he had found in the jungle west of Pong, Phayao province, Ml 64, 11, not far from a withered windscreen, however he said that he never cought sight of the Mlabri themselves.

Fig. 6. Lissu farmer with a spear he had procured from a Mlabri somewhere north of Mae Ai, Chieng Mai, province, just inside Burma.

Fig. 8. One of two Thai border police men, our protection for eight weeks in 1970, when the struggle with the Communists was still going on in the mountain jungles.

Fig. 9. During the first visits many districts were accessible only on foot, especially in the rainy season, when streams each year turn into torrents.

Fig. 10. Our first meeting with the Mlabri in B. Kum, M1 70, 19: Ut, Ajan, Muang, Paeng and the two boys, Ton and Lat.

Fig. 11. The frame of the windscreen is made of bamboo culms, which are covered with banana leaves. Big pieces of bark are put on the ground to sleep on.

Fig. 12. Women spend most of the day with their children. In front 'e-Si (Som's wife) an old mother (Khamla), daughter (Not) and girl, behind Hramla and to the right Lungsie with a small boy. They were very shy claiming they had never had non-Mlabri visitors before (1977).

Fig. 13. Father Lek sleeps nearest the entrance to the windscreen. The small boy and girl sleep between him and his wife, while a teenage boy stays two metres behind the mother. Lek's son from a former marriage, not included in the photograph, slept five metres further away due to a severe illness.

21

Fig. 14. A band of 16 persons; four couples with their children, occupying four windscreens (1978). They were situated north of B. Bow Hoy in a clearing made by the Mlabri for the Hmong to grow rice in the coming spring.

Fig. 15. In this case, in 1994, all the band's windscreens were joined into one 11 metre-long construction, making communications easier between its 12 members. Ut's band, Hui Yok, Ml 87, 61.

Fig. 16. Single men or women some-times choose to stay in their own, small windscreen; here the widow Thobitoa.

Fig. 17. A platform for four teenage-boys to sleep on. Beneath it, glowing charcoal to keep warm through chilly nights. January 1977, Ban Baw Hoy.

Fig. 18. Once loin covers were made from tree bast (Gaeo and Pha). Now they are made of rags.

Fig. 19. A loin cloth is worn by the old men; previously made of bast, but from the 1960s made of rags. Once women made a skirt of banana leaves when visiting the other hill tribes; now they wear a sarong.

24

Fig. 20. Most Mlabri have a deep nose root and in several the lower part of the face is prognathic. The colour of the hair is matt black, but some of the infants are medium blonde (fig. 23).

Fig. 21. Never having had visitors before, these two woman had put ash on their faces to look less attractive and they were trembling from fear as they thought that we might abduct them (1977).

25

Fig. 22. Patot, by far the oldest Mlabri (1982). He died in 1988, about 75 years of age.

Fig. 23. Infants less than 2-3 years of age are carried by their mother all day, and never left alone. The survival of the children is decisive for the survival of the whole group.

26

CHAPTER 1

Material and Social Culture

The Mlabri first appear in the ethnographical record in the writings of the Danish long-time resident of Thailand, Erik Seidenfaden 1919 and 1926. Seventeen years later, in 1936, they were actually visited for about a week by the German ethnographer Hugo Bernatzik, 1938 (see bibliography). Two decades later they were once more contacted by scholars, but only briefly, notably by the Australian explorers Goodmann and Weaver, 1956. In 1962, and again in 1963, a team from the Siam Society led by Kraisri Nimmanahaeminda (Boeles et al. 1963, pp. 133-201) also visited the Mlabri (Ml).

When we first met the Mlabri (Ml group) in 1970 (figs. 10-11), they were still living exclusively as itinerant forest gatherers and hunters, divided into about eight bands. Occasionally the men had brief contact with other mountain peoples in order to exchange honey and medicinal roots for a little cloth, salt, tobacco and iron. But, because of hostility from many sides, they were extremely shy and afraid of all outsiders. For this reason, their women and children were rarely seen by other mountain peoples until the mid-1980s, when the Mlabri started to work regularly for some Hmong villagers, clearing the forest cover in order to create rice swiddens.

Today, all the Mlabri families are employed for some months every year in swidden work. But, when they are not working for the Hmong villagers, they continue to roam the dense mountain forests, still maintaining the skills necessary to survive as hunter-gatherers. Nonetheless, their traditional social structure and religious beliefs seem to be rapidly disintegrating. This is due to the dramatic changes which have occurred in their environment, so they have come to depend for their subsistence on rice obtained from the Hmong. Since the late 1980s, the Mlabri have received regular visits from various scholars, and a growing number of tourists.

From the literature, as well as from my own travels, it appears that there are Mlabri-like groups with somewhat different languages and cultures, both in Thailand and in neighbouring countries. However, as the prayers in this book derive only from two groups now living in Northeastern Thailand, I shall restrict myself in this chapter solely to these two groups. Furthermore, most of the descriptions will cover the larger group, Ml, which has been better able to maintain its traditional culture than the smaller refugee group, M3. We first traced the latter group in the Nam Yao refugee camp north of Nan city in January 1977. Since then we have stayed with both groups during each visit to Thailand. As regards the other Mlabri groups contacted, see Appendix 1.

Names, Location and Number

Both groups call themselves mla' bri "people forest", but to outsiders they will use either Khon Pa "people forest" or Kha Thong Leuang "aboriginals of the yellow leaves". The last two names are also used by the Thai and Laotians, who also use Phi Thong Leuang "spirits of the yellow leaves". This is, however, strongly resented by the Mlabri themselves. The Hmong call them Magu, while the T'in call them A'yo.

Until 50-60 years ago, Mlabri-like groups were seen in many localities in Northern Thailand, as we know from our own investigations in 1970, when we visited almost every province there, but today they seem to appear only in and around the Nan province (except perhaps, for a small group in the Uttradit province). The Ml group stay in the mountain ranges dividing the provinces Nan, Phrae and Phayao within an area of about 20 by 50 km, whereas the M3 group live about 50 km northeast of Nan city (see map on last page). When we first encountered the main group, they preferred to live above the 600 m contour and to range up to 1,500 m, according to the season of the year, trying to avoid malarial tracts. Nowadays, however, they are compelled to remain further down, while clearing forest for the Hmong swiddens. The Mlabri still prefer to stay together in three or four nuclear families, but otherwise the bands have lost much of their importance since the 1990s.

It seems that most of the Mlabri of the main group have lived within the same general area at least since before the Second World War. Some of their few old people, as well as some Hmong informants, have related to us how the Mlabri, crossing the River Mekong, arrived in Thailand from Laos around 1916 when their oldest member, Patot (about 70 years old in 1982), was still a child. This would, incidentally, have been only a few years before we have the first reports of the Mlabri living in the Nan province.

Before 1919, when Seidenfaden wrote about them, we have almost no information about the relationship between the Mlabri and their mountain and lowland neighbours. Several old Northern Thai people told us in 1970 that these forest dwellers were once more numerous than they are today and the old Mlabri themselves say that when they were young they primarily maintained connections with Khamu, T'in and Lue mountain peoples. But, since the arrival of Hmong, contacts have been more numerous with the latter two than with other hill peoples. The Mlabri have also interacted for quite some time with a number of hill-dwelling Thai communities. Elder Mlabri recount that, for many years, they would approach only small and distant Hmong and Thai villages to procure the most essential goods, such as iron, salt and tobacco. Mountain Thai, as well as the Mlabri themselves, have told us how they would take great precautions not to be seen before entering a Hmong or Thai settlement, sending one or two emissaries ahead of the main party, never staying overnight and almost never taking their women and children along with them.

Such limited interaction between the Mlabri and their neighbours continued well into the 1970s. But then they were compelled to seek regular work from these neighbours because first the forest animals began to disappear and, subsequently, the forest itself. From the middle of the 1980s nearly all the Mlabri have worked as underpaid farm workers for 2-4 months a year, mostly employed by the Hmong, who often treat them harshly. In 1982 the population of the M1 group was around 140, comprising 20 more or less related families and eight bands, thus with an average of 17 individuals per band. The small group, M3, consisted of three families of 18 persons in 1975, which was reduced to only 11 persons in 1994.

The M3 group originates from the Sayabouri province of Laos, east of Nan province and just across the border, where they say some of their people probably still remain. In 1964 Michel Ferlus recorded a short list of Mlabri words in a village in westernmost Laos (see Rischel, 1995, p. 35). Our old friend Oy of the M3 group told us in 1978 that his first encounter with a westerner took place near Ban Nam Min and Ban Nam Hung, when he was still young. This fits well with the recordings of Ferlus, for Oy was born around 1938.

He claims that before the flight from their former habitats there were about 22 families. This would correspond to more than a hundred individuals, showing how rapidly their number is being reduced. His group then consisted of four families of 28 persons, and his own band had eight members. We have recorded the names of 36 individuals in Oy's group, but in 1994 only 10 persons remained in Nan, while three had moved down to Uttradit. Two young girls have married T'in men, while others have married Thai farmers, demonstrating how the disintegration of the Mlabri groups may also have taken place during the 19th century.

However, prior to 1970 the Communists and the Thai forces were already involved in a bitter guerrilla war, which took place across the frontier, squeezing the population of that area from both sides. At some point it was necessary to remove most of its people, and in 1975 more than three thousand Hmong, Yao, T'in and Lue, with the remains of our M3 group, were ordered to move down to Pua, until they were put into the Nam Yao camp six months later. Oy explained that many of his group died during these years, and when we found the Mlabri in the overcrowded camp in 1976-77, they were starving and in a critical condition, both physically and mentally. Fortunately, not long afterwards they were allowed to stay outside in the jungle about 20 km east of the camp, where we met them again in 1978.

Actually, back in 1970 we traced another group of Mlabri (M2) in Sa (south of Nan city) consisting of three males, two women and two children, and now and then we have come across remains of other groups, one as far away as in Loei province in 1982 (M5). In 1989, when staying in Ventiane, we were taken some hours by car to visit a young Mlabri woman, (M6), and on this occasion we were told that there are Mlabri-like people in several provinces of Laos, although their alleged number, 800 persons in 1970, seems to be exaggerated.

From time to time we have also obtained some evidence of Mlabri (M7) living on the Laotian side of the border facing Nan province. One group is called kri', both in Laos and by people living close to the border in Nan. Our two groups (M1 and M3) call them tha lae or kha lai people "people striped", since they have stripes of dots on their upper arms and legs. These Mlabri live mainly by hunting with their spears, for the jungle is still dense on the Laotian side. The Hmong at Don Prai-wan in Nan describe them as very fierce, adding that until recently they would sometimes kill and eat humans, but this is not unanimously supported by those few old Hmong and T'in who have actually met them. From what we have been told, they do not seem to be much different from the Ml group.

Meanwhile, a reliable Thai informant told us that he saw a Mlabri-like person on the Laotian side of the border in 1988. The person was quite heavily built, had but a skin over his shoulders, carried a spear, and probably belonged to a hostile group. This somewhat conflicting evidence raises the following questions: Are there more than two ethnic different groups of Mlabri on the other side of the border and was our Ml group just as peaceful 50 years ago as it is today? The two oldest men of the M3 group told us that whenever they met the "spear group", previous to their flight from Laos to Nan, they had to give whatever these Mlabri (which they called Kha hawk (Th) "the spear people") wanted, or they themselves would be in great trouble.

Today, some of the Ml bands have also disintegrated, and one day the group endogamy will no longer exist when the Mlabri have become dispersed in small hamlets as underpaid day labourers, like similar villagers of Thai, T'in and Lue (Lü) origin. This will be the end of a long process. Thus in remote parts close to the Laotian border we have found many individuals resembling the Mlabri; indeed Thai officials here told us that some mountain tracts hold people who were properly Mlabri only a few generations back.

In the following pages the two groups are dealt with separately, but to avoid unnecessary repetition, descriptions and data of the smaller group M3 are referred to only insofar as they differ substantially from those of the bigger group. As regards the other Mlabri-like groups in Thailand and adjacent areas, see specifically Appendix 1 with conclusions pp. 233-244.

Physical Characteristics

The larger group, Ml

Physically, they are mostly well built but of short stature. Men average 155 cm in height, women 144.5 cm. Women and children often have alveolar prognathism (fig. 20) and frequently an oblong occiput (back of head) and adult males have heavy brow ridges. Both sexes have broad cheekbones and a flat nose, imparting a typically triangular impression to the face. Skin colour is light brown and of a faint reddish tinge when living in the forest, but it becomes very dark brown when exposed to sunlight for long periods during work in the Hmong swiddens. Teeth are quite small and could be said to be "Melanesian".

Blood samples show a very complex pattern, perhaps due to isolation and genetic drift within these small, purely endogamic groups. Of the 80 persons we have investigated (belonging to various Mlabri groups, but mostly to the Ml group) all but two were of blood group A rh. pos. The few exceptions were AB rh. pos. Fingerprints were thoroughly investigated by the late Charles Vogelius Andersen, a real specialist in this field. They are extremely interesting and characteristic, with almost no arches and with one of the highest percentages of whorls recorded anywhere in the world (men: whorl 84.7%, ulnar loop 14.7%, radial loop 0.4% and arch 0.2%; women: whorl 76.6%, ulnar loop 22.6%, radial loop 0.4% and arch 0.4%).

As so often with the application of anthropometry to the peoples of Indo-China, the results of our measurements of the Mlabri are far from easy to interpret. However, taken together, they resemble those obtained from some of the Orang Asli groups living much further south, along the Thai-Malaysian border. The anthropometric data, along with certain cultural evidence (see pp. 244-245), suggest that the various Khon Pa groups are probably descendants of an ancient Austroasiatic population (Sundadont), once dominant in mainland Southeast Asia, but subsequently broken up by massive Palaeo-Mongoloid penetration from the Chinese landmass, a question to be further discussed in the Appendix 1 and 7.

Whereas our own anthropometric investigations, such as the fingerprint patterns, show beyond doubt that there are old traces of Negrito blood among the Mlabri (see also G. Olivier 1968, p. 38, who indicates widespread localities on the Indochinese Peninsula where there have been reports of Kha Thong Luang (Th)). I suspect that the apparent Mongoloid genetic influence on their physical characteristics is of relatively later date (see also J.B. Birdsell 1975, p. 521). The Mlabri themselves say that there is a religious ban against their marrying into other mountain peoples. On the other hand, we do have on record the case of a Mlabri group trying to kidnap a girl from an isolated upland Khon Muang village community (p. 197) as well as rapes of Mlabri girls by the other hill people.

Despite periods of hunger, young Mlabri usually seem quite healthy, especially when subsisting on their varied forest diet. But there are only a few old people. This is the result of the depredations of tuberculosis, malaria, various parasites, tigers and snakes, and even simple fatigue, resulting from having to change camp site so frequently. In the case of serious illness, Mlabri mostly relied (before 1990) on the help of the spirits, making offerings of meat and roots. For curing head-, tooth- and stomach ache they use a number of special roots and herbs (ca 'a, etc); for burns they may apply squirrel blood, and they also know of an extract from a red mushroom to treat earache. One band applied a special kind of large, white larva, called tom kan, to wounds, probably because it contains antibacterial substances; see further in Appendix 5, p. 286.

Until recently, the Mlabri very seldom washed themselves, but dried away their sweat near the fires. Due to this lack of sanitary habits, it is not surprising that they suffer from skin diseases, stomach ulcers and worms. With increasing contacts to the outside world, infectious diseases may present an even more serious threat to the Mlabri, who may not have sufficient resistance to them. This has already happened with tuberculosis which killed many Mlabri from the 1960s onwards.

The small group, M3

The number of individuals is too small to furnish any statistical data, but the five adult men averaged only about 146 cm in height, and the five women 135 cm, when they were measured in 1977. Otherwise, they resemble the larger group in most respects with regard to their physical dimensions, teeth, etc. However, the colour of their hair is more matt black and resembles that of Laotians in general. But they have the same general blood group pattern as Ml, less extreme fingerprint patterns, but still quite a large number of whorls (67%). Without going into detail here, it can be said that the two groups seem to be physically related, although not so much as to have originated from one common group within several hundred years. The members of the small group are less healthy than those of the larger one. This is mainly due to a heavy addiction to opium, which they grow for their Hmong employers! Incidentally, none of the members of this group had holes in their ears, but we were told that it was the custom previously when they were told that otherwise the spirit of their parents would cut off the "thick of the ear", i.e. their ear lobes.

The Band, its Camp and Social Organisation

The information in the following pages relates primarily to the main group, but most of the details probably also applied to the small group perhaps only half a century before. Until about 1975, the Mlabri lived almost exclusively as wandering forest gatherers and hunters, organising themselves socially and economically on the basis of bands numbering between 12 and 25 people. In fact, these people still maintain their band organisation when they are living by themselves in the forest. A typical (and actual) example of a band is that consisting of an old man (a widower), his two married sons and their wives, a male friend and his wife, and the children of these three couples, two of whom had already married each another, see drawing below. Thus, this band comprised three generations and 18 individuals, and occupied five windscreens, in which its members lived for about a week before moving on.

Windscreens are built by erecting two posts in front, which carry a lintel, and another two sticks behind to support the back of the screen, which is covered with

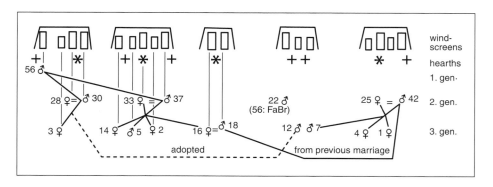

Fig. 24. The social organisation of a typical Mlabri camp with indication of each member's position, sex and age (* major and + minor hearths).

banana leaves or palm fronds (fig. 11). Inside, the floor is covered with palm leaves, rags or large pieces of the outer bark of trees. As the floor always slopes slightly downwards, the Mlabri set up a wooden plank to act as a foothold in order to prevent the windscreen's sleeping occupants from sliding down into the fire in front of it. The fires are used for cooking, for warmth during chilly nights and mornings and, not least, to keep off wild animals and insects (figs. 25-26). It takes two or three people about forty minutes to erect such a windscreen and prepare the necessary underlay of bark or banana leaves.

Different kinds of windscreen are made from small versions to larger ones. A small screen measures about 1.5 by 1.7 m and can accommodate two people, while the larger ones may measure 2 by 5 m and have seven occupants. Sometimes a band constructs just one long windscreen, actually 3-5 windscreens built together, and once we came across a band staying in a 13 m long 'double' windscreen, a sort of primitive longhouse. However, in the dry season all the band members sometimes just sleep under small trees. For further details of the various types of windscreens and their construction, please consult Appendix 2.

In the example of an actual Mlabri band fig. 24, the (relatively) old widower shares a windscreen with one of his married sons, and the latter's wife and daughter. Another son, his wife, their son and two daughters occupy the second windscreen. A third shelter is occupied by a young childless couple, he being the son of the male friend by a previous marriage and the wife the granddaughter of the old widower, while a male friend, his wife and two daughters stay in the fifth windscreen. Finally, in the fourth shelter sleep three unmarried males: the brother and son of the male friend and the adopted grandson of the old widower. The five windscreens have, between them, ten hearths; but only four of these are major hearths used for cooking as well as for warmth. The unmarried males eat with their respective families and so do not keep a major hearth in front of their windscreen.

Within the windscreens, men occupy the flanks to protect the others against wild animals, women are positioned so as to care for their small children, and the older boys and bachelors are stationed somewhat away from the married couples. While relative positions may change when the band moves to a new camp site, the general occupation pattern remains consistent with these practical and psychological concerns! The size of a band depends very much upon circumstances. Successful men tend to have large families and may attract other families as well as individuals to their band. On the other hand, during the dry winter months, when food becomes increasingly difficult to find, a band may split up.

Already during our first visits we were told that individuals, especially when they are on their own in the jungle for two or more days while hunting for example, make a nest of branches in a tree in which to sleep, using vines to secure the construction as well as themselves. Somehow it seemed incredible, but during our last visit more Mlabri from both groups said the same thing, adding that once single women sometimes went to sleep in a tree ('ɛm tul lam "sleep point (up) tree"), even while staying with their own band, from fear of wild animals or from being sexually exploited by the young, unmarried men. In times of danger, old and young alike may take to the trees, and young men climb acrobatically very high and are able to jump from one tree top to another!

There are no shamans or other religious leaders among the Mlabri. Within the band, the only real authority is that held by parents over their children and, to a lesser extent, by grandparents over their grandchildren. When extra-familiar disputes do arise, these are settled by the older men. If two men are having a dispute, they may select a trusted person to judge the case. If judged guilty, the wrong-doer has to leave the band for ten days, but when he returns the matter is not to be mentioned again by anyone. An important mechanism for social control is the Mlabri principle that any individual or family is free to join another band. Theft is very rare among the Mlabri, and anything resembling violent crime almost non-existent. But we did record an interesting case, said to have occurred long ago, of a respected person killing a troublesome band member while out on a spurious hunting expedition.

Although all Mlabri are related to each other in one way or another, there are no traces of a comprehensive 'tribal' organisation, but once there were annual meetings of all the bands (see also G. Young 1962, p. 72, and Ahmad, 1981). Such meetings allowed the younger generation to find marriage partners and the older folk to exchange news. There have also been occasions quite recently when two or more bands have camped in close proximity to each other. Thus, in January 1977, we came across four bands, totalling 65 people, who were all camped close together. However, there is no proof of the former existence of an institutional chief of all the bands, but we have heard of persons who almost obtained such a status, such as phaw ("father" Th) Phan, who died around 1970.

Fig. 25. Fires around the windscreen during chilly nights also keep off wild animals and insects. Sometimes the temperature fell to only a few degrees centigrade in the high mountains, when everyone suffers.

Fig. 26. Paeng and Gaeo's families eating together, the older members ensuring to that the small ones get their share.

Fig. 27. Gui arguing about the size of the coveted pig with our Thai guide – a tiresome business as we were often greatly overcharged by the Hmong villagers.

Fig. 28. At least some Hmong treat the Mlabri well. Here Paeng laughing at one of Lao Toa's jokes.

34

Fig. 29. Mlabri women (here Thobi-toa) were scared of any passing stranger well into the 1980s, in this case a dubious looking Hmong man.

Fig. 30. How jealousy starts! Women continued until the 1980s to breast-feed their children for 2-3 years during which time they only rarely had another child.

Fig. 31. When by themselves they are more relaxed and enjoy a good laugh.

Fig. 32. In the old days Mlabri men visited the other mountain peoples to beg for food and rags. In return they imitated Thai (or Lao) dancing (1977), but they never stayed over-night in any village. From left to right: Lek, Gui, Pang, Pha, Pat, Ta.

Figs. 33-34. Their own style of dancing is to jump from one leg to the other while singing in counterpoint and clapping their hands.

Figs. 35-36. We had some difficulty in making the women sing for us, which they did in a high pitch, but we have never seen them dancing.

Fig. 37. Gui with his huge pipe soon exhausted my Dunhill tobacco! Most Mlabri, including some women and children, smoke.

Fig. 38. Our Danish friend, Dr. Ryon Sørensen, helped us by collecting the many anthropological measurements and blood samples.

Fig. 39. Patot (fig. 22), the oldest of all Mlabri. Using his hands for digging roots has turned them into claws.

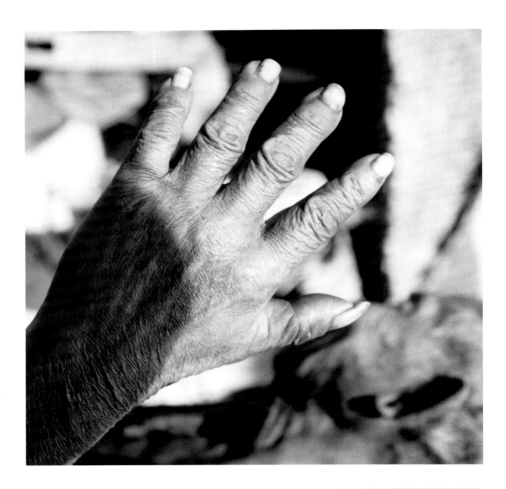

Fig. 40. Casts of 24 Mlabri teeth impressions were obtained in 1982 together with photographs, here of a 45 year old man, showing no signs of carries. Previously they had no access to sugar.

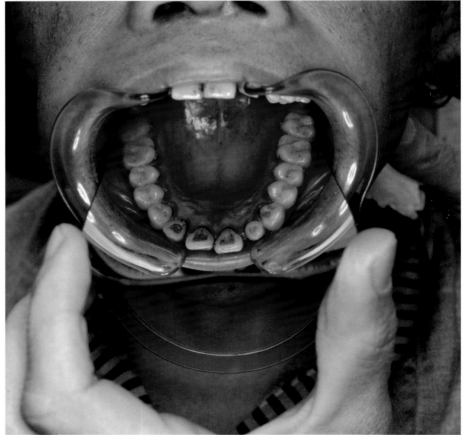

40

Fig. 41. For identification of the ca. 140 members of the main group (MI), fingerprints of almost everyone were taken in 1982. Incidentally, these have specific patterns resembling those of of the Semang Negritto (Orang Asli).

Fig. 42. Drawings of humans were obtained from many members as in this case from Suk, who we were told was stabbed to death in 1988 by his Hmong employers. At first the Mlabri drawings did not resemble humans – rather the dismembered parts of the body, but later on more and more so (see also Appendix 6, e.g. Suk's drawing fig. 162).

Fig. 43. Colour tests from about 50 Mlabri showed that everyone had a perfect colour vision, indirectly proving that they were born to be – what they themselves claim – jungle dwellers, as families with such dificiencies would sooner or later disappear.

Fig. 44. Discussing names and properties of animals. From left to right: our Khon Muang interpreter, a Hmong, a T'in and a Mlabri (Oy, of the small group M3); each a quite typical representative of his ethnic group.

M3 group

This small group also lives under windscreens, but sometimes they utilise a different construction in which the windscreen is placed on a slope with a small platform made of split bamboo, with the front of the platform raised about 60 cm above the ground. At the rear, where the roof almost touches the ground, there is also a small fireplace. To our surprise, a platform of only about 2.0 x 1.8 m could accommodate three adults and two children (fig. 70). I doubt whether any other people make do with so little. It was added that previously the camp was situated in the deep jungle on a slope for fear of elephants, that the fire was kept low, and that everyone had to talk in a very low voice. Thus, incidentally, was still their habit in 1994.

Mating, Marriage and Divorce (M1)

Most of what is said in this section applies only to the main group, for data are lacking with regard to the smaller one (M3), owing to its limited number. Small boys and girls have little direct contact with one another, because in day-to-day life the girls stay with the women, and the boys either play with one another or join the men. However, when they are thirteen to fourteen years old, they meet when bands meet, or a boy may even be permitted to visit another band for the very purpose of finding a girl. Young people are allowed to have premarital sexual contacts, and select their own partners.

Marriage is an informal affair. When a young couple wishes to get married, the boy's father talks with the girl's parents, who normally give their consent, provided the couple are not close kin. Nowadays the boy does not need to give the girl's parents anything, but he will usually offer them some meat, rice, tobacco or cloth. Formerly he had to bring home some animals, a wild pig or a deer, to show that he was able to support a family of his own. If the girl's parents did not agree to the match, it would not occur. Also, we were told, if the boy and girl met a tiger just before their intended marriage, this was traditionally considered such a bad omen that their union would not take place. Mlabri almost never marry non-Mlabri. They believe that, if this happens, the rain will not come and everything will dry out. We have but one recorded incidence of a Mlabri man marrying a Hmong girl, by whom he had a son. After a short while she died, probably from poisoning by her own family, the Mlabri said. The child was then adopted by that family.

We have repeatedly asked about marriage ceremonies, and always received the same answer, that there are neither ceremonies, nor any celebrations connected with marriage. The young couple simply make their own windscreen, usually in the camp of the girl's band to ensure that the man treats her well. It is our experience that, quite often, the marriage is not a success, and the couple therefore split up, even if the girl is already pregnant. If, however, the two get along, and provided they have a child, they receive a joint name from the elder men in the band, indicating the start of a new nuclear family (see p. 48). But still no ceremonies are held. After six months to one year, the couple moves to the band of the husband, where they usually remain more permanently.

All Mlabri of whom we have enquired have mentioned something in particular, primarily different kinds of meat, which should be avoided during pregnancy. Surprisingly, nobody in either group of Mlabri seems to know about the nine-month period of pregnancy! When a woman is about to give birth, she walks a short distance downhill from the camp, accompanied by another woman who assists her in various ways, by making a couch, fetching wood and boiling water. The umbilical cord is cut with a bamboo knife, and the afterbirth is buried, although previously it was left in a tree. Interestingly, this roughly corresponds to the disposal of the dead; now they are buried at the request of the Hmong, but formerly they were either laid on a pile of leaves or placed in a tree.

The new-born child is placed in a small depression covered with banana leaves. Nowadays the midwife, together with the mother and child, returns to the camp on the same day, but previously the party had to move away from the camp and stay there for three days, possibly because they feared that the spirits of the camp might harm the soul of the new-born. At first the Mlabri denied that they ever suffered miscarriages or gave birth to deformed babies, until one of our most reliable informants suddenly announced that deformed or very weak infants were killed and buried by the mother. Even one of twins were killed once, because Mlabri believed (as do some of the Lissu for instance), that twins share only one soul, and as a matter of fact we have no examples of twins in our records. In 1994 a Mlabri woman denied that practice, and explained that if a woman gives birth to twins, it is because she likes to eat twin fruits!

When we first met them they said that husband and wife abstained from sexual intercourse for 1-2 years prior to and after a birth to avoid secondary infections. Intercourse was also avoided during menses as they explained that the woman's blood will cause her husband to sicken. During these periods the husband could have sexual intercourse with other women in the band (e.g. an unmarried sister of his wife – see further below), but the Mlabri are, not surprisingly, reluctant to discuss such matters. Now the pre- and post-natal taboos are no longer upheld by the Mlabri after having settled and working more permanently for the Hmong, exactly for the reasons explained below by Geoffrey Benjamin, 2002, pp. 36-37, see pp. 247-250.

Our informants did not agree on the details concerning the naming of a new-born child. Possibly this is because it is done in slightly different ways. From our own records, we find that some children do not have other than a nickname before they are five to six years old. The bringing up of children is just as uncomplicated as most other aspects of Mlabri life. They do not receive much instruction, but simply learn by imitation. Parents cherish their children, whom they may scold but almost never beat. The children, for their part, treat their parents with considerable respect.

Almost all Mlabri marry several times; women usually three times, men up to five times. The average length of a marriage is about six years. There is, however, a wide range of variation in the length of marriages. The reason why some men may marry more times than women is due to the fact that women stop marrying and having children before they are 35 years old, whereas men generally live longer and often marry women much younger than themselves.

A man may leave his wife at will, and a woman may leave her husband if he is often sick and cannot take proper care of his family. But she is also able to leave him for other reasons. A Mlabri man told us that if a man stays away for some days, perhaps while hunting, and comes back to find his wife with another man, he will possibly firmly ask the intruder to leave. But if the latter refuses to move, the cuckold may ask his wife to choose between them, and if she prefers her new partner, the husband has to leave her. A divorced single person or a widow or widower often occupies his or her own windscreen (fig. 16).

Divorce is not so serious a matter among the Mlabri as with most other peoples, because it is so common and, importantly, there are almost no material belongings to share. Moreover, they have only a few things that cannot be produced by anyone, such as bamboo containers, a wooden spear or a knife. However, the children may present a problem. Small children stay with their mother until they are 6-8 years old, when their father might insist on having them, because they theoretically belong to him. But the present rules are not as rigid as they used to be, and teenagers now choose where to stay. If small children lose both parents, they are adopted, often by their grandparents or an uncle.

Probably due to the absence of social stratification and a freedom to believe as they like, there are fewer tensions and jealousies among the Mlabri than among the Hmong, Thai or most other peoples. A divorce may be painful enough, but for a woman the problem may be eased by the fact that there is a surplus of men, and consequently she will not stay single very long, provided she is under 35 years old. Single men for the very same reason sometimes have to wait until they find a partner. From the rapid turnover of some marriages, with nobody being left alone, we realise that two couples might exchange partners, in which case the more powerful man and woman make their choice, while the two others have to agree more or less willingly.

Kinship Terms

Kinship terms reflect basic economical, social and psychological features of any society, and kinship is generally of greater importance among hunter-gatherers than in modern societies, because they have no other sources of support than their families and friends at times of crisis. The kinship terms of the Mlabri Ml and M3, the two groups from which the prayers were recorded, are basically rather alike, just as their languages are probably merely two dialects of one and the same precedent language.

Usually the Mlabri do not use anything but simple words for family relations when they are among themselves in the band, such as uncle, aunt, father, mother, boy (for brothers), girl (for sisters) and child, or for anyone (kɔm, km.bɛr), as also related by Bernatzik, 1933, p. 167. The main group also use their Mlabri family name or local Thai or Hmong first names (see p. 43), while the members of the smaller group have only a local name. In the main group, most adults know all the adult members of the other bands and, approximately, their inter-relationships. This is rather important, because they have to ensure that marriage does not take place between close kin. That this is not an easy task can be seen from the fact that we have sometimes come across individuals who could not even remember the name of all their own children or their changing Mlabri names.

Therefore, there are various means to help the Mlabri trace their relationships. The approximately 140 members of the main group are divided into 8-10 family lines, mostly named after their grandparents, and they are again subdivided into 2-4 nuclear families. All adults know to which of the family lines they belong, but perhaps to make sure that no mistakes are possible, the adult men had at some point (before 1970) their particular family code tattooed on their underarm, the tattoo also served to ward off danger. The nuclear family name (see p. 43) is, furthermore, aimed at making it possible for the family and their friends to trace descent, although only two generations back. This has, on the other hand, the advantage that the descendants are thereafter more free to select spouses, which is always a big problem because of their small number and traditional incest taboos.

In the following, the kinship terms are described in some detail for the main group (Ml), but more briefly with regard to the small group (M3), as they were treated in detail by Rischel, 1995, pp. 115-131. However, the differences are not very substantial, although they are interesting in other respects, for example for linguistic purposes, showing how a language develops in small isolated hunter-gatherer communities.

The kinship terms have, for several reasons, caused us considerable trouble. At the beginning we often made the mistake of confusing two quite different situations, i.e. when the Mlabri describe how they will address a relative, as against how the relationship is referred to when talking to somebody else. Secondly, there are only a few, fixed lexemes. Rather, the Mlabri utilise additional terms of various kinds to furnish the particular sort of information needed in a given situation. Therefore, when the researcher tries to record a specific term, different answers are often the result, even though the question is correctly interpreted. This is clearly demonstrated when two informants are employed at the same time, who often present two different, but adequate, responses to the same question. Thirdly, when it comes to more complex family relations, some of the Mlabri, not knowing the proper terms themselves, try to explain using a long sentence, exactly as other people and we ourselves would do! Furthermore, they have adopted kinship terms from their immediate neighbours, the Thai, T'in and Hmong.

The work of collecting kinship terms began in 1976-77, but due to language difficulties I have hesitated in dealing with our data until they became more transparent. In despair, because of the seemingly conflicting answers, various approaches were tried. On our last visit, we collected all the available bottles in the camp, from large ones for foodstuffs down to small medicine bottles. These were then arranged so as to visualise different kinship situations, the large bottles representing grandparents and the smallest their grandchildren. This actually helped in keeping everyone involved on track.

In Mlabri there are no more than a dozen, single kinship lexemes. However, these constitute only a part of the kinship system, as already mentioned. By adding different groups of modifying words, it is possible to address any kind of relationship, still keeping in mind that this can be achieved with differing results, hopefully meaning the same! I believe that the Mlabri themselves seldom use complicated kinship terms. These are rather obviated by the context.

With few exceptions, kinship terms cover only three generations: the preceding, the speaker's own and the subsequent one. Already here we are faced with another characteristic of the kinship terms (known from most other languages), namely that one term often covers two or more different relationships. Although such pairs mostly represent the same number of steps away from the reference point, there may be practical reasons for their very existence. As seen from the kinship terms, page 46, both an uncle and grandfather are called ta', and aunt and grandmother ya'. Therefore these pairs are somehow equals, or equally close and important for the child in question. This is manifested in several ways, and clearly if the child's parents are dead or have divorced, because then it is usually adopted either by the grandparents or by an uncle and aunt.

J. Rischel, 1995, p.122, mentions another example concerning parents-in-law, who are called mɤm thaw ("father grey") and mɤ' thaw ("mother grey"), in other words respectful terms, placing such persons almost on a par with one's own parents. The main group use the same terms, and the importance of parents-in-law is demonstrated by the fact that without their consent no first marriages of their girls are accepted, and after the marriage has finally taken place, the young man will live together with the parents-in-law sometimes for one or more prolonged periods of time.

KINSHIP TERMS AND COMPONENTS, MI & M3
(If terms are used by only one of the two groups this is indicated)

Relative generation	
ta' ya'	Grandparents or ancestors, also 'at tio yong, lit. former male relative.
ta'	Grandfather and uncle, also 'at jyong, mɯm (father). When spoken to, may use chak.km ruc "old" (MI), chak.km.ruyh "uncle" (M3)
ya'	Grandmother, aunt or use mɣ' "mother" or droy (MI), hnya' (M3)
mɯm, jyong	Father (also young "male"), mɣ' mɯm or 'uy yong "parents".
mɣ'	Mother, or 'uy "female or mɯhl (hmal mɯhl "female tree spirit") Father's relatives 'at mading, mother's relatives bn.hnɛ' kɔm.bɛr. Fa El Br: ta' Fa El Si: ta' Fa Yo Br: ding Fa Yo Si: ding (M1) Mo El Br: ta' Mo El Si: ya' Mo Yo Br: ding Mo Yo Si: ding Fa El Br: ding Fa El Si: mɯlh Fa Yo Br: roy Fa Yo Si : mɔn (M3) Mo El Br:ding Mo El Si: mɯlh Mo Yo Br: mɔn Mo Yo Si: mɔn (Fa: father, Mo: mother, El: elder, Yo: younger, Br: brother, Si: sister).

Words indicating sex & approx. age	
To be combined with terms of related-ness to speaker or third person (see below). Used for same as or younger generation.	Married man: bung dong. Man before marriage: baw, Young man: ta roc (MI), ta reng (M3), burbur, biot (M3) Son: 'ɛw la met. Title of senior woman: ya female or woman: mənying, hnrɣ' (M3) Young married woman: gɯtgɔt (MI), Young girl: lungguh, Daughter: 'ɛw mənying. Baby: lɛng. New-born baby: 'i cho (M3). Child: 'ɛw, dik theng (M3) Child of relative or somebody else: kum.ɔm (no indication of sex).

Relative age	
ding (-bɛr)	"Elder", term used alone or as modifying lexeme, applied to anyone older than oneself, e.g. an elder brother or sister, or the elder of two or more of one category, such as father's or mother's elder brother or sister, or an elder brother- or sister-in-law, e.g. elder brother: ding yong, or 'ay plus the local name (e.g. 'ay Ton), elder sister: ding lungguh, ding mɯlh (MI and M3), ding 'uy (MI), ding 'ɯy (M3) while ding bɛr often denotes a married elder sibling and his or her spouse.
roy (-bɛr)	"Younger", term applied for anyone younger than oneself or the younger of two or more of one category, such as a younger brother or sister, a younger brother- or sister-in-law, or a cousin, e.g.: Younger brother: roy yong. roy bɛr denotes a married younger sibling and his or her spouse, as well as nephews and nieces; da droy is also a younger sibling (M3).
ding roy; roy ding	"Brothers, sisters, relatives" of the same generation as the speaker.
no' (-bɛr)	"Grandchild, nephew, niece" (can also use 'ɛw and roy).

Relations by marriage:	
Elder generation and their children.	Father & mother-in-law: mɯm thaw, mɣ' thaw, one source che bɣr. Fa El Br: ta' & wife: ya' & children: nong (MI) Fa El Si: ya' husband: ta' roy Mo El Br: ta' wife: ya' roy Mo El Si: ya' husband: ta' roy Fa Yo Br: ding wife: ding nɔ Fa Yo Si: ding husband: ding nɔ' Mo Yo Br: ding wife: ding nɔ' Another informant said Fa Yo Br: ding bɛr, his wife: ding khy. When inquiring about the terms for in-laws of one's elder generation we obtained conflicting answers. But it seems that both the MI and M3 just called their father and mother in law, respectively mɯm thaw ("father grey") and mɣ' thaw ("mother grey"), see next page.

Same-as generation	El Br and El Si: ding, their spouses: ding bɛr and children nɔ'.
	Yo Br and Yo Si: roy, their spouses: roy bɛr, and children nɔ'.
	(Elder) brothers-in-law: 'ay + local name.
	(Elder) sisters-in-law: 'uy (M3 ɯɣ) + local name.
	Sister-in-law: also yo', e.g. elder sister in law: yo' ta bɛng (MI)
	Rischel 1995, says p. 123: 'ɛw bɛr may be used to denote one's child and the child's spouse, more specifically 'ɛw yo' is an in-law, while yo' bɛr is the couple. One may also use 'at bɛr (lit. the second one) for the daughter's husband or 'ot 'ɛw di (g)lang (my daughter's husband).
Half siblings	In-laws (+half-siblings?) 'em roh (ruc) husband of one's niece. (M3)
Divorced family members	Divorced man or widower taram, their children 'e ram.
	Divorced woman or widow: yaram, their children 'e ram.
Younger generation	Daughter 'ɛw 'uy, her husband khɣy and their children nɔ'.
	Son 'ɛw yong, his wife 'ɛw man (man married in Thai) and their Children: nɔ'. (MI)
	Oy (M3) called his daughter-in-law nɔ bɛr, and she called him ta' while he called his son-in-law 'ɛw yo' and the young man his father-in-law rum hluak. Oy's wife called her son-in-law roy mon, and her daughter-in-law: bɛr. For grandchildren they used the general gloss: nɔ'. (M3)
Groups of people	(MI only):
kɔmbɛr kɔmti	Boys and girls
kɔmbɛr kɔmcingto	Men and women (cing to "meat body" or syn. for "women") Men and women, when addressed (mother's relatives bn.hnɛ'
bn.hnɛ' kɔmbɛr	kɔmbɛr) if father's relatives specifically 'at ma ding).
grok kɔmbɛr	Relatives, group of Mlabri, the band.

Two very important and much used modifiers indicate whether the person in question is older or younger than the speaker or the person referred to. It is the so-called ding-roy system, which can be applied to almost any member of the Mlabri, including in-laws. Among siblings ding and roy indicate whether the person in question is respectively older or younger than the speaker (e.g. ding ta' roc "elder brother"). With regard to parents, the two terms are used to indicate whether an uncle or aunt is older or younger than one's own father or mother. But as these modifiers are relative terms, they are also used when talking about someone's relatives.

A further qualifying lexeme is to indicate the gender. Besides, the lexeme usually holds a vague indication of the absolute age, e.g: 'ot ma ding baw "my elder young man" (12-16 years). Among the Mlabri MI there is steady competition to attract the best partner; for women until about their forties, but for men into their fifties. Strength, reliability and a sense of humour are the qualifications most appreciated by both sides. Material objects are correspondingly much less valued than among other peoples, because they do not give the owner much improved status. However, the provider of food for everyone has a high status.

The last important group of kinship terms comprises those covering relationship through marriage. One way is to use a kinship term + bɛr "two" or "friend", which may mean the couple, but more often his or her spouse (e.g. nɔ' bɛr "daughter-in-law"), ding bɛr and roy bɛr are an older and younger sibling respectively plus his or her spouse, but both expressions may be used when talking to or just referring to two persons of the same category, such as two older or younger sisters.

Just as among siblings, there is a hierarchy among the family members of some of the other categories of relatives, especially when these members are spoken to. This system has, incidentally, contributed to confusing our recording. Thus an uncle older than one's own father or mother, is addressed ta' and his wife ya', and likewise an aunt older than one's own father or mother is ya' and her husband ta'. However, uncles and aunts younger than one's father or mother are addressed ding; they are in away, 'degraded' to the same level as one's elder brother and sisters. An elder brother and his wife are both ding, and a younger brother and his wife are both roy. A person's elder sister is ding; her husband is bɛr or ding bɛr. The younger sister is roy, but her husband is roy baw (also 'degraded', because baw is usually an unmarried person).

A son-in-law may be called roy khoy (Ml) while a daughter-in-law is 'ɛw man. There also seem to be traces of hierarchy in the terms for the spouses of uncles and aunts, and with regard to their children (being of the same generation as the speaker). Incidentally, it is of interest to note that (elder) females-in-law are called muɩh (Ml and M3), but this is an old word and now not often used. There is another term for in-laws. I have roh bɛr brother-in-law, but according to Rischel, 1995, p.123 roh may also be used to refer to half-siblings (both Ml and M3), adding that it may indicate a further step away from the speaker. Half-siblings are very common among the Mlabri, due to the usually many marriages (three or more) during their lifetime.

Especially with regard to terms for males and females, there are considerable differences between the two groups of Mlabri (Ml and M3). In Mlabri M3 a baby is called 'i cho, a girl not yet married is hn.rɣ', when married ma ying (from Hmong), while a woman is pɛl or bɛl (or muɩh). A boy is hnum (or baw from Thai), a young man is biɔt ("soft"), however a married man bung dɔng ("swollen penis") as in Ml. But on the whole, kinship terms of the two groups of Mlabri are organised in the same way. The differences are not at all surprising, when we consider the small size of the M3 group and the resulting lack of necessity for using kinship terms among the few members left today. What counts even more is that the two groups have shunned each other as long as anyone can remember and they left their former common territory about 90 years ago. During this time they have been exposed to different ethnic groups, in the case of the M3 group, especially to the T'in. We have been told that for several years prior to their escape to Thailand in 1975 they worked for the T'in, and since about 1988, two of their girls have been married to T'in men.

Naming System, Kinship Diagram, Preferred Modes of Marriage and Statistics (Ml)

All the Mlabri Ml are related to each other in some way or other. Of the 140 persons alive in 1982, we have obtained data for about 130 individuals; their names and those of their parents and their approximate age, in addition to anthropometric measurements. Moreover, information on 40 of their deceased family members was recorded. Based on this material, the various family lines and their inter-connections were established to produce two kinship diagrams, figs. 45-46. However, these contain only 108 individuals or 76% of all the members alive in 1982, as it is already rather complex to represent a three-dimensional network for these in a two-dimensional diagram.

Due to the frequent inter-marriages among the Mlabri they are not always able to remember their complicated family relations, especially when marriages took place many years ago. As a result there are bound to be some mistakes and omissions. Even with these reservations the main issues of the Mlabri naming and marriage modes can be demonstrated quite satisfactorily in the diagram.

Local Names and Mlabri Names

All Mlabri more than 12-14 years of age have one, or sometimes two, local Thai or Hmong names, given to them by their employers. These names are rendered with initial capital letters, whereas the Mlabri names are given with small letters; they are just combinations of short syllables and do not refer to anything in particular, such as animals or plants. Mlabri names have a social rather than a religious function and are seldom referred to in the prayers. When a couple marry and their first child is born, the three of them acquire a joint name, e.g. luan. To distinguish them from one another, the father is ta luan (ta' "uncle"), the mother is ya luan (ya' "aunt"), while the child is 'e luan if a boy and 'i luan if a girl; however 'e luan is often used for both sexes and 'i for babies.

The family name has a different function for the father, the mother and their children. Thus the family name indicates the father's formal ownership of his children, whereas his wife is not his property and, consequently, if he dies she reverts to her maiden name. If the parents divorce and they are not too old, they will usually not wait very long before remarrying, whereby each of them will obtain a new different family name, whereas the children from the divorce will keep their parents' joint name, so they will always know which partnerships to avoid in the future. Both full and half siblings usually maintain close connections throughout life; they often stay together in the same band and support one another. To further confuse the whole naming system, many families have nicknames for their children as well as for their dogs – short easy ones like chɛ' "much", thɛh "good", wet "chamelion".

Function of the Naming System

Before discussing various modes of marriage, a few examples from the kinship diagram fig. 45, and 46 are mentioned to show how the naming system works. Phan, once the famous leader of the Mlabri (uppermost left side), was married at least three times, when he was called respectively ta prec during his first marriage, and then ta mɛt where he had Patot, no. 66, and ta man where he had Gaeo (elder one, deceased before 1980). Gaeo was called 'e man when he was a child, but received the name ta bet when he married for the first time. Therefore his wife was called ya' bet and their children 'e bɛt, Muang no. 9 and Ajan no. 44. Then Gaeo divorced and married Thobito, no. 85, and they received the family name to (ta' to respectively ya' to) including their daughter 'e Saeng, no. 2. Gaeo's last marriage was to Aila, no. 45, 25 years his junior, and their family name became krɯl to, and thus their children 'e krɯl to.

Thobito, no. 85. After her marriage with Gaeo, she married Po and they had the family name gu gup, because he had been adopted by the family of Gu, no. 50. But a few years later Po died (around 1980) without having had any children. She was then called ya' to bɯl, or widow, but returned later to her maiden name 'e to, and became the industrious supporter of her daughter 'e Saeng, no. 2, and this young woman's children with Paeng Taw, no. 1 (see diagram fig. 46).

Marriage Modes

Like most other people, the Mlabri endeavour to avoid marrying close kin. Thus we have not encountered marriages between full siblings and seldom between aunts and nephews and cousins. But as we shall see there are bound to be some exceptions among this small endogamous group, where suitable mates are not always available. This was the case with Som, who was about 27 years old when we met him near Ban Baw Hiew in 1977. He went out on a long trek from Nan to the Pha Yao area when he was 16 or 17 years of age (around 1967) with the sole purpose of finding a girl among the Mlabri, also from Nan, who had stayed in the high mountains behind the famous lake for quite some years until their return to Nan in 1967-68 (see also p. 223).

Traditionally, it was the custom for the man to ask the parents of the girl for permission to marry her whenever a marriage was to be established. Since the 1980s this tradition has only been followed in respect of a girl's first marriage or in case of somewhat odd marriages.

Usually first marriages start when girls are 14-16 and boys 15-17 years old. Women marry up to three times, until they are 35-37 years of age, while men remarry until they are about 50 and up to four times, but seldom more. The latter was the case for the above-mentioned Som, who was said to have married six times prior to 1994, when he was 44 years old. But then even the sexually tolerant Hmong also said that some of the young Mlabri were indeed now becoming somewhat promiscuous.

Strong and greatly respected persons were selected as band leaders, and they attracted both males and females, producing family lines, among others that of deceased Phan, ta prɛc and his son Patot, no. 66 (who died in 1989 at the extraordinary age of 77), deceased Gaeo (father ta' man), Ut, no. 231, Paeng Taw, no. 1, and Pha, no. 6. However, only the first-mentioned Phan was said to have attained virtually the status of a leader for all the Mlabri, Ml. Band leaders are often the ones who have had most wives and married rather young girls, as for example Paeng Taw, who was about 47 years old, when he married 'e Saeng, no. 2, when she was only 16 years old. But we have no records of women marrying much younger men.

There are some special and even preferred kinds of marriages, where quite close family members marry each other; thus Kham (no. 6, the younger brother of Patot, no. 66) married the daughter of his father's first wife, and Mun, no. 74, likewise married the daughter of his father's fourth wife Lit, no. 68. It also happens that a man marries his stepmother when his father dies, especially when they are about the same age, as we have seen in the case of Ajan, no. 44, and we have one further example. Two young men from one family line may also marry two sisters from another family line, see no. 52 and 53. It also happens that a man is first married to one of two sisters and then to the other, and in the same way a girl may marry two brothers, one after the other.

Let us consider a more special case: Gu, no. 50 (above the centre of the diagram fig. 46) married Lot, no. 51, some time ago, but he complained of her son from a former marriage, Long II, no. 49, who was now living with Gu's daughter, Dung, no. 52. Long said however: "When Gu can take my mother, I might as well take his daughter." Eventually Dung and Long married each other.

We have met only few cases of polygamy. Thus Som and Gui (Pang) each had two wives in 1990 (not included in the diagram). When Gui's elder wife died, he took her

Age of induviduals	70-60		60-50		50-40		40-30		30-20		20-10		10-0		Total
Sex	♂	♀	♂	♀	♂	♀	♂	♀	♂	♀	♂	♀	♂	♀	
In the kinship diagrams	1	0	3	0	9	5	5	14	6	12	11	13	19	10	108
Also recorded	0	0	1	0	1	2	2	0	1	3	4	2	2	4	22
All Mlabri Ml recorded (alive in 1982)	1	0	4	0	10	7	7	14	7	15	15	15	21	14	130

Age and sex distribution for each of the decades between 0 and 70 years (reference 1982).

daughter from a former marriage as his second wife. However, these cases are unusual and disapproved of. When a man wants to have a second wife he has to obtain permission from the parents of his first wife. It should also be mentioned that it would be impossible in Mlabri society for a woman to have two husbands as happens, for example, among the Lissu.

The Mlabri have always claimed that there is a religious ban on sexual relations with the other hill people. But after having recorded several cases of love affairs and rapes involving the Mlabri and the Hmong, Khon Muang, Khamu, etc. I can say that such relations are not approved of and most often end in disaster. Nevertheless, they have taken place once or twice every ten years or so during the last fifty years. In the kinship diagram fig. 46 we have the following examples: Paeng Taw, no. 1, claimed that his grandfather was a Khamu (see under the centre of the diagram), and Paeng's first wife was allegedly abducted and was never found again, even though he searched for her for several months. Lat, no. 228, bottom right corner, had a boy Lao Daeng no. 88 (fig. 46) with a Hmong girl, who was killed in 1979 by her Hmong family, who brought up the boy. Yet another sad case is that of Suk, no. 43, upper right corner, who also had an affair with a Hmong girl. This enraged her family so much that they stabbed Suk to death!

Khon Muang farmers in turn relate that there have been incidents in which their girls have disappeared and perhaps been abducted by the Mlabri. This may be true, considering the case from Tagor, see p. 197. These cases are interesting from another point of view because it strongly suggests that both the Mlabri and the other hill people, including the Khon Muang, may but rarely have exchanged genes.

Statistics

The kinship diagrams fig. 45 and fig. 46 cover the main part of those Mlabri encountered in 1980 and 1982. These are listed in the first line of the table below,

whereas those Mlabri not included in the kinship diagrams, or those who were recorded in 1987, 1989 and 1994, are listed in the second line, but only persons alive in 1982 and with their age adjusted to that year. To arrive at the total number of Mlabri Ml living around 1982, we only have to add those we have met with only briefly or just heard about, probably no more than 10-12 persons living beyond Po King, bringing the total to about 140 persons.

Age group 0-20 years

Regarding juveniles, there are 50% more of each sex relative to men and women of 20-50 years of age. Actually, many infants were not investigated during our first stays, as the Mlabri often tried to hide them for fear that we would take them. Quite a few of these children were not recorded subsequently as they died within months or a few years of being born. Thus a higher birth rate than previously observed seems to have compensated for the fact that many infants still died in the early 1980s due to the unsanitary conditions after their birth as well as various children's diseases and malnutrition.

Age group 20-50 years

The decrease in number especially of males is mainly due to about ten men having been killed by the other hill tribes during the 1970s and 1980s.

Age group 50-70 years

As expected, there are not many Mlabri exceeding 50 years of age, in fact only five men and no women. This is simply because the latter are worn out due to their many obligations during the changing of campsites every seven to ten days under difficult circumstances, bad weather, lack of food, etc., while snakebites, malaria, tuberculosis and landmines were also responsible for some early deaths. These, however, affected both sexes.

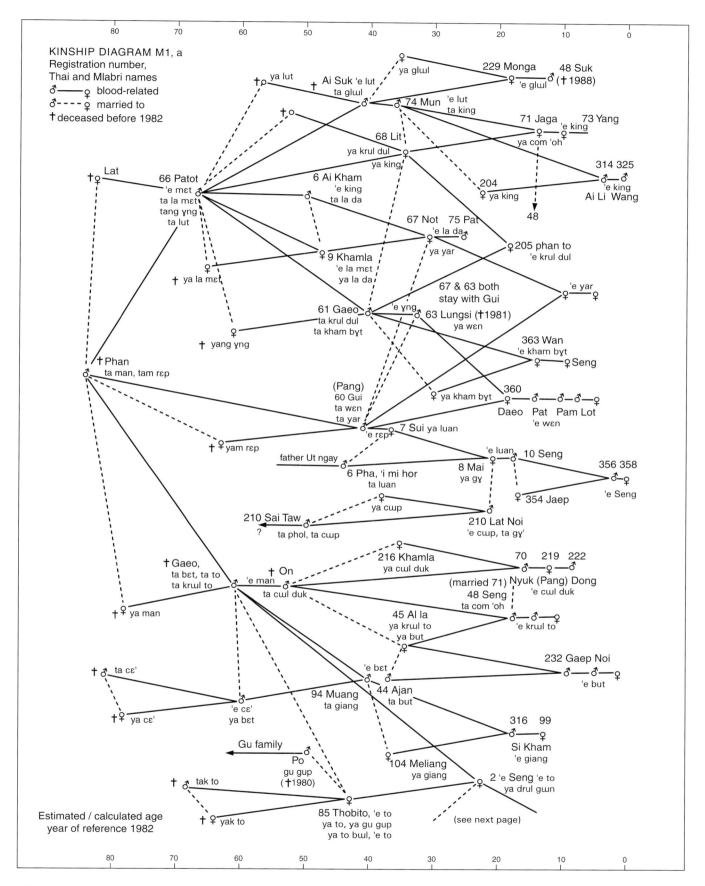

45. *Kinship diagram M1, a.*

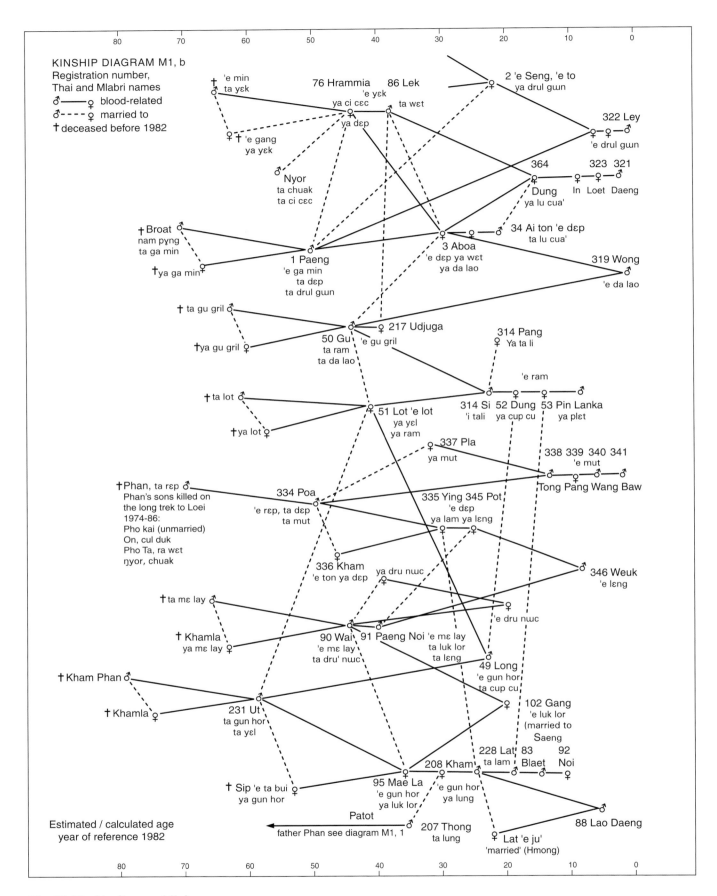

Fig. 46. Kinship diagram M1, b.

Quite apart from the above-mentioned problems there is also the question of inbreeding. There is evidence both of the hereditary blood disease *thalasemia* as well as of hereditary disconfiguration of the facial crania, *dysostosis mandibulofacialis*. See for example the fine contribution on "Mlabri Anthropometric Genetic, and Medical Examinations" by Gebhard Flatz in Kraisri Nimmanahaeminda, 1963, pp. 162 and 167-168, based on examinations of 18 Mlabri men. However, thalasemia is seldom homozygous with the Mlabri, but heterozygous, viz. the milder form, and we have only seen disfigurement of the facial bones in four men of Patot's family, namely Kham, no. 6, Mun, no. 74, Pat, no. 75 and Thong, no. 207. There are two reasons for these problems not being more pronounced. As mentioned earlier, severely handicapped misfits are not allowed to or cannot survive in the harsh environment of the Mlabri. The other reason is that the Mlabri probably derive from a previously larger population in Laos, as one of our Hmong informants told us, see p. 195. He claimed that there were more than 300 Mlabri who came into the borderlands between Laos and Thailand at the beginning of the 20th century. Moreover, we have recorded a number of instances where Mlabri girls have been raped by Lao, Khamu and Khon Muang farmers, which has also meant that inbreeding is genetically less critical.

Still, the Mlabri (Ml) are inter-married to such an extent that the members are very closely inter-related. Our anthropometric measurements also show very clearly, especially the blood tests and the fingerprints collected from about 2/3 of all the M3 we have met. Due to their limited number, and the old taboo among the main group against marrying any non-Mlabri, they constitute almost one super family. In addition to some interesting physical characteristics, this also has several social consequences. For example, they have experienced an extraordinarily high degree of self-determination and have neither religious leaders nor very dominant band leaders.

Kinship Diagram, Naming System and Marriage Modes, M3 group

The diagram on fig. 47 shows the members of the M3 group we have met, as well as some of their deceased family members, a total of 35 persons. Only those investigated anthropometrically, etc. have numbers in the diagram, nos. 22-31.

At first glance it appears that they use only common local names, probably because there are so few members left and there is therefore no longer any need to use Mlabri names similar to those of the Ml group to avoid mistakes when mating. However, a closer inspection reveals that there are residues of their former Mlabri names, especially among the elder, deceased members: 'e ta, 'i chɛ', 'i ca, 'e cha.hen, ta' oh and perhaps also with Kit's two children 'e lot and 'e lit. Just like the language itself, this points to the common origin of the two groups of Mlabri, Ml and M3.

As regards marriage modes, the M3 Mlabri seem, to a very great degree, to have observed the same customs as those of the Ml Mlabri. As with the Ml group, we also have an example of a man, Oy no. 25, who first married the elder of two sisters, and when she died he married the younger sister. However, as related by Kit, no. 25, couples normally stick together and only remarry if their companion dies. The lack of proper mating is demonstrated in the case of Oy's two daughters, nos. 30 and 23, who are both married to T'in men, but have remained childless so far (1994). Also Syom was said to have come from somewhere else.

It may be relevant at this point to repeat what Oy related, that their group had 120-130 members when they lived in Laos when he himself was a child. But the members of the present group split away from their original group due to lack of food, and trekked slowly south-west and then westwards into the undemarcated border areas between Laos and Thailand around 1960. However, during the next ten years tension built up between the two countries and fierce fighting developed around the border. As a consequence, the Thai authorities removed about three thousand hill-tribe people, including Oy's group, to the refugee camps in Chiang Kham and Pua, both 90 km north of Nan city, in 1975. During this operation and the difficult life in the overcrowded refugee camps, about one third of the Mlabri Ml died from stress, starvation and disease. When we met them in 1976-77 there were 14 persons left, in 1994 only nine and in 2007 but three.

Contrary to the Ml group, almost all the deceased members of the M3 group seem to have died from natural causes (starvation included). Thus Oy said that one of his grandparents was killed by a tiger, and his mother Pim died because her baby got stuck during birth, while Won probably died from a kidney disease. Kham (Oy's father), Sum, Thong, Nyu, Peua and Dyom died from fever (including malaria), Sa of cancer and Noan

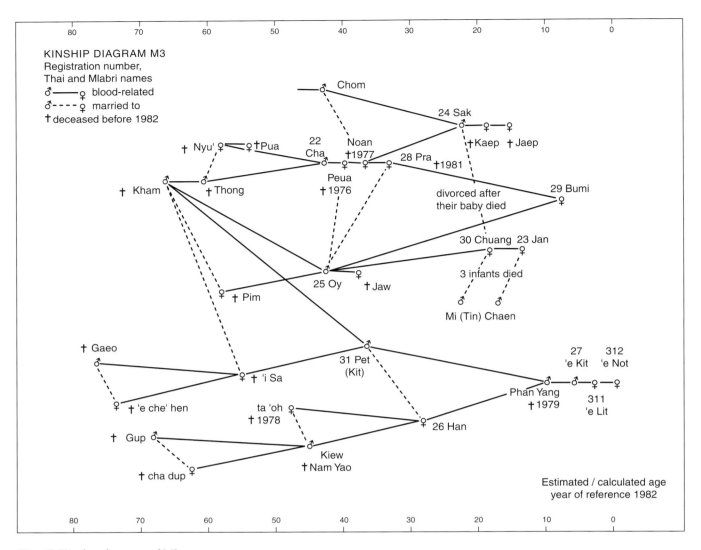

KINSHIP DIAGRAM M3
Registration number,
Thai and Mlabri names
♂——♀ blood-related
♂----♀ married to
† deceased before 1982

Fig. 47. Kinship diagram of M3.

from eating rotten fish. Soon, the M3 Mlabri will have vanished completely and people may wonder that such modest food collectors ever lived on the formerly jungle-clad mountain slopes where now only rice paddies and wasteland with shrubs remain!

Economic Life, Tools, Arts and Daily Routine, Ml Mlabri

The main diet of the Mlabri traditionally consisted of easily obtainable game animals, like bamboo rats (fig. 50) and other rodents, along with forest plants: yams, various roots, bulbs, vegetables and fruits. Previously, wildlife was much more plentiful and Mlabri hunters sometimes killed larger game such as deer, gibbon, bear and wild pig (fig. 49). Birds were also a part of their

traditional diet – along with large spiders! They seldom ate fish, being afraid of deep water, but they did catch small fish, crabs, turtles and frogs in or near streams. The men also climbed tall trees, at great risk, in order to hunt smaller animals, to collect honey and beeswax (fig. 52). Previously they went hunting quite far off, sometimes staying away for several days or even weeks at a time with the aim of finding new mountain tracts for their band to exploit.

According to early reports on the Mlabri (see Seiden-faden, 1919, p. 50), and as also mentioned by the people themselves, their traditional weapons and utensils were made entirely of wood and bamboo. The Mlabri claim never to have used objects of stone. But since at least the 1950s they have also used iron spearheads and digging tools (fig. 57). They would obtain the iron from other hill peoples and were able to forge it using a simple double bellows device made of bamboo internodes (fig. 58). During periods when they were totally out of contact with settled hill villagers, they were able to obtain small pieces of iron by searching the latter's abandoned swiddens.

Until about 1960, they applied poison to their spearheads. The poison could be made in different ways, one of which involved four ingredients: a rubber-like oil from the Yanong tree, the white marrow of a young palm tree called taw, poison from the head and tail of a centipede, and snake venom. The mixture was first tried out on a frog, and the spear left in the mixture for some days. Others said they would use a poison from the sap of the bark of a tree, *Antiaris toxicaria*. Mlabri men traditionally hunt with spears (figs. 5-7, 10, 19, 49). They have related that they have also tried to use bows, but rarely crossbows. We saw their first and I think only blow-gun in 1982 (fig. 54).

In the Mlabri's traditional daily routine, three or four men leave the camp early in the morning to hunt small game, dig out bamboo rats, collect roots and honey and, occasionally, to catch fish from a small stream. Sometimes they go hunting farther afield, staying away for several days at a time. Within the band the most successful hunter usually becomes their leader, who decides when and where to go hunting as well as planning the hunt itself. Previously the person having killed a large animal, e.g. a boar, was not allowed to eat any of the meat for fear of the spirit of the forest, wɔk pha, the guardian of its animals. As compensation he could choose any woman in the band to sleep with until the meat was finished, yet another means to avoid nepotism on his behalf when directing the sharing of the meat (see also Appendix 1, p. 196).

Ranging only 500-1,500 m from their temporary camps, two or three women and teenage girls collect roots, edible plants, crabs, etc. (fig. 67), but they also hunt small animals like rodents. In this way they might provide almost as much food as the men, besides collecting wood for the fires (fig. 61) and taking care of the rest of the band in or near the windscreens, where they also tend the small children, the sick and the aged (fig. 22). The children spend the day playing with pieces of wood as well as with big knives and fire.

Around noon, the women who have been out collecting return to their windscreens to cook for the children, who receive three meals a day, even if the adults do not. In the afternoon, when the men return to the camp (sometimes they may have been away for two or more days), the food which has been collected and hunted is shared out among all the families. Each family usually eats separately. After eating, they drink water from long bamboo containers, smoke tobacco and chat. As there are only a few preparations to be made for the next day, the camp members go to sleep early. Indeed they often take short rests. One of our biggest surprises, when we first met them, was to see how children could also sit passively watching the forest for a long time. With their increasing contact with the other mountain peoples, this is no longer as apparent as before.

Until quite recently (about 1980) the Mlabri firmly believed that if they made any attempt to cultivate plants they would be punished by the spirits. Neither do the Mlabri domesticate animals, except for their dingo-like dogs, which they keep to warn them of the presence of tigers, bears, snakes and strangers. Bamboo internodes are used to collect and store water, as cooking utensils and receptacles for their scant belongings (figs. 57-60, 63): tobacco, strike-a-light and salt.

Since around 1960, some Mlabri have learned from others to make finely worked baskets and mats of rattan, as well as string bags of bark fibres (figs. 64-65). But even today, only some of them are able to produce such items. The Mlabri previously made their own textiles, but the young men said that, until the mid 1980s, when staying by themselves, they wore no clothing at all! However, we have only seen this once. Thus the Mlabri demonstrated how, in the past, when the men had to visit a village settlement, they would make a loincloth of bast, while the womenfolk, on their exceptional rare appearances, would don a skirt of banana leaves (figs. 18-19).

Mlabri artistic expression, as among other Mlabri-like groups, is remarkably limited. It is true that they draw some simple geometric designs on their bamboo containers, pipes, etc. (figs. 146-148). Incidentally, these are strikingly similar to, although not so well executed as, those made by some of the Orang Asli of peninsular Malaysia (cf. Skeat and Blagden 1906, I: Pls. 426-427). Once the Mlabri made stripes on their arms and legs using a needle and the sap of a tree, and some of the men still bore crude traces of these as well as finely executed examples made by Khamu and Thai villagers (figs. 11, 84)). Previously, all Mlabri men had a hole in each ear-lobe or else, so it was said, small twigs would start to grow from their ears. Since the 1980s, this custom has been abandoned by the younger men as they do not wish to be too easily recognised as Mlabri. They make no jewellery, or other art objects, except for attractive beads made of dried seeds for women and girls, see figs. 146-49, 151.

Hunting and Gathering. M3 Group

The M3 Mlabri gather very much the same items from the jungle as the larger group. However, there are some important differences. First of all they very seldom hunt anything larger than bamboo rats, and previously the bulk of their food consumption comprised roots and vegetables, spiced with small fish, crabs and frogs found in or near streams (fig. 72). But since 1982 their main staple has been rice. Incidentally, climbing together with them in the steep, dense mountain jungle and watching how they are able to find all sorts of edible materials, including special leaves and rotten wood, provided some of our best experiences. Furthermore, we were also told that they previously ate a chalky substance when they could not obtain anything else and were very hungry (fig. 304). The fact that meat was less important is attested to by their lack of weapons. Apart from digging-sticks, now furnished with a small spatula of iron at the end (Mlabri: cho'), they have only short knives and no spears. This difference is significant and has been so for at least the last thirty years. This can be seen from the fact that they distinguish themselves from the larger group by calling them mla' kɔt "people spear" whereas they themselves are mla' cho' "people spatula". However, Oy said that their group also had small spears in his parents' time.

Whereas the larger group has some division of labour when hunting, making baskets, etc., the small group drifts through the jungle together and stays together most of the day. They work for the Hmong for most of the year and therefore stay near the latter's villages. But for some months each year they move out in the jungle where they feel more at ease. Otherwise, many of our observations from the larger group also apply to the smaller one, still bearing in mind that of the latter only two families remain. We feel privileged that we have also had the opportunity of staying with this small, timid but graceful group, who probably have had fewer material possessions than any other people in the world!

The traditional Mlabri culture is not remarkable for its technological or artistic achievements. Rather, it is outstanding because of its lack of attachment to material items and of social and, especially, religious organisation, combined with the high degree of Mlabri individuality. All of this is reflected in their concept of their spiritual world.

Developments in the 20th Century, M1 Group

The Mlabri themselves said that they have always been hunter-gatherers and that hunting has been their primary source of protein as far back as their tradition extends, as they had been banned from growing anything until quite recently. Being constantly on the move and choosing to hide themselves on steep, jungle-clad mountain slopes when moving from one area to the other in order to avoid hostility from other hill tribes, has required their possession of material objects to be as light and minimal as possible.

Starting in the 1930s and 40s, the sparsely populated lower mountain areas of Northern Thailand were invaded by the other hill tribes from the north and northeast, as well as by Thai farmers from the south who wished to acquire virgin land on which to grow mountain rice, etc. At that time almost everyone also went hunting, so the Mlabri had to withdraw to the remaining mountain jungle higher up. It was therefore crucial for their survival that they kept together, supported one another and shared their precious protein reserves. This is mentioned again and again in their prayers, see e.g. p. 145.

As the animals in the jungle were decimated during the 1980s, all the Mlabri had to take work, especially from their neighbours – the Hmong – who on their part needed more land to pay back their rising debts for trucks, grains, etc. Therefore, the Mlabri were used as part-time workers, especially during the winter months, to clear the jungle and thereafter plant rice. In the 1970s the Mlabri worked for the Hmong for only about one month each year, During the 1980s this became 2-3 months and during the 1990s 4-5 months. When acquiring a pig from the Hmong in payment for their work it was, and still is, the band leader who ensures that each nuclear family obtains its share, even if this requires someone walking quite far to deliver it.

In the 1990s, Mlabri traditional life disintegrated further, to the consternation and sorrow of the elders, while the younger men put it this way: "Today we live a safer life, but previously it was more fun!" Another way of demonstrating the radical changes in Mlabri lifestyle is to look at their food consumption decade by decade during the years of transition:

	Larger animals & rodents	Turtles, fish & crabs	Hmong pigs	Roots & tubers	Vegetables & fruits	Hmong rice	Other foods from market
1970-1980	23	4	3	44	16	9	1
1980-1990	15	3	5	35	13	26	3
1990-2000	10	2	7	24	10	41	6

Estimated consumption of various foods 1970-2000 in % (by weight).

As seen from the table, the most conspicuous changes are the reductions in 'wild meat' 27-12%, roots and tubers 44-24%, vegetable and fruits 16-10% and the increase in the consumption of rice from 9% to a rather higher 41%. Altogether this represents quite a change to a less varied and less healthy diet. However, what is more important is the deterioration in the Mlabri's self esteem.

Recent Developments

We have made several further trips to Thailand, the last being in 2000. However, we have not visited the Mlabri since 1994, but we still follow developments in Nan, realising that deterioration in the jungle and the conditions of its people has continued. I think the best way of describing the present situation is to cite the Thai anthropologist Sakkarin Na Nan's statements to journalist Sanitsuda Ekachai, printed in *Bangkok Post,* December 2006. Sakkarin spent two years living with about 150 Mlabri from 20 families:

"The once close-knit band is drifting apart as each family must spend most of its time working in the fields of the Hmong. The elders have lost their traditional leadership roles because the community no longer needs them for hunting-related rituals. Meanwhile, the provincial authorities are using the Mlabri's Stone Age image to promote local tourism."

"The Mlabri children grow up with low self-esteem, looking down on their ancestral culture. Now living and working as farmers and wage labourers, the Mlabri need to have land of their own. Their children also need higher education, so they can have better job and life opportunities. But this is difficult as their parents don't have the needed resources to support their children."

"Ironically, poverty and the draw of consumer goods have forced the Mlabri to play along with the tourism operators, posing as Stone Age hunter-gatherers for camera clicking tourists." (Note: It is not likely that the Mlabri ever made tools of stone).

"As hired hands, the Mlabri are employed all year round, which has quickly made the former hunter-gatherers experts in chemical farming, thus exposing them to several health hazards."

"Some Mlabri", Sakkarin says, "fight back by growing their own rice on small plots of land they received after converting to Christianity. Although the yields are inadequate, they help relieve the dependency on the Hmong. Interestingly, the yields are not kept for individual consumption, but shared with the whole Mlabri community."

"Despite the deteriorating forests that offer little in return, Mlabri fathers take their boys out to teach them the ways of the wild. They said that they can no longer call themselves Mlabri if they don't know how to hunt."

"We must also question the state system that takes away the forest, land and other natural resources from the locals and marginalises indigenous people", he adds.

A National Park and a Refuge for Animals, Plants, Trees and the Mlabri

When we first stayed in Northern Thailand in 1970, little did we anticipate that its fascinating mountain jungles were about to disappear, but only ten years later it was already evident that the destruction was accelerating at an alarming speed. To compensate a little for the damage already incurred, the Thai authorities should be able to find an area of still intact mountain jungle of at least 25 by 25 km in Nan or Prae province for the creation of a National Park. This should be accessible only to zoologists, botanists, the Mlabri and their personal guests, until it has been fully established, perhaps after 15 years. Thereafter it could be visited by anyone provided this takes place in the form of guided tours. What could be a more obvious solution than employing the Mlabri to look after and take care of the park's fauna and flora under the supervision of a small staff of the necessary specialists? The justification being:

1) The Mlabri know the jungle better than anyone.
2) Traditionally they have taken care of the plants and trees by only utilising parts of them, enabling regeneration. They intensely dislike cutting down big, old trees, as these are considered to be the abodes of their deceased parents.
3) The project does not require special buildings or complicated technical facilities, but a fence around the park and an electronic surveillance system are both essential.

It is difficult to say how many Mlabri might be interested in joining such a project, but probably no more than 2-3 bands (about 30-40 persons including women and children) are needed to work in the park, together with a moderate sized staff of specialists and technicians.

Fig. 48. Some Mlabri men are formidable tree climbers. If possible they choose slim trees or vines to mount tall trees while hunting or collecting bees' nests. They are also able to jump from one tree top to another, which they do by swinging the tree top from one side to the other and jumping when they have obtained the neccesary momentum.

Fig. 49. The spear is seldom thrown, but is rather used for stabbing. In case of dangerous animals, such a bear, a tree may serve as protection for the hunter's body (Pha).

Fig. 50. Catching bamboo rats requires hours of digging (Phaeng and
Suk).

Fig. 51. In case of an immediate danger, such as a wild boar or a bear,
and not long ago tigers too, old and
young took to the trees in a matter of
seconds.

60

Fig. 52. Climbing for honey, using burning leaves to chase away the furious bees.

Fig. 53. By cutting down the forest for the Hmong, the Mlabri bring an end to their own traditional life.

61

Fig. 54. Long with the first gun of his band (1982). About five years later there were only a few larger animal left however due to Hmong hunts and felling.

Fig. 55. Mlabri climb very tall trees at great risk to find bees' nests, birds, etc. In this case it was just a demonstration, but now Ajan said there was actually a greater risk of falling down when there was nothing to catch!

Fig. 56. Especially the women and children were very afraid loosing their way in the dense jungle. As a consequence the others made signs on trees to show the direction etc. of their whereabouts, also using flutes of bamboo to call for their missing band members.

Fig. 57. Mlabri have been able to work small pieces of iron at least since the 1950s. They use a fire and simple bellows, made of two hollow bamboo internodes, to obtain the necessary temperature.

Fig. 58. Making fire using a small
piece of steel, a quartz stone and dry
scrapings of bamboo as tinder. It took
Poa less than half a minute.

Fig. 59. Making containers for salt,
tobacco, etc., from bamboo internodes (Som and his son). They are
often decorated with various designs
of a type much resembling those of
the Semang and the Senoi (Orang
Asli) living in Malaysia (see figs. 146-
148).

Fig. 60. Father (Muang) and his son while carving a flute, the only traditional musical instrument of the Mlabri. The boy has put a (Hmong) slingshot around his head.

Fig. 61. Mlabri woman are hardworking. They collect most of the roots and vegetables, leaves for covering the windscreen not to forget firewood.

65

Figs. 62. Digging for a great variety of roots and tubers, which are cooked or roasted. Roots were the main staple previously, but now it is rice.

Figs. 63. Water often has to be fetched from far downhill. This load was about 30 kg.

Figs. 64-65. Handicraft is not important among the Mlabri, but some of them are able to make strong baskets of rattan or flexible, very durable and attractive net bags, made of jute. Threads are made by rolling the soft inner bast on the legs.

67

66. During the tiresome work of digging for roots Maiga, Pha's wife, also had to carry their son while Pha went hunting.

67. *While the men sometimes leave their families for several days, for example going hunting, the women gather various roots, tubers, bamboo shoots and crabs not very far from the camp, here with Seng (Paeng's wife) as their leader.*

CHAPTER 2

Supernatural World

This chapter of introduction to Mlabri culture deals with the supernatural world. After giving an outline of Thai and Mlabri concepts of the human soul, as well as that of animals, I shall enumerate all the Mlabri spirits known to me, and attempt to classify them so as to gain an idea of their interdependence and function. As one of the main purposes of this book is to present and explain the prayers, some of the details related below are repeated when the specific prayers are dealt with in Chapter 4.

Our data on the religion of the main group (Ml) are much more numerous than those for the small group (M3); this is for several reasons. Apart from the main group being about ten times larger, we have stayed with this group for longer periods and always in its own camps. But most importantly, the small refugee group has been less able to maintain its former culture, including its religious beliefs. The latter seem not to have been too different from those of the main group perhaps only a couple of generations back. The description of the Mlabri supernatural world therefore primarily concerns the main group, bearing in mind that much of it would probably also apply to the smaller group some time ago. This is apparent from the fact that most of the important spirits are identical, and that the prayers are more alike than one would expect, considering the difference at present with regard to the material and social cultures of the two groups.

Thai Beliefs – the Spiritual Heritage

The faith of the majority of the population of the Indo-Chinese Peninsula is a mixture of old animistic, Hindu and Buddhist ideas which were present there long before the Tai people arrived in Thailand. However, the invaders adopted many of the religious traditions of their conquered predecessors, the Mon and the Khmer, while in turn developing their own traditions and influencing the beliefs of the hill tribes, a process still going on today.

According to traditional Thai ideas the soul, khwan, develops gradually after a child is born. About a month later there is a ceremony in which the parents tie a string around the child's wrist to bind the soul to the body, a ceremony which may be repeated at critical times later on in life. It is said that a healthy person has 32 different souls, each residing in the most vital parts of the body, but usually they are referred to as a single entity. However, there are still other kinds of souls, one for example covering the vague inner being, jit or jai' or jit jai'.

When a person dies, the soul becomes very weak or disappears, whereas the "spirit-soul", vinyan, survives. With the help of a monk, the vinyan is persuaded to leave the body to find rest somewhere else and to be reborn, preferably into a better situation, material as well as spiritual. Most Thai believe that the spirit, phi, of the dead person stays for some months or years where he or she has lived, and that it may haunt the people there, especially if the deceased has been unfortunate or bad, for which reason these spirits or ghosts are greatly feared. Such ideas have penetrated deep into the religious world of the peoples of Indo-China to the extent that many of the Mlabri also believe that they themselves may be reborn as animals or humans.

As the Mlabri religious concepts of the soul, mind and spirits have so far turned out to have several elements in common with those of the Thai, I would like to quote at some length two distinguished scholars, one Thai and one American, on these issues. The citations start by tracing the meaning of relevant terms and are thereafter arranged in the same order as those of the prayers (Chapters 4-11), i.e. by following the souls and spirits through birth, disease, death and rebirth. For comparison, a few comments on the Mlabri beliefs are incorporated below, before their beliefs are presented in a separate section (see p. 75).

Phya Anuman Radjadhon, 1968, p. 202, begins his chapter on the soul and its ceremonies:

"The khwan, as vaguely understood in a confused way, is an unsubstantial thing supposed to reside in the physical body of a person."

This short, but terse statement is important to remember, for it will apply to most people anywhere, hence the various opinions of the nature of the soul. Furthermore it is said, p. 207:

"Traditionally a person has 32 khwans. This tradition is known among the Thais of Thailand particular in the North and North-East also, among the Laos and perhaps to the Shans, but so far it is not found among the Thai in the central area including Bangkok."

I may add that many of the hill tribes also count 32 souls. In Thai there are additional aspects or kinds of souls, whereas in Mlabri there are only two slightly different ones and one post-mortem. Ruth-Inge Heinze, 1982, p. 17, writes more specifically about the soul:

"The khwan has been defined by Thai informants as the "essence of life", a principle vital and essential for all sentient beings. Insubstantial and indestructible by nature, the khwan is supposed to reside in a physical body, which it can leave during sleep, illness and death. Without a khwan a person would not be complete. As a child grows, its khwan will also become stronger and more attached to its body."

Not only humans are considered to have souls. P.A. Radjadhon, 1968, p. 202, says:

"The khwan is not confined to human beings only. Based on certain ceremonies, which are performed in connection with the khwan and also on certain expressions in the Thai language, we may say that some kinds of animals, trees and inanimate objects useful to man have individual khwans."

The Mlabri for their part say that all animals, the larger ones at least, have souls, whereas certain trees and inanimate objects have only spirits. But now let us turn to the origin of the terms for souls and their meanings. Ruth-Inge Heinze, 1982, p. xii, writes:

"In Thailand, ... no contradiction is felt that the khwan, a permanent individual entity ("soul"), is a concept which cannot be found in Therawada Buddhism."

Therefore we have to look somewhere else to find a connection. P.A. Radjadhon, 1968, pp. 203-204, gives the following interesting information:

"By comparing the word khwan with that of the Chinese word khwan (old Chinese sound kwun or gwun), which means soul or a spirit, one is inclined to believe that the Thai khwan and the Chinese khwan are one and the same word. On this presumption we may safely say that the Thai khwan was a soul in its original meaning. The Chinese word kwun is composed of two characters meaning vapour and demon. As the English word spirit and atman or soul in Sanskrit means etymologically breath (compare the word atmosphere) one is tempted to think that Thai words ghwan (soft aspirated sound in gh) and ʃwa (hard aspirated ʃ) meaning smoke or dream respectively have derived from the same source as that of khwan."

As will be demonstrated later, smoke, mist and fog have connections to soul and spirit in Mlabri as well. Meanwhile Ruth-Inge Heinze, 1982, pp. 33 and 38, adds:

"It was Radjadhon (1962, 120-121) who discovered similarities between the Thai word khwan and the Chinese ghwun/hun ("soul, manes, spirit"); [note 23, p. 135: Modern Mandarin, hun; Dioi, hon; Ancient Chinese, yuen; Mak, kwan; Sui, kwan; Lungchow Tai and Tai in Nanchao, khwan (Textor 1973 b: 34.2)]. The sign for hun is composed of two characters: "goblin, demon, spirit" and "vapour, cloud". Both characteristics fit the phi. The Chinese envision the hun, however, as a clinging and an expanding "soul", and this concept carries features of the khwan" ... "The Thai words ghwan ("smoke") and fwan ("dream") seem also linguistically to be derived from the Chinese hun. The Chinese, however, moved into the area south of the Yellow River later than the Thais and, when the Chinese language was unified in the second century B.C., not only homonyms and synonyms of different regions but also of different ethnic groups were amalgamated. Therefore, the Chinese may have adopted these words from the Thais as well." ... "It [hun] rises after birth and forms itself with the inhaled air, similar to the khwan who gradually becomes attached to a body. The hun has, however, triple characteristics – intelligence, the inhaled, and the exhaled breath."

In Mlabri, Ml & M3, spirit soul is hmal while (h)lon has a slightly different nature, probably rather representing "mind", just as khwan is "soul" in general, and hun (hon) somewhat resembles "mind", as may be concluded form the cited material. The Mlabri also say: "hmal resides in all the body, but (h)lon only in the head." Note the similarity to hun (hon). In this connection Radjadhon, 1968, may again be quoted, p. 85:

"In adopting words of exotic origin into the Thai language the Thai have made use of their old device of forming "synonymous couplets", probably to translate their newly adopted foreign words by juxtaposing them with the Thai indigenous ones which have similar meanings."

One may underline similar, but not necessarily identical meanings – as frequently found in the Mlabri prayers as well (e.g.: gʌm ki to (h)lon to hmal "don't harm mind & soul"). Already at this point it should be mentioned that in one of the two languages of the T'in people, Mai and Lua (or Pray), mal (long a) is also "soul", while mla "human, person" perhaps is an older word for "soul" among the Mlabri themselves.

The Souls of Newborn Children and of Sick Persons

Through the critical stages of life – birth, mental difficulties and severe illness – most of the peoples of Indo-China will contemplate arranging for a ceremony (in Thai tham khwan) to recall the soul of the person in question. Ruth-Inge Heinze, 1982, p. 42 says:

"Because the khwan is the "essence of life" its independence is threatening to the well-being of an individual. To call, to propitiate and to bind the volatile khwan is, therefore, the major motivation to conduct khwan ceremonies." And p. 83: "In summary, we can say that the symbolic act of tying the wrist, at least, has the following functions: (1) to keep the khwan inside the body of the recipient and to strengthen the essence of life; (2) to protect the recipient against evil forces from the outside; (3) to seal a contract between the individual and the supernatural and (4) to assure the recipient of the care and the goodwill of those close to him by means of a socially sanctioned rite."

When describing the ceremony in Thailand, P.A. Radjadhon adds, 1968, p. 214:

"For instance, in Northern Thailand the tham khwan is called choen khwan, i.e. the invitation of the khwan, while in the north-eastern part of Thailand, where its culture meets that of Laos and also in a southern direction that of the Cambodians, it is called su khwan, i.e. the invitation of the khwan."

Su khwan was exactly the Thai term used by the Mlabri when they explained the ceremony in Khon Muang. Ruth-Inge Heinze, 1982, p. 3-9, describes the ceremony for a newborn Thai baby in detail, usually to be conducted about a month after its birth, which basically does not differ much from that for a newborn Mlabri baby:

"He [the father of the child] took a small bundle of lighted yellow candles and waved them three times around the baby's head. ... Then the baby's wrists had

to be tied, each, with pieces of unspun cotton threads. ... While the threads were being tied around the right wrist, the khwan was invited to come; while the left wrist was tied, the khwan was invited to stay."

We noted that the Mlabri also use candles and make string of unspun cotton for such ceremonies, but there are other similarities. Thus P.A. Radjadhon, p. 222, writes about the use of eggs in the tham khwan ceremony:

"The khwan egg ... may be a symbol of vitality or a second spiritual rebirth if partaken ceremonially by the owner of the khwan."

When the ceremony for a newborn Mlabri child is about to take place, the parents collect eggs, evidently with very much the same purpose, as mentioned above, i.e. to strengthen the vitality of the soul of the child in question (see p. 152). In the event of severe illness, the Mlabri perform ceremonies again to tie up the soul, and according to the situation more or greater offerings are presented to tempt the unstable soul to remain with the physical body, a precious offering being a pig, just as the tradition was previously among the Thai.

The Soul after Death

After having discussed Chinese beliefs Ruth-Inge Heinze, 1982, p. 37, writes:

"In the Thai case, the khwan becomes a phi after death and its power decreases in proportion to the offerings it receives."

However, the sequence of events is not quite so simple. When a person dies, the soul (some call it "spirit-soul" or vinyan) is very weak and leaves the physical body to stay in a remote place, while the spirit of the deceased stays in the locality where he or she has lived, to receive offerings regularly. Hereby the spirit gradually becomes weaker, which will make it easier for the tiny soul in the far away place to be reborn in the female body of another living being. Probably most Thai believe only partly in these transformations, which may explain their sometimes conflicting answers to the question, whereas those of the Mlabri, who believe in reincarnation, agree with the explanation.

Meanwhile, there are other aspects or properties of the soul or the mind, thus Ruth-Inge Heinze says p. 20:

"The chitaphud is the soul as shadow or reflection (Frazer, 1951: 220ff), "the footsteps behind you", an insect (cricket, firefly, caterpillar, spider, etc.), leaving the sleeper or the dying by the nostrils, mouth, crown of the head, or the feet. Everyone has four chitaphud. Rad-jadhon related them to be the four elements or the four humors (1962: 124). Villagers, however, see in the chitaphud the fleeting characteristics of the khwan."

As will be demonstrated below, the Mlabri think that animals can be carriers, both of souls and of spirits. For instance, it is believed that the weakened soul of a sick child may be carried away by an eagle. This will cause the death of the child. The spirits of deceased parents, who come to receive the offerings from their children, are seen as the insects (e.g. beetles) coming to eat the food placed on the altar. Ruth-Inge Heinze also relates pp. 37-38:

"The other Chinese soul, the houen (French) or hun (English) written with the character for 'cloud' and 'spirits', separates from the body after the death. It is said that after the death the hun becomes a shen and does not perish unless made to suffer hunger. ... The spiritual soul, hun, does not have a human form but is often conceived as an animal. ... We hear that it is possible to capture the hun of a living person and thereby kill that person; ... In later folk beliefs it is assumed that the death-god captures the hun-soul and thus causes death. ... The hun like the khwan therefore, persists with the desire to be reborn."

The above houen or hun and Mlabri (h)lon probably have the same origin, but I have no further evidence to corroborate the connection than that already mentioned. With regard to the other kind of soul, khwan, Ruth-Inge Heinze says p. 17:

"Between earthly existences, the tiny khwan lives in a tree under the care of a female spirit, Mae Syy."

Some Mlabri also share the belief in trees being the temporary abode of the khwan before rebirth (concerning tree-spirits see p. 80), and they also know of the female spirit Mae Syy (Th) inhabiting special trees in far away places.

Vinyan is a Pali word meaning consciousness in its original sense. Ruth-Inge Heinze, 1982, p. 18 writes:

"With the arrival of Buddhism, the Thais began to use the word vinyan (from the Pali word vinnana) to denote a more abstract soul that incorporates the concepts of thought, perception, and consciousness. It is believed that the vinyan is that which transmigrates and, in rebirth, enters a mother's womb to give rise to name and form. The Mon of Lower Burma, the Shan, the Burmese, the Lao, and the Cambodian are, in fact, still using the word vinyan for "soul". The areas in which these people live encompass almost exactly those of the Mlabri, and they likewise say that vinyan is that part of the soul which transmigrates. Further on, p. 41:

"The vinyan presumably carries the kamma from the one reincarnation to the other, but the khwan remains an immaterial entity which decides at will when and for how long it wants to reside in which material body."

The Mlabri do not seem to know the word kamma (Pali: "fruit of one's thoughts, words and actions"; Sanskrit: karma), but they are well aware that people may sin, and they say that it is their former major (mythical) spirit, tharago', who decides from looking at the deceased's excrement or bones, whether the person has been good or bad and, accordingly, is to be reborn or not.

Spirits

In Thailand much has been written about spirits and the ceremonies to pacify them or ask for their help. Only two citations on this subject will be quoted here. These also show that the Thai and the Mlabri have quite similar ideas. Ruth-Inge Heinze, 1982, p. 21, and p. 32:

"The power of a phi is feared and admired, and it is always advisable to propitiate a phi when his presence is felt – for a variety of reasons. Sometimes a Thai will go to the area (e.g., mountain, tree) where a powerful phi is supposed to reside and ask him for personal favours."

"The power of each phi decreases over time. It is believed that this is connected with the decreasing amount of offerings to him. When the spirit's power is completely exhausted, it is assumed that the phi has been reincarnated. This is why some Thais tend to call a khwan between reincarnations a phi."

The above discussion on the nature of souls and spirits among the Thai and their neighbours leads to the following conclusion, that khwan, the entire soul, is identical with hmal in Mlabri, while the Chinese hun (hon) is probably related to Mlabri (h)lon, coming closest to the western conception of the mind (jit-jai in Thai). Vinyan is that part of the soul which is reincarnated, and which is called hmal (h)muul ("soul spirit") in Mlabri (see p. 53), while phi is spirit and synonymous with Mlabri wɔk (often termed cɔnre for the spirit of dead persons). It is evident that the Thai and the Mlabri have many basic religious ideas in common, but as will be demonstrated, their spiritual worlds are quite different since, among others, the spirits themselves are chosen according to local needs and developments.

The Mlabri Concepts of Souls and Spirits

The Mlabri have few material belongings and anyway have cared little about them until recently. To be healthy, respected and liked by others is more important, and they avoid discussions and quarrels with anyone. Selfish persons are those who do not share food with others ('oh hak 'ek "I (one, who) separately take). When in need of something, the Mlabri simply ask for it, and if they cannot have it they resign gracefully. During our many sojourns I cannot remember any quarrels with them, nor have we seen children being punished. Thus they have great respect for the personalities of other individuals.

As already mentioned, Mlabri believe that both humans and animals possess souls (Thai: khwan, Mlabri: hmal), which are formed after birth and grow gradually to maturity. One Ml source said that before birth the baby is a spirit and that they give eggs to strengthen the feeble soul of the new-born. We were once told that hmal is situated "all over the body", while lon belongs to the head, for which reason, among others, I think it is closer to "mind". Lon is especially mentioned in connection with the prayers for very sick people, nevertheless many Mlabri claim that hmal and lon are the same. Bernatzik, 1938, pp. 170-173, writes that the Yumbri considered humans to have immortal souls (see also p. 78), but without going into details of their nature. J. Rischel, 1995, has in his M3 vocabulary p. 258: "hmaal: spirit (word used in rituals addressed to a particular spirit)"; and p. 288: "lon the personal spirit of an individual", however rather "(spirit) soul" and "(spirit) mind" respectively.

Some think that during a dream the soul leaves the body to experience everything dreamed, and that dreams may come true the following day. Likewise, the spirits of parents may come to talk with their children during dreams. One M3 Mlabri said that if they dream, it is because the soul is bad, but if they dream about a dead, close family member, it means that the person asks for an offering. Communicating with the major spirits is also of great importance on critical occasions such as during a thunderstorm, a divorce or in case of serious illness. Indeed, the prayers are communications of this kind, during which the Mlabri sense the reactions of the spirits, rather than conventional formulas.

When a person is in great distress or very ill, the Mlabri think it is because the soul is about to leave, and if the soul disappears into the jungle, the person in question will die. Therefore some of the most important prayers are connected with offerings to bring back the soul and the mind of sick people. Persons are only believed to be possessed by a spirit if they are vicious. When such persons die, they may become spirits or ghosts (e.g. a tiger), who may haunt people.

Souls of wild animals are considered to be powerful, the more so the bigger the animal is, for example elephant, wild ox, deer and wild boar. With the exception of elephant or deer having red colours, all these have been used for offerings, but the Mlabri say that they prefer domesticated animals, since they have less strong and vengeful spirits, namely after sacrifice. A band often willingly works for one week to obtain just one pig from the Hmong for an important ceremony. Dangerous animals or animals which are carriers of spirits (for example boars) may also be called spirits, while some special animals believed to be the property of the most important spirits (e.g. the sky spirit) are sometimes called wɔk, because they are not to be touched.

According to two of our informants, the idea of sacrificing an animal, as in the case of severe illness, is to support the person's weak soul by adding the soul of the animal offered during the ceremony. However, it is very difficult to obtain an unambiguous answer when discussing these complicated issues, for the Mlabri themselves are not too sure about them.

When a person dies, he or she becomes a spirit, wɔk buɪl "spirit [of the] dead" (Ml, M3) within a short time, which is the reason the Mlabri hurry away for fear that the spirit may take another one from their midst. The Ml group moreover uses the word cɔnre buɪl, and cɔnre itself means spirit and may be used for all kinds of spirits, but is mainly used for those of the dead, and therefore it is quite possible that originally it was used exclusively for such persons. Thus Egerod and Rischel, 1987, p. 48, have (Ml): "chnre; to cover with earth, bury, corpse." However, we have asked the Mlabri several times, and they always said: "wɔk gʌh mɛn, cɔnre gʌh mɛn: wɔk is right, cɔnre is [also] right", or that the two words have the same meaning.

Afterlife

When somebody dies, it is a commonly accepted idea that the soul then vanishes, but the spirit of the deceased stays in or near the grave. Only when dissatisfied with the offerings from their living kin will the spirits of dead family members come to trouble the Mlabri to remind them of their duties, or the spirits might be asked to come and help their family in case of danger. This is in accordance with the information obtained by the Australian explorer W. Weaver, who met a small group of Mlabri near the large sandstone mountain plateau, Phu Luang, down in the Loei province; see Weaver, 1956, p. 295. He says the following about the ancestral spirits:

"These are good spirits, but they can cause the clan considerable difficulty and suffering. The spirits cannot locate food for themselves even though they roam the jungles as their living descendants do. And when the ancestors become hungry, they inflict illness upon the living people to let them know they need food. The clan must then sacrifice an animal."

Let us return to the above-mentioned term vinyan in Thai, which the Ml group call hmal hmɯɯl (by some scholars called "soul spirit"), viz. that part of the soul, so to speak, which leaves the body after death to move far away, and which many members of the Mlabri of the main group (Ml) say is reborn as another living being. Incidentally, the old man Oy, from the small group (M3) also stated that hmɯɯl is the same as vinyan, even though he said that he does not believe in reincarnation, thinking that the soul after death has only a limited existence before it vanishes (he said: "goes upwards"). J. Rischel, 1995, p. 238, has (concerning the M3 group): "chɯɯr mɯɯl: a person's soul (which leaves the body after death)", which word and meaning is not far from the above-mentioned, hmal hmɯɯl. P. 259 it is said: "ɣh lon 'ɣh hmɯɯl: perform ceremony for personal spirit" but should rather be: "perform [ceremony] for mind and soul".

When Mlabri are asked what they imagine the existence of the spirits of the dead would be like, it is mostly maintained that they stay in or near their graves, but that they may materialise as a small spirit animal (e.g. a kind of beetle) harbouring the spirit prnah kae "long time old (deceased)" coming to eat of the offerings presented by their living family members (Ml). One M3 Mlabri told us he believes that after death his spirit goes around visiting all the places remembered from his life, after which it "passes upwards" after two or three years.

Many Mlabri (Ml) thought previously that there is some sort of hereafter or heaven in the west where the deceased live a carefree but shadowy existence, while others claim that they believe in reincarnation (Ml and M3). Of the latter, some say that the soul of a dead person moves to a newborn baby, while others say they are reborn as animals – boys as squirrels, girls as tortoises,

old men as deer and old women as small deer (pohl). These ideas of reincarnation surely point to ancient Indian influences, which are present everywhere as a general cultural heritage of this part of the world. The reason why Mlabri have no fixed answers to the nature of the afterlife is that they have no religious leaders to tell them what to believe. Therefore anyone is free to choose among various alternatives, deriving mainly from their changing contacts with other peoples.

The Other Spirits

Anything bad happening to the Mlabri is, or rather once was, considered to be due to the malicious spirits, who may cause storms, falling trees, sickness or animal bites, especially if the Mlabri have done something wrong. I have also asked what they think the other spirits look like. But apart from saying that some of them may form an entire family (e.g. the sun as the father, the moon as the mother and the stars as their children), most of them say they do not know. Therefore, I think that to the Mlabri a spirit (wɔk or more rarely cɔnre) is simply synonymous with anything bad affecting their life or mind. Also, they believe in sheer good or bad luck, for example when hunting. They seldom use magic (Ml: mʌ' tʌt, mʌ' mon; M3: mʌ' lon), and we have heard of only one example of using black magic (for killing an elephant), but they are somewhat concerned about the magical powers of the Khamu or Hmong. Some of the older men have had lucky spells tattooed on their breast and back by some Khamu or Thai, besides those simple ones made by the Mlabri themselves.

Not all of the many different spirits receive a mention in Mlabri prayers, so I had to ask the men over and over in order to discover which of them are commonly accepted. I have also repeatedly asked my informants to distinguish between the various spirits to make it possible to categorise them – but usually in vain. Therefore, the spirits have been divided up according to their nature and spheres of influence (fig. 69), which has proved to be of some help in understanding other features, such as their interconnections.

In the following pages I shall discuss the spirits, largely in the order in which they appear in the table, fig. 68. Only those names that are actually used in Thai and in Mlabri are listed. It is to be noted that when anybody does something very wrong (Ml: "sin" mak ngay; M3: bap (from Th)), the Mlabri think that one of the important spirits will send a message in the form of a sign or a

MLABRI SPIRITS, M1 & M3		(m): masculine (f): feminine	
Kind of spirit,	Thai: phi	MI: wɔk (or cənre) +	M3: wɔk +
sky sun, moon; star thunder rainbow (dragon-like) red evening sky wind	pha pha nug lom	klar, (kɔk) klar ki' (sun also tal); chəmɔny kɯr, (pir, pɣr) pang (connected with kroc) lɛng dɣng rəmut (kul kwil "whirlwind")	klar ki' (or "sun" tal); chəmɔny kɯr pum pang twɛng dɣng (m), lɛng dɣng (f) fff)) rəmut
mountain mountain pass mountain cave big stones	doi kiw	chohboh chung ("high mount." mount.") gətwʌt, prowʌl, also kiw luh kɛp, kɛp kɛp (ding)	chohboh rulɔh tor kɛp (m), hok kɛp (f) kɛp ding (m), kɛp blay gong (f)
water (river, streams) waterfall pool wet soil hot spring	nam pong	wɣk (old name: ji'rʌk) wɣk hɔt tong ruʌt kuh, lɛng	ji'rʌk, ruʌng ("river") tong ruʌt kuh, lɛng
forest big tree; trunk bamboo creepers, rattan	pa mai	bri, thɛk (drnʌl) lam (kɔk lam), ton ("trunk") tatri, trlu', etc. mʌ' (in general), trak	bri, thɛk lam ton, ("trunk") mʌ'
spear and sword	hok, tap	kɔt (wɔk kɔt, wɔk naw)	kɔt, naw
field Hmong tea plantat. windscreen fire; fireplace drugs and medicine	suan mieng 'ya	chu'ʌn, (or chən) mieng gɛng 'ohl.hnke' 'ya lah hɯl pyɛr to, old word	chu'ʌn mieng gɛng 'ohl, bɔk, hnke' 'ya lah hɯl pyɛr to,
earth death grave termite heap dead persons, e.g.	din tai fang mae, phor (mother & father)	bɛ', kɔk bɛ' ("spirit") bɛ' bɯl (bul), lukh ma bɛ' ("earth"), kr'ung km.puc mɣm, mɣ', ta', ya', 'ɛw, no', etc.	bɛ' bɯl bɛ', bontu, kr'ung km.puc (like M1)
sin man-like spirit: giant man-like, stay with tiger ghost in mountain walls animal-ghost, pig-like dragon, giant crocodile	bap	mak ngay ("like easy") taragɔ' (ding "big") kha seua, mok tok, khon tok ba'a' dəkat, do kroc	bap (from Th) tarago' ba'a' dəkat kroc

Fig. 68. Diagram showing the interconnections between the major spirits.

"spirit messenger". The sky spirit, for example, sends thunder (Ml and M3). If the wrong-doer does not respond to this message by making an appropriate offering, the offended spirit will send a more severe punishment.

Spirits of the Sky, Sun, Thunder and Weather

Possibly only a generation back both groups considered taragɔ' (Ml) or tarago' (M3), a giant man, to be the supreme spirit, who would come to rescue the Mlabri in times of major crisis. Among the few older persons in group M3 this is still the case, whereas there is some confusion about the matter among the members of the Ml group. But Muang from this group said

in 1994 that taragɔ' can distinguish between good and bad persons by burning their excrement, and from the bones of deceased people he selects those who have been good, to be reborn, while the others are burned. However, the sky spirit is the only supreme spirit mentioned in the prayers. Still it is quite possible that the sky spirit and taragɔ' are somehow related (the latter perhaps being a son).

The sky spirit, Mlabri believe, sees everything people do, even at night (M3 think that tarago' also has that capacity). It is also this spirit, along with the earth spirit, which makes people sick, when they have done something wrong, for example lied. Once, when I asked our old friend Paeng (Ml) what would happen if one of them killed somebody, he took me aside and whispered that

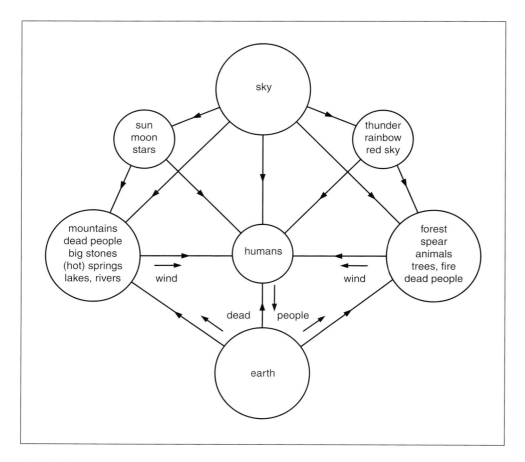

Fig. 69. The Mlabri world of spirits, showing each one's particular abode. Humans are spirits only before birth and after death until they are eventually reborn. If the spirits disapprove of someone's behaviour, he or she is informed, often through a messenger, which itself may be a spirit (thunder or strong winds), an animal or something else. When people do not respond to such signs, they are punished by encountering accidents, sickness or even death only to be prevented through offerings and prayers.

the jungle would be raised towards the sky, so that the sky would come down on them, and anyone committing a murder would have crazy children. The M3 Mlabri say that if they drown bees or cut ants, the sky spirit will punish them. As referred to further on, some animals are the property of the sky spirit, and therefore should not be harmed in any way (applies to both Ml and M3).

In times of a real crisis, the Ml group makes offerings to their supreme spirit, for example if someone has become seriously ill. Meanwhile, no outsiders are permitted to be present. We have therefore had to rely on what our informants told us. A bamboo altar (Ml: tɛk, M3: rɯh ta') is constructed and decorated with flowers, and a pig is provided to be sacrificed to ask the sky spirit for mercy. To increase the plea, dots of charcoal may be put on the sick person's ring- and middle fingers, cheeks and forehead. Near the windscreen of the sick person, the sacrificial pig is hung up, head down. While the other families in the band now move out of sight and keep absolutely quiet, it is slaughtered. If the blood stains someone during the operation, it is not to be removed. The head and some other pieces of the pig's carcass are cooked separately and put on the altar, and a prayer is said. The beginning runs as follows:

hmal muɯ   //   gʌm to lon   to hmal   //
Soul return,   don't harm mind   & soul;

wɔk klar   wɔk bɛ'   gʌm   ma   tit   ma bɛ'   gʌm di jur
spirit sky   spirit earth,   don't come stick to touch,   don't attack (come down).

Then all the band feasts on the meat, but the offerings are not to be touched until two days later.

We have enquired of Mlabri dozens of times as to what they believe the sun, moon and stars to be. They have invariably replied that they do not know or that they are not interested, except that some consider them one family of spirits: father, mother and their many children. Once, when Paeng was asked whether Mlabri engage in sexual intercourse during daytime, he answered that it is not good, for "the sun would feel ashamed". On another occasion we were told that once the red planet (Mars or Jupiter) was considered to be a sign of danger. Previously, there was a prohibition on killing animals with red colouring, and nobody was allowed to wear anything red (Ml). During our first visits we were told not to buy red blankets for the Mlabri, but after about 1982 they rather preferred to wear red clothes!

The spirit of thunder is also feared, because thunderstorms are a threat to the exposed Mlabri. It is said to show, for example, that they have eaten beef. Even today, the Mlabri will get very afraid and start praying intensively during thunder, as we have experienced when staying with them (see also p. 107). In the old days, according to several informants, they would beat on bamboo internodes. If that did not help, they would burn some old rags, so the bad smell could tell the thunder spirit that being poor people they should not be plagued. Sometimes they 'close' their windscreens, covering the front with big palm fronds against the lightning and heavy rain, as they explain, because "uncle thunder" is angry. Furthermore, they think that if they start quarrelling, hail may strike them. The M3 group said that previously they would put ashes on top of their heads while asking the thunder spirit to have pity and leave them. Also strong winds have been regarded as spirits which may carry fever.

A red evening sky is a sign of danger, and sun and rain at the same time show that the sky spirit is angry. A rainbow is a particularly bad sign and thought of as being the blast, wɔk pang, from a dragon-like spirit, which the Mlabri call wɔk kroc. Actually kroc is "crocodile", probably as they have no special name for dragon. But they said that it looks like a huge snake with two heads – one at each end – and that it is of the same kind as one sees on fences protecting Thai temples, where they are made of bricks or a concrete wall! The spirit stays where the rainbow ends, a place of all sorts of mischief, and here the spirit is said to consume the body odour of anybody who happens to be there, thus killing the unfortunate person. Alternatively, the victim may be bitten by a tiger or a snake. It was added that the rainbow often ends near water, where this spirit likes to stay, and that anyone drinking of the water will become ill (Ml). Moreover, because Mlabri believe that kroc can eat the roots and animals of that place, they will quickly abandon the area. One of the old men, Muang (Ml), related that when he was a child (in about 1950) they had special ways to make the rainbow leave. They either put up a sort of doorway of two branches "with cut-through leaves" (a fern) – an exit for the rainbow – or they wrapped a stone in dirty old rags

Spirit of Mountains, Caves and Stones

The spirits of mountains are often referred to in the prayers (Ml), and they are, for example, considered responsible for rolling large stones down upon the Mlabri, but it is remarkable that the M3 group seldom mention these spirits. The Mlabri Ml, in particular, do not like to stay in caves, which they consider to be cold and unpleasant as well as the abode of spirits. It is also this group who say that they are not allowed to hunt animals just outside such caves. Some unusually large or strange stones are likewise considered to have spirits, and birth ceremonies are said to have formerly taken place in front of them (Ml).

Water Spirits

The Mlabri know perfectly well that they sometimes get sick from drinking water from streams, which is thought to be due to the water spirits. This might be the reason that they may collect water from hollows in large bamboos, or they may make a hole in a wet area and take the water from there, the immediate surroundings acting as a filter. They are also afraid of waterfalls and large rivers, which are likewise considered to hold spirits. Perhaps for the same reason the older generation almost never immerse themselves in water. Incidentally, they say that insects make more trouble when they themselves are not covered with a layer of dirt and grease – sweat being dried away by the fire.

Spirits of muddy riverbeds, wɔk ruʌt, and of pools, wɔk tong, receive special mention in prayers (Ml), since they are thought of as being the source of sickness (e.g. dəkat bri "malaria" see p. 113). Thus it is believed that trees rubbed by muddy wild pigs (or wild oxen, elephant and deer) might transfer these evil spirits to anyone who touches the trees, and they should therefore be strictly avoided. In some places in the jungle there are hot springs with salty deposits, which animals come to lick. One of the oldest Mlabri (Ml) said that when the spirit of such places, wɔk ku' wɔk lɛng, is invoked, they think it is transported by the wind, and that once special rituals were performed in such places.

Spirits of all the Forest, Large Trees and Creepers

The mighty spirit of all the jungle is called wɔk bri, and contrary to most other spirits it is benevolent. Nevertheless, the Mlabri have not told us much about it, but they offer, for example, eggs to this spirit after a birth to keep the mother and baby alive. Therefore, the forest spirit might be the custodian of life in the Mlabri universe. This may also be deduced from the fact that it is the jungle spirit who has ordered them never to cultivate anything or to tame animals, except their dogs.

All Mlabri believe that some large trees hold spirits, wɔk lam or wɔk ton. They often construct their altars leaning against such trees, where they make most of their offerings, such as those to their dead parents (figs. 78-79, 98-101, 104) and to the spear spirit (figs. 81-82). A sign showing that a tree has a spirit is that animals come to play under it. This is also indicated if a large branch has stuck itself into the soil. It should then be avoided or they will get a headache or a stitch in their side. Likewise, fallen trunks may have a spirit, and should therefore not be crossed, but circumvented in order to avoid a headache.

If part of a large branch has stuck itself into the ground, it is necessary to remove the earth around the hole; and if someone cuts the branches of spirit trees, he or she may be punished by falling branches. We have also heard that a child might be killed by such a tree turning over, if the tree spirit feels lonely and likes to have the company of the soul of the child! In that case the close family has to bury the dead child under the tree, because otherwise they themselves may fall down from other trees later on (Ml). Parents of the M3 group tell their children that swinging on a branch makes the tiger come.

I have asked several times where the spirit of a tree is situated, and if it has any particular shape. Most Mlabri agree that the central roots of especially large trees are the home of this spirit, but there are conflicting answers with regard to its nature. Some just said that such trees may be inhabited by one or more human-like, green spirits, sometimes making up a whole family – a father, mother and their children. Pha, our best informant, gave me another answer. He said that the tree spirit stays inside a sphere resembling a wasps' nest, and that it is situated between the central roots of the tree. He even took a piece of paper and made a ball of it to demonstrate what he meant (fig. 85). It was added that it shines "like the sun", but if the shell breaks, the spirit emerges and brings bad luck, which is one of the reasons not to make wind-screens from large trees. This story and much other evidence shows that tree spirits play a major role in the supernatural world of the Mlabri. Incidentally, there are several examples of spirits talking together. Thus the spirit of a strong wind may discuss with a tree spirit whether or not a person should be punished by a falling branch. This, however, may be denied by the tree spirit as it may hold the spirit of the parents.

A tree having spiralling lianas (such as rattan), especially if they move in the wind, should be avoided, for the plant has a spirit, wɔk mʌ'. If someone walks under lianas, the Mlabri (M1 and M3) are convinced they might get a deadly dizziness unless the lianas are partly cut down and a small offering is presented to the spirit of the creeper. Some of the roots might also be cut away and likewise sacrificed to the spirit, but its central part, the home of the spirit itself, is not to be touched or the Mlabri will be in deep trouble. Both the M1 and M3 group say that going close to banyan trees, ji'ri, produces nausea. They agreed that these trees also attract unpleasant animals.

The Bamboo and the Spear Spirit

The Mlabri utilise 15-20 different species of bamboo, from very thin to very robust ones, and for all kinds of utensils, e.g. for making their windscreens or as firewood. Unfortunately, this strong and elegant material may also injure them, and I have myself had a large splinter cut through the lower part of my leg. This was the play of the bamboo spirit, wɔk ta.tru' (M1).

Until about 1985, the M1 group still used spears with an iron tip, but before 1920 these were probably made entirely of hardwood or bamboo. As spears were used for killing all kinds of animals and even quite big ones, they were also considered to house a spirit, wɔk khɔt. Each spear belonged only to one person, and no other person was allowed to touch it. If this should happen an offering should be made. To make sure that its spirit should be able to find the animals but not harm its owner, this spirit received regular offerings either before or after the spear was used. As the spear tip was often poisoned, it was all the more important to look after it properly.

As already mentioned, the Australian explorer Robert Weaver encountered a small Mlabri-like group near the mountain range of Phu Luang in Eastern Thailand in 1955. It is interesting to read his observations of the importance of the spear and its spirit, which agree perfectly with ours with regard to the larger group, M1 (see Weaver, 1956, p. 295). One of the men from the M3 group said that about 40 years ago they also had short wooden spears (lɛm), but seldom for killing anything other than small animals. At that time, they stayed in Laos and sometimes came across the spear group (Mlabri M1 and M7) who did not tolerate that they hunted larger game!

Spirits of Fields, the Lowland, Camping Sites, Windscreens and Fireplace

Just like the other mountain peoples, including the Hmong and the Thai, the Mlabri believe that fields have their own particular spirit, wɔk chuʌn wɔk mɔn. Another spirit is that of the Hmong's tea fields, wɔk mieng.

When coming to a new area the Mlabri used to make an offering to the spirit of that particular place, wɔk leua (Th) "spirit [place] left over" (vacant land), especially if they sensed that dangers were present. A few roots were considered sufficient for the purpose, as we were told when the small ceremony was demonstrated (M1 & M3, see also Bernatzik, 1938, p. 171). In a few cases we have come to know of a ceremony by chance. After having watched the big offering to the parents' spirits (see p. 188), we observed that a tiny altar had been squeezed into one of the corners of a windscreen (fig. 90), where some pieces of meat were left to its spirit, wɔk gɛng, and yet another prayer was mumbled (M1).

Fire is a necessity for the Mlabri to keep away wild animals and insects, to cook by and to warm themselves through chilly nights. But their habit of sleeping close by the fires all too often produces bad burns, especially among infants. When that happens, so they say, it is the play of the fire spirit, wɔk 'ohl (unusual closed vowel ô), or that of the fireplace, wɔk hnke'. Previously there were special rules for extinguishing fires, thus it was not permitted to beat down the fire because of its spirit (M1).

Spirits of Drugs

Alcohol and drugs, such as opium and medicine (wɔk 'ya), which have an influence on the human mind are, or rather were not long ago, considered to hold spirits (M1). This once again demonstrates that spirits are all such influences – physical and mental – which affect the life and mind of the Mlabri.

Spirits of the Earth, of Death and of Dead Persons

The spirit of the earth, wɔk bɛ' or wɔk din (Th), is said to be red and lives in holes in the earth (red being the colour of danger). It is the one mostly connected with sickness and death. It is greatly feared, and in the prayers it is requested again and again that this spirit should not come to trouble the Mlabri. If a person has been good, it is believed that he or she will die peacefully, but if he or she meets with a violent death, the person has been bad. When someone dies, the body is disposed of in a hurry, and the band decamps immediately for fear that the spirit should take someone else. A generation back, the Mlabri did not bury their dead. They just made a pile of branches and placed the corpse on top. Even though most Mlabri flatly deny this practice, we note that Bernatzik, 1938, p. 159, describes very much the same procedure. Once they sometimes placed the dead near termites so as to enclose the corpse in a termite heap, km.puc, as has been explained by the older men (M1). In the old prayers we indeed find the word wɔk km.puc, the spirit of the dead enclosed in such a structure.

In areas with tigers, the Mlabri previously wrapped their dead in a mat of bamboo, which was hoisted up in a tree (M1 and M3), or the dead were put behind some big stones, while infants were sometimes put in holes in trees, all with a view to preventing wild animals (which later on might also be hunted and eaten) from feeding on the body, or tigers from acquiring a taste for humans. Meanwhile, since the 1970s, dead Mlabri have been buried, owing to the influence of their Hmong and Thai neighbours. The dead are placed in spots unlikely to be crossed by anyone. Bushes and small trees nearby are cut down and burned to indicate "no entry".

The spirit of death is called wɔk buɪl (buɪl), a term also used for the spirits of dead people in general. The spirits of deceased family members are called wɔk (M1 & M3) or cɔnre (M1) plus their designation for father, mother, uncle, aunt, child, etc. Theoretically, no one dares take over the belongings of a deceased person, but in practice some do – nowadays at least (M1).

Spirit of Sin

There is yet another spirit, the one of sin, mak ngay (M1) and wɔk bap (M3), which does not occupy any particular place, like the other spirits. This spirit will punish a person who, for example, has been hurting an elder or has told a lie, both of which are strongly condemned by the Mlabri. Incidentally, the only occasion when we have caught them in a lie was when we asked them where they camped. For the safety of their band, they might then indicate a wrong direction and a much exaggerated distance, when they do not like to be visited in their camps.

Spirits of Ancestral Heroes, Man-like and Animal-like Ghosts or Spirits

Some of these spirits do not belong to the same hierarchy as the other spirits, and not all Mlabri believe in them. Besides, they are almost never mentioned in the prayers. They rather belong to the limited number of Mlabri legends or myths. One example is of two very powerful giants, of which day ("almighty") is the taller and has a huge face. He is a friend of the sky spirit, and when he breathes, he makes the wind blow. The other giant, jay (jai "big", Th), comes from the earth and is the friend of a spirit animal, wɔk kroc, whom he feeds and who is connected to the rainbow spirit, wɔk pang. One day these giants will come to rescue the Mlabri. Still another spirit, wɔk ba 'a' ("bad, polluted"), lives in holes in steep mountain walls; with its long tongue it is said to be able to pull people down while they are climbing the mountain.

Mok Tok, Ang Tok, Khon Tok (khon "people" (Th)) some say are man-like spirits only about two feet high, while others say that they are as tall as Mlabri children (M1), and that they are real people, who lived in their jungles further to the east one or two generations back. Several of my Hmong and Thai sources speak about such people, and even E. Seidenfaden, 1952, p.136, has a short note on similar people (Butr Daeng probably: puht daeng "the naked red" [children, Th]). Personally, I think they are similar to the M3 group, who are quite smaller than those of the main group (on average 10 cm for both sexes). Actually, these kind of Mlabri were previously met with, albeit in small numbers and briefly, in many places of northernmost Thailand even up towards the border with Burma.

The Mlabri also know some myths, much the same as those related by the Thai, about the phi kha seua lit. "spirit people [staying with the] tiger"(Th), whom Mlabri call wɔk pa bay seua (Th), lit. "spirit forest big tiger". They are said to stay with the tiger, and to be half man and half spirit. The Hmong call these spirits blong chong.

DANGEROUS ANIMALS OR SPIRIT MESSENGERS (mainly M1)			
	Mlabri 1: wɔk+	Mlabri 3: wɔk +	Special properties
tiger	roay	roay	Most feared animals may also be a spirit.
bear	bɛk	birk	Dangerous.
boar	ngay	ngay	Brings illness when muddy from the wet soil.
deer	pohl	pohl	Previously not to be hunted due to red colour.
anteater	'bor	'bor	Eats termite mounds formerly used as graves.
peacock	tr.lok bo, ngol	trɣl, kwɣng	Should not be harmed because of its colours.
parrot	giang	dun.ring	Same as peacock, both property of sky spirit.
woodpecker	to dɛo'	pok	Warns Mlabri of snakes and other dangers.
hornbill	'i' hurl, pɔc	pɔc	Strange appearance (there are two species).
eagle, hawk	tr.lang gung	kalang gung	May carry the soul of a sick person away.
snake	tom 'o''	tom 'o'	Killed many Mlabri previously.
centipede	kəndeb	kəndeb	Bites are very painful.
scorpion	hmukbok	hmukbok	Stings are painful.
spider	gec, pompway	gec	Much disliked, especially by women.
lizard	wet, pagoy	wet, pagoy	Two species, property of the sky spirit.
bee	yɛk	yɛk	Property of the sky spirit.
hornet	takul	mɛng.pu'	A few stings may be fatal.
butterfly	rɣl.phɛp	'u 'ʌ'	Strong colours, property of the sky spirit.
termite	trɯny	thɯbɯr, trɯny	Once protected buried people inside heaps.

The spirit – wɔk kroc, who is to be found where the rainbow touches the jungle, has already been mentioned, while dəkat ("cold") – is a pig-like ghost with white ears, who can be encountered in cold places such as dried-up river beds (see also p. 78 and Bernatzik, 1938, p. 171). Both were greatly feared before, but hardly any Mlabri believe in them anymore.

Even though there are not so many animals left in their jungles, they still play a major part in the minds of the main group (M1), as shown very clearly by our Rorschach-tests. Like most hunters, the Mlabri have respect for animals – at least the big and powerful ones to which they also attribute strong souls. If offended, the animals may take revenge. One man from the M1 group said: "Before going hunting, we have to pay our respects to the animals", by which he meant that they will make a small offering. When a large animal is killed, the thrusts with the spear should be few, and the blade should not be plunged into the body. After a successful hunt of big game, the hunter himself was previously not permitted to eat the animal, for he would become seriously ill, or would have bad luck subsequently while hunting (M1). Children are incidentally still told that they will not be able to eat if they laugh at copulating animals. Within the M3 group, animals do not have the same importance, at least not today, but reminiscences of their spiritual properties as held by the main group are still recognisable.

Normally, not even the most dangerous animals are regarded as spirits, but some animals are termed wɔk

under special circumstances. Thus all the permanent spirits can send animals as their messengers to warn the Mlabri of their misgivings (whereas, for example, the spirits of the deceased parents are not able to send the thunder spirit). Some animals, if eaten by the Mlabri, make them sick, in which case they may also be termed spirits, including also a few rare or strange-looking animals. Others with many bright colours are said to be the property of the sky spirit, and they should not be touched either. Not many years ago, it was not permitted to kill animals with a red colour. In the table above, all those animals termed spirits we know of are listed, but there are surely more. A few of them require special mention.

The M3 group, just like the main group, M1, use the tiger to prevent bad behaviour in their children, "or else the tiger will come to bite you", such as when the children start swinging on a big branch or playing with their food. Neither the tiger nor the bear should be mentioned while walking in the jungle, or else they may be encountered shortly afterwards. Instead they refer to these two animals as "the striped" or "the long-nosed", and if the Mlabri step on the footprints of a tiger, it may get "hot and dangerous".

Very bad people, when they die, are said to turn into a fierce tiger or a bear spirit. Also the boar is very fierce and quite dangerous when hunted. Even though its meat is very good, this animal is believed to be able to transmit the two spirits, wɔk ruʌt and wɔk tong, causing sickness, i.e. when the pig is muddy and thereafter rubs itself against a tree which in turn is touched by humans. Anteaters should also not be touched, perhaps because they may have eaten those termites that make their heaps protecting the bodies of dead people. Rather, the termites should be fed with leaves. Which is said to give energy to the Mlabri when walking uphill (Ml)!

Several birds, especially ones bad to eat, for example owls, were previously termed spirits, whereas two or three other kinds of birds are their friends, because they may warn the Mlabri of dangers such as the python. This is for example the case when they hear the gɛ' gɛ' gɛ' of the woodpecker to dɛo', which they say also starts to make a noise when friends are approaching. Other birds, such as eagles, are said to be able to carry away the souls of the Mlabri, especially those of their sick children (Ml). Unfortunately, I have no further details on this interesting subject, but something similar is related by the Khamu (see Kristina Lindell, 1984, p. 169) and the Orang Asli (Senoi), living in Malaysia, see pp. 246-250.

One species of lizard, wɛt ("long"), as well as colourful or black butterflies, are believed to be the property of the sky spirit (Ml and M3). Mlabri children are asked not to play with or laugh at these animals, or else the sky spirit will strike them with fever or lightning, just as we hear in the prayers against them. Something similar is said about bees, especially when they come to drink from streams (M3).

Myths

We have only recorded a few myths, because members of both groups explained that their parents seldom told them any. The most interesting ones are about how the world was created and why the Mlabri are what they are, although our sources on this subject are confined to only a few persons, of whom the most important is Lat from the main group Ml. Incidentally, he is the only Mlabri who, to our knowledge, has had a child with a Hmong woman. He told us the following about the creation of the world:

"At first there was only one Mlabri family. Trees and everything were very small, and the land and the sky were close together. The couple had only one boy and a girl. One day, when the father went hunting, he fell into a river and drowned, because at that time there was no sun, so it was all dark. His wife was very sad and died soon afterwards. The boy and girl stayed together, and one day when hunting the boy saw the other people and returned to tell his sister. When the strangers came to

their windscreen, the sky spirit made the present world, and the sky retreated from the land. When in the morning they could see everything clearly, they became very afraid, also because now they could really see the other people. Therefore they went into the deep jungle, where they had a daughter. But a tiger came and ate his sister (and wife), and now he had to wait to marry his own daughter, with whom he had many children, which was the start of all the Mlabri."

Besides describing the creation of the world, we hear about the fear of other peoples and of the tiger, as well as of the difficulties of finding a suitable mate among their tiny population. The next two myths are also from Lat and further elaborate on how the world was created, and that outsiders are not to be trusted!

"In the beginning there was nothing on the earth except rocks and hot water. Then two male spirits came to make the land dry, after which they created the stars, the trees and all kinds of animals as well as humans. One of the men, day or ta pru' wɛw, is the taller and has a huge face. He is friend of the sky spirit, and when he breathes, he makes the wind blow. He has only one son. The other man, jay ("big") or ta pru' phlaw ("precious"?), is not quite so big, but both men are very powerful, and they are able to uproot big trees. Jay comes from the earth and he is a friend of a huge snake phi nug (Th), which he feeds and which is connected to the rainbow spirit or wɔk pang. He has two children."

"One day the two giants went to see the Thai people to get food, because they were very hungry. As the Thai did not have enough water, they tried to shoot at a big stone (a mountain wall?) using a crossbow, to obtain water from the inside. Not succeeding themselves, they persuaded the two giants to try by promising them the wanted rice. Already the first shot with the crossbow made the water come out, but the Thai were jealous and wanted to kill the two men. Therefore they took them to a hot spring to drown them in the hot water. But by utilising sugar canes the giants crossed the hot spring. The next day the Thai invited them to come to the market for a meal, but the many people there cut them down with their swords so they died."

Others, from both groups, relate similar stories about their former mightiest spirit tarogɔ', whom the M3 group call tarogɔ', saying that they still consider this spirit to be the most important one, whom they may call on at times of crisis. Obviously, this spirit and the above-mentioned two giants belong to the same myth (being the father and his two sons?), perhaps a story taken from some former neighbouring people and modified to fit Mlabri ideas.

There are a number of stories to explain why the Mlabri do not grow anything, the most important reason being that the spirit of the jungle, wɔk bri, has forbidden them to do so, or to domesticate animals – their dogs mainly being kept to warn them of dangers. Our old friend, Paeng, related the following in 1982:

"About seven generations back, both the Khamu and the Mlabri each had a handful of rice. While the Khamu got real seeds and were able to grow rice, the Mlabri only had husked rice and therefore their crop came to nothing."

Pha (Ml) gave very much the same explanation in 1989, saying that they formerly stayed close to the Khamu and the T'in. "Even when the latter gave us rice again and again we never succeeded, and at last the officials asked us to go back to the jungle." Lat gave a slightly different version in 1987:

"Once, the Mlabri and the Khamu both worked in the fields and the governor gave them rice for planting. Whereas the Khamu put it near the fire to dry it and later planted it, the Mlabri cooked it first and then planted it. When the governor demanded the tax, the Khamu were able to hand over some of the crop, while the Mlabri could not, and therefore they had to run away into the jungle."

Although what we are told here could reflect some realities, I rather think that the stories are 'excuses' for the fact that the Mlabri have always preferred to live in or close to the deep forest. Until now, they have not endured staying for any length of time in any locality. When Lat was asked, he agreed and added that to his knowledge they have always been on the move. This result is more important than it may appear at first, because some scholars have suggested that the Mlabri could be refugees from village life (see for example Boeles et al., 1963, p. 171). However, this is very unlikely, taking our present linguistic, anthropometric and cultural evidence into consideration. Indeed it may not have been more than a century ago that some of their neighbours, e.g. the T'in, also lived mainly from hunting and gathering, as we have been told.

What has been said about the lack of success or rather lack of interest in growing anything is supported by the small group (M3). Thus Oy from this group, about 55 years old in 1994, explains:

"The first village people our group met with were Lue and T'in, and only quite late the Hmong, in about 1950. It was the Lue who introduced the taste of rice to our group through one of my father's friends. He went to visit the Lue, who began to teach us how to grow rice. We tried with a small and irregular field, as we did not have the tools to cut down the jungle. After sowing and waiting for the rice to get ripe, we were shown how to cut the rice plant with a sickle, to let bunches of the grass dry in the sun, and finally to put the bunches on banana leaves to beat away the rice grains. The Lue also showed us how to pound the grains by hand and to cook the rice. Although we tried for two or three years, we did not have good results."

Comparison with Bernatzik's Material

H.A. Bernatzik, 1938, was not only the first, but is also among the very few who have written in some detail about the Mlabri spiritual world. Therefore some of his results are discussed in the following. He writes, pp. 170-73, that his Yumbri consider humans to have immortal souls. The soul of a deceased, bad person is called mla, and it hurts living people, whereas the soul of a deceased, good person, mla te [tɛh "good"], may help them. According to our own results, the Mlabri (Ml and M3) normally make a distinction between souls and spirits, and in the prayers they almost always do so. A deceased person's spirit is called cɔnre (Ml) or more rarely wɔk (but among M3 always so). The immortal soul Bernatzik speaks of is possibly vinyan "soul spirit", in Mlabri hmal (h)mɯl, or that part of the soul staying temporarily with the female tree spirit before it is reincarnated into another living being.

It is moreover said that an evil person after death may turn into a tiger. We heard similar stories, but then such people were claimed to be non-Mlabri (e.g. Hmong). However, it is a mistake when it is said that offerings are presented only to deceased, evil persons (i.e. persons who were bad when alive). All the various groups of Mlabri we have encountered or heard about make offerings to their beloved, deceased parents, true enough in order not to be harmed by their spirits, but at the same time they also ask for their support, as clearly demonstrated in the prayers.

But as Bernatzik writes, and we also heard, their dead are seldom seen, but are said to look like humans. He mentions, p. 171, two evil spirits, dkat (dɔkat "cold, sickness") living in dried-up river beds and looking like small cats or dogs, and Baa (boo "bad"), as well as one good spirit, gruray, residing in trees, who protects the Mlabri and helps them find food (our wɔk lam). The Ml group also mentions dəkat, and also says it resides in dried-out river beds, but is a pig-like animal with white ears. It is interesting that a distant source connects the two slightly different descriptions. Thus Mr. Khambai, an anthropologist at the Institute of Cultural Affairs in Ventiane, told us in 1989 about a Mlabri group in the Borophar province near the Vietnamese border. This group is called 'a rɛm by others and kri' by themselves, and they have many habits and some words in common with the Mlabri of Thailand. Their most sacred animal, mo.lɣng, was said to be a pig-like animal with claws like a dog, just as related by the Mlabri Ml.

Bernatzik remarks that there are no priests, that the Yumbri have neither white nor black magic, that they do not believe in prediction and that animals and plants have no magical power. Thus most of these results are similar to ours with only minor differences (on magic). However, he writes that his Yumbri do not believe in spirits in the sky, in thunder, in mountains, in stones, in water, etc. While it is quite possible that 'our' Mlabri might have adopted these spirits from, among others, the Hmong, it is unlikely that this happened after 1936 (the year of Bernatzik's contact), because our old informants say that they had ceremonies for these spirits already in their childhood. This is also indicated by their prayers. Actually, the Mlabri M1 and M2 seem to have originated from one and the same group before the M1 group crossed the undemarcated border around 1916 and entered Thailand, while the M2 group remained in Laos.

Another explanation could be that the group of Mlabri, which Bernatzik and his party encountered, differs from our Ml and M3, but this is also unlikely, for we know from our investigations that the Mlabri Ml were in the area just west of the Thai-Laotian border where he met the Mlabri in 1936. We rather believe that the Mlabri he talked with during his limited stay did not dare to reveal all their secrets, exactly as we experienced during our first visit in 1970. It took us a long time before we obtained a coherent understanding of their many spirits and ceremonies. Later on, the Mlabri themselves told us that previously they were very scared of the spirits, taking all sorts of precautions before allowing strangers into their camp, such as advising their band members not to reveal their ideas of the supernatural.

As is apparent, changes in religious ideas and practices are continuously at work. This becomes even more obvious when the small conservative M3 group and other sources on the subject, such as Weaver, 1956, are included. Examples of comparatively new elements might be the belief in reincarnation. Other examples are those of burying their dead below ground and making fine, decorated altars provided with Hmong-style small parcels for the spirits. But on the whole, the cultural impact on the Mlabri from the outside world only began to change their former beliefs radically in the 1980s.

When comparing the large M1 group and group M3, which arrived later from Laos, we note that, in spite of the language and the religion of the two groups having much in common, there are many differences with regard to physical features, material and social culture. This leads to the conclusion that these two groups, both deriving from the Sayaburi-area of Laos, already there belonged to two, somewhat different ethnic subgroups, mla' kɔt and mla' cho' (viz. the spear and the spatula group), as also emphasised by our M3 informants.

Evidently, the Mlabri in Thailand are closely related to similar groups in Laos, and from linguistic evidence it is likely that they were also already in touch with the other K'muic-speaking peoples of the area, the T'in and the Khamu, centuries ago. Paeng, our old Mlabri informant, put it like this: "The Khamu are our cousins". Subsequently, the Mlabri have had connections with Lue, Tai, Yao and Hmong, but it seems they have not taken their religious ideas from any of these people in particular. The Mlabri have rather adopted a few elements here and there during brief contacts with other mountain peoples, when exchanging forest products for iron, cloth and salt.

Meanwhile, similarities with the religious ideas of the other hill tribes are worth noticing. Thus Walker, 1992, p. 342, when talking about Lahu Nyi, says that they believe spirits may bite a person's soul, and alternatively, the spirit may capture it victim's soul, enticing it from the body of its rightful owner, or even take up residence in the victim's body. Furthermore, Walker adds, p. 388, that the Lahu Nyi believe in numerous lesser supernatural beings, and says: "Most of these latter they term "spirits", which they frequently conceive as being masters or owners of particular natural phenomena: hills, streams, rainbow, sun, lightening, etc." We recognise all the above-mentioned elements from the Mlabri spiritual world, but also Thai, Hmong and

Yao believe in many kinds of spirits of animate and inanimate objects in the sky, mountains, water, forest, trees, tigers, birds etc. And they also place great importance on the worship of their ancestors, elements which may be almost as old as mankind.

The significance of the Mlabri is not only that they have, until recently, constituted small groups of remnant, wandering food gatherers, but rather that there were once considerably more similar groups to mix with the successive swarms of primarily Mongoloid tribes coming down from the north and having a technologically more advanced culture. Evidently, the autochthonous peoples on their side have contributed substantially to the melting pot of races, including the Tai people, in all of Indo-China (see also Walker, 1992, pp. 18-19).

Whereas Mlabri prayers primarily reflect their traditional beliefs, their confidence in the spirits is diminishing almost as fast as their jungles are cut down and burned, making us remember what our old friend Pha says: "When the forest disappears, we will all be punished by the Great Spirit or tha'rago'), everything will dry out, including all the spirits of the jungle". In other words, most of the former Mlabri supernatural world is vanishing, as their belief in the intricate transmigrations of the souls of humans and animals into spirits and *vice versa* have no longer sufficient media by which to function. However, they have preserved to the present day an extraordinary psyche, very different from any of their immediate neighbours.

In the search for possible connections with other hill tribes, I wrote twenty years ago about the similarities between the Mlabri and the Orang Asli, more precisely the Semai Senoi, who live in and around Malaysia (Trier 1986, p. 262). Only quite recently have I come to realise from literature sources that the similarities between their material – as well as spiritual – cultures are so numerous, even in detail, that their connection is beyond any reasonable doubt. In the Appendix pp. 244-246, on the origin of the Mlabri, we shall return to this subject.

CHAPTER 3

The Mlabri Language

No deeper understanding of any hunter-gatherers' spiritual culture can be achieved without some knowledge of its language, for this, more than anything else, reveals their ideas and feelings. The translation of the prayers, Chapter 4, does not consist of complete English sentences, but rather of telegram-like word-by-word renderings, which better suit the understood, short and abrupt style of the prayers themselves which then, all the more, require detailed commentary on their interpretation. Therefore, this chapter provides a sketch grammar of certain aspects of Mlabri, as well as a description of the transcription system used. The brief outline of the syntax and morphology of Mlabri given below is meant to help the linguistically inclined reader to obtain a fair idea of the details of the prayers. Before that, some notes on previous investigations of the language, as well as on our own experiences with this kind of fieldwork, may be appropriate.

Except for the somewhat inaccessible word lists of Hugo Bernatzik 1938, pp. 237-240, Mlabri was almost an unknown language until 1963, when Kraisrii Nimmanahaeminda published some preliminary notes and word lists on the Mlabri Ml language, see Nimmanahaeminda, 1963, 179-184 with appendices. Here, Mlabri was placed among the vast group of Mon-Khmer languages of the Indo-Chinese Peninsula. It was also stated that Mlabri has borrowed quite a number of words from the neighbouring hill peoples: the T'in, Khamu and the Khon Muang. This is in accordance with the much more detailed results obtained by Theraphan L. Thonkum, Søren Egerod and Jørgen Rischel (see References), although the specific relationship of Mlabri to the other Mon-Khmer languages is yet to be determined.

However, from linguistic as well as other evidence it seems probable that Mlabri is related more closely to languages spoken by other jungle peoples living east of the present habitat of the Mlabri in Thailand, i.e. in Laos, whence they derive and where there are said to be similar groups of them. Some early reports, by among others Catholic missionaries, document the presence of similar people there (see References, e.g.: Guignard, T. 1911 on the Taccui, and Fraisse, A., 1949, on the Yumbri). At the Institute of Social Sciences in Ventiane I was told in 1989 that there are various, small Mlabri-like groups of hunter-gatherers in several provinces of Laos and one in Vietnam (see also G. Olivier 1968, pp. 36-40.

The seven groups of Mlabri we have met or obtained information about have been labelled consecutively M1-M7. Their origin and reciprocal connections are discussed in detail in Appendix 1 (see pp. 195-251). But the recorded prayers derive from only two groups, the Ml Mlabri with about 140 members, and the M3, probably belonging to an older stratum and consisting of about 15 members in Thailand in 1976 and only three now (2007). Both avoid each other and insist that they have not intermarried, which our anthropological investigations at least do not contradict. Whereas all the other hill tribes in Northern Thailand have been used to talking to many kinds of strangers, this was not the case with the shy and elusive Mlabri during our first years with them. Furthermore, they naturally thought that some of our questions were strange.

Just like the Mlabri themselves, their language has a number of interesting 'archaic' features relative to the other Mon-Khmer languages of the area, so it was not surprising to learn, when we first met them, that no one from the neighbouring tribes is able to speak or understand Mlabri. Fortunately, already in 1970 it turned out that some of the Mlabri men could make themselves understood in Northern Thai, which is a sort of lingua franca among the many hill tribes of Northern Thailand.

Already during our second visit in 1976-77 we compiled word lists and transcribed simple sentences. However, acquiring the ability to understand just everyday Mlabri turned out to be more difficult than anticipated. One can only agree with the trained Thai linguist Dr. Theraphan L. Thongkum, when she writes (1992, p. 57):

"I myself have a great deal of experience in field work, but when working with the Mlabri I found myself very frustrated, almost giving up on several occasions. … In addition collecting data is problematic and very time-consuming."

During our fourth expedition to Thailand in 1980, now also visiting the M3 group in their windscreens, we realised that the Mlabri were about to lose interest in their former beliefs. It became imperative for us to concentrate our efforts on recording the prayers and having them explained phrase by phrase and word by word by the older Mlabri. Consequently, the need for direct communication with the Mlabri developed into a desire to know not only what was actually said in the prayers, but also what was implicitly understood.

When it came to the prayers, other problems emerged. Apart from being recited very quickly, sequences might be abbreviated as understood. Even the Mlabri themselves had their doubts about some phrases. Fortunately, it turned out that our many talks with the Mlabri on religious issues often made way for clarification of the prayers as well.

Structurally, the Ml and M3 dialects are very close. There are almost no differences in morphology and segmental phonology, but the dialect of the larger group Ml has much greater variations of intonation (pitch, duration and stress), and an extraordinarily long-drawn falling pitch of declarative or emphatic sentences. However, many words are the same for the two dialects, especially the basic ones, while more modern words and loanwords from Khamu, T'in and Northern Thai are often different. This is not surprising, because the two groups have been separated geographically since about 1916, when the Ml group arrived in Thailand proper and primarily had contacts with the Khon Muang (the mountain Thai) and the Hmong, whereas the M3 group mainly stayed with the T'in and the Hmong, both before and after their transfer from Laos to Thailand proper in 1975.

Bernatzik 1938 accomplished some interesting pioneer studies during his stay with the Yumbri in 1936. He also collected a small vocabulary of Yumbri words, pp. 237-240 of his book. When his list is examined word by word, the close relations to both our Ml and M3 vocabularies are recognisable. Apart from some little used words, most of the remaining ones or about two-thirds, are almost identical. If loanwords, a few misspellings, misunderstandings and, above all, the separation of the three groups in time and space, are taken into account, it is evident that the three 'dialects' or variants are more closely related than it seemed to us initially. Rischel, 1989, pp. 68-71, rendering many illustrative examples of words for comparison, arrives at very much the same conclusion, adding that Bernatzik's Yumbri is the most 'conservative' type of Mlabri, then comes M3 and, as the most advanced, Ml.

While the linguistic evidence from the three groups does not reveal their connections within say the last century, the anthropometrical measurements certainly do. When Bernatzik's material, including his photos, is studied, I find that his Yumbri and the Ml are likely to belong to one and the same group. Bernatzik found an average height for men of 158 cm and for women 144 cm, while we measured 156 cm and 145 cm in the Ml group. Furthermore, the total number of Khon Pha bands he met or heard about, on the whole, fits the Ml Mrabri, as well as the time and location west of the Thai-Laotian border (see map of their distribution on the very last page).

As regards the average height for the 15 members of the M3 group remaining in 1975, we found only about 145 cm for men and 135 cm for women. However, our collection of fingerprints are perhaps even more decisive since they reveal that, although they follow the general Mlabri-patterns, there is no chance that the Ml and M3 belong to two closely related groups.

The words in the prayers are transcribed on the whole following the IPA conventions for the transcription of speech and along the lines of Jørgen Rischel's thorough work from 1995. The main exception concern the two consonants dʒ (IPA) and j, where I have instead chosen respectively j and y to avoid misinterpretation among English- and Thai-speaking readers. For glottal attacks and stops, apostrophe ['] is used instead of IPA [ʔ].

Consonants

Initial consonants with examples of words current in both Mlabri Ml & M3:

Stops:

voiceless, aspirated:	ph (phalɛk "lightning")	th (thɛng "monkey")	ch (chat "stab")	kh (khɔt "spear")
voiceless, unasp.	p (pak "prick")	t (ta' "uncle")	c (caw nay "official")	k (ka' "fish")
voiced:	b (bɛr "two")	d (ding "big")	j (jak "walk")	g (gʌl "ten")
voiced, glotalised:	'b ('bu "slowly")	'd (dɯn "lazy")		

Nasals:

voiceless:	hm (hmɛ' "new")	hn (hnʌm "year")	hny (hnyɔt "rain ceased")	hng (hngke' "firewood")
voiced:	m (ma "come")	n (nak "much")	ny (nyʌ' "that")	ng (ngam "listen")

Fricative: voiceless:			s (see "colour" Th)
Liquids: voiceless	hl (hlɛk "iron")	hl (hlɛk "iron")	hr (hr.lɛ' "laugh")
voiced:	l (lam "tree")		r (rew "strong")

glotalised:	'w ('wɛk "macaw" (Ml)		'y ('yɛk "bee")
	('wɛ' "own child"(M3))		
Glides: voiceless:	hw (hwɣ "salvia")		
voiced:	w (wʌl "return")		y (ya' "aunt")

With the consonants b versus p, d versus t, j versus c, and g versus k, there are special problems; these pairs being difficult to distinguish even in syllable-initial position in stressed syllables (see also Egerod and Rischel, 1987, pp. 39-40). Following the same source, as there are no minimal pairs separating the sounds sh (IPA [ʃ]) and ch (IPA [tʃ]), they are transcribed using the same ch, which represents a palatoalveolar affricate but is frequently spoken without oral closure as a palato-alveolar. The sibilant s (as e.g.; see "colour" (Th)) is of Thai origin and is only applied to Thai loanwords.

A further problem is that some of the nasal consonants with g, h and k are sometimes difficult to hear, and r is usually trilled. Moreover, in stressed syllables beginning with b, g, h, k, m, p and r, the initial consonant is often pronounced more emphatically. I have chosen j to be pronounced as in English "job", whereas y is everywhere pronounced as in "you". Initial and final glottal stops are indicated by apostrophes [']. As their status as distinctive consonants is difficult to establish, this has not been done consistently. Words in T'in, Hmong, and Thai are rendered as in English-Thai dictionaries, see Farland 1944, the latter words with an appended (Th), especially when it is of interest to indicate the provenience of the word.

Final consonants with examples valid for both M1 and M3 (with three exceptions):

Stops:

| Voiceless, unasp: | p (chop "ask") | t (blɛt "rattan") | c (gac "nine", Ml) | k (chuʌk "salt") |
| Nasals: voiced: | m (pam "fight") | n (poon "much") | ny (peny "shoot") | ng (pang "rainbow") |

Oral Continuants:

with final aspirated:	lh (rɛlh "root")	rh (buɯrh.rɛlh "heavy", M3)	yh (gayh "nine", M3)	
Fully voiced:	w (baw "young man")	l (buɯl "die")	r (buɯr "two")	y (ngay "boar")
Glides: voiceless:	h (bɔh "ashes")			
Stop:	['] (bɛ' "earth")			

Vowels

The vowels contribute substantially to making Mlabri difficult to decipher, because there are often but slight differences between them, as for example ʌ and ɔ, and their pronunciation also depends on the speaker as well as the preceding and succeeding consonants.

	Unrounded		Rounded	Mlabri word examples			English word examples	
	front	back	back					
Close:	i	ɯ	u	ki "sun"	kɯm "throw"	gul "seven"	fish (s.b.)	bull
Half closed:	e	ɣ	o	'e' "yam"	dɣng "look"	pon "our"	set	work (s.b.)
Half open:	ɛ	ʌ	ɔ	bɛr "two"	gʌl "ten"	wɔk "spirit"	bear (s.b.)	cock
Open:	a				lam "tree"			(s.b.)
(s.b.: see below)		ə	(schwa)		balak "white"			adjust

For the above vowel symbols i, e, u and ɛ it is easy to find illustrations in English, while ɯ, ɣ, o, ʌ, ɔ, and a require comment. Thus ɯ is pronounced almost as in German "über", but the tongue is placed further back, while ɣ is pronounced as in "work", but more closed, and o as in French haut "high". ʌ and ɔ are easy to remember from their shape, since ʌ is a half-open, unrounded back vowel, pronounced somewhat as in gallows but further backwards and more open, while ɔ is a half-open, rounded back vowel, pronounced as in "cock". Especially in Ml, ʌ has been steadily moving towards ɔ, and a has no corresponding phoneme in English and is completely open, unrounded and unstressed, approaching the a in French "allez" ("go").

Double vowels indicate long vowel length. As their status is unclear, they are included only when they serve to separate two otherwise identically sounding vowels such as in: ngam "nice" and ngaam "listen" There are a few vowels with aberrant values such as in the word klaec "tricky", where ae, IPA [æ], is pronounced somewhat as in English "slang", and is quite common in Thai and a loanword in Mlabri (e.g. daeng "red"). Finally, the presyllable ə (schwa) represents a short and indistinct vowel with reminiscences of all those already mentioned.

There are also some diphthongs. Egerod and Rischel 1987, p. 42, or Rischel 1995, p. 67, include only a few "true" examples (see below). However, if some phonetically falling diphthongs as sequences of vowel plus final (-y) are included, there are many more such as 'uy "woman, wife, female" or rway "tiger", and they are often found among emphatic words for close family relations or for special animals.

First vowel		Second vowel of diphthong						
		ɯ	ɣ	o	ɛ	ʌ	ɔ	aa
i	M1		jiɣk "carry"	jiong "father, sun"		miʌang "tea"	tiɔng "all"	
ɯ	M3	biɯk "bear"	ciɣk "grasp"			jiʌɣ "chew"	ciɔr "pull"	ciaak "deer"
	M1, M3					mɯʌng "country"		
u	M1		cuɣy "see"		cuɛh "badger"	chuʌk "salt"		chuaak "tie"
	M3		gruɣ "things"			chuʌk "salt"		

(According to Rischel 1995, pp. 68-69, words with iʌ, uʌ and uɣ are loanwords from Thai).

Syllable Structure

Mlabri words consist of one or two – seldom more – syllables, each consisting of: consonant (+ consonant) + vowel (+ consonant), the maximal structure being CCCV-VC or, as a minimum, a glottal attack indicated with an apostrophe plus a vowel IPA ['V]. In disyllabic words the first syllable is unstressed, whereas the second is usually stressed and longer, with the result that the vowel in the first syllable is often variable, indistinct and may approach extinction, whereby the word is reduced to a monosyllable with an initial consonant cluster. This is especially a problem with the prayers, which are often murmured at a great speed with up to five syllables a second! In addition, Mlabri contains many similar, open or half-open indistinct vowels, for which reason some of the prayers had to be replayed more than 30 times. With Mlabri songs, there are the same and other problems to cope with. For this very same reason they are not included in this book.

The vast majority of syllables occurring finally in stress groups are closed syllables. Rischel 1989 (50), p. 84, says that an important difference between Mlabri and Thai or Sino-Tibetan languages is the inventory of final syllables, where Mlabri has richer consonant patterns and many more disyllabic words with reduplications or other sequences of presyllable plus main syllable.

Intonation

Mlabri is non-tonal, but both tone level (frequency) and amplitude vary considerably, for example when someone becomes agitated or many people talk together (Ml). Then syllables of important words might become very drawn-out with a characteristic falling tone as is, to an extraordinary extent, the last syllable of most sentences. Less prominent words, such as grammatical particles, have less stressed syllables and here the vowels become short and indistinct. Particles cannot occur finally in a stress group; they are always short and of the simplest structural type: consonant + vowel (+ consonant). An important example is the causative marker ba or pa, as, for example, in: buɪl "die" and thus: pabuɪl "cause to die" or "kill".

The general pitch is still high today, especially among some of the old people, as well as with women and children, but it is interesting to note that when we first met the Ml group, they talked at a still higher pitch than now. At that time, only men of about 25-40 years old met briefly with the other hill tribes to exchange their wild products for cloth, iron, salt and tobacco. Mlabri can be characterised as having a very conservative phonology with features that have been lost in most other Mon-Khmer languages of the area (Rischel, 1995, p. 63). While the languages of the Ml and M3 at first sounded very different, with great variation in articulation and vowel length of the larger group in contrast to those of the timid and softly speaking small group, these differences turned out to be largely superficial.

Word Formation and Syntax

In the following pages some of the main points of Mlabri grammar are dealt with, mainly on the basis of the works of the two linguists Therephan Tongkum, 1992, pp. 50-57 on M1 Mlabri and Jørgen Rischel 1995, pp. 83-99 and 148-189 on Mlabri M3. In the introduction of the latter, p. 83 it is said:

"Although Mlabri is a predominantly isolating language like other contemporary languages it has a rich and in part transparent morphology. These features may give the language an 'archaic' flavour and they contribute in some cases to mark a difference between nouns and verbs. As for word formation mechanism, one encounters infixation, apparent and real prefixion, reduplication and apparent and real compounding."

Until the present (2008), the M3 language was the best documented, while the prayers of the Ml Mlabri are by far the most numerous in my material. For this reason examples of words and sentences in this chapter are preferably rendered in both dialects, except when the two dialects of a sentence do not differ.

Infixation

Infixation with one or more of the consonants rn, r, mn, n after the stem-initial consonant occurs on many verb stems. It is a genuine typological characteristic of Mon-Khmer languages, the pattern of infixation found in Mlabri being almost proto-typical. Suggestive infixals -n- and -ra- are probably put in the original word bling "raw, unripe" to form the word bnling "green, grey, light blue" or with -ra- in braling "pale-bluish, green". There are some near synonymous verbs which are suggestive of a -p- infix, e.g. gwɛc "poke", gip wɛc "to scratch softly" (M3). The most frequent function is to form deverbal, particularly abstract nouns, e.g. gla' "to speak" and grla' "speech".

Prefixation

Mlabri has a richness of pretonic syllables, but there is only one instance of entirely transparent prefixation, that of causative formation. This involves the transitivization of verbs by means of the prefix pa- before stem-initial, voiced consonants, e.g. buɪl "die" and pabuɪl "kill", while ba – before a voiceless consonant, as kuɪm "throw", produces bakuɪm: "throw away".

Reduplication

A much used device is to reduplicate words in order to underline their importance, to indicate plural, or to indicate movement. Without vowel alteration:
di dii di ngam (Th) nyʌ' prnah prnah (Ml) "[get] well, here as long time back"
po' po' plil "push push vagina" or "to have sexual intercourse" (Ml).

While an example with vowel alteration, is for example: butbɔt "trembling" (M3).

In the prayers there are also interesting double phrases, e.g. words repeated in both Mlabri and Thai (as in the first of the two adduced examples above) which are believed to make the prayers more powerful. There are also examples of chains of double words in Mlabri of much coveted animals, which serve the same purpose (see, for example prayer, p. 144).

Compounding

As in other languages, compounds are made from noun + noun or verb put together to form new words which may have a similar or different meaning from those of the original words, e.g. wɣk "water" plus yek "bee", and therefore: wɣk yek "honey".

Personal Pronouns

There are only simple first and second person pronouns in singular and dual but no real third person pronouns:

	Pronoun	Possessive adjective
First singular Second singular	'oh "I, me, my" mɛh "you", br.mɛh "your" bnhnɛ' "You" (politely)	'ot "my" mɛt "your" (e.g. child)
First plural Second plural Third plural	thɣng (Ml), 'ah "we" (M3) bah "you two, you" (plural) bn.hnɛ' kɔmbɛr "relatives" or members of the band (Ml)	

bn.hnɛ' (Ml) is commonly used as a respectful form for second singular "you", while bn.hnɛ' kɔmbɛr is vaguely used when talking about the relatives or the members of the band. In Mlabri M3 hnɛ' "He" is a respectful form, used when referring to the creator of the Mlabri world, but also when speaking to the elder men in the old days. I venture to say that hnɛ' is the original form, to which the Mlabri Ml have added the prefix: bn, properly deriving from Thai boon "merit, virtue, good deeds".

Pronouns, Adverbs and Prepositions (including only the most frequently used ones):

	this	here	that	there	over there	like that	in, at, with	in, at, into	to, into, with, on	(enter) into
Ml:	gʌh	gʌh, rih	nyʌ'	nyʌ', rih	nyʌ'	yʌk	ni	ti	lɔng	blʌk
M3	gʌh, nɛh	gʌh, nɛh, rih	nyʌ'	nyʌ', rih	dɯgʌ'	yʌk	ni	ti	lɔng	blʌk

Possessive Constructions

Possessive constructions are common. Frequently, a possessum precedes the modifier as in mla' bri' "men (originally: souls?) of the forest". However, if it is intended to emphasise the possessum, di is put between the possessor and the possessum as in: mɣm di khot "father's spear", or in: 'oh lom di mɣ': I love (my) mother". di is also widely used in complex predicate constructions, often together with imperative verbs (meaning "be good" or "get", or pleading for something as in the prayers).

Articles

dɔ indicates an indefinite quality or number, as in: 'a dɔ dii (Ml, dee (Th)), 'a dɔ thɛh (M3) "get well, everything good": dɔ mla' gʌh, lit. "some people [time] this" or "people nowadays". 'ak (Ml), 'at (M3) is used as a definite article, as in 'at hngɛ' "the branch".

Affirmations and Negations

'ɣ is used for both affirmative responses such as: 'ɣ 'oh pa bɯl cabut: "Yes, I killed (the) pig" (Ml), as well as for negative responses:

'ɣ 'oh kɔ bɔ 'ɣ 'yuk: "Yes, I am not going to eat rice", as it is customary among the generally polite Thais to first say "yes" to acknowledge the question! Others: ko' 'yes' (M3), 'a mɛn: "(is) right" and chi: "want to" (however also "feels pain").

Negations are more diversified and their use is more complicated:

Negative predicate	Negative preverbs for negating verbs inside clauses
Ml: bɔ (Th) "no" 'a nɔny "no (left)"	ki "not", ka bɔ, ki bɔ "not", chak "not, unable" ki mɛn "not correct"
M3: bah "no" 'a nɔny "no (left)"	ki "not", ki bi "can't You", met "not", chak "not, unable" ki "also, in fact", kɔ "also" or "then" (preverbal)

gʌm ki or merely gʌm for prohibitive commands or conjurations.

Questions

There are two types of question: absolute and relative, lɛ is used for absolute questions, while there are a number of possibilities for relative questions. The most important ones are:

	who	why, what	where	when
Ml:	dɔm mla', mən hnɛ'	pi' nyʌ, cingde'	gɔlɛng	tal 'dɣ
M3:	'itɯ mla' (which), mla'	ti pia'	ganɛng, gilɛng	pan 'dɣ

Some examples from Tongkum 1992, (Ml), pp. 56-57, both on this and the next page:

mɛh kɔ bɔ' 'ɣ' yuk lɛ, lit: "You do not eat rice" or: "Aren't you going to eat rice?" ak pi' nyʌ' lit: "go why" or "Why (are you) going?" dɔm mla' nyʌ' ba to' hng.ke' "Who lit (the) fire"?, where the interrogative particle nyʌ' is positioned inside the sentence.

jak gə lɛng "Where (are you) going?"; jak tal 'dɣ "When (are you) going?"

'ɣ is used for affirmative responses to both affirmative and negative questions, e.g.:

'ɣ 'oh pabɯl cəbut "Yes, I killed (the) pig."

'ɣ 'oh kɔ bɔ 'ɣ yuk "No, I (am) not going (to) eat rice".

Commands

For giving commands di +verb is generally used as mentioned on the previous page, or as in the short sentence jak di 'yɛ' "go far away" (Ml), or without di: jak wec (M3) often by stressing the first word and lengthening the second. However, the command di is less used in Mlabri M3. Mostly, their commands or requests are unmarked as in: bong "eat"!, but if necessary they can also say: di bong "eat!" This phenomenon might be due not so much to a difference between the two dialects, but rather to the fact that the members of the small group are less outspoken than those of Ml Mlabri, and therefore do not want to press their arguments too far.

For prohibitive commands or conjugations gʌm ki (M3), or just gʌm is frequently used in the prayers for all the evils the Mlabri do not want to happen and which they try to persuade the spirits to nullify (e.g. "spirits don't make thunder").

Sentence Structure

Mlabri is an SVO-language very similar to that of Thai, where intransitive sentences have the unmarked order S V as in: "'oh 'a jak "I leave" and: 'oh 'ar jak "I go in advance". It seems that whatever the number of constituents present in a sentence, the unmarked order is in accordance with the overall scheme: (S) V (O), the constant structure being that the subject in a noun phrase is immediately proceeding the verb, as in: rway krɔb chrkɛng "The tiger bites (the) chicken" (Ml). If one is focusing on the object, the order can change to: O S V: chrkɛng rway krɔb "It is (the) chicken (that the) tiger bites".

In clauses or sentences having both a direct and an indirect object, the latter normally comes before the former object, as in:

> mɛh ma' 'oh pol "You give me (a or the) blanket" (Ml),
>
> mɛh ma' 'oh gɯncay (M3)

But with the connective di the order is reversed: 'oh ma' pol di 'ɛw "I give (or gave the) blanket to (the) child". (Ml)

The subject of a sentence may be a noun, pronoun or a noun phrase, with the structure: noun + modifier or modifier + noun, where the modifier may be an adjective, a demonstrative or a quantifier (classifier):

> brang dɣng 'a bɯl "dog big is dead". (Ml)
>
> 'uy chakkamruc pa koh hng.ke' "woman old cut firewood".
>
> 'ac gʌh bong jʌc "bird this (for) eating (is) delicious".
>
> 'ac chɛ' pʌr jak "bird many flew away".
>
> kwʌr chɔng mla' thəlɛw wɣk "strangers, two persons, are bathing."

In indicating the possessive in Mlabri, word order is as in English, i.e. the possessive pronoun precedes the noun, e.g: mɛt 'ɛw jak toc ka' "Your child went (to) catch fish". The object of a verb may be a noun, pronoun, or a noun phrase, as also applies to the subject. Negative preverbs are situated between the subject (if any) and the verb. But if the construction involves a modal auxiliary, the order (disregarding the subject, which is often latent) is:

> Verb + (Object) + (Negation) + Auxiliary:
>
> 'ɣ' yuk ki bɔ day "eat rice not can" (Ml), or:
>
> bong yuk mɛt bɣn (M3).

Vocabulary

When studying various vocabularies of the Mlabri language, it is important to remember that these peoples have probably always lived in very small bands, each of about 12-20 persons, and that there are no more than about hundred people within one large area. With their very limited material culture, there would have been little need for certain semantic fields, for example for specific tools. But within other categories, such as animals and plants, they have a great variety of words.

However, the Mlabri have always had some contacts with other peoples. Nevertheless, these connections might have been very limited for long periods of time, because of fear of their technologically superior neighbours trying to kill or exploit them, in the same way as they still do today. This is also seen from the vocabulary, which seems to consist of a core of a limited number of old Mlabri words, on which layers of loanwords from their changing contacts are superimposed. The fact that the M3 language has developed less than the Ml language may be seen from the fact that it has retained more words with both a masculine (m) and a feminine (f) form:

"banana-leaf dress" tɛb (m), 'yɛt (f);   "buttocks" kldɯl (m), gɔt (m);
"hole" dol (m), hok (f);   "throw" kɯm (m), tɔl (f);
"bring back" toc bruk (m), toc lɛ (f);   "to roll" krlkrel (m), kulkol (f).

Since the 1990s, the cultural impact from the outside world has been overwhelming, and this is also apparent in the vocabulary, especially in words for all sorts of modern items such as cigarettes, sweets, radios – even tape-recorders! Further back, we find words from Khamu, T'in and old Northern Thai (words for family relations, colours, etc.), but the Mlabri also construct words themselves. When going through our word lists with them we have often experienced how they would make a new word on the spot, if they did not remember or did not have the Mlabri equivalent.

The Mlabri's linguistic abilities are indeed extraordinary, and now most of them are able to speak Thai and some Hmong as well, while the M3 group also speaks T'in. Some of the elder Mlabri, like Poa (Ml), are able to sing long and complicated mocking songs, and young Mlabri sing very well in Mlabri, Thai and Hmong. Sometimes the young men really surprised us by repeating part of our own conversation in almost perfect Danish! Like others, the Mlabri often pronounce one and the same word differently, or they may have, or may construct, slightly different words for one and the same thing, for example for headache gly' gret "head pain", kɯr gly' "thunder head", kɯr gret "thunder pain".

Life in the jungle seldom requires the use of numbers above five or six, except for the notion "many" (chɛ'), and when we first encountered the Mlabri, only some of them were able to count from one to ten in Mlabri without making mistakes. Mlabri Ml and M3 numerals are almost identical:
moy "one", bɛr "two", pɛ' "three", pon "four", thyng "five", thal "six", gul "seven", tii' "eight" (also meaning all the fingers except the two thumbs), gac (Ml) and gayh (M3) "nine", and gal "ten".

As a matter of fact, these words bear some resemblance to those of their neighbouring Mon-Khmer speaking people, in particular to T'in Sagad (see, for example, Kraisri Nimmanahaeminda in Booles et al. 1963, Appendix I) which, together with their limited use, may show that they are not very old acquisitions. When, for example, the Mlabri previously made appointments with the Hmong to do some work, they cut a number of small bamboo sticks according to the number of dawns (or nights) before they had to appear. By discarding one stick every subsequent morning they knew when it was time to show up. This procedure was also used in 1970, when we had arranged with Mr. Phujaka to meet them after 11 days at the deserted village of Ban Kum (see p. 199). Now the Mlabri use Thai numerals when discussing payments for their work, but for many years they had only a vague idea of amounts above ten, e.g. 10 Bath, as they seldom received money for their work but rather rice, old clothes and, occasionally, a pig.

It was more surprising to find how little colours are used and matter in their culture. When we first asked the Mlabri for these names, it transpired that they had only a few fixed terms, which some of them did not even know. Often they merely named the colours after objects having similar colours. During the years 1976-1987 we questioned 24 Ml Mlabri and seven M3 Mlabri about the colours, always using the same colour tables.

With regard to the Ml group, there are no fixed terms except perhaps for "white" palak, and "red" lɛng, the colour of danger. "Black" is variously designated, the main form being tokwek, while padam, the Thai word for "black", is also used; others use trlɔh "(black) pot". Green and blue shades are more or less treated as the same colour, (bn)ling, but many other suggestions were proposed, while yellow obviously presents to the Mlabri a mixed colour, being perceived by some towards red, but more often considered to be close to green and blue; a few called yellow yak yek, "beeswax". Other colours, such as orange, pink and brown, were discussed as well, but the answers were rather confusing. L. Theraphan Thongkum, 1985, mentions only the four most often used names from the larger group, which is rather an over-simplification.

There is closer agreement as regards our results for the small group when these are compared with those obtained by J. Rischel, 1995, p. 112. Just as the Ml group, the M3 group see green and blue as almost alike, but the terms are not fixed, except to some extent for twɛng "red", lɛng "yellow-orange", bn.ling "blue-greenish" shades, bəlaak "white" and chɛng "black" (Rischel, 1995, also has braliing "pale bluish-green").The two groups seldom use colours, even when describing or giving names for plants and animals. More often they describe them or derive their names from the shape (e.g. wet "long" for lizard), or with regard to animals imitate the sounds they make. For the very same reason, many names for animals are ono-matopoeic, as they say, because the sounds are of greater use, animals being heard and identified long before they are actually seen in the dense jungle!

We have also investigated the Mlabri for colour blindness using some special charts developed for testing airline pilots and similar. Though about 50 persons were carefully examined, not a single person had difficulty with any of the 20 colour charts, a highly unusual, but very significant result! This means that the gene for that deficiency has never been allowed to spread among the Mlabri, which is typical for isolated, permanent jungle dwellers. This indicates that they have always been what they themselves believe – jungle dwellers, but contrary to what some writers have suggested based, however, on dubious Thai legends.

CHAPTER 4

The Prayers (M1 & M3)

Definitions and Purposes

"Prayer" best covers the kind of prayer the Mlabri use, as according to my Oxford Dictionary: "invoke", v.t. call on (God etc.) in prayer or as witness; appeal to (person's authority etc.) summon (spirit) by charms, ask earnestly for vengeance, help, etc.)"; whereas: "Incantation, n. (Use of) magical formula; spell, charm" is more connected with magical operations, which the Mlabri said they did not practise and which they feared, especially when used against them by the Khmu.

Almost all the prayers are concerned with urging the spirits to obtain food or with evading bad weather, accidents, sickness and death, and they all require some kind of offering. This is also the case with the prayers prompted by the birth of a child or the subsequent name-giving, which centre on the health of the child and its mother. The attainment of maturity or marriage is surprisingly not celebrated at all. In the case of marriage, this is probably because it is first really acknowledged when a large animal has been killed, because then the Mlabri will use the opportunity to offer some of the meat to the most important spirits, especially to those of deceased parents.

The spirits of the deceased parents are also informed about important events through prayer-like talks, which might serve psychologically to justify the actions of the praying person. It is believed that the spirits then might show their disapproval, if the persons in question meet with difficulties shortly afterwards. If, for example, a couple met a tiger shortly after their marriage it was previously considered a sign from the spirits that they disapproved of the union, in which case it had to be annulled.

As demonstrated, there are a number of taboos which previously were undoubtedly much more numerous and strict. One group of taboos concerns hunting: how to handle the spear, to make offerings to its spirit and to share the kill with all members of the band. Another group of taboos is concerned with avoiding dangerous obstacles such as cliffs, waterfalls, hanging creepers and special animals. Yet another group concerns bad behaviour like telling lies or quarrelling with old people. Above all, every means – including prayers to the dead and not using their belongings or approaching their graves – should be employed to prevent the spirits from remaining with their living kinsmen, which Mlabri believe may cause further deaths.

Structure

Introducing each prayer, there is brief information on the year of recording, the registration number of the tape recording and the name and approximate age of the person saying the prayer, derived from our photographs taken during each of the eight expeditions. As it is always the men who take the lead while praying, their prayers are the only ones presented in this book. However, the women repeat them, but in much shorter versions. Besides, the women are usually very shy and, therefore, I have only a few incomplete recordings of females. The locality of the recording is not relevant and therefore not mentioned, since most of the bands moved camp endlessly.

There are some interesting individual differences of language, style and content among the members of the main group (Ml), but as far as I have been able to trace them, they have mainly to do with the age of the supplicant and from whom he obtained the prayer – not necessarily his father, but perhaps an uncle or the leader of the band. As one might anticipate, it is generally speaking the few old men who know the prayers best. But it is the younger men who are most willing to reveal the secrets of their tribe as far as they know them, because they do not fear the spirits to the same extent as their elders. Therefore, as already mentioned, I have played the tapes over and over again, while asking both old and young men for their comments.

The vocabulary of the prayers is rather limited, as they are used mainly in times of crisis. They follow more or less the same pattern: a) calling on the spirits, b) asking for specific favours such as bagging many animals, averting dangers in the jungle or sickness, c) presenting the offerings in return, d) asking the spirits not to follow their band, and e) wishing for a good and healthy life. The Mlabri try to persuade or rather beseech the spirits, but they rarely thank them for anything they have done! Otherwise there are only a few rules for their composition, with frequent improvisations, no two prayers being identical.

The words of the prayers are usually grouped together in 2-3 words of 2-5 syllables to give the prayers a rhythm (mainly iambic), thereby helping the Mlabri to remember the phrases. To give the reader the impression of the cadence I have used a short interval between the single items in a word group, whereas there is a greater interval between word groups. Finally, there is a double slash (//) at the end of longer utterances, not necessarily identical with the end of what we call a sentence.

The prayers, as they are presented here, are rendered in word-for-word translations in order to preserve some of the flavour of the prayers but also to avoid more interpretation than our material warrants. To compensate for this shortcoming, I have added explanations for special words within rounded brackets ( ) as well as at the end of each prayer. Words in the translation might be lacking, either because they are grammatically or semantically implicitly understood; these are supplied within square brackets [ ]. In addition, there are commas, semicolons and full stops whenever it seems appropriate to improve comprehensibility.

To facilitate a comparison of the many prayers, they are divided into specific groups (Chapters 4.1-4.8) according to the spirits invoked and especially to the occasion requiring the prayer, nearly all of them to counteract hunger, various kinds of dangers in the jungle, ill health, death and when addressing deceased parents. For each category of prayer, first those of the main group (Ml) are dealt with, thereafter those of the small group (M3).

When the prayers of the two groups are compared, the difference of pitch and voice is at first misleading, because after translating word by word it becomes evident that both composition and content are very much the same. Also, most of the glosses are identical, those of the smaller group merely representing a more 'conservative' Mlabri. But as it has been stated in Chapter 1, and will also be demonstrated in Appendix 1, the two groups are culturally quite different in some respects.

4.1 Prayers Invoking Several Spirits

Some of the prayers involve more than one or two spirits, especially when the Mlabri have killed a large animal, such as a pig, and they like to use the opportunity to make an offering to two or more of the important spirits. In the literature there are very seldom references to details of any of the religious ceremonies. However, Weaver, 1956, p. 336, has an interesting description of a sacrifice to the spirits of their spears as well as to those of ancestral parents. This ceremony is, apart from some minor differences, almost the same as one we recorded in 1980 (figs. 78-79, 98-99).

"After we had been with the Phi Thong Luang several days, we prevailed upon them to perform their sacrificial ceremony, using a pig which the expedition provided. After the pig had been killed, a bit of its blood was caught in a large leaf and given to an elderly man. He remained seated upon the ground and repeatedly wiped the blood across the point of a spear. In a low voice he directed lengthy incantations to the spear spirit. As soon as this phase of the ceremony was completed, the pig was dismembered, and each person, grasping a piece of raw meat, walked around the old man in a circle and waved the meat in the air, inviting the ancestral spirits to come to the feast. The elderly man remained seated and seemed to be inviting the ancestral spirits through more formal incantations."

"The pig meat was then placed in large sections of green bamboo over the open fire. As soon as it was partly cooked, it was removed and carefully placed upon a small bamboo platform that had earlier been woven and erected under the front centre of the lean-to. It was left there overnight so that the spirits could feast upon it, and what was left the next morning was removed and shared by the clan."

The first two prayers by our old friend Paeng are among the very first ever recorded and translated. He was one of the most prominent Mlabri personalities, and until about 1985 he was the leader of his band of 15-20 persons. It was individuals such as Paeng who led the ceremonies.

On the day of the ceremony he had spent two hours making an altar of split bamboo (fig. 105), finally placing a few offerings on top. Whereas the members of the large group (Ml) make crude altars as a result of influences from the other hill tribes, this is not the case with the small group (M3), who just place their offerings on a stone or some banana leaves – at least when we met them in 1977 (fig. 77).

Several other important spirits are mentioned in these first prayers, which is the reason they are dealt with in this chapter. The prayers concerning specific events are covered in the subsequent chapters. There are close connections between the Mlabri and the powerful ancestor spirits of some tall trees as well as the spirits (or soul) of their spears. When we eventually had the opportunity to witness not only a demonstration of the spear ceremony, but the actual ceremony itself, the altar (similar to that on fig. 82) was constructed leaning against a tall tree, which was said to hold the ancestors' spirits.

1978 (year of recording), 5a (tape no., first side), 097 (counter), Paeng (aged about 48):

'o cənre'   lam ding   lam dɣng   chən 'a mɔn   ki gɔt   gʌh jay (Th)
Oh, spirits   tree big   tree watch   field has cotton,   not [come]   behind this soul,

   ngam na' (Th)   'a chaboh chung (Th)   chaboh long lɔng   ngam (Th) na' 'a
   [get] good [life];   [spirit] mountain high   mountain (into) low   [get] good [life] please,

gʌm ki dəkat   gʌm ki naw   di thɛh di ngam (Th)   wɔk thɛk wɔk bri'
don't [get] sick   don't [get] cold,   get good [life] very best;   spirit jungle spirit forest

ki gɔt   gʌh jay   lam ding lam dʏng   chən 'a mɔn   // wɔk ruʌt wɔk tong
not [come]   behind this soul, [sp.] tree big watch   field has cotton; sp. wet soil & pool

ki gɔt   gʌh jɔc   chən 'a chohboh chung chohboh long lɔng   ki gɔt gʌh jɔc
not behind, that [is] nice; [sp.] field,   mountain high   & low   not behind that [is] nice.

'ɔ' pia' chɛ' pia'   kha' lam   ki gɔt gʌh jay   'ɛ di   thɛh di ngam
Bag [with] much meat, tree spirits   not behind this soul,   yes get   good [life] [same in Th]

nyʌ prnah prnah   gʌm ki dəkat   gʌm ki naw   gʌm di rih
as long time back [indeed];   don't [get] fever,   don't [get] cold,   don't [spirit come] here,

di rang (Th) jang (Th)   di chəring   di rih di rang jang   di chəring
go to trail energetically   to mountain crest,   hither to trail energetically   to mountain crest.

After the spirits have been asked to come and receive the offerings, they are requested to give the Mlabri a good life and not to follow them, thereby causing them accidents or fever, but rather to go somewhere else, viz. to the far mountain ridge, chəring (last line) the backbone of a pig and also a mountain ridge, owing to their similar shape.

1st line: There are two names for spirit, wɔk and cənre' (ə is often heard towards e or i). Egerod and Rischel 1987, p. 48 have: "chnre" to cover with earth, bury, corpse", which does, however, have other designations. The two terms mentioned for "spirit" have the same meaning, but cənre' is used specifically for spirits of dead family members. The Mlabri M3 only use wɔk, probably being the older term. chən (M3 chuʌng) 'a mɔn "field has cotton" is a reference to unspun cotton used for the offerings together with food, etc. ki gɔt gʌh jay "not behind this soul". Even though the Mlabri themselves could not explain this expression satisfactorily, it probably means not follow them or come to deceive them, jay (Th) being "soul, mind" in Thai.

2nd line: long lɔng "into descend" meaning "low" (mountain).

3rd line: di is an imperative marker meaning "on, in, to" whereas dii, dee "good" (Thai).

6th line: 'o' is a small bag made from a strong leaf for the offering of meat. kha' lam are the spirits consisting of their deceased family members believed to inhabit large trees. Some of the old family members said that these spirits were seldom seen, but if the Mlabri did not include them in their prayers they might inflict various mischief upon them. pia' "edible (meat)".

Last line: Polite way of asking the spirits of deceased family members to stay away.

1978, 5a, 718, Paeng (aged 48):

Several spirits are included in this prayer together with those of me and my family. The Mlabri told us some years after the recording that they believe that the spirits of strangers – not least those of the much-feared Hmong – could harm them, and that they had to ask the spirits not to punish their band before bringing strangers into their camp. For the very same reason it took many years before I was allowed to go collecting food with them in the jungle.

cənre' khɔt	cənre' naw	ki gɔt	gʌh jay	//	lam ding lam dɣng
Spirit spear	spirit sword	not [come] behind	this soul;		[spirits] tree big watch

chən 'a mon	chohbɔh chung chohbɔh lɔng lɔng	ki gɔt	gʌh jay //
field has cotton,	mountain high & mountain low	not [come] behind	this soul;

wɔk ruʌt wɔk tong	ki gɔt gʌh jay	//	lam ding lam dɣng
spirit wet soil & spirit pool	not [come] behind this soul;		[spirits] tree big watch

chən 'a mɔn	ki gɔt	gʌh jay na'	cənre phala' phalang
field has cotton,	not [come]	behind this soul please	spirit stranger

ki gɔt	gʌh jay	na'	//	'ɣ	di thɛh di na'
not [come] behind	this soul	please;		yes,	good [living] please.

4th line: Many of the phrases end with the word na', of which my Thai vocabulary says: "please, polite word used at end of requests, etc., often not translated." phalang or farang (Th) is a distorted form of the word for "French" or "foreigner".

The next prayer was recorded when the Mlabri had received a pig for the ceremony for their deceased parents – so we thought. But it turned out to be one for several other spirits as well. We were led to a spot in the jungle above the camp, where a fine altar had been constructed leaning against a big tree. The altar, made of split bamboo, was decorated with flowers and various cups of wood, bamboo and leaves containing offerings of meat and rice (figs. 78-79). Paeng Noi and his father, Ut, were standing in front of the altar and started invoking the spirits shortly after we had arrived. It was repeated over and over, but with some variations every time.

The spirits of the big tree, together with those of the empty and full pool, those of the field and those of the deceased relatives, are asked not to come and bother the members of the band, but to receive the offerings. The spirits of the parents are also asked to help the Mlabri find the most coveted animals (10th line: kum 'ɣh "support") i.e. by guiding the spear when they go hunting. Halfway through the prayer old Ut joins Paeng Noi. Besides their repeating some of the already mentioned phrases, we are requested not to harm the Mlabri or bring sickness or parasites, and finally they are all, including the spirits of us – the strangers ("master official") – asked to go far away to the mountain crest, viz. to stay away. The Mlabri later told us that they were afraid we might annoy the spirits, so that the Mlabri themselves would get punished. As is apparent, the prayers have but one main purpose – to secure simple survival in a world where even minor accidents may be fatal.

1987, 9a, 745, Paeng Noi (aged 42), partly together with his father Ut (aged 62):

'o lam ding lam dɣng	ki gɔt	gʌh dii	wɔk ruʌt	wɔk tong ki gɔt
Oh, [sp.] tree big watch	not [come] behind	this [is] good;	sp. wet soil & pool	not behind

gʌh dii	mɛh rɣm	ki ma tit ma thal	'ot chak 'ot chuʌk	chenyʌk ki thɛh
[is] good;	you follow	not stick to follow	my body mine tie up,	likewise [is] not good;

mɛh rɣm	ki gʌm ma kawak chuʌk	mɛh keh ma kham	ma glɣ'	ma kham
you follow	don't come across tie [us] up,	you break come across	[my] head	come across,

chenyʌk ki thɛh	'e mɣ' 'e mɣm 'e roy 'e ding	'a bɯl 'a tay	'ek mak na'
likewise not good.	[Honour.] mother, father & relatives	have died,	take like please

105

'a bong 'a thɣng   wɔk mla' bri'   ki gɔt   gʌh dii   mɛh rɣm ki ma tit
we [give to]   spirits [dead] Mlabri,   not behind this [is] good;   You follow not stick to

ma tae   //   'o wɔk ruʌt wɔk tong   ki gɔt   gʌh dii   wɔk lam ding
& touch.   Oh, spirit wet soil & pool   not [come] behind this [is] good;   spirit tree

lam dɣng   ki gɔt gʌh dii   wɔk chən wɔk mɔn   pyang pia'   'oh 'ar 'ɣ'
tree watch   not behind this [is] good;   spirit field sp.cotton   present food   I have eating

'ar ma'   'ar pyung   'ar pia'   prwar   'ar ma' 'ek   mɣ' 'ek mɣm   'ek cin
have given,   have presented   eating   honest (straight),   have given,   mother & father   take meat

pia dɛ' 'i dɣ'   sa' la' də yu'   ki chu   'ek ni   kɔm nay   də ka' də kɣl
animal edible,   sacrifice (Th) rice   not buy;   bring here   master official   fish, crab,

də ching   choboh cin ching   cama to ta   chɯ cama   //   ma' də mla'   kum 'ɣh
pig much   ("mountain") fleshy pig   will person   buy will.   Give to Mlabri   support

kum bɛr   kham (Th) ma koh   pia' 'dɛ 'i 'dɣ   bɔ koc   bɔ hnɛl   gather
help friends,   meet come share   animals edible: carry bamboo rat,   rat,   squirrel

koh gachong   wɔk 'do'   wɔk thri'   //   //   ngɔr kɣ ma kawak
share turtle,   spirit (two kinds)   porcupine. (Paeng Noi and Ut)   Footpath not come across

chuʌk   mɛh rɣm   ki ma kham   kɔmbɛr kɔmti'   'ot chak   'ot chuʌk chenyʌk
[us] tie up;   you follow   not come across   children [and]   my body   tie up, likewise (is)

ki theh 'a   //   'o wɔk lam ding   lam dɣng   ki gɔt   gʌh dii   wɔk ruʌt
not good.   Oh, spirit tree big   tree watch   not[come] behind, this [is] good;   spirit wet soil

wɔk tong   chenyʌk   ki theh   ///   Interval, then   ///   'o wɔk   lam ding lam dɣng ki gɔt
& full pool   likewise   not good.   Paeng alone: Oh, spirit   tree big   watch, not behind

gʌh dii   wɔk ruʌt wɔk tong   chenyʌk ki theh   mɛh rɣm   ki ma tit
this [is] good;   spirit empty & full pool   likewise not good,   you follow   not stick to

ma thal   kɔmber kɔmcing   to rɣm bɛ'   chenyʌk   gʌh theh   jaw nay (Th)
follow;   men & women   get together   likewise   [is] good;   official master

'o ta chɯ   jaw nay   mɛh rɣm   ki ma   goh ma   bɛr nɛh   gʌm ki ma khay
things buy,   [but] master   you follow   not come   break   us here;   don't bring fever

ma phanyʌt   kɔmbɛr   kɔmching to   chenyʌk ki theh   kɔmbɛr ching to di dii
bring parasites   [to]   relatives,   likewise [is] not good;   relatives get good

di ngam   di rɛ'   di rang (Th) jang   di chring   //   di rih di   rang di jɔng
very best;   run   to trail energetically   to mountain crest,   here to trail   forth & back

di hrlɛ'   mɛh rɣm   ki khon   jao khon nay (Th)   mɛh rɣm   ki tit   ki tae (Th)
laughing.   You follow   not person   (stay) master official,   you follow   not stick   to & touch

kɔmbɛr kɔmching to   chenyʌk   ki theh   di rɛ' di rang jang   di chring
    relatives,   likewise   not good;   run to trail energetically   to mount. crest,

di rɛ'   di rang jang   di jɔng di hrlɛ'   'o wɔk ruʌt wɔk tong
run trail   energetically   forth & back laughing.   Oh, spirit wet soil sp. pool

ki gɔt   gʌh dii   wɔk lam ding   lam dɣng   ki gɔt   gʌh dii   wɔk chən
not follow this good,   spirit big tree   tree watch   not follow   this [is] good,   sp. field

wɔk mɔn   chenyʌk ki theh
spirit cotton   likewise is not good.

There is a loud, distracting noise from myriads of cicadas, but the terrific speed of praying with 5.5 syllables per second – the highest recorded – makes it even more difficult to distinguish the details of pronunciation. Among the problems are:

2nd line: mɛh rɣm "you together" or "you follow [us]", ma thal "come long" or "follow". chak "body", (notice chruʌt "chest", resembling chuʌk "tie, tie up").

3rd line: ma kawak (Ml), ma kham (Th) both meaning "come to cross" or "to intercept".

4th line: tay, tai "die" said in Thai to strengthen the appeal. 6th line: tae' "touch" (Khon Muang) and tit (Th) "stick to" (as a glue).

7th line: wɔk chən, in M3 chuʌn (when spoken fast resembling chən), while mɔn is the reference to the cotton string to fix the soul to the body during the ceremony.

7-8th line: 'oh 'ar 'ɣ' 'ar ma' "I have eating have given", viz. in advance and therefore has to be pronounced 'ar, because it is followed by a translocational verb, according to Rischel 1995, p. 333.

9th line: pia' dɛ 'i 'dɣ "[any] edible animals".

10th line: to ta chɯ, where to is "body" and ta is stative verb, see Rischel 1995, p. 315.

12th line: wɔk 'do' wɔk thri', two species of porcupine, previously considered to be sacred.

19th line: phanyʌt (Th) "parasites" (for infection Mlabri use the Thai word 'ak cep).

4.2 Thunder, Wind, Rain, Hail and Rainbow

All these natural phenomena were once considered to be the spirits signalling that someone had done something wrong, requiring propitiation. The prayers urging these spirits to keep away are still remembered, but the Mlabri no longer take further measures against them as we have been told they did a generation ago, and as it is related in the prayers.

Everyone is afraid of thunder when it comes too close, but for the Mlabri it may well be fatal, because often they cannot help having their windscreens close to big trees, and they may also camp on a high mountain. My party had such an experience in 1987 when staying for three weeks with the Mlabri (Ml) on Doi Sathan at an altitude of about 1,300 m. One evening, a thunderstorm raged over the mountain for two hours, during which lightning struck a tree only one hundred metres away. It may be of interest to note that until then the Mlabri had flatly denied that they still used prayers against thunder. However, when it was closest, and the lightning illuminated our camp in a series of flashes, we could see them sitting wet and close together, as well as hear them repeating the prayers over and over again in terror.

1980, 4b, 175, Seng (aged 18):

'o la (Th) kur mɛ'   gʌm hot chɔh   //   sa' la' (Th) kɔnding
Oh, leave thunder & rain, don't fall lightning,   sacrifice front loin-cloth [lit. navel]

neh di pang   sa' la' kwang   mɛh də dɛl sa' la' rɣ' yɣl
this to rainbow [spirit], sacrifice behind [loin cloth] you cut & sacrifice dust head;

107

gʌm ta' tʌn(y)	na ta' ya' (Th) chɔh	gʌm ki poh roh poh ray (Th)
don't uncle speak [thunder],	please grandparents lightning	don't split fiercely.

To show "that we are very poor people", so they said, some old rags or dry leaves with deer excrement on top were burned to make black smoke, which is also the way to signal to the rainbow spirit to leave. The smoke produced is supposed to rise up to please the nose of the rainbow spirit. The Mlabri perceive the thunder to be their mythological grandparents, ta' ya' (lit. "uncle-aunt", sometimes only the uncle is mentioned), who are requested not to speak, i.e. not to thunder too much. Incidentally, many of the natural phenomena are said to belong to whole families of spirits comprising father, mother, uncles, aunts and children. Thus the sun, for example, was said to be the celestial father, the moon to be the mother and the stars their children.

1st line: chɔh, heard rather as cɔh, the Mlabri gave various explanations of this. Egerod and Rischel 1987, p. 48, have however: chɔh "burn, start fire, smoke, singe, scorch", all of which could be the effects of the lightning and therefore, as we were told, a symbol of this. The word could also be an imitation of the sound of lightning and somehow it is connected with lightning, because some of the Mlabri shouted the very same word whenever I used my flashlight in the evenings back in 1980! sa' la' "sacrifice" (Th), kɔnding "navel", i.e. sacrificing the small piece of cloth covering the loins of males.

2nd line: kwang "broad, wide" (Th) was translated "[cloth] behind" (while khwan "smoke" (Th)). na' "please" (Th), polite word used at the end of requests etc., but often not translated, rɣ' yɣl was said to be "above head", but is rather "dust head", viz. smearing the head with dusty soil and, as the Mlabri said, an older way to ask the Thunder God for mercy.

1980, 4b, 218, Seng (aged 18):

sa' la' kɔnding	ni di pang	sa' la' kwang	di dɛl	sa' la' rɣ' yɣl
Sacrifice front cloth	to rainbow spirit,	sacrifice behind [cloth]	divide,	sacrifice dust head;

gʌm ta' tʌny	na' ta' ya' chɔh	gʌm gɛ'	poh ro' poh ray (Th)
don't uncle speak,	please grandparents lightning,	don't break	split fiercely,

chabay	poh chuh
carry shoulder	splitting down below.

Here, the thunder spirit is asked to carry the thunder away on its shoulders to the lowland.

1980, 4b, 224, Lek (aged 40):

chɔh	ta' ya' 'dɣ pɯh	gʌm ma poh mo' puʌk	//	lungbɛr lungti'
Lightning,	grandparents all wake up;	don't split & 'throw up'		[thunder on] children;

'ek 'ɣh	'ɛw wɛt	tek pa goh	di pɣr	gʌm ma poh	lungbɛr lungti'
take	small lizard	hit & break	get lightning;	don't split	children,

rih di rɯm	di gɣh sik	dɣ 'ɣh jak	di jɔr di jɔr //	hik pɣr
hither go away,	over there (?)	all send,	pull (rep.) far away;	very much lightning

gʌm ma poh	lungbɛr lungti' //	di pɣr di pɣr	di jak	di jar loh jar
don't break	children.	Lightning (rep.) much	go fast	search for

108

cho gɔt	cho' wɛt	cho tɛt cho' wɛt	chɛ'	chak kɣɣ chak lungguh
(small) child	hurting lizard,	child cut hurting lizard,	much	disable children & women;

di pɣr	'oh mak	hnguh	ma poh
lightning	I want	stop	splitting.

As usual the older generation knows the prayers better than the younger one, some of the latter claiming that they hardly believe in the spirits any longer. Thus this prayer is somewhat more elaborate. Killing or merely playing with lizards as well as with butterflies, which belong to the sky spirit, is considered a sin and is punished accordingly by sending the thunder spirit.

1st line: Some said that "uncle thunder" is the brother of the sky spirit, while the sun is termed: jiong "father". puʌk "throw up, full" possibly Northern Thai: uak (onomato-poeically).

1st, 4th & 6th line: poh "attack, hurt, kill, split"; at the very end of the prayer poh is as usual drawn-out.

2nd line: pɣr "lightning", the common word being grɯlbo, but Gui said that pɣr is especially used when there are very dark clouds and lightning.

5th line: cho' "cut, hurt", while chogɔt "baby, female", compare gətgɔt "young woman".

6th line: hnguh "sit, stay, cease, stop".

1980, 4b, 265, Ton (aged 17):

mɛ' pang	'ek koc jak mla'	//	mla' rɛ' jak	khɯn	'a chohboh chung
Rainbow (sp.)	take bamboo-rat leave people,		[from] people	run up	[to] mountain high.

The Mlabri have never told us about offerings of animals to the rainbow spirit, but it seems that this happened previously.

1980, 4b, 280, Ton (aged 17):

mɛ' pang	'ar khɯn	//	'a pung	yɔng	mɛ' ba 'a'	khon pa (Th)
Rain rainbow	has gone up,		[wind] blow	back and forth,	rain bad,	thick

'dɣ rɯm ding	//	mɛ' 'a	'oh ni	pang	khɯn 'i	//	rɛ' jak di 'yɛ'
several days big.		Rain have	me leave,	rainbow	[sp.] go up,		run away far,

//	mla' jang (Th) karɔl	'ek mla'	mla' 'ɛ bɯl
	people many swallow,	take persons,	persons yes die.

It is said that the rainbow has already swallowed many people, because the Mlabri believe that where the rainbow ends in the jungle another spirit, grɔc, a kind of dragon resembling a giant snake, may wait for them to swallow any person nearby. This is probably an inheritance from the old Indian belief in their water gods, the Nagas. Others believe a tiger may be present. Seng said that when the rainbow spirit smells the various roots the Mlabri eat it will take all the roots so they have to leave the area. Only the sky spirit can order the rainbow spirit to leave.

1st line: khon "thick, concentrated" (Th).

2nd line: ba 'a' "bad, rotten", wɔk ba 'a' "evil spirit".

3th line: jang "very much, many'" (Th).

1980, 6b, 110, Som (aged 28):

kɯr	gʌm hot	pa gʌm	jak jur rəmɯt	kɯr pʌr lom (Th)
Thunder	don't fall,	don't descend	wind (strong),	thunder fly & wind retreat (from]

bɛr komti'	nak cərɔng
boys & girls	very small.

1980, 6b, 130, Som (aged 28):

kɯr	gʌm di jur parɛl	gʌm 'i jur lom (Th)	//	di gɯn jak
Thunder	don't [come] down & hail,	don't descend wind;		return [away from]

lunggɔt lung gəndɣl	kɔmbɛr kɔmti'	nak chərong	nak lɛng
young woman & married woman,	boys & girls	very small & smallest (babies).	

bɛr komti'	nak cərɔng
boys girls	very small.

1980, 6b, 160, Som (aged 28):

toc pang	gʌm jak gʌh na'	jak bɛ'	loh	tom.'o' krʌp
Catch rainbow spirit	don't come here please,	go earth,	watch out	snake bite.

As referred to already, the Mlabri think that where the rainbow ends a tiger or a big snake may be waiting for them.

1980, 9a, 635, Muang (aged 42):

'ek chərek	phatɛp (Th)	phatɛp chal	pahtɛp pamɯy	//	di rɛ' di jak
Take tear	cloth,	cloth smelly,	cloth make smoke;		run go away

wɔk kɯr	wɔk lom	gʌm ki ma poh	mo puʌk kam
spirit thunder	spirit wind (Th),	don't come split &	stay throw up across

kɔmbɛr kɔmching to	nak cərong nak lɛng
relatives & very small	& smallest [children].

1980, 9a, 640, Som (aged 28):

chərɛk phatɛp	(interrupted by Muang, but continues)	chərɛk chong	phaw phay
Tear cloth,		tear trousers	when danger,

bato' hngke	//	dor chal phatɛp	chal pamɯy	//	wɔk kɯr pʌr
make fire fireplace,		throw [on] stinky cloth	[make] stinky smoke;		spirit thunder fly

kɯr mʌc	gʌm ki ma poh	mo puʌk kam	kɔmbɛr lɛng chingto
[when] thunder see,	don't come split	throw up across	relatives;

di chal	to' muk	chal kup	ma //	chal tɛr	chal yak	chal nɔm
get stinky,	burn smelly,	stinky cloud	come [being]	stinky bad,	stinky shit	& stinky piss.

When the thunder spirit sees and smells the stinking smoke it does not come to harm anyone.

1st line: phaw phay "when danger" (Th) and possibly included as a sort of explanation. This is also heard on the tape from the minor interruption and lowering
of the voice by Som.
3rd line: kɔmbɛr, km.bɛr "men", lɛng "babies" and chingto "fleshy body, women"!

1980, 9a, 721, Muang (aged 42):

chɔrɛk phatɛp pa muy //	dok lah dɣng //	chal	pa muy	yak gret
Tear cloth [make] smoke,	hang up [to] look [sp.],	stinky	make smoke	shit bad;

wɔk kuɯr	wɔk lom (Th)	di rɛ'	di jak	di 'yɛ'	di gɣtwʌt
spirit thunder & spirit wind	run,	leave	far	to mountain pass.

The burning rags are thrown on the earth or hung up in a tree: "to show the thunder
spirit that we are only poor people and therefore should not be harmed". Muang
added in 1994: "When the smoke comes up to the nose of the spirit of the thunder
it is pleased and stops thundering."

1982, 5a, 620, Gui (aged 37):

'ay	mɣ'	'i mɣm	'dɣ jak	di 'yɛ'	di gɣt.wʌt //	'o mla' bri
Honourable mother & father	send [thunder] far away	to mountain pass.	Oh, people forest

mla' tɛ (Th)	ma duk	ma yak //	mɛ' ki 'dɣ	gʌm juɯt
& former ones	have difficult & hard [life].	Rain not any (more)	don't angry,

rəmuɯt ki 'dɣ	gʌm jɔng //	'i mɣ' 'i mɣm	di jak	di 'yɛ'
wind not any,	don't go back & forth;	mother & father [spirit]	send	far away

di gɣtwʌt //	'oh 'ek nɔn (Th)	pia' lam pia' ton
to mountain pass	I (take) sleep	[near] any tree & trunk.

Here, the appeal to send the thunder away is directed at the deceased father and
mother spirits, or perhaps to the mythological grandparents, who might also be
called mɣ' mɣm. The last line is to underline the danger of staying near big trees
during thunderstorms.
1st line: 'ay prefixes names of adults during conversations to show respect.
2nd line: mla' tɛ probably tae kawn (Th) "people former ones", as the Mlabri put it
"the fixed ones" viz. those in their graves, but in other circumstances it may also
mean the other mountain people living in their villages. The dead Mlabri are
said to have a difficult existence, because they have to depend on the offerings
from their children since they cannot provide food for themselves.

1982, 5a, 700, Gui (aged 37):

kuɯr lom (Th) parɛl //	di rɛ'	di jak	'oh hom (Th)	hnguh gʌh
Thunder, wind, hail	run	go away,	me protect	staying here;

phi phor	phi mɛ (Th)	cɔnre 'uy	cɔnre yong	di rɛ' jak
spirit father	spirit mother,	spirit mother	spirit father	send running [away].

1st line: hom "cover up the body with clothes, blankets, etc.", according to my Thai
dictionary, here probably meaning "protect", but when Gui was asked, he said

that in case of strong wind and rain they also covered the windscreen with leaves
or blankets.

2nd line: Here we find again the not often used combination of the same phrase in
Thai and in Mlabri to make the prayer more powerful.

1982, 5b, 725, Gui (aged 37):

wɔk bang wɔk wɣk	//	gʌm ma tit ma thal	//	'ot ta'	'ot rɔy
spirit water		don't stick to follow,		my relatives (old & young)	

bɯl 'i tay (Th)	//	rɛ' 'yɛ'	pit (Th)	'yɛ'	di gɣtwʌt
die cause pass away		run far (away)	turn off	far	to mountain pass.

In this prayer also the spirit of water is invoked, which may be responsible for sickness, as well as when the Mlabri happen to drink from polluted water.
1st line: thal "long", ma (come) thal "follow".
2nd line: 'i "in order to, cause", tay, tai "kill, pass away" (Th).

1982, 5b, 746, Gui (aged 37):

wɔk bang	wɔk wɣk	//	gʌm ma tit ma thal	//	wɔk chǝhboh chung
Spirit rainbow	spirit water		don't stick to & follow,		spirit mountain high

chǝhboh lɔng lɔng	//	'ot ta'	'ot rɔy	'ot 'ɛw	'e dǝkat 'e naw (Th)
mountain descending,		my relatives	(old & young)	my children	oh (get) fever, cold,

'e bɯl 'e tay	//	rɛ' jak	di 'yɛ'	di gɣtwʌt
oh die pass away		run	far away	to mountain pass.

1982, 5b, 756, Gui (aged 37):

chɔh	gʌm ma 'ɣh	ma poh	kɔmber lɛng ching to	cǝnre kɯr
Lightning	don't come	split	relatives	[you] spirit thunder

cǝnre lom	//	rɛ' jak di 'yɛ'	di gɣtwʌt	//	gʌm gʌm ki	ma 'ɣh mɛ'
spirit wind,		run far [away]	to mountain pass;		(really) don't	send rain

hot chɛ'	hot na (Th)	//	'ɛ tɛ	rɛ' jak	di 'yɛ'	di gɣtwʌt	'ot ta'
fall much	fall thick;		yes truly	run far	[away]	to mountain pass	my uncle [thunder],

'oh to	dǝkat dʌm thɛk	//	lam ding lam dɣng	'i gɔy tom	'i bɯl
my body	(get) illness malaria;		tree big watch	before trick [someone]	in order to kill.

Very much the same prayer, but with the addition that diseases, including malaria,
should also be absent, perhaps due to the fact that many Mlabri, young and old alike,
catch this disease. Only the old refer to the spirit of the wind, which is also believed
to carry diseases. The last line indicates that falling trees have previously killed
people; the Mlabri often refer to this. It is still believed, at least among the older
generation, that the spirits may punish them by sending all sorts of misfortune,
especially if they do not make sufficient offerings.
4th line: dʌm thɛk lit. "head jungle" synonym for malaria. tom "trick someone"
(Th slang) perhaps related to the similar word: thom "clog, choke up" (Ml).

1982, 5b, 785, Gui (aged 37):

wɔk lom   wɔk kɯr   //   gʌm ki 'ɣh ki leh   kɔmbɛr lɛng ching to
Spirit wind spirit thunder   don't make bad here   [to] relatives,

rɛ' jak   di 'yɛ'   di gɣtwʌt   //   bɛr lɛng   di dɔkat   dʌm thɛk
run   far away   to mountain pass;   [or] children   get sick   malaria;

'i bɯl 'i tay (Th)   lam goh lam tom
   die [if]   tree break tree trick.

1982, 9a, 1368, Paeng Noi (aged 37):

'o la   jak dɔk   ma lam ding   //   'i mɣ' 'i mɣm   ding roy   bɯl nom (Th)
Oh, finish   put down   come tree big;   oh, mother & father relatives   died young

'nah pr.nah   //   to kum joy   kum dɔk   poh lom(Th)   poh rəmɯt
'long time back;   body hold help,   hold down   splitting wind   splitting wind,

'gʌm ki gɛ'   gʌm ki goh   'a di   pa lam pa ton   di kum kum
don't branch   don't break (fall down),   must   make tree trunk   hold (really)

kum dɔk   //   krom ding   lom dɣng
'hold down;   fat, big   wind watch (out).

The prayer is directed at the deceased relatives to beg for the wind to calm down as well as urging the spirits to support the trees so they do not topple.

The remaining prayers of this chapter on the Mlabri, Ml, are all by Poa (aged about 45 years in 1987), a pleasant and interesting person. Together with his band, he had been away from the main group further to the south for quite some time (1972-1984). As this band was moving through hostile areas due to the fighting between the Thai soldiers and the Communists, it was kept very isolated. Thus, apart from not being in touch with the other Mlabri, it was also less influenced by the surrounding hill tribes. This could be the reason for Poa's higher pitch (see introduction on language p. 83), and his fine language. By mere chance we caught a short glimpse of a boy from this band in the Loei province in the spring of 1982, not knowing the connection until five years later.

1987, 10b, 1250, Poa (aged 50):

chɔh   ta' ya'   gʌm ma poh   mo' puʌk   //   kɔmbɛr kɔmti'
Lightning   grandparents   don't split   keep throwing up (lit: full)   children [have]

poh wɛt   'o pagoy
split lizard,   oh, lizard (big species).

The thunder has come to strike, because one of their children has killed a lizard. This is very bad because, as already mentioned, lizards are considered to "belong to the sky spirit", who is the most powerful of all the spirits. Poa addresses his deceased grandparents, who in turn may 'ask' the sky spirit to stop the thundering. Only when in great distress do Mlabri invoke the supreme sky spirit directly (see p. 78).

113

1987, 10b, 1252, Poa (aged 50):

chɔh	ta' ya'	gʌh pa klol	'oh kwang (Th)	//	cho' gɔt	cho' wɛt
Lightning	grandparents	this cause head	me afraid (lit. "big");		hurt child	hurt lizard

tɛt tɛt jep lungguh	poh baluh balak	ta' ya'	to klol to kwang 'oh
(much) cut hurt [has] girl,	split angry & white	grandparents,	afraid (heart big) me.

On this occasion, Poa also agreed that they previously burnt old clothes to tell the thunder spirit to keep away. It seems that he is worried, since he may be blamed because his daughter has hurt the lizard.

2nd line: balak "white" and probably an allusion to "lightning", to klol to kwang "heart big" or "agitated, afraid".

1987, 10b, 1261, Poa (aged 50):

chɔh chɔh	ta' ya'	gʌm ma poh mo puʌk	kɔmbɛr lɛng chingto	//
(Much) lightning	grandparents	don't split throw up [on]	men, children & women;	

poh pa 'oh wɛt	'oh pagoy	//	jak long ru' ngɔr	dʌm hnguh	no (Th) gɛng
split have I lizard	I lizard (big spec).		Go into footpath,	long time stay	my windscreen,

'ɛw gɛng nyɔ'	//	ta' ya'	gʌm ma poh	mo poh puʌk	kɔmbɛr
small windscreen here.		Grandparents	don't come split,	stay & throw up	[on] men,

lɛng chingto	gʌm kul gɛ' 'ɛ	pya' lam	pa ton	to lon	to lɛn (Th)
children & women,	don't roll branch	any tree,	cause trunk	body shake	body move

to gɔt	dʌm	gənduɪl
behind	my	back.

2nd & last line: dʌm "onwards in time" or "brain", and then syn. for "my".

1987, 16a, 1064, Poa (aged 50):

'o kuɪr gʌm ki juɪt	rəmut gʌm ki jaw (Th)	gʌm ngɔr	gʌm ki	glɣ'
Oh, thunder don't angry,	wind don't perforate,	don't [this] way,	don't [hit]	head,

'oh gʌm ki kul	gɛ' 'ɛ	pa lam pa ton	tɛ 'ɔn	di khuɪn	jak di 'yɛ'
me don't roll	branch	tree & trunk;	indeed softly	[thunder] rise	go far away

di gɣtwʌt	//	mɛh gʌm ki ma guɪt	ma poh	kɔmbɛr lɛng chingto	//
to mountain pass.		You don't consider (think)	come splitting	relatives;	

mɛh di rɛ'	jak di 'yɛ'	di gɣtwʌt	//	mɛh gʌm ki	ma 'ɣh	ma' kul
you run	go far away	to mountain pass.		You don't	make	roll

gɛ' 'ɛ	lam pa don	//	mɛh di gɣn jak	də 'yɛ'	də	di di dɔy (Th)	//
branch	tree trunk.		You return back	far away,	go	indeed to mountain.	

gʌm ki	lom (Th)	rəmut 'oh
don't	fall down	wind [on] me,

Another iteration recorded about two weeks after the previous ones. As seen, the words are somewhat different, but the composition is almost the same.

2nd line: tɛ 'ɔn "indeed (right) softly".

114

Mlabri M3

The next four prayers were obtained from the small group of Mlabri refugees, brought down by the border police from the areas bordering Laos around 1975, and who we found already in January 1977. For the sake of convenience, they are designated M3, as they are the third group of Mlabri we have traced. As already stated (see Chapter 3, p. 53), their language is quite similar to that of the main group, Ml. Although intonation, vocabulary and a number of other features are somewhat different, these do not warrant seeing the two languages as other than mere quite closely-related dialects.

1987, 1b, 1120, Sak (aged 31):

krɔ'	wɔk mɣ' wɔk mɣm	di gɯn jɔy	gɯn kum 'oh	kum lam
Excuse (ask for) spirit	mother & father	return help,	return hold me	& hold trees &

kum ton	dɣng yɣl dap	'oh kampong	'ɛw	kambong	ngwɛ'	'a chung //
hold trunks,	watch [if] head hit	my skull	(your) child,	head (own)	child,	high (spirit)

gʌm tɛk	wʌl dap	'ɔt gɛng	wʌl bɔ' krɔ	tɛk 'yak
don't hit	return [stop] hit	my windscreen	return carry [away] please,	hit bad

lam baw //	kɛt	kɛt lam	kɛt ton	'ɛ goh tɣp	'oh kampong
other place;	afraid,	afraid tree	afraid trunk,	yes break cover	my head,

kr'ung 'oh	mɣm wʌl jɔy	'ot 'ɛw
inside me;	father return help	your child

In this prayer, the spirits of his deceased parents are also asked to come to prevent trees and branches from falling down upon them during thunderstorms, exactly as was explained to us at the time of recording.
1st line: Both gɣn and wʌl mean "return", while kum "hold, support"
2nd line: kampong is really "skull", but Sak said "head". M3 has a separate word for one's own child: ngwɛ'. chung "high" (spirit) or "please".
4th line: kr'ung "hole, inside".

1987, 2a, 875, Kit (aged 44):

This, and the next two prayers, begin with a sort of explanation in Thai of five or six words unciated in a low voice. In both prayers the sky spirit is asked not to send thunder – the mythological grandparents are exactly the same concept as that of the main group. But here they put ashes on their heads instead of burning old rags to plead for pity. However, the difference is not that great for we have been told that the main group once also smeared ash on their faces to ask for pity under especially critical circumstances.

ao' khi' thaw (Th)	ni chay wai (Th) ///	toc	ya phor	gʌh lɔh
Take (grey) ashes	this put in place, keep.	Catch [thunder]	grandparents,	this near

kambong //	ta' ya'	gʌm ki poh	ki pɣn lɛng	ki chay //
head.	Grandparents	don't split,	not shoot orange (lightning)	& not put on [us],

gʌm	ki krɔ' ma kr'ung	'yɛ'
don't	damage come inside,	[go] far [away].

1st line: The first phrase is not in Mlabri but in Thai, in explanation of the short ceremony, and therefore khi has a different meaning than ki "not", but rather derives from khee "waste material" (in general, Th). thaw "ashes, grey" (Th). chay "put on" according to the Mlabri, probably from Thai: sai "put on".

2nd line: pɣn the Mlabri said was "split" but rather derives from Thai peun "rifle, to shoot" and the light and sound of lightning as compared with those from a rifle. lɛng is the colour "orange (female language)", as in lɛng dɣng "red evening sky".

3rd line: kro' "damage, bad" compare krom: "dense (jungle), shade", kr'ung "inside".

1987, 2a, 890, Kit (aged 44):

ao' khi' thaw (Th)   chay la kha (Th) ///
Take (grey) ashes   put on, don't kill.

'ɣh   ta' ya'   gʌm ki poh   ki p'lɛng   //   yah 'ar thɔp
Yes grandparents don't split not shoot orange   We have burned,

'a bɔh   'a ta' ya'   'a klol di gong di thɛh klul thɛh klol
have ashes, have grandparents, have heart good get good heart happy

Sak, the younger of the two men present, was also asked to repeat the prayer, but said that he could not, because he had never learned it!

1st line: thaw or thao (Th) "ashes", while bɔh in Mlabri. la kha "say farewell, take leave" (Th), here in the meaning of: "leave (don't) kill".

2nd line: p'lɛng is a contraction of: peun (Th) lɛng "shoot orange".

3rd line: thɛh klol "good heart" or "happy"; Ml also has klul klol "happy". The physical brain is: cin klol "meat brain", while Ml has: klol 'on "brain soft". The mental brain is dʌm (M3).

1987, 2a, 900, Kit (aged 44):

'oh ni' chay khi' thaw ///   'ɣh ta' ya'   gʌm ki poh   ki pɣn lɛng
I this put on ashes;   do grandparents don't split, not shoot orange

ki chay // gʌm ki kro' ma kr'ung   ya' thʌp 'a bɔh   pa ta' ya'
not put on; don't damage come inside, brought burned ashes, cause grandparents

klul dii klol dii klul dii gong // 'ɛw dik theng   nɛng tɛk baw
hearth happy & hearth good.   Small children and unruly boys

poh cɯ   poh mʌc   // tak yʌk   wʌl yʌk   ta' ya'   //
not know not understand (see). Now as before [goodness] grandparents.

3rd line: nɛng "all, altogether" (nɛng hmu "group of people"). tɛk "hitting, unruly" (?)

4th line: tak yʌk wʌl yʌk Kit said means: "now as before"; J. Rischel has "in the past".

Fig. 69. In search of food in the mixed mountain jungle (Oy, Kit and Oy's wife Pua). These people often use walking sticks, as they have weakly developed knee joints due either to malnutrition or from eating some specific roots, probably containing toxic substances, as part of their daily diet. They also eat various species of leaves directly from the trees.

Fig. 70. This tiny windscreen accom-modates five persons, but usually they are somewhat bigger. M3 fig. 70-77.

Fig. 71. Previously banana leaves were used instead of a loin cloth (Kit and Sak).

Fig. 72. This group has specialized in finding small animals living in or around mountain streams.

Fig. 73. Digging for roots using only a wooden stick.

119

Fig. 74. Making a very simple mouse trap. This group never hunts large animals, at least not anymore.

Fig. 75. A display of the food collected, including various roots, marrows, wild fruits and crabs.

120

Fig. 76. Using a sharpened bamboo stick as a saw to produce enough heat to ignite scrapings of dry bamboo (Kit and Sak).

Fig. 77. Oy presenting an offering of some roots, put on a stone, while praying to the spirits of his deceased parents.

121

Fig. 78. Old Ut and his son Paeng Noi during the long prayer for all the most important spirits (see p. 105). (M1: fig. 78-87).

Fig. 79. The finely arranged altar attached to a big tree. On the platform there are offerings of bamboo cups with rice, meat, alcohol and parcels of various kinds

Fig. 80. The Mlabri said that once they sacrificed a little food every morning to gain protection during the day.

Fig. 81. Paeng demontrating the spear ceremony by holding the spear above the sacrifice, placed on a stone or, as here, a leaf.

Fig. 82. Poa during the real ceremony for the spear spirit. Offererings of meat are placed on the small platform and in the parcel hanging on the spear sheath.

Fig. 83. Som and Muang explain how a person, bitten by a tiger, is placed in a tree (see the arrow) to be abandoned soon after by the band.

Fig. 84. Gui demonstrating how the tiger climbs the tree to jump at the unfortunate person. The protective tattoo, also effective against tigers, was made by one of the other hill tribes.

Fig. 85. Pha made a ball of paper, imitating the shell, said to house the tree spirit. He said that the shell looks like a wasps' nest and that it is situated between the central roots of the tree. If someone breaks the shell, the spirit will emerge bright and shining and brings bad luck. Therefore the central roots are not to be touched (see p. 134).

Fig. 86. Skin diseases are very common. The back of this boy's head was one big wound caused by scabies. Many Mlabri have infections due to their insanitary habits.

Fig. 87. A young man, Lek's son, suffering from a kidney disease. His family did not allow us to take him to the hospital in Nan, and he died 14 days later.

127

Fig. 88. Thobitoa, an interesting and charming woman, said that elderly, disabled persons, who were not able to follow their band or had unbearable pains, made a poison of a plant-prym.

Fig. 89. Demonstrating how a burial takes place. Previously there were several other ways of disposing of the dead (see pp. 168-169).

4.3 Snakes, Tigers, Swamps & Creepers

In the 1970s the mountain jungles were still much bigger than they are now and had a very varied fauna. At that time, the Mlabri spent most of their lives in these jungles and were therefore exposed to a number of dangerous animals and obnoxious insects. The large and powerful animals were, and still are, considered to have strong souls (Ml), but usually they are not believed to hold spirits, except when they are sent as some kind of messenger by the most important spirits (those of the sky, mountains, earth, deceased parents, etc.) to warn the Mlabri of their wrongdoings or to punish them (see, for example, p. 105). Neither do the Mlabri agree as to the kind of spirit animals may possess. Some maintain that tigers, for instance, are simply very dangerous animals, while others say that they can sometimes be ghosts, a concept shared by many Hmong and Thai people in the area. One of the old men said that a bad Mlabri, when he dies, might turn into a dangerous bear ghost and a Hmong into a tiger ghost!

In the mountain jungles there are other hazards threatening the Mlabri. Apart from the obvious ones such as steep cliffs and waterfalls, there are swamps, hanging lianas and fallen trees, all of which have spirits to be placated with offerings and prayers under special circumstances.

Snakes

With one exception there are no prayers specifically directed towards snakes, but they are sometimes included in the prayers among the evils the Mlabri ask the important spirits not to send. If a child sees a snake he or she may say: ding ta' tom.'o' "elder (father, uncle, etc.) snake"; and if he or she is bitten:

ding roy   tal gʌh   tom 'o'   'a tal   krʌb 'oh   katong   gʌm lɔh   blʌk   bah tɤŋ di rɛ'
Relative now (today) snake   just   bite me.   Jump   don't [go]   near enter,   you run.

Tigers

The first two prayers are used against the large, striped tiger, which was last seen in about 1975, and which the Mlabri feared more than anything else. A group of tigers could easily kill two or three members of a band of 15-20, and the Mlabri therefore had to take strong counter-measures to prevent the tigers from following them. First of all they preferred not to stay more than a week in one place, as they had to move before their windscreens turned yellow. Otherwise the tigers would find them by their smell. Just mentioning the word for tiger while walking in the jungle was considered enough to be attacked.

If a tiger had injured someone in the band, the unfortunate victim was abandoned or placed in a tree – dead or alive – in such a manner that the attacking tiger was subsequently trapped either by a pitfall or by being impaled (see figs. 83-84 and Trier, 1986, pp. 31-32). One may wonder why the otherwise so reasonable Mlabri would leave their companions to such a fate, but obviously they had very little choice. Otherwise the tigers might further reduce their already small number. The Mlabri said that the wounded persons accepted their fate voluntarily, because it was their duty to enable the rest of the band to escape.

1982, 9a, 1340, Paeng Noi (aged 37):

'ε la' roay   //   bah thɣng   gʌm ma   poh blʌk   //   'i mɣ 'i mɣ gʌ'
Yes, leave tiger,   us   don't come   split (into).   Mother & father there

gʌh lah   gɯn 'ɣh   gɯn jɔy   lɔng 'εw   //   gʌm   to   kli'   bɔ' roay
up above   do return   return help   (lit. into) child;   don't   animal   bring   carry tiger

bɔ' plεng   //   ki ma 'ɣh ma 'ɣh   ma krʌp   'a tɣng
change (direction)   don't send indeed (rep.)   bite   (have) us.

This short prayer is interesting because it shows that, on the one hand, the deceased parents are asked to come and help their children against the tiger while, on the other hand, it is said: "don't bring the tiger". This is very likely because the Mlabri fear that the spirits of the parents might be angry, perhaps because they have not received sufficient offerings. Anyway, this was an explanation commonly shared by our informants.

1st line: 'i is used in speech when addressing elders; in other circumstances 'i is a
    female prefix, with i also used for infants.
2nd line: gʌh (gɔh) lah "this up above", poh roay "splitting tiger" or "fierce tiger".
3rd line: bɔ' plεng (Th) viz. carry and change tiger's direction away from the
    Mlabri.

1982, 9a, 1360, Paeng Noi (aged 37):

'o 'i mɣ'   klɔ' 'i mɣm   gʌm ki to kli'   bɔ' roay   bɔ' plεng (Th)   //   to bih
Oh, mother & father (spirits), don't bring animal, carry tiger change direction,   person cut

pa bɯl   'ar tay (Th)   gʌm ki ma 'ɣh   ma krʌp 'εw   gʌm ki   klol kli'   klol klap   //
killed,   have died [before]   don't send [to]   bite children;   don't   hearth bring   & trap.

'i mɣ'   'i mɣm   to kum jɔy   kum jak dɔk   bɔ' roay   bɔ' plεng (Th)   //
Mother & father   body hold help,   hold put away   carry tiger   change direction,

gʌm ki   ma krʌp   //   gʌm ki ma krʌp   mʌr gεng   bɔ mɣm   //   mɣ' mɣm
don't send   [to] bite,   don't come bite,   crawl windscreen   of Mr. father.   Mother father (sp.)

mʌc 'ɣh hak   bɔ' jak   gʌm mεt roay   bɔ' plεng   di 'ɣε'   di gɣt wʌt
see to both carry [away], don't your tiger   carry [our] direction,   go far away   to mountain pass.

Again the spirits of the dead mother and father are asked not to bring the striped tiger, but rather to send it far away to the mountain pass.

1st line: klɔ' is a classifier.
2nd line: klol "hearth" is used in various connections to describe states of mind, e.g. klol thεh "friendly, happy". gʌm ki klol kli' klol klap:"don't hearth bring to trap (the Mlabri)". Rischel 1995, p. 276 has: klap "hold (something) by squeezing it" viz. with a similar meaning.

Som, Muang and Gui also demonstrated some of the main points of what happens when the band leaves a person who has been attacked and wounded by a tiger (figs. 83-84). Somehow we had the feeling that Gui had heard it from someone who had actually seen this happen when he was a child. Anyway he mentioned the name of a person who had suffered this terrible fate. In the next prayer it is said that the

130

person is being lifted up into the tree, that the others in the band have to forsake him, and that this is done to rid them of the tigers, which may otherwise follow the members of the band. After the band has left, one of the tigers will probably climb up to jump on the unfortunate person causing both of them to fall down and be impaled on a number of pointed bamboo sticks set around the trunk of the tree. The latter has been stripped of its outer bark to a height of three to four metres!

1994, la, 237, Gui (aged 49):

roay krʌp	roay krʌp	pa khɯn	dɔmɔy	jak hnguh	//	khɯn	'a yong
Tiger bite	tiger bite,	bring up,	alone	[to] stay.		Up [in the tree]	have men

yok gʌh 'uy	yok gʌh	jak hnguh	lah dɣng	//	nɛh roay	khɯn rih	khɯn rih jak
lift this female,	lift this	[to] stay	upwards.		This tiger	climb up	hither climb up;

ni' rɔb.yu	rɣm glɯn	ja' (Th) luɣy	rɣm bakdor	//	nɛh roay	lah klap
[others] flee jungle	together support;	shall straight	together leave.		This tiger	above trap

hɔt jur	krʌp mla'	nyʌ' hot jur	roay bɯl	mla' goh	bɯl
descend down	bite person,	that one fall down,	tiger die,	person break	[also] die.

1st line: pa khɯn (kheun in Thai) "make go up".
2nd line: yok "lift, lift up" (Th), while dɔk lah dɣng "put on up, hang up".
3rd line: ni' rɔb.yu "flee jungle", is the rest of the band, who hurry away. glɯn "lean to, support", luɣy "pointed" or "straight", pakdor "leave, forsake".
4th line: hɔt jur "arrived down", hot jur "fall down" after slipping on the slippery inner bark.

Swamp and Water Pools

The spirits of wet soil or swamps, wɔk ruʌt, and of natural water pools, wɔk tong, are greatly feared and are among the most frequently mentioned in the prayers. This is with good reason, since these places are breeding grounds for malarial mosquitoes and because water taken from them might be tainted. The Mlabri said that the two spirits should not adhere to them. This might happen: "when the wild pigs are muddy (from the wet soil or the pools) and come to rub themselves against trees". It is believed that, as a consequence, the bad spirits are deposited there, so when children or others touch these trees their souls may be captured. Incidentally, boars are hunted, but as they may have strong and vengeful souls and because they may hold these spirits, the Mlabri insist on using domesticated pigs for their offerings. Paeng, one of the old men, told us that the wind, like the wild pig, might be responsible for transmitting the diseases caused by these two spirits. Prayers against them were also used together with a small offering when a band arrived in a new area and before they went hunting in that locality, as demonstrated in the next example.

In the following two prayers we shall see that the Mlabri believe, moreover, that spirits can reside in their belongings, such as their sack or trousers, just as the spirit of dead persons still occupy their previous belongings, which is one of the reasons for not removing these from the grave.

131

1980, 8a, 1815, Som (aged 25):

'ɛ wɔk ruʌt wɔk tong   bɛr lɛng ching to   kɔmbɛr kɔmti   'oh pa gʌm
Yes, spirit wet soil, spirit pool,   relatives,   children &   me don't cause

rɣm tit   rɣm tɛ' (Th)   'ot tong   'ot dɛo'   //   jak tɛ   pa 'oh   jak tɛ mʌc
follow stick to & touch [or]   my sack   my trousers;   go truly   make me   go truly find

pia' 'dɛ   'i 'dɣ   //   koc   hnɛl   gather   gɔchong   ngay   ciak
edible   animals: bamboo rat,   rat,   squirrel,   land turtle,   wild pig &   (Sambhar) deer,

'oh bɔn ngɔr   bɔn thang (Th)   //   mɛh hak   wɔk ruʌt   wɔk tong
I meet footpath   & road   You both (separately),   spirit wet soil & spirit pool,

'oh   ki rɣm tit   rɣm tɛ' (Th)
me   not follow stick to   & touch.

1st line: kɔmbɛr lɛng ching to "men, babies and women" is often used loosely for "relatives"; Coincidently ching also means pig, allegedly as the women (ching to) should be as fleshy as their most coveted meat animal!

2nd line: tɛ' "touch", probably from tae' tawng (Th) "touch". dɛo' "trousers" said Som.

4th line: bɔn "together, meet, dance".

1980, 8a, 1820, Muang (aged 42):

'ɛ wɔk ruʌt wɔk tong   wɔk khray sang (Th)   'ay chɔng (Th)   gʌm ki tit
Oh, spirit wet soil spirit pool,   spirit some boar   these two [spirits],   don't stick to

ki tae'   //   kɔmbɛr lɛng ching to   'oh di dii di ngam   nɛh pr.nah pr.nah
not touch;   relatives &   I get very good [life]   as long time back.

gʌm ki tit   ki hong   pathong pothay   //   ma poh   koc   poh hnɛl
Don't stick to   not stay   sack (for collecting)   Come kill   bamboo rat,   kill rat,

gather   gɔchong   'ɛ man   di dun di dar (Th)
squirrel,   mountain turtle   yes, luck   a lot.

Here the connection between the two first-mentioned evil spirits and that of the boar is clearly demonstrated. Finally, it is said: 'e man di dun di dar. Muang translated this into: "roots a lot" (man "root" in Khon Muang). However, man also means "luck" in Mlabri, whereas dun, (Th) could be "a weight of twenty pounds", and dar, "full, abundant" (Th), thus both meaning "a lot".

1989, 5a, 600, Si and Ton (aged 31 and 29 years):

ngay jak   lɛp ruʌt   jak ma huut lam   gʌm jak   pa tit (Th) wɔk
Boar gone   dip wet soil   & come rub tree;   don't [You] go   stick to spirits.

lɛp "dip (put into)", while the Mlabri just said "into", which is covered by other terms, however.

Ton confirmed that when the wild pig crosses into a muddy place, gets dirty and then rubs itself against a tree, it transfers the bad spirit, wɔk ruʌt. Therefore, children especially are advised not to touch the tree or they might become very ill. This time it was added that the elephant and the wild ox are also able to produce this problem, although it is always the boar that is referred to in the prayers.

Creepers

Creepers such as rattan, with their long, winding lianas, are believed to house a special spirit, wɔk mʌ' which, if not treated properly, causes severe headaches or even death. The spiral forms of the lianas obviously represent the feared dizziness of the mind. If the Mlabri have to walk under them, they should cut the lianas and some of the roots to offer to the tree spirits, in order not to develop a deadly headache. Furthermore, at least part of what is under the earth, i.e. the central parts of the roots, the centre of the spirit itself, should not be touched. This procedure actually ensures that the rattan trees survive. Once again we see that religious concepts often suit practical purposes, since rattan is used to make baskets, etc.

1987, 6b, 950, Gui (aged 42):

mʌ' lɛc	gɯn 'a blʌk	//	thang.ɔt glɣ'	trɣl bɯl dʌm	pɣc
[Big] creeper	returned [after] entering,		[got] dizziness,	pain kill brain.	Cut [for]

cɔnre cɔnraw	jak 'ɣh	jak pɣc	jak pa 'e'	//	gɯn 'a	ki bɯl	ki pa 'e'
spirit,	make	cut	feed (offer).		[If] return [camp],	not kill	not feed;

//	cɔnre lam	cɔnre ton	cɔnre mʌ'	cɔnre thrak lah grɔk kɔmbɛr
	spirit tree	spirit trunk,	spirits (two species)	creepers up above, relatives &

kɔmti' bɯl	na glɣ'	bɯl dai (Th)	//	cɔnre mʌ'	cɔnre thrak
children die [if]	much headache	die can,		due to] spirits	(two species of) creepers.

If someone walks under the creepers without making the appropriate offering, it is said they might develop the devastating headache, even after having returned to their camp. In that case they are advised to return to the place of the hanging creepers to make the offering.

1st line: mʌ' is a general name for creepers such as rattan, while lɛc (keua' in Thai) and thrak are very large species, gɯn "return, give back", probably from Thai: kheun. thang.ot glɣ' "dizziness" is similar to car sickness as explained by Gui, where thang is the withdrawal of a part of the mind from the axis of the body (Th). 'ɔt "poor", and glɣ' is "head". trɣl bɯl dʌm is some kind of deadly headache, where trɣl "pain", bɯl "kill" and dʌm "brain, head".

3rd line: lah "up above". 4th line: na "thick, much" (Th).

1987, 6b, 978, Gui (aged 42):

cɔnre blʌk	cɔnre mʌ'	cɔnre lam	cɔnre mʌ'	cɔnre lam blʌk	//	gʌm ki
Spirit enter,	spirit creeper	spirit tree,	spirit creeper	spirit tree [come] into,		don't (enter)

glɣ' ki tɛk	di dii di ngam	nɛh prnah prnah	//	wɔk mʌ'	wɔk thrak
head not hit;	get good [living]	as long time back,		spirit creeper & big species.

1st line: We notice again that spirits are either called cɔnre (also: cɔnraw) or wɔk.

2nd line: gʌm ki glɣ' here meaning spirit not enter or take over the head according
  to the Mlabri.

1987, 6b, 986, Gui (aged 42):

cɔnre mʌ'   cɔnre thrak   //   gʌm ki   berlɛng ching to blʌk   gʌm ki glɣ'
Spirit creeper   spirit (large spec.)   don't   relatives enter,   don't head

ki thɛh   di dii di ngam   nɛh pr.nah pr.nah   //   pɛc lat 'a lɛn   pa 'e' yɔng
not good;   get good [living]   as long time back;   cut finished,   feed & offer

    phi (Th) ni dii   //   cɔnre mʌ' cɔnre thrak   'a na   (then mixed with Thai:)
[to] spirit, this [is] good. [If] spirits (two species of creepers) are thick   [and therefore]

bə phan   pa tat   bə khwang ni   bə yɔng   phi yɔng   yang ni 'oh
cannot pass by & cut,   cannot put away,   not offer [to] spirit, offer   in this way, [then] my

khon   pen nak   nak bay   //   pen khon   nan man   yu dii
people   surely get   difficulties big.   Able persons   long time luck   & stay good,

man kheu   thae kawn (Th)   ma' lam   phi kheu khaw (Th)   ki cɯ'
luck have,   really long time   give [to] tree   [when] spirit has requested,   sp. not entcounter.

2nd line: yɔng "put something up" as when offering to the spirits (Laotian).
5th line: man "root" (Khon-Muang), but obviously also syn. with "luck".

According to Gui, walking under the creepers, especially if they move in the wind,
may create great difficulties if they are not cut down and a sacrifice is made. But it
is finally said that honourable people who keep sharing their food with the spirit of
the creeper will not receive any trouble. The second half of the prayer is mixed with
Northern Thai words (Khon Muang) to make it more powerful.

    The next prayer is a good illustration of a long example. It is actually in two
parts, of which the first two-thirds are about the danger of walking under the creepers and how to avoid the deadly dizziness. The remaining third comprises a request
to the spirits or perhaps rather to us for money, because the Mlabri receive so little
from working for the Hmong farmers that they barely have enough rice to eat.
Ultimately, Gui expresses his hope for the future that the Mlabri may become more
plentiful and become as wealthy as us – the strangers!

    The big creepers have to be cut down, except for the central parts of the root
stem, after which an offering is made of, for example, some meat, flowers and roots.
It is explained, moreover, that in the case of a deep root of the plant, one has to dig
deep and cut away the side parts to offer to the spirits. We also hear that if the earth
is removed around the rootstock, and the latter is lifted up from the ground (using
a long rod), everything should be all right, provided an offering is presented to the
creeper spirit of rice and meat. But if the main part of the root (the home of the
spirit) is cut or pared off, the Mlabri think they are in great trouble.

    Incidentally, the same procedures are employed when removing the large branch
of a tree, which has fallen down and become stuck in the ground and has to be
removed immediately. It is worth repeating at this point what Pha told us in 1987
(see fig. 83), viz. that the soul of the big creepers is situated at the centre of its root
and resembles a honeycomb.

134

1987, 6b, 995, Gui (aged 42):

pɣc pɣc 'a lac pa 'e'   //   kɔmbɛr lɛng ching to   gʌm ki glɣ' gʌm ki buɩl
Cut, cut, finish feed (offer),   relatives [creeper spirit]   don't head [occupy] don't kill,

ki tay (Th)   pa 'e' cənre te'   'ɛ tɛk   'ɛ te'   pa 'e'   pɣc   //   thang 'ɔt glɣ' gʌm ki
not die,   feed spirit soil   yes beat   yes soil   feed,   cut.   Dizziness [if] don't

pɣc   ya thang 'ɔt glɣ' buɩl   //   mʌ' ji' gʌh   ji' 'dɣ jəru   khɔn yak
cut,   bring dizziness die.   Creepers [even] belonging [to]   any deep   trunk difficult,

    khɔn te'   khɔn wɔk bak   ching hn.tel   nɛh pa 'e'   chuʌk kl.dul   //   nɛh
trunk [into] soil   trunk spirit dig deep,   side parts   this feed,   dig big,   [if] this

    'a lʌh   thuɩ' mɣk   gʌh chual   //   bɛr lɛng ching to   khon jak kwɛhl   poh koc
[part] get up,   [be] good   & relieved,   relatives people   go search,   split bamboo rat,

    poh te'   'e' mal   phakkat ləbo'   //   khuɩn 'a mɣk   gʌh ki jak pɣy
split soil [get]   yam, taro,   lettuce such ones.   Lift up have [trunk],   this not eat,

    khɔn gʌh   ki jak plut   kɔmbɛr kɔmching to buɩl   //   nak chərɔng chəgɣh
trunk this   not skin off,   [then] relatives die.   Very small, similar(ly)

nak hluak luɩ'   nak hluak chərɔng glɣ'   nak chərɔng   te' 'dɣ jak   pɣc pa 'e'   //
very grown big   very big & small root   very small,   soil all go   cut feed (offer).

    khɔn nɛh   jak kruɩh   nɛh 'a thuɩr mɣk   'ɣ' jak bong   jak 'ek ma   //
[When] trunk   dig out,   this should [be] alright,   eating rice & meat   bring (offering).

'khuɩn 'a khɔn   gʌh ki jak plut   mʌ' gʌh   ki jak pɣc   ji 'dɣ   gʌh ki
up have trunk   this not skin off,   creeper this   not go cut,   anyone   this not

'jak pa 'e' 'ɣ'   kɔmbɛr kɔmching to   buɩl   paduk patiɔng   gʌh   tɛ bɣn wʌl
feed on, eat   relatives   die   altogether,   [if] here   indeed return

    krum krum   hɛk 'a glɣl klɛh   ///   mla' bri   mla' tae   mla' grɔk   mla' ma
dense, (really)   many get headache.   People forest   & former   people band,   people got

duk ma yak (Th)   ki gʌh gʌh   pɣ' ngɣn   pɣ' khang   //   chuʌn mɔn   gʌh ki bi'   //
difficult [life],   not this here   have money   satang (Th).   Farm (field)   this not (give) full.

    kwʌl gətheu   pɣ' ngɣn   pɣ' khang   krɔ gruɩ'   dɔ ngɣn   di dɣn   dor jo'
Stranger carry   have money   satang,   ask for   money   big give away,   this want.

    yu' pi'   gʌh chɛ'   mla' bri'   ki chɛ'   ki nak (Th) 'ɣ'   ///   gʌm 'ɣh   gʌm tɛk
rice husked   this much;   Mlabri   not much   not much eat.   Don't do [bad],   don't hit

gʌm paluh   ///   rak sɔng (Th)   rɣh jak   kɔmbɛr kɔmchingto   nɛh ki 'dɣ
don't quarrel   Make love two   wait [for]   relatives;   these not any,

    ki ngɣn hluak   suɩm suɩ (Th)   theung theung   (Th) jak   'ɣh jak kwʌl
not money much;   [when] little by little   very much   get, [we]   become [like] strangers.

1st & 7th line: glɣl (glɣ') "head" as well as "root" (dɔm, dʌm "brain, and klol "heart").

2nd line: cənre te' 'ɛ dek 'ɛ te' pa 'e' was said to be a kind of spirit trap made of pieces of split bamboo, but it rather means: "earth yes beat yes earth feed" dig for

135

getting the roots, perhaps because the Mlabri had replied on my next question as to where the offerings to the creeper spirit were put, viz. besides the spirit trap.

6th line: poh te' 'e' mal phakat ləbo' the translation rendered is the same as that of the Mlabri.

12th line: krum "fat, thick, dense", the idea probably being that if the creepers get too dense they will cause trouble. glɣl klɛh "headache", where the Mlabri said: "finish", however which fits with klɛh "to strike" (the head tangentially). mla tɛ (tae in Th) "people formerly, deceased".

13th line: ngɣn is lit. "silver", while khang was said to be satang, an old Thai name for money.

16th line: rak sɔng (Th.) "love two" (or "have sex"), which the Mlabri translated into "feed baby", however this is an understandable transliteration (while "breast-feed" ma' bo' or bo' bo' ma' 'ɛw "breast give child"), rɣh jak "wait for".

1987, 11a, 693, Poa (aged 50):

| pɣc pɣ' mʌ' | pɣ' 'i mʌ' | tal gʌh | kɔmbɛr thang 'ɔt glɣ' | // |
| Cut have creeper, | have creeper | today, | person dizziness (turn around head); | |

| gʌm ki klol glɣ' | gret dɔm (dʌm) | gʌm ki thang 'ɔt glɣ' | trɣl buɪl dɔm |
| don't [enter] head, | pain brain | don't dizziness | pain deadly brain, |

| di dii di ngam | nɛh | pr.nah | pr.nah |
| get very good (life) | here | [as] long | time back. |

Mlabri M3

Animals

As already mentioned, hunting and the animals themselves are of much greater importance for the members of the large group than for those of the small one, who have subsisted rather by catching small animals and collecting roots, tubers and plants. When the latter meet dangerous animals, they run away instead of fighting them, as would the members of the large group, if need be. Therefore, the small group does not have many stories about the animals or prayers relating to them – at least now. However, reminiscences about the animals having souls or spirits or being spirit messengers are also found among the old members of the small group. For instance, they also believe that butterflies should not be killed or the sky spirit will kill those responsible. They also think, like the members of the large group, that big birds should not be sacrificed least the birds carry their souls away.

Moreover, we have the following example of a short prayer used after killing a python. This has to be done by using two sharp forked bamboo sticks. One is pushed into the earth over the neck of the python in honour of the death spirit, wɔk bɛ', while the other is pushed in over the tail in honour of the mighty sky spirit, wɔk kuɪr (these sticks are called yuɪm lom "stay blocked".

Kit, 1994 (aged 44):

| huɪl hʌl | gɔy hnguh | gɔy tom (Th) | nom ray | jak glɣ' | lʌh, lʌh, lʌh |
| Pull out tongue, | soup settles | soup boil, | [meat] tender much; | go up [spirit] | up, up above. |

136

The python is cut into pieces and cooked in boiling water, which after being cooled is sipped. The meat is said to be a delicacy. Probably the spirit of the dead python is asked to leave before the soup and the meat can be eaten. I was told that huɪl hʌl is the name of the spirit of the python, but J. Rischel, 1995, p. 257, has: "put out the tongue in order to cool off ", which in the present case might be done to ease away the spirit of the python. Kit added that if these procedures were not followed the sun would go dark. They are also performed to ensure that the spirit of the python will not harm their group, but go far away. Incidentally, the mountain people have many stories about large cobra and python who they say may take their revenge after encounters with humans.

Creepers and Trees

The small group also fear to pass under or near large, hanging lianas, especially if they move in the wind (mʌ' guɪn luɪk), which may produce a deadly dizziness. Kit said that if they become dizzy or have a bad headache, in spite of having cut down the creepers and returned home to the camp, they would take the trouble of going back the same way, even including all their itinerary of the preceding day, to make a small offering of a bamboo rat, silver and gold leaf (!) and betel (see the next prayer) to the spirit of the creeper and set up a bamboo spirit trap (Th: thong lit. "flag"), before again returning to camp.

1994, 02, 250, Kit (aged 51):

lɛo wɔk mʌ'	wɔk thrak //	'a thang 'ɔt glɣ'	thang 'ɔt glɣ'	ta wɔk mʌ' //	
Finish spirit creeper	spirit rattan,	have dizziness	dizziness [much]	Mr. spirit creeper,	

'ao lɛo	wɔk mʌ'	wɔk trak	pɣc mʌ'	'ar tat (Th)	yah 'ar pɣc mʌ'
want finish	spirit creeper	spirit rattan,	cut creeper	having cut	we having cut creeper

'ar tat 'ar nuny //	'ar jak mʌ'	'ar lɛn ngɔr	'ar lɛn chɛm nɛ	'ar jak 'ar lɛn ngɔr
cut finished.	Left creeper	finished way	finished feed yesterday,	left, finished way,

lɛn chɛm	'ar pa 'e'	mʌ' wɔk mʌ' gʌh pa 'e' //	di thɛh di mɣk	gʌm ki
finished feed,	made feed	creeper, sp. creeper this feed.	Good living,	don't get

thang 'ɔt glɣ'	thang 'ɔt dʌm	'at lɛn ngɔr lɛn chɛm	wʌl toc to ngɣn
dizziness (head)	dizziness (brain)	end of way finish feeding;	[when] return take silver,

to 'iyo	to di pru'	to wɛm	to di pru'	to khondɛb	gʌm ki mak nyayh
gold,	betel [leaves],	(plant species),	betel	& saliva;	don't like to sin [therefore]

'at lɛn ngɔr	lɛn chɛm //	'oh whi' jak di wʌl	'oh di 'a tɛ (pr)war di
at the end of way	finish feeding.	I hurry to return,	I must make real straight,

jak di wʌl war di	rɣm tɛ klɣng	gʌm chɣl	tɛ hnɛ'	//
going return straight.	[If] all good afterwards,	don't believe	certainly Him [that spirit].	

1st line: thang 'ɔt glɣ' "dizziness or car sick" exactly the same words as the main group use.

2nd line: pɣc "cut at a right-angle", while sɔm "cut" tangentially, and tat "cut" (Th).

3rd line: 'ar lɛn ngɔr lɛn chɛm "finished way finish feeding", to which Kit added:

"that there was no other way to finish with the headache"; ngɔr "footprint" (e.g. ngɔr gling "way, road").

5th line: An additional offering, including thin silver and gold leaf (as in the Buddhist temples) and betel leaves, is presented to the spirit of the creeper.

6th line: kɛndɛp "betel nut" according to the Mlabri. 'at is the definite article, so while lɛn "finish", at lɛn "end". nyayh "resent" or according to Kit "to sin".

last line: klɣng "behind, afterwards". chɣl probably from cheua "believe" (Th). If he is unaffected after having passed under the lianas, he does not think they had a spirit.

1994, 2a, 065, Kit (aged 51):

| gɔy gla' | gɔy pa 'e' | gɔy pa 'e' | wɔk mʌ' | // ao' (Th) thang 'ɔt glɣ' |
| Slowly speak, | slowly feed, | slowly feed | spirit creeper; | got dizziness |

| pa tak nɛ | 'oh thang 'ɔt glɣ' | ya (Th) 'oh | thang 'ɔt glɣ' | ya 'ot mʌ' |
| caused yesterday, | I [got] dizziness, | don't me | [get] dizziness, | don't my creeper |

| nɛh 'ot ngɔr | 'oh jak nɛ | jio | gʌh loh nɛ | gʌh loh yɛng (Th) |
| this my way, | I go yesterday, | a while ago, | this search for yesterday | & this noticed. |

| 'oh thang 'ɔt glɣ' | jak pɣc nyɔ' tak | loh pɣc | 'a jak dor | 'ot ngɔr |
| I got dizziness [when] | go cut rambutan, dig up, | look for cut | have put away | my way |

| gʌh gʌh gʌh | 'at pɣc mɛt | 'at ngɔr gling | 'at pɣc pɣc pɣc pɣc | // kham ngɔr |
| this, this, this, | cut your | footpath, | cuts, cut, cut, cut. | Cover trail |

| 'at lɛn 'at pa 'e' | // | pɣc ma' tat | 'at pa 'e' | laeo (Th) wɔk | mʌ' wɔk thrak |
| at the end feeding; | | cut, make cut (Th) | offering, | finish spirit | creeper (two species). |

| // gʌm ki 'ɣh | gʌm ki mak nyayh | gʌm ki | thang 'ɔt glɣ' | thang 'ɔt dʌm | // |
| don't do bad, | don't like to sin, | don't [get] | dizziness | dizziness. | [When] |

| wʌl toc to ngɣn | to 'iyo | to tɔl 'oh khondɛb | gʌm ki 'ɣh | gʌm ki mak nyayh | // |
| returning, take silver, | gold [leaf], | betel mine & saliva; | don't do bad, | don't like to sin; |

| gʌm thang 'ɔt glɣ' | thang 'ɔt dʌm | // pa di whi jak di wʌl | pa di rɣm thɛh |
| don't [get me] dizziness, | head & brain. | Make fast return, | make all together good |

| glɣng 'oh gʌh jak wʌl | 'oh 'a thɛh | pa lɛn | ngɔr | lɛn chɛm | // |
| afterwards I myself return. | I [feel] good, | finished | way | finish feeding. |

1st line: gɔy gla' "speak slowly" probably a repetition of my request to Kit to better understand the following prayer!

4rd line: ngɔ' (ngaw, Th) "rambutan".

5th line: kham "cross (Th), cover".

8th line: glɣ' "head" (feminine form) while dʌm "brain" or "head" (masculine form).

9th line: rɣm, Egerod and Rischel, 1987, p. 75 have: pon rɣm, 'ak rɣm "all of us".

last line: chɛm "feed" (e.g.: chɛm 'ɛw "feed up baby"). A branch that has fallen down and become stuck in the ground (lam hot chɯt "branch fall leaning") is also said to produce the deadly dizziness or a pain (jɛp hng.ther "pain piercing") in various parts of the body. If this starts, one must hasten to remove all such branches, even the smallest, in order not to become very ill. Just like the main group, the members of the small group, M3, also do not cross fallen logs but circumvent them for fear of malicious spirits causing, for example, a sprained ankle.

4.4 The Spear

For the Mlabri, who really live on the edge, the overriding concern is food and this is all too often a problem. During severe drought or heavy rain the situation may become critical if they cannot obtain help from neighbouring peoples. We were told that during such periods adults often become dizzy, while the children cry from hunger. Actually, many of their children have, due to malnutrition, died following an otherwise non-fatal disease. The most prized ability among the Mlabri – men and women alike – is therefore the ability to find food. In the old days, the person who brought back most animals – the great hunter – and was willing to share with others, was the most respected of all. A man returning home after searching for food might say.

1980, 6b, 490, Som (aged 28 years):

dingroy	jak kwehl 'e'	kwehl mal	kwehl koc kwehl hnɛl //	jak 'ek gurk	'ek nam
Elder	go find yams	find taro	find bamboo rat find rat;	take container	fetch water

ma 'ɣ' ma bong	kɔmbɛr kɔmti' nak chərɔng nak lɛng	'oh gɛng 'oh mɯm
come eat rice & meat	children very small & smallest child,	my windscreen, father's.

1st line: dingroy is lit. "elder & younger" or "relative", but is often used for "father" or "elder relative".
2nd line hnɛl "rat, mouse", even though the Mlabri Ml also eat mice, they only go to hunt various kinds of rats, even some quite large species.

Almost all the literary sources on the Mlabri, including the very first ones from the beginning of the 20th century, just mention that they use spears, without giving details of the worship of the spear spirit. However, this is not surprising, because by revealing too much information, the Mlabri would offend this spirit, and would not have any luck when hunting. An exception is the Australian explorer Robert Weaver and his companions who, in 1955, traced a small group of Mlabri M3, probably belonging to the last remaining members of this kind of Mlabri in the Loei province. Actually, we also heard about them when visiting the area in 1982, close to the locality indicated by Weaver. He succeeded in recording and photographing part of the spear ceremony during the few days he spent with the small group, which comprised six men, one woman and a boy. Weaver writes, 1956, p. 295:
"Everything, with the exception of their spears, was shared equally. Each spear was sacred to its owner. If anyone else should touch or handle a spear, its spirit would be quickly offended. This was serious, because the spirit could either guide or misguide the weapon in flight. An animal would then have to be sacrificed to pacify the spirit. And for purposes of general insurance, such a sacrifice would be addressed to all the spear spirits, whether they had been offended or not. ... The [ancestor] spirits cannot locate food for themselves even though they roam the jungles as their living descendants do. And when the ancestors become hungry, they

inflict illness upon the living people to let them know they need food. The clan must then sacrifice an animal."

It is interesting that most of Weaver's observations are in complete agreement with our data on the main group (Ml), and this is also true with regard to his information on the spear spirit. Right from the start, we ourselves had many discussions about the spear and its spirit, and induced the Mlabri to recite the prayers. But for many years they were reluctant to perform the real ceremony, because they were afraid that the spear spirit would turn its deadly virtues on them through accidents while they were preparing the poison for the spear tip or hunting. It was not until 1987, after staying with the Mlabri Ml for a long time, that we were shown how to forge the spearheads (fig. 57), as well as perform the complete ceremony (fig. 82). However, in this chapter I will only deal in detail with the manufacture and use of the spears, as far as it is directly relevant to the content of the prayers themselves.

A good spear is one that kills the animal with the very first blow and such a spear is sacred to its owner. The spirits of the spear and sword are asked to come, but not to bother either the band or those (us) who have come to visit the Mlabri. This was actually our very first stay with them in their windscreens. One of their main concerns with having strangers in their camp was the possible unfavourable reaction of the spirits.

1978, 5a, 712, Paeng (aged 48):

wɔk khɔt	wɔk naw	ki gɔt	gʌh jay (Th)	falar phalar phalang (Th)
Spirit spear	spirit sword	not (come) behind	this soul.	Westerner

pa ma 'ɣh	ma phɔm (Th)	mɔ' klay (Th)	mɛh 'ɣh	di buɪl di tay (tai Th)
come [to]	see me;	sneak close	you [spear spirit]	go kill

nɛh prnah prnah	//	na (Th)	di chi	di chɔng	jɔng dor	hr.lɛ'
as long time back.		Much	want	walking	forth & back	laughing.

1st line: ki gɔt gʌh jay, where jay "soul, inner being". Originally, none of the Mlabri
    seemed to be sure of the translation but gave various slightly different alterna-
    tives such as: "don't come here" or "don't come to harm us", but in another con-
    nection Paeng said that he was afraid that the malicious spirits might sneak
    behind them, and he himself had become too deaf to hear the tape recording in
    1989. Incidentally, this remarkable person died in 1993. However, Egerod and
    Rischel 1986, also have: gɔt "behind".
3nd line: na "thick" (Th), but is used by the Mlabri as well for "much, many".

1978, 5a, 758, Paeng (aged 48):

On this occasion Paeng demonstrated how he would put small pieces of meat on a stone and by holding the spear over the offering, he would then ask the spirits of the spear and sword to guide him to stab the animals mentioned (fig. 81).

'ɣh cɔnre khɔt	cɔnre naw	mɛn leh keh	tɛ pa buɪl	//	cɔnre lam ding
Oh, spirit spear	spirit sword	yes, come break,	indeed kill.		Spirit tree big

lam dɣng	chɔn 'a mɔn	mʌr klay	chɛ' glɛc	chɛ' kham rih (Th)	//	chat
tree watch,	field has cotton,	sneak slyly	much slyly	much crossing hither.		Stab

140

poh thri poh　　'do' cing nyʌ' gʌh thɛh　　　　chat kruwɛk krul wʌl　　　　pulang
porcupine (2 spec),　like this [is] good,　stab bearcat (2 spec: Th: hen, hen lom),　turtle

chapa'　　　ka.ohm　//　nɛh jak chung　　nyʌ' tʌny na' (Th)　　chəboh chung
soft shell　& water turtle.　These get much　　as asking please　　[spirit] mountain high,

chəboh long lɔng　//　na' pa dɣng　　bɛr ching ta'　　pia' 'dɛ 'i 'dɣ
mountain low;　　please make see　relatives　animals edible.

3rd line: krul wʌl is a small, black animal with long hair, while pulang is a small,
　flat water turtle; cing nyʌ' "similar, like that".
4th line: nɛh jak chung "this go high" or "get much", long lɔng lit. "into descend-
　ing".

The following pages do not deal with real prayers, but are rather conversations
between a father and son. The latter asks to borrow or to keep the spear belonging
to the father. Two aspects are worth noting. One is that this sort of conversation is
kept in a form very much like that of the prayers which, incidentally, are mostly
quite informal. The other is that a son might also "ask" his already deceased father
for permission to take his spear. This underlines the importance of the spirits of the
dead parents, a subject dealt with below in Chapter 4.8.

1980, 5b, 944, Seng (aged 17):

In this example, Seng asks his father to lend him his spear to go hunting. Possibly,
the spear spirit accepts that a father can lend his spear to his son. Otherwise the
spear is a very personal item, since its spirit can have only one owner.

roh 'oy　　jak khɔt　gʌh　ta　mʌc　　pia' 'dɣ 'i to　//　to koc　to hnɛl
Young man　give spear　this　[to]　find　animals edible:　bamboo rat,　rat,

to gather gachong　　　to pye　to pia'　　to 'yek to prɛng　　to 'ɛk to mʌc
squirrel,　land turtle,　lizard [meat] edible,　bees & nest,　take find (lit: see).

1st line: ta preverbal particle with stative verbs, Rischel, 1995, p. 315.

1980, 8a, 1290, Som (aged 28):

Som then demonstrates the conversation between a son and his father who, in this
case, is also presumed to be still alive. However, the father declines to give him his
spear, because he is not able to make another one for himself, since he has no iron
bars left. Respectfully, the son apologizes, saying that he should not have asked:

'a wal 'oh krɔ　　//　bay jak　　　bn.hnɛ' bɛr　　jak paluh　//　'ot roy
Son: Give (return) I ask;　[if] much take　honourable friend　get angry.　Your child,

hmɔng 'ɣy 'at krɔ　　palɔy chop　　'a lɔ' krɔ　　lɔ' ngam　　'i ding roh
blood yours (?) excuse　know [if] borrow,　sorry ask for　sorry all right;　elder (men)

mɛh palɔy　　jam (Th) tɛk　//　'a dɣng　　kəbɔ loy　　jam tɛk　　'oh jak
you know,　remember beating;　have seen [but]　not know　remember beating,　me give

ruhm rang 'a mɔy　　'a dɣng 'a jam nɛ (Th)　//　ma' hlik　　　ma' hlak
in advance have one,　have seen & remember surely.　Give much [or]　nothing [anyway]

pa bn.hnɛ' bɛr	'a man	///
cause friend (respectfully)	have luck.	

'a ding roh chaw	'oh kə ta bɔ ma'	//	'oh hlek hlak	'oh gɔh
Father: Have elder hungry,	I not give		I iron finished	myself,

'kəbɔ lɔy	tɛk	gret gʌh
not know [when]	forge [again]	sorry this.

chɛ' 'a leh lac	ding roh	'a tɛ	'a kə tɛ	bɔ krɔ
Son: Much have already (never mind),	elder have	indeed	have really	(should) not ask.

2nd line: hmong 'ɣy "blood yours" translation uncertain; chop "ask for, borrow".

4th line: hlik, hik "very"; hlak "lost, finished, empty", while hlek "iron".

8th line: leh lac "come finished" or "already", and roh seems here to mean just "elder".

Formerly, it was the custom to leave the few belongings of a dead person in or beside their grave, because, at that time, nobody dared to keep anything belonging to a dead person. However, the spear was so important for survival that it was tempting for a young man to ask for it, either when his father was still alive, or to remove it just after his death. Som explained (see below) that if the latter took place they would feel bad about it, but by asking the spirit of the father they might ascertain psychologically whether the request would be acceptable or not. This is very much what happens in the prayer. The son evidently feels bad about asking his deceased father for his spear, and at the same time he is somewhat worried that the spirit of his father will punish him after he has taken it.

1980, 8a, 1279, Som and Muang (aged 25 and 42):

'ɛ ding roh mɛn (Th) mɛh juy	mo' bɔ khɔt	pɣ' naw	ma' mɛn mɛh
Yes elder, yes you help,	[I] keep no spear [or]	have sword;	give yes you

jam 'ɣh jam tɛk	//	mɛh pa buɫ	'ar tay	'oh pa di	lɔ' krɔ	lɔ'
know to forge (beat).		You already died	have died,	I therefore	sorry ask for,	sorry

'ɛk jak	//	mɛh gʌm	rɣm rap	rɣm tit rɣm jak	gʌm guɪn rɣm rap jak
to take.		You don't	follow chase,	stick to & follow,	don't return follow chase

grok roy	br.'oh ching to	'i nɔ'	nak cərɔng	nak lɛng	//
band's young persons,	my women,	children,	very small,	very smallest (babies).

'oh	lɔ' krɔ lɔ' 'ek	jak khɔt naw
I sorry	ask for sorry [to]	take spear & sword.

2nd line: lɔ' "sorry, sick", krɔ "ask for", while lɔ' krɔ "excuse" (loh "look for, search for" and lɔh "near by").

1980, 8a, 1304, Som (aged 28):

mɛh pahak buɫ	//	ding roh	'a di jak khɔt	'ek jak naw	tɔ' jo'	//
You separated, died;		elder [father]	have to take spear,	take sword,	knife & machette.

142

mɛh	pajak 'ɣh	jam tɛk	mɛh pabuɪl	'ar di	rɣm krɔ
You	already made,	know beat (forge),	you died,	[I] had to	altogether ask

'i jak	//	jak kwɛhl	chat 'ɣh	chat bong	koc hnɛl
in order to take [tools].		Go find (hunt)	stabbing	stab meat:	bamboo rat, rat,

ngay bɛk	bɛr kɔmchingto	roy	cho 'e' chamal	'oh krɔ 'i jak
boar & bear,	[as] men, women,	children	hungry & thin.	I ask in order to take,

mɛh gʌm	rɣm rap	rɣm jak
you don't	chase follow [us].	

Som explains to the spirit of his deceased father that he had to take the spear, sword, knife and machete, because they are needed to support his relatives. Still, he is somewhat worried about having done so.

1st line: tɔ' is a pointed spear blade, while jo' is a kind of machete with a 3-4 cm, blunt edge on top; both have just one sharp edge (fig. 56).

2nd line: rɣm "together, follow" (Khon Muang).

3rd line: 'i is a preverbal conjunction "(in order) to".

4th line: cho 'e' "hungry", where cho' (chaw) is "pain" and 'e' is "tubers".

1980, 8a, 1340, Som (aged 28):

mym pahak buɪl	//	mɛ gʌm	rɣm pang	rɣm loh 'oh	//	'oh krɔ
Father separated, died,		you don't	follow play	search for me.		I ask

'i jak mɛt khɔt	'oh jak kwɛhl	chat 'ɣh	chat bong	koc hnɛl
to remove your spear.	I go look for	to stab,	stab meat:	bamboo rat

gather gɔchong	//	mɛh hak	rɣm buɪl	rɣm tay	mɛh kɣ rɣm
squirrel & land turtle.		You separated,	staying with	[us] died,	you not follow,

kɣ jak kwɛhl	'ek kwɛhl bong	mɛh pabuɪl 'a tay	mɛh pa blʌk kim
not go find,	take meat [for yourself]	You died have died,	you [put] into grave,

blʌk km.puc	//	'oh krɔ 'i	jak khɔt
into termite heap.		I ask in order	to remove spear.

Very much the same speech as the previous example. In the last line there is a reference to the dead father, who was interred in a termite heap. Som explained that he was merely buried under a big pile of dead leaves covered with a thin layer of earth in a place with many termites. In a fairly short time the termites had turned the pile into one of their characteristic constructions. This procedure ensures that the bones are not removed by wild animals. Som himself was a boy when this happened, viz. in about 1960, and the Mlabri abandoned the practice about ten years later.

The next two prayers are both important and tricky. They mention primarily the spirits of their deceased parents to help guide them to the animals, and they are of the kind of prayer the Mlabri would once say before going hunting. Certainly (just as with the two prayers on pages 144 and 145), they are to the spear spirit, since Paeng now held the spear over the sacrifice placed on a flat stone and called the spirits. All the animals desired are mentioned, and Paeng says that since everyone in the band gets hungry, it is necessary to share. If the hunter keeps everything for

143

himself he will develop a headache and the others in the band will develop stomach ache. Even giving only a little is better than nothing. We have often seen ourselves how food is shared, and that a young man, for example, who had received some meat as payment from us, set off to present it to his father who lived one day's walk from his camp. Giving food is by far the most important virtue for obtaining respect among the Mlabri. Together with the frequent intermarriage it has been decisive in keeping them together

.

1982, 2b, 866, Paeng (aged 52):

'ɣh cenre'   'ɛ wɔk na'   // jak di mʌc   pia' 'dɛ 'i 'dɣ   'ek mɣk   'ek wʌl
Do spirit, hey spirit please,   go to find   animals edible, take good, take back;

jak dɛl 'ɣh   dɛl gʌm cho 'e' chamal   // 'ek 'dɣ   'ek wʌl mɣk   pia' 'dɛ 'i dɣ
go [to] share, share don't [anyone] hungry. Take anyone, return good animals edible:

koc knɛl   gather gɔchong   koc   mo' mʌ'   mʌ' ko' bɛk, bɛk ngay
bamboo rat & rat, squirrel land turtle, bamb.rat keep python, python yes bear, bear boar,

ngay thri', thri' krwɛk,   krwɛk   chapa', chapa'   ga.ohm, ga.ohm thawa',
boar porcupine banana   bear cat,   soft-shelled turtle   water turtle macaque,

thawa' thɛng,   thɛng kr.wɛk,   kr.wɛk hn.kle', hn.kle' pɔk, pɔk   chɔro',
macaque white gibbon, banana bear cat, small black bird, woodpecker, bamboo bird

chɔro' chɔpa', chɔpa' ga.ohm, ga.ohm pye, pye pia', koc   hnɛl,
(rep.), soft-shelled turtle, water turtle, lizard edible, bamboo rat & rat,

ga.ther gɔ.chong,   ma' 'ɣ' ma' bong   cho 'e' chamal   chi 'e' chi pia'
squirrel land turtle; give eat rice & meat hungry (roots), want edible animals

dɛl man   dɛl gʌh   dɛl bɛr   bn.hnɛ'   tɛk klɛh   tɛk nɔy   // gʌm
share luck share this [with] friends, everyone cut small cut little [bit each]. Don't

hak 'ɣ', hak bong   chi chi yɔy chi thapul   'at trɣk 'ɛng hmɔng 'ay   //
separately eat rice & meat, pain gut & pain stomach ribs & blood honourable

bn.hnɛ' 'e bɛr   gʌh loh gʌh lay (Th)   ya 'dɣ   'dɣ 'i mɣk   pia' 'dɛ 'i 'dɣ
Everyone this search for many, bring all good living, animals edible.

'ar to blʌk koh rap to man 'e bɛr bnhnɛ'   //   thɛh kan thɛh (Th) jɔ' khon jɔ'
Have (into) divided luck [with] others;   good for each, [even] people not much

kɔdah khon kɔdah   // ki tit   gʌm hak 'ɣ' hak bong   'e' cho' 'e' pi
[or] little, people [get]. Nobody don't separately eat rice & meat, hungry husked rice

che 'e' che.pia'   // ma' leh bn.hnɛ' 'e' bɛr   chɛ' bɛr   si' lek (Th)   si' nɔy, si' lek
hungry edible [meat]. Give here everyone, each little bit, [so] no

khon che 'e'   che.pia'   // ma' 'at 'ɛ la'   'ɛ blɛng   'ɛ theng 'a thawa' thawa
people hungry edible meat; give shoulder [or] arm [of] gibbon & macaque,

gʌm ma'   bun mla' thɔng glɣ'   // ki dɣ' gɣn   hak 'ɣ'   hak bong
don't give honourable person dizziness. Nobody return separately eat rice & meat,

bi' di blɣhl   // gʌm 'ɣh pa cho 'e' chamal   ki 'dɣ khon che 'e' che pia'   //
get full (stomach); don't cause hungry (tubers), no person hungry edible meat,

ma' to mla' thɔng gly'   //   koc hnɛl kadɛl   gɔchong   chərɔ'
give people dizziness.   [Want:] bamboo rat, rat, squirrel,   land turtle,   (bird:) banana

    bɔk   'um gleb 'um klɔ'   'i hurl chərɔ' bɔk   chapa' ga.ohm   koc
& hornbill, gaeng & nyung (Th) hornbill & banana,   soft & water turtle, bamboo rat,

hnɛl,   gather, gɔchong   pye pia'   // ma' leh bn.hnɛ' 'ɛ bɛr 'at trɣk 'ay hmong 'ay
rat,   squirrel, land turtle, lizard edible;   give come everyone, ribs & blood honourable.

2nd line: cho 'e' chamal "hungry roots" ('e' "yams", mal "taro"). mɣk "good" (cf.
    with the almost synonymous word: mɣ' "mother").
5th line: pɔk is the big Rhinoceros Hornbill, while 'i. hurl (18th line) is Northern
    Pied Hornbill.
7th line: che 'e' che pia' "hungry meat", pia' "edible meat").
9th line: at trɣk 'ɛng hmɔng 'ay (or 'ɣy) which the Mlabri said means "young and
    old family members". I have: "ribs & blood honourable" ('ay is used when talk-
    ing to elder persons), which gives almost the same meaning. trɣk "ribs" (Ml) or
    ji 'ɛng (M3), viz. both glosses are known to the Mlabri Ml.
11th line: 'ar to blʌk koh rap to man "have divided luck" (with others in the camp).
    thɛh "good", kan "each other" (Th); jɔ' "not much".
13th line: si' emphatic word (Th), usually not translated.

1982, 2b, 880, Paeng (aged 52):

Like the previous prayer, the next is also very narrative. At the very beginning it is
said that the offering is placed on a leaf, exactly as we have seen Paeng do when
demonstrating the prayer for the spear spirit. While the first half has many of the
same phrases as the previous prayer, the second half relates, with fatalistic humour,
some of the various kinds of troubles the Mlabri has to cope with – the cold of the
winter nights, the difficulties of hunting birds, that the collected roots have worms,
the meeting with a snake on the trail, that the sack for collecting food is empty, that
the smoke from the fire gives him a headache, that he misses his target while hunting, and now he is finally sleepy. Paeng was a kind of leader, not only for his own
band but for about half of all the Mlabri, until about 1980. Thereafter, he rather
became the charming and popular grandfather and leader of his own band until his
death in 1993.

    'ek bɔ' 'ang dɔk   //   'ɣh cɔnre ma pia' 'dɛ   'i dɣ koc hnɛl ga.ther
Take carry bamboo put up [altar] do spirits send animals edible: bamboo rat, rat, squirrel,

   ga.chong ma' lɛng ta'   ching roy gɯn 'ɣ' gɯn bong //   mɛh hak bong
land turtle, give relatives,   [give in] return rice & meat.   [If] you separately eat meat

di dii dəmɔy   'ɛ chi' chi' 'i chi' pia' //   ma' lɛng   hn' da'   lung 'ay   lɛt nit
well alone, [others] hungry edible meat;   give children, relatives uncle elder, little bit

gərit nɔy /// lam ding   lam dɣng jak gri' chən   ki mɔn   ki kon ki mʌ'   //
each.   [Sp.] tree big   watch   go trail to field, not get lost, not logs or creepers [cross].

ya mʌc   pia' 'dɣ   'ek wʌl   gʌm ki   mʌc gʌh lɔ'   wʌl day   // hn' ta' 'ay
Bring find animals take back, [if] don't find this sorry, (but) return can;   relat.(lit."tail")

kre' 'i mɯɯm	ya to blʌk	koh way (Th)	to ma'	gərit nit	gərit nɔy	ki 'dy
hit tomorrow,	bring animal,	share all,	give	little bitq	each,	[so] nobody

chi' 'i chi' pia' //	'e ding hn.roy	ta' 'i gʌl	hi' to poh	'i kwehl ki to
hungry meat,	old & young relatives,	uncle aunt.	If animal kill	look for & nothing

poh	wʌl day //	'ar dor	mo mʌc	mo ma'	'ɣ' cənre
killed,	return can [also alright].	Have given away &	remain find	to give,	feed sp. dead

cənrɔc //	roy chak	'ɛw chɛ'	'ɛk kɯr jak ///	'ɛk wɣk	'ɛk nam (Th)
sp. young.	Young unable,	children many,	take side part,	Go take water	take water,

mo ma' mɔ' thɣl mɣln tɔn //	nɔn nɛh lɛk nɛh chɣl	gʌh dəkat kɣ naw //
keep bamboo container only section.	Sleep this late this sunset,	here shivering cold;

jak rap	pa dəlao	gʌh mʌc koc //	jak rap	pa chot	gʌh mʌc
Search (chase)	bamboo spec,	here find bamboo rat.	Search (other)	bamboo spec,	here find

thong klep (Th) //	jak rap pa chɛk	gʌh mʌc gəchong //	jak rap pa pyong
net bag	Search for rattan tubers,	here find land turtle.	Search fruit (spec.),

gʌh mʌc kan chərɔ' //	'ar jak rap pa hn.ga' də kəh	gʌm mʌc tac
here find then bamboo bird.	Have gone searched for pheasant far,	don't find hornbill

pɔc //	khana' (Th) ro' khana' chring	bin 'ac pʌr //	cuʌk mal gʌh kʌh
(bird);	Then (up to) pass mountain crest,	fly bird fly [gone].	Dig taro this worm [has]

gla' khon 'ay day thal //	mʌ' kul 'i di grɣng	dɣng thong krl.dɯl ki klɣp
cut off thick parts get late.	Python roll middle [of road],	sack [is] bad, also box

'u ki ta //	wrɣl yak thang 'ɔt glɣ'	'ɣ' ɛ gʌh ki bi' //	tɛk tik
[is] ugly.	Smoke dirty [give] dizziness;	eat root, this not enough.	Beat porcupine,

gʌh chibut //	chuʌk trut	gʌh ta ma' tɔn //	mɯɯ 'a lɛo	ma nɔn 'a leh
this missing.	Dig (spec.) root,	this get [only] partly;	Return finish,	sleepy become.

3rd line: hn.ta' is "thin" also "tail" and an allusion to the children following behind the adults as they walk from one camp to the next!

bong "food or meat" depending on the situation.

4th line: mɔ', mʌ' "creepers" is variously pronounced, but among the Mlabri Ml as here, often mɔ', whereas among the Mlabri M3 mʌ'. jak gri chən (when more carefully pronounced chuʌn M3). ki mən (go trail field) "not get lost", mɔn "cotton" probably synonymous for confusion (due to its winding fibres!). Moreover they should not cross over large logs or under hanging creepers.

5th line: gʌm ki mʌc gʌh lɔ' wʌl day "don't find, this sorry return can", meaning that if someone does not find animals after having tried anyway it is alright, as they will receive meat from someone else.

6th line: mɯɯn or mə.ɯɯn "tomorrow". blʌk koh way to ma' lit: "into parts cut, able body give" or: "keep sharing, able to give something", exactly as we have seen, how the meat is cut up very carefully and divided, so that each family or household has an equal share (fig. 97).

8th line: 'ɣ' cənre cənrɔc "eat spirit dead, sp. young (newborn persons)" because both have especially vulnerable spirits and souls.

12th line: pa pyong in Thai: mak kom (lit: "fruit bitter").

146

13th line: chəro' "bamboo bird" (Th: nok kok). tac pɔc is another name for or species of "Hornbill".

14th line: khana' (Th) "this time, then". bin "to fly" (Th), pʌr "to fly" (Ml), while the interpreter said "go to the valley" (Th).

15th line: gla' khon (Th) ay "cut away ends" of the dead roots, i.e. what worms have eaten.

Last line: chibut "missing the stroke", trut, in Thai: man leuang "root yellow".

1982, 6a, 052, Kham (aged 54):

wɔk khɔt wɔk naw   // 'oh tɛk   'oh bɯl bɯl   tɛ plung tɛ rawn (Th)   jak gʌm ta'
Spirit spear sp. sword   I hit,   I kill (really)   indeed hot indeed hot.   Go, can't uncle

koh bay   gʌm ma'   gʌm pa chrkeh pa hmal   //   jak tɛ di to mʌc   tɛ jɔt
break big,   can't give,   can't offer anything [for] soul.   Go, indeed animal find   and stop

to ngay to bɛk   chat tɛ li' di   toc pa bul   chat tɛ li' di to   pa 'ɣ' pa bong   //
boar & bear.   Stab indeed find   catch & kill,   stab indeed find body;   [we] give food.

cho' yuk cho' bong   mɛh hak jam (Th)   pa 'ek ma' thɣ (Th)   //   wɔk khɔt
Hungry rice & meat,   you separately remember   offering, give again.   Spirit spear

wɔk naw gʌm ki   'ɣh ki phlat (Th)   lah (Th)   gʌm ki   'ɣh ki phlat   'ɣh bih
sp. sword don't bad,   not missing;   above all   don't bad,   not missing   cutting,

cing nyʌ' ki thɛh   //   wɔk bɛ' wɔk pa tae   di ki ngam   cin di luang (Th)
likewise not good.   Spirit earth sp.former (Mlabri)   not good [giving]   meat in advance,

mo' ma'   kahpa ma'   //   cin cəbut wɔk khɔt gʌh to gʌ'   wɔk bɛ'   gʌh to gʌ'
keep give,   cooked rice give.   Meat pig spirit spear this is there,   spirit earth   this is there.

An interesting prayer in which Kham says that if he cannot capture any animals then, of course, he cannot offer anything to the souls of the spear. We notice that the spear spirit may not be relied on if not offered to and the spirit of the earth also receives a sacrifice, as it must participate in deciding the killing of the desired animals.

3rd line: li' "find" (Khon Muang?).

4th line: ma' thɣ (Th: thee, M3: cɛɛm) "give again".

5th line: gʌm ki 'ɣh ki plat, was first translated as: "don't make sound", as I thought it was in Thai: "prat (3) onomatopoeically from the sound of struggling or flapping wings (as when fowls are trying to free themselves)". However it is rather phlat "misusing or missing" (Th) the target as when throwing the spear. Maybe the similar phrases are allusions to related problems while going hunting.

6th line: luang (na) "in advance" (Th). mo' ma' kahpa ma' "keep giving cooked rice" as previously when the Mlabri made offerings of a little food to the spirit of the parents every morning.

1982, 6a, 095, Kham (aged 54):

lah cənre khɔt cənre naw   cənre bri   cənre tae (Th)   //   gʌm ki ma tit ma thal
Up above spirit spear sp. sword;   spirit forest   sp. former Mlabri   don't come stick to follow

di li' mo' li'   mo' li'   ma' 'ɣ' ma' bong   //   gʌh dɛk   gʌh to gʌ' cəbut
find stay   find stay (rep),   give eat rice eat meat;   here altar   this is there, pig

gʌh to gʌ'   khɔt gʌh to gʌ'   //   whi gʌm ki bet   to bɯl   tɛ pran   di mo'
this is there,   spear this is there.   Hurry (?) don't cry,   body kill   indeed hunting   keep

di wʌl   //   chimo li'   'uh ('oh) jak 'ek ma' 'ar   kɔm jaw kɔm nay pa ma' 'ɣh
returning.   Pig (raw meat)   I bring, given have (in advance)   master   official   have given

mo' ma'   //   'oh gʌh   'ɣh gʌh   m(a') bo' 'ek   cənre khɔt   ma' 'ɣ' ma' bong
keep giving.   I myself   do this   feed bring   spirit spear: give eat rice & meat;

lɔng ngay to diʌk   to bɛk to mo (Th)   //   gʌm ki pa dəkat   pa tat naw   //
kill (descend) pig, deer,   bear & sow.   Don't cause illness,   catch cold,

cənre bɛ' cənre pa tae to kʌh   cənre klar   cənre klar   //   'oh pa ma 'ɣh
spirit earth sp. former [Mlabri], up there   spirit sky   spirit sky.   I keep on coming

ma' pa 'ek   //   cənre khɔt hn.ta'   cənre tɛng ding 'e ta' bɯl   mla' prim
give [offering]   spirit spear thin (lit. tail)   spirit married uncle (who) died,   person old

mla' bi 'a   gʌm ma tit ma thal   gʌm ki mo   ma' 'ɣ' ma' bong
person full (age),   don't come stick to follow,   don't stay;   (we) give eat rice give meat,

to yu'   to pi'   to cin   cəbut cəbut
cooked rice   husked rice,   meat,   pig much (rep.).

The various spirits are asked not to follow, adhere to or remain with the Mlabri, but to receive the offering in return for good luck during hunting. It is also related that I ("master official") have bought a pig just as many times before. Thereafter, he asks more specifically for various animals and not to get ill. At last he will call the various spirits, including those of the sky and the deceased family members, to come and eat the offering – but not to remain

1st line: lah or lʌh "up, above" as when the spear is held over the altar during the ceremony to ask for good luck while go hunting. Kham pronounces "spirit" chnre' or less clearly cənre' like many other Mlabri.

3th line: gʌm ki bet "do not cry", meaning when hunting one should not make any noise but work in earnest. te pran probably means "right hunt" as pran is "to hunt, hunter" in Thai. But a similar word is prang "to keep quiet (for the purpose of deceiving)". The connection of this word with the hunter's luck became plausible when a Mlabri of the small group (M3) also told us that: jak 'ɣh di pen di pran means: "go! get luck" (see also note to the next prayer, p. 149).

4th line: chimo li' Gui said means a "raw" pig, i.e. one which has not yet been killed.

6th line: The Mlabri insist on obtaining a tame pig from the Hmong; preferably a sow as these contain more fat!

7th line: cənre bɛ' cənre pa tae "spirit earth & spirit former [people]" the spirit of the earth together with those of the dead, which agrees with the translation by the Mlabri: "spirit earth & spirit inside the earth".

8th line: tɛng "married" from Thai: taeng ngan, here probably meaning Kham's uncle (ding 'e ta') to whom the spear originally belonged.

1987, la, 262, Poa (aged 50):

'o wɔk kɔt   wɔk naw   ki gɔt   gʌh dii   tɛ pohl   tɛ pran   gʌm ki 'ɣh
Oh, spirit spear sp. sword not behind this is good, indeed luck, right hunting; don't make

ki pran   kɔmbɛr lɛng ching to   //   di 'ɣh di wʌl   di mo' di wʌl   gʌm ki
no luck [to]   relatives (men and women).   Come back   keep returning,   don't

jak 'ɣh jak hnguh kɔmbɛr kɔmching to // di 'oh   dii pong   ngam nɛh pr.nah
hurt & hide (from)   relatives,   me [give] good meat   good as long time

prnah   di jɯn (Th)   di jɔng jɔng   di hr.lɛ' jak jal   kre' lam   paton
back;   keep on walking forth & back laughing, cleverly hit (straight as) tree trunk,

gʌm ki   jak 'ɣh jak leh   gʌm ki   tm.'o' ki ma   ki 'ɣh   ki yɔh   //
don't [sp.] make bad come,   don't (send) snake not come, nothing bad not spit.

tɛ pohl   tɛ pran   di mo'   di ya chak   ya chruʌt
Indeed luck,   right hunting, keep on bring animal (body) bring myself (lit. chest).

Poa asks the spirit of the spear and the (short) sword not to give them bad luck or to hurt anybody. As he is the owner of the spear it should attend exclusively to his fortune.

1st line: Neither pohl nor pran means literally "luck". However, pohl was variously translated as the "deed" of the spear spirit or as the "right strokes" of the spear, guided by its owner and the spear spirit. During our last stay in 1994 someone said that tɛ pohl tɛ pran means "soul up", which also suggests "good luck". Yet another Mlabri rightly pointed out that pohl is lit. "barking deer" in Mlabri. It was added that the hunters once took out the 'stone', or the Adam's apple, of this animal to keep in a bamboo container to obtain good luck while hunting. Therefore the translation rendered.

4th line: yɯm, yeun "stand" or "keep on" (Th). kre' lam pa ton "hit [straight as the] tree trunk".

1987, 1la, 275, Poa (aged 50):

'o tɛ pohl   tɛ pran   gʌm ki 'dɣ   ja' la   jak 'ɣh   yak pran   kɔmbɛr lɛng
Oh, indeed luck, right hunting don't any shall leave, making   bad luck [for] relatives

ching to   kɔmbɛr lɛng ching to   bɔ loh 'ɣ'   bɔ pyal   bɔ mla'   bɔ glɣ' cin
(twice: men, children, women) not search eating, bad meat, no people no brain meat,

cin chapa'   ja' la   cin jɛ' sa   'a chapa'   khom chal.mɛn   di mo' mo' li
meat no taste shall leave meat bad   have no taste, bitter & smelly;   keep on finding

di ya pohl   ya pran   nak khom   nak chring   //   tɛ pohl   tɛ pran
bring luck   hunting,   much sharp   big backbone,   indeed luck right hunting

jak wʌl tok   ple dɛl   di gʌh   gʌh dii   'yak cəbut   'yak ching
bring back fall (many as) seeds to this [place] that is good, dung pig dung pig (luck).

//   wɔk bɔh   wɔk bakdor   wɔk glɛw   to thupru' to mak (Th)
    Spirit ashes,   spirits share   liquid chew   betel leaves & seeds.

This short, tricky, but interesting prayer attempts to persuade the spirit of the spear not to give the Mlabri bad meat from animals that they eat only when they have nothing else. Afterwards, he offers betel leaves to chew. Note that words like alcohol, tobacco, betel and medicine were previously prefaced by wɔk (spirit), because they may all affect the mind!

1st line: ja' la probably derives from Thai: "shall leave, be absent".

3nd line: chapa' "bland, no taste".

4th line: nak khom nak chring "much sharp, big backbone" is a symbol of a big, much coveted pig. Again he asks for good luck (synonymous with as many animals as there are seeds in a flower). Directly in the next line we find yet another symbol of good luck:

5th line: 'yak chəbut "dung pig", which they said brought good luck, probably due to its strong smell overshadowing the smell of the hunters. At this point we were told that once they actually dipped the spearhead in pig dung before going hunting to prevent the animals from smelling the hunter as he approached his prey.

The next long prayer was recorded after we had brought iron rods up to the Mlabri, who forged them into spears and knives during the course of the next three to four days. A small altar was constructed leaning against a large tree, and various pieces of meat from a pig, slaughtered shortly before, were put into small parcels of palm leaves and placed on the altar. The spear tip had another parcel with some meat hanging around the cover of rattan. Poa, standing, now placed the spearhead directly over the offerings on the altar and began invoking its spirit by quickly reciting the prayer (with 4-5 syllables per second). It was repeated to several times the length of what has been transcribed below.

The prayer is a long chain of wishes for luck during hunting, alternating with all the bad things he does not want: that the thrusts of the spear miss their targets; that they should follow bad animals; that the other spirits should interfere in a bad way, or that the spirit of the spear should leave him to reside with another person. It is quite obvious that the spear spirit is considered to possess a will of its own, but if treated properly, i.e. with care and with regular offerings, it will bring luck to its owner.

1987, 16a, 825, Poa (aged 50):

'o tɛ pohl   tɛ pran   gʌm ki 'ɣh   ki chak chat   'dɣ poh pran   kɔmbɛr lɛng
Oh, indeed   luck right   don't make   no good stab,   any split luck,   relatives

ching to cin cəbut cin ching   ko' to dii   thɛh roy   wɔk lam   wɔk ton   ki gɔt
[give] meat pig, meat fleshy,   yes animal   good much,   spirit tree   spirit trunk   not behind

    gʌh dii   'yɔh glɛw //   wɔk bɛ' wɔk pa tae' (Th)   tɛ pohl tɛ pran   dɛk keh gʌh
this is good, spit chew. Spirit earth sp. former persons   right luck & hunt, altar plaited here

'ek bong   tɛ cəbut jong   katong leh   po' lon po' hmal   //   ja' la pa ma'
take meat,   truly pig male   put up   cup for mind & soul.   Shall finish give [many as]

chrɣl wɔk   poh chrɔny lɔmbo   poh chən (Th) 'a   poh bɛk poh thri' poh 'do'   //
palm spirit   split seeds tree (spec);   kill such as have   kill bear & porcupine (2 species)

wɔk khɔt   jɛk sa' la' wɔk lam   wɔk ton   ki gɔt   gʌh dii   tɛ pohl tɛ pran
Spirit spear   sacrifice, spirit tree sp. trunk not behind, this is good, indeed luck & hunting

wɔk khɔt   wɔk naw   ki gɔt   gʌh dii   gʌm ki ma' 'ɣh   mo' pran kɔmbɛr lɛng
sp. spear   sp. sword   not behind,   this is good,   don't make bad,   keep luck,   relatives

ching to   hnguh   di dii di ngam   bong tɛ cin cəbut   cin ching   //   gʌm ki ja 'ɣh
        stay   very good,   eat indeed meat pig   fleshy.   Don't send

   jak cho' ngɔr   kɔmbɛr lɛng ching to   'oh bong dii   'oh di bong ngam   prnah
bad trail [of animal].   Relatives & I eat food good,   I want food good [as] long

   prnah   di juŋg   di jɔŋg jɔŋg di hr.lɛ'   //   jɛ' ram jɛ' wut.chi   gʌm jak na
time back,   walk forth & back laughing.   Hungry shivering cold,   don't get much

də mɛh də mɛh   //   tɛ 'ɣh   tɛ wʌl   tɛ pohl   tɛ pran   gʌm koh   jak chak chat
oneself (really).   Indeed return   luck and   hunting   don't break   make unable stab,

   ja' pohl phra'   wɔk khɔt wɔk naw   ki gɔt   gʌh dii   //   ja' la   wɔk lam ding
bring luck honourable sp. spear & sword,   not behind this is good.   Leave   spirit tree big

lam dɣng   ki gɔt   gʌh dii   gʌm ki 'ɣ' ki pran   kɔmbɛr lɛng ching to   hnguh
tree watch,   not behind   this is good,   don't make no luck,   (for) relatives,   stay

di dii di ngam   //   gʌm ki ja' la   jak wʌl bɯl   jak ma' di to di ləbo   di mɣk
    very good.   Don't (spear) leave,   give away kill,   give to some other (owner),   good

di wʌl   //   wɔk khɔt   wɔk naw   ki gɔt   gʌ dii   tɛ pohl tɛ pran   gʌm ki jak
returning.   Spirit spear & sword   not behind this is good, indeed luck & hunting don't go

chak chat   ja' bɯl phra'   ja' la gʌh dulu 'ɛ   ləbo pyal bə glɣ'   'oh cin ja' la
bad stab,   kill honourably;   leave this root (Th: hom)   any bad meat as brain;   I meat leave

   'a jal 'a chapa' ple' pok ple' dɛl   //   wɔk ruʌt   wɔk tong   ki gɔt   gʌh dii
cleverly bad taste many [kinds] as seeds.   Sp. wet soil sp. full pool not behind   is good

sa' la'   tɛ pohl tɛ pran   mɛh gɣh   ja' la dʌm   jak də mɛh   wʌl to mɛh
sacrifice indeed luck & hunting,   you not   leave long time   by yourself, return yourself,

gʌm ki ma' 'ɣh   mo pran kɔmbɛr lɛng ching to   kɔmbɛr lɛng ching to   gʌm ki
don't make bad,   keep luck [for]   relatives   (men, children and women);   don't

jak 'ɣh   ja' chak pohl   cha' kr.dɔl   cheng.yʌk   ki thɛh   tɛ pohl   tɛ pran
make bad   bring no luck,   pain elbow,   likewise   not good; indeed luck & hunting

wɔk khɔt   wɔk naw   ki gɔt   gʌh dii   mo bong   'dɣ cəbut to ching
spirit spear   sp. sword   not (follow) behind   this is good,   keep eat   any pig fleshy.

There are the following problems of translation with this prayer, which was uttered
with up to five syllables per second!
3nd line: keh "woven bamboo strips", where the offerings are placed.
4th line: cəbut jong katong leh "pig male put up (on the altar)", as it was explained
   by the Mlabri, but actually katong "jump" and as well "put up, place". po' is the
   cup made of bamboo leaves to be put on the altar. In the next line Poa asks for
   as many animals as there are seeds in fruits from the *lombo* tree, which has red
   fruits.
6th line: sa' la' "sacrifice" (Th).
9th line: Mlabri believe that if they come across footprints of a dangerous animal
   it may get agitated and start chasing their people.

12th line: ja' pohl phra' (Th) "bring luck honourable". The Mlabri explained at this point that it means "not missing the target by using too many strokes".

14th line: The spear or its spirit should not leave its owner to reside with another person, and:

18th line: The spear spirit should not depart on its own and thereby become lost.

Mlabri M3

The Digging Implement

As already stated, the members of the small group have not had real spears for many years and, therefore, have no spirits or prayers connected with the spear. Instead, the multipurpose cutting and digging instrument, cho', is their main tool. It is also the case among these Mlabri that preferably no belongings should be removed from the grave of a dead person. Accordingly, a ceremony has to be performed in order to legitimate the necessity of nevertheless taking this treasured object. When someone dies, the living may 'ask' the deceased for a particular item, just like when one of persons from the main group asks his deceased father for his spear. However, their ceremony and prayer are different. Instead of just talking to the spirit of the deceased, two persons, located one on each side of the grave of the father, throw the desired item back and forth between them over the dead body, while uttering the following short prayer. However, in the same way as with the Mlabri M1, they know from their own feelings whether the dead person will allow them to take the tool:

1994, 02, 100, Kit (aged 51):

kan (Th)	(pr) war yok	cuʌk dɯb	gum cho'	yah mɔy, bɛr
Together	straight lift,	dig grave,	throw spatula,	bring one, two,

'at pɛ, pon	'ar toc jak
three, four (times),	thereafter fetch [the tool].

1st line: kan "one another, together" (Th); prwar "straight (in a horizontal position)", (pa) yok, "lift up, raise" (M3 and Thai).

4.5 Birth, Naming, Marriage and Divorce

There are but few ceremonies connected with some of the most important phases of life: birth, puberty and marriage. A brief ritual is enacted some days after a birth to support the weak soul of the newborn and again some months or years later when the child is given a kind of first name usually of Khon Muang or Hmong origin, to be employed everywhere in the area. The reason for waiting this long is that a great many Mlabri children do not survive their first critical years, and therefore there is no need to hurry, perhaps unnecessarily. The Mlabri gave the explanation that the soul of the child develops only slowly, and therefore one might just as well wait.

No rituals are performed when a young person reaches maturity or when a couple get married. Indeed, the Mlabri seldom have celebrations. Only when they sacrifice a pig, as they do to the spirits of the parents, do the whole band feast on the for once plentiful meat. They drink a little alcohol, talk and sing a lot and feel happy. Often they use such an occasion to give the infants a name. Much the same happened when, in the old days, the band had the good fortune to kill big game such as a deer, a bear or, very rarely, a wild ox.

Overall, it seems that the prayers are primarily concerned with the dangers threatening them, including the spirits. These are all capable of harming them, whereas only a few are beneficial, first and foremost the spirits of their deceased parents. This does not necessarily mean that their life is as dismal as it may appear to others. Especially when they have enough to eat and they are by themselves, there is a great deal of shouting and laughing, but the situation may change dramatically whenever strangers, such as their Hmong employers, are around. Then they feel insecure and often unhappy (fig. 29).

Newborn & Naming (Ml)

1980, 7b, 020, Som (aged 28):

'ɣh gʌh 'i	nɔ' roy	tɛ pro'ɔng	gʌh 'ɛk Khamla	mo' 'oh 'ɛk	//
Do this (female)	niece,	right name	this take (name)	stay [with] me, take	

gʌh	klɔ'	'i	nyʌ'
this	(classifier)	girl	that one.

When a pig is sacrificed to the deceased parents, whose spirits are called from far away, the opportunity might also be taken to give the child – here a girl – its own name (until then it has only the family name of the parents). An altar is made of bamboo and a string is tied to the wrist of the child to bind the soul to the body. While the hand is held above the altar the prayer is uttered. The offering is usually a chicken or some eggs. Som said that first he had called the spirits of the deceased parents from far away.

1982, 3a, 000, Gaeo (aged 48):

'o nɔ' roy	gʌm ki	dəkat ki naw	di dii di ngam	//	cəbut yong katong
Oh, nephew	don't [get]	fever nor cold,	get well very best.		Pig male put up (offer),

wʌl phom (Th)	ja' a	pɔ' lon pɔ' hmal	//	gʌm ki	jak dəkat jak naw
return [soul to] me,	shall finish	push mind & soul.		Don't get	fever [or] cold,

gʌm ki	jak hnguh	lam ding	lam dɣng	gʌm ki	jak hnguh	kulkol drol
don't	go stay [with]	tree big	tree visit.	Don't	go stay	rolling very end

kulkol ruʌng	di mɣk di wʌl
rolling stream;	to health return.

1st line: katong "jump" or "put up", as when offering; phom "I, me" (male speaker only).

2nd line: ja' la (Th) "shall finish" or "leave" according to the situation. Both lon "mind" and hmal "soul" are weak after the child is born and are therefore asked to remain with the body. Incidentally, hmal and mla' ("person") are quite close and could have the same root (see also p. 75).

3rd line: Gaeo adds that the soul of the newborn should neither be taken by the tree spirits, which he explained "like to have some company": lam dɣng "tree visit" (lit. "tree see"), nor should it go far away – metaphorically speaking – downstream to the very end of the river, because in both cases the child may loose its soul, i.e. die.

4th line: mɣk "health", notice the almost similar word mɣ' "mother". In the next prayer, also by Gaeo, it is said that the soul of the child should not go far away (along the river) or stay with the parents' spirits in the large trees – who like to have the company of their grandchildren – or those spirits of water pools and wet soil, the latter being responsible for causing sickness.

1982, 3a, 056, Gaeo (aged 48):

kuuk hmal muu	nɔ' roy	//	gʌm ki	dəkat	ki naw	ding	ta'	gʌh	pɣ'
Call soul return	nephew,		don't [get]	fever	not cold,	elder	uncle	this	want

gʌh mi (Th)	//	gʌm ki	jak hnguh	ja' la	kulkol drol	kulkol ruʌng
this have;		don't	go stay	leave [for]	rolling very end	rolling stream.

cəbut yong katong	wʌl pɔ' lon pɔ' hmal	// to gʌm ki jak hnguh
Pig male put up [offering],	return push mind & soul	person don't go stay

di di dɔ mɔy	//	to di muu di wʌl	ta' ya'	gʌh pɣ'	gʌh mi	//
on & on alone.		Person return (keep) returning,	grandparents	this want,	this have.	

to gʌm ki	jak hnguh	lam ding	lam dɣng	wʌt wɔk ruʌt wɔk tong
Person don't	go stay [with]	[sp.] tree big	tree visit,	tie to wet soil & full pool,

ki gɔt	gʌh dii	//	to di muu di wʌl
not [get]	behind		(to) body (indeed) return.

1st line: kuuk (pronounced with a high pitch) is used to call back the soul and the same expression is used among the M3 Mlabri. It is interesting to note that the similar word kup "mist, cloud" is also connected with spirits just as guh "shell, skin" and, as related on p. 59, the soul is compared with the invisible interior of an empty shell or with the insubstantiality of mist which nevertheless has a shape when seen from outside.

3rd line: katong "put up, put down", i.e. while offering on a stone, respectively an altar.

1982, 4b, 1315, Kham (aged 54):

jak 'ek	chr.kɛng	'ek na' 'ar kha (Th)	na' pabuɪl	kɔmber kɔmti'
Take	chicken,	take please have killed	please (Th) killed	[for] child,

nak cərong nak pɣ'	//	'ɣh di dii	di ngam	gʌm ki buɪl	ki tay	//
very small smallest,		do get well	very best.	don't die	not die.	

hnguh	gʌm lom (Th)	di di bɔ' chə'um	'ar chuʌk no (Th) ti' long lɔng	//
Stay,	don't [soul] fall down	get carry stinky smell,	have tied small wrists together.	

gʌm ki	gʌh ki	jak hnguh	jak ni'	sam prang (Th)	ten lon di long prem
Don't	this [soul]	go staying	away	repeatedly confused	& walk soul until worn out;

pa 'ar	jak 'ek	chr.kɛ' chr.kɛng	//	che' 'e' cəbut	'ek ching	kɔmber kɔmti'
have	taken	chicken (the offering).		Hungry pig	fleshy,	child

154

gʌh gʌˈ chərɔng	gʌh pɣˈ	//	pa maˈ chuʌk tiˈ	chuʌk dʌm bɔn	gʌh ˈa
this [is] there small	this have;		make tie wrist	tie brain together	this have

di hn.taˈ	//	hnguh long di	long di yong	di lang	di hn.taˈ	long di ˈuy
to relative.		Stay together	together father,	husband,	relatives,	together with mother

di dəmɛh	huguh	di dii di ngam	gʌm ki bɯl ki tay	//	ˈar chuʌk	naˈ ˈa
& yourself,	stay	well very best,	don't die not die.		Have tied,	please have

chr.khɛˈ chr.kɛng	ˈar lac ˈar lɛo (Th)	//	ˈɣh cənreˈ	mʌr lon	mʌr hmal
chicken (indeed)	have finished already.		Do spirit	crawling (weak)	mind & soul,

gʌm ki jak	hnguh	jak sam prang	bɔˈ long luah	long bri	kɔmbɛr kɔmtiˈ
don't go	stay	repeatedly confused	carry into jungle	into forest,	friend child

gʌh bɔn [lit. "dance"]	mɛh cɯˈ	//	chr.kɛng gʌh to gʌˈ	cəbut	gʌh to gʌˈ
here together	You know.		Chicken this [is] there,	pig	this there;

pa ˈar chuʌk	ˈar hnguh	//	mɛt lon	mɛt hmʌl
have tired	have [already] done		your mind	your soul.

Kham is one of the oldest of the Mlabri men and therefore he knows the old prayers, as is apparent from this example. He said that the ceremony takes place shortly after a birth, during which either a bird or some eggs are sacrificed. Incidentally, the offering should preferably be of domestic animals (e.g. chicken), as they are not considered to have such strong souls as those of wild animals. If wild animals are used for the offering, the soul of the child may be carried out into the jungle by the spirit of the sacrificed animal. The father binds the soul by tying a string around the left wrist, and sometimes also the right ankle of the boy, in very much the same way as has been the custom among the other hill peoples, including the Mountain Thai.

3th line: lom (Th) "fall down". It was said that a particular bad smell from a baby might betray a critical infection. no (Th) "rat, mouse", also used to mean "small" for children.

6th line: dʌm is both "brain" and "onwards (in time)".

7th line: hn.taˈ "tail" or "relatives" as the generations are viewed when a band walk in a line from one place to the other with the adults in front and the children behind.

9th line: cənreˈ mʌr lon mʌr hmal, the Mlabri explained in various mutually conflicting ways. As mentioned previously, the mind and soul of an infant have not developed much, so if the child is becoming ill there is even a greater risk that it may loose both, i.e. it will die. Quite a few Mlabri use the expression "spirit soul", probably to indicate that the soul is in a state of transition, i.e. the person may either recover or die. As related on p. 74, many Thai also used this term for the tiny, weak soul of a dead person before it is reincarnated.

Marriage (Ml)

As already stated, there are no religious ceremonies invoking the spirits when a young couple get married. In fact there is not even a celebration in the family! However, I have included the admonitory speech of the father of the bride to the bridegroom because of its resemblance to the prayers.

1987, 11a, 558, Poa (aged 50):

mɛh mo'	'ek 'ot 'ɛw	//	nɛ (th) gʌh	'oh klol	gʌh day	'oh chi buɪl	mak 'ɛw
You keep	take my child,		This here	I feel	this can,	I really want	happy child,

'ek gʌh	dɔk di	//	'oh klol chiw	'ek gruɣ	'ek cəbut	mo' ma' 'oh
take this &	hang on to.		I (hearth) happy,	take cloth &	take pig	keep give me.

1st line: klol "hearth, feel" (used in various expressions of emotions). day, dai (Th) "can" or "all right". chi buɪl lit. "want deadly" or "really want".

2nd line: He asks for cloth and a pig, which is the customary gift for his wife and himself.

1987, 11a, 588, Poa (aged 50):

mɛh ja'	la 'ʉn	mo' tɛng ngan (Th)	//	jak 'ek tɛ 'dɣ	mo' ma' 'oh	//
You shall	leave tomorrow	keep married.		Take indeed	keep, give I	

'oh guɪr ma' 'dɣ 'ɛw	//	mɛh jak hnguh krum	gʌm 'ɔn rɣ' di.	'oh kro'
I wish give child.		You go stay fine (fat),	nothing bad ahead,	I feel (into)

klol chiw	//	gʌm	bɔ phit (Th)	pɛ' say (Th)
hearth happy;		nothing [with]	"Mr." wrong,	all right.

Another example of what the father of the girl might say.

1st line: My Thai vocabulary has: taeng ngan "marry".

2nd line: rɣ "wait, waiting" or "ahead".

3th line: pɛ' say "all right" from Thai: "clear or not disturbed".

1987, 11a, 601, Poa (aged 50):

hnguh	sɔng blɛng	di dii di ngam	gʌm jak 'ɣh	jak baluh	gʌm 'ɣh
Stay	two united,	[get] very good [life];	don't made bad	quarrel (angry),	nothing bad,

gʌm bak dor	//	'oh di dor pec chəkamruc chak mʌ'	//	gʌm ki ja' la
don't separate.		I give cut away [being] old, disabled & bent.		Don't [young man] leave

rɛ' jak	rɛ' mɣ'	wɛ' chaw bɔ nay	jak 'ɣh jak leh	//	hnguh thɛh
run away,	run [to] mother,	just married 'master',	must come forwards.		Stay truly

sɔng blɛng	leh dor bɔ' tak bɔ' roy	//	bo' jak dor pɣ'	kɔmbɛr kɔmchingto
two united,	get in time carry children.		[when] breasts become,	(get) boys & girls.

Poa has a great sense of humour and he is also able to compose long contrapuntal, satirical songs. Perhaps because the Mlabri marry increasingly more frequently nowadays than a generation ago, he urges with kind irony the boy to stay on together with his new bride – rather the habit of former times also in this far away place!

1st line: hnguh sɔng (Th) blɛng lit.: "stay two arms [united]". During the small ceremony the new couple are joined with a cotton string in the old Indian and Thai fashion.

2nd line: mʌ' "creeper" lit. "bent"

3rd line: wɛ' "just married". chaw "citizen", nay "chief, master" (Th) said ironically!

156

1987,11a, 617, Poa (aged 50):

'ek see (Th)   ya bur   mo' mo' hnguh song blɛng //   gʌm ki   jak 'ɣh gʌm bakdor
Take woman young man, keep   staying two united. Don't make bad, don't separate,

    di dor   hɔ' jar hɔ' jar nay   // gʌm ki   jak 'ɛh   jak paluh gʌm ki jak
throw away   master official [ironically].   Don't make bad quarrelings;   don't

chak mak nay   po' yɛk po' preng gʌm ki jak   pɔ' hɔt   pɔ' bɔng // phɣng jak
reject master   honey   nest;   don't go   push fall   get swollen.   Rely on

    hak dɣng   kɔmbɛr kɔmchingto 'ɛw to di ta'   hɔt dii   hɔt hluak
separately see   relatives,   small & elder   get good   get full.

//   jak pabo' pɔ' nom   khon la (Th)   hnguh sɔng lɛk   pon lɛk   rɛ' jak
   Get breast push milk; person neglect stay away two [or] several nights run away,

hnguh   sɔng lɛk   pon lɛk   rɛ' jak 'oh khet hɛk di // way(Th)   sɔng blɛng
stay two nights [or] several days run away, I fear much.   Please [keep] two united,

ja' la   phor   gɔtgɔt   kro' gn.dɯl 'ek tang ban (Th)   tang mɣk
shall leave father,   daughter [turned] into woman, take different home, different life.

This longer speech to the young bridegroom has some remarkable points: When he says: "don't reject honey nest", he means: "don't give up the good things in store for you", and likewise when he says: "don't fall down and get stung (while collecting the honey)" it is a warning that the young man is going to meet new challenges and responsibilities. Poa adds that the couple should rely on and support their family.

1st line: see (Th) emphatic word usually not translated. bur "young man".

5th line: The meaning is somewhat ambiguous. It is actually said that the boy should not run away for some days or visit another girl, which is really a problem among many of the Mlabri youngsters nowadays! sɔng lɛk "two evenings" i.e. "tree days". la "neglect, leave, abandon"

6th line: pon "four" (Th), but here meaning "several". khet "afraid" (old language as in M3). 7th line: gn.dɯl "woman" (lit. buttocks). tang "foreign, different" (Th), ban "house, home" (Th).

Divorce (Ml)

In the following two prayers, or rather talks with the spirits of his parents, Gui demonstrates what he said to his now divorced wife as reasons, or rather excuses, for leaving her.

1994, la, 047, Gui (aged 49)

'oh 'ak bakdor   mɛh hak jak   mo' malam (Th) // 'oh hak jak mo'   mo' myu'   //
I (divorce) leave, You separate, kept "singing".   I separately stay, [family] keep wife.

    yak pɣ' 'ɛw   kɔmbɛr kɔmching to mla' mɛh   klol bɯl   loh mi (Th)
Difficulties have child & relatives.   Person your heart [is] dead, tried have much

bɯl patok pationg // gʌm rɛ' dɛo   gʌm gɯt   ya' ya'   jak mo'
much altogether.   Don't run excited, don't think (plan) [Gui's] mother go to keep

komom lɤng mot [Th] 'uy   //   mla' gʌh yak (Th) mo'   mɛt khoy ma yom

child together with finished wife.   Person this difficult to keep   not in law come stay.

1st line: bakdor "separate, divorce"; malam "singing" or "complaining".

2nd line: loh mi buɪl "searched have much", viz. for a solution, buɪl "die" is used to underline the meaning.

3rd line: dɛo "excited, shaking" (Th?). ya' ya', by which is meant Gui's own mother.

4th line: mot "finished, used up, all gone" (Th); yom, yɤm "stay" (M3).

1994, la, 90, Gui (aged 49):

myˈ mɤm chin.deh   'ek ki bo phit   //   mɛh gʌm   bakdor   song (Th)

[Spirits] parents know,   take not wrong.   You don't   disagree   sending away

kot dɛo (Th)   //   mɛh hnguh   bo ka dii   di dor pɤy   'i nɔ' bɛr   nak chərɔng

oppressed & exited.   You keep on   not good   to feed   child   very small &

nak pɤ'   //   jak kwehl   ma' koc   ma' hnɛl 'e' mal   mo' ma'   mɛt myu' bɛr

smallest.   Go find   get bamboo rat,   rat & tubers,   keep give   Your wife's group

'ɤ' bong mɛt 'ɛw bɛr   //   jak tan (Th)   'oh 'a mo'   bɔ' ka dii   //   nɛ' 'a

[give] eating your child.   Got choked up,   [if] I had [to] keep not good.   Yesterday had

mo sɔng myu'   //   gɤn 'ar   mɛh hnguh   mo' myu'   gʌh klol chiw   //

kept sending away wife.   After returning, You stay   keep on wife,   this [I] feel happy.

mo' myu' 'oh klol blung   mɛh gʌm dʌm   nɛ' 'oh 'ar bakdor

[By] keeping wife I am angry.   You [parents sp.] don't mind, [that]   yesterday I divorced.

1st line: chin. deh "know, idea"; 'ek bɔ phit "take not wrong" or "don't be mistaken". bakdor "separate, disagree, divorce". song "send, see someone off" (Th).

2nd line: kot dɛo "oppressed (and) excited" (Th). nak chərɔng nak pɤ' lit. "very small, very have – i.e. smallest".

5th line: klol chiw lit. "hearth happy" (whereas klol blung "heart hot" or "angry").

When a man has asked his wife to leave him, he must also explain it to the spirits of his deceased parents to obtain their approval – we would say psychologically! He starts by saying that the parents know he has good reason for his move: that his wife has not provided enough food for their child, and that she makes complaints to others about him, two serious accusations in any human society. Therefore he had to return her as well as their child to her own family. Obviously, he still feels guilty about the divorce and perhaps he tries to find excuses because he may have found another woman. Talking to the deceased parents at times of crisis is much more common than we had recognized during all the previous visits. Curiously enough, this phenomenon is more common anywhere in the world than most of us are aware of!

158

Mlabri M3

Newborn & Naming

As already mentioned, this small group comprised only 18 members when brought down from the border (around Nam Wa) to Phua, and thereafter to a crowded refugee camp near Nam Yao also in the Nan province, around 1975, due to fighting between the Thai forces and the Communists. Only 11 persons remained in 1994 (three in 2007). Therefore, their traditional social structure has almost completely disintegrated and their ceremonies are practised less nowadays. However, two of the older men still remembered quite a lot, including some of the prayers.

After a birth, both the child and the mother are in danger of infection. Under the hardships prevalent in the jungle this has reduced their number considerably. This prayer is also for the mother and Kit expresses the hope that she will survive this birth like the previous ones, and he repeats ji' nɛh several times, which means "that's for sure" or "be such".

1987, 1b, 660, Kit (aged 44):

kuuk hmal mɯ   mɛ (Th)cho   ji' nɛh   //   kuuk hmal mɯ   mɛ' cho   wʌl yɣm
Spirit soul return   mother (with baby), be such,   spirit soul return   mother,   return stay

wʌl chɯ'   kap chak   kap chruʌt   gʌm keh   ma yɣm   to bri   to tɛn (Th) 'ye'
return here   with body   with chest;   don't break   (away) stay   forest   jungle far away.

ao' (Th)   wʌl yɣm   wal chɯ'   na 'uy na yong   //   bun 'ɛw   bun 'wɛ'
Want   return stay,   return here   please mother father;   good deeds child,   newly married

ji' nɛh   //   jong   kha' na' hnguh   mɛt hmal mɛt lon   wʌl yɣm   thɛh di mɣk
be such.   Walk   thereafter stay   your soul & your mind,   return stay   good living.

This prayer is for the mother of a newborn baby and is recited three to seven days after the birth. Although some words are different from those of the main group in Thailand, the composition and substance are very much the same.

1st line: kuuk "spirit" is pronounced with a high pitch to call the spirit from near or far. Kit repeats ji' nɛh several times. This was said to mean "that's for sure", in Thai: nae jai' "sure". cho (long vowel). The Mlabri could not agree upon this, but they said it is not "pain", which is cho'. It is actually used to indicate a newborn baby or its mother.

2nd line: kap chak kap chruʌt is lit. "with body with chest" meaning that the soul of the mother should stay with her body. thɛk (Ml), tɛn (M3), is "dense jungle", while almost the same word, daen "land" in general (Th).

3rd line: na (Th) "please". bun, bn "much, merit, or good deeds", from Th: boon.

4th line: kha na "at a certain moment, then, thereafter" (Th). hmal and lon were both translated into "soul" just as it is often the case with the Ml group, but lon is mostly used to indicate the unstable mind of a sick person. thɛh di mɣk "good and suitable", while Kit said "good living".

1987, 1b, 720, Kit (aged 44):

kuuk hmal muu	'e cho	//	wʌl yɣm	wʌl chuu	kap chak	kap chruʌt
Spirit soul return	girl newborn;		return stay	return straight	with body,	with chest,

kap yong kap pɛl	//	gʌm chak yɣm	ta prat	ta krɣng	wʌl yɣm
with father & mother.		Don't stay	mountain ridge	halfway;	return stay

wʌl chuu	kap yong kap pɛl	kap gɛng	kap phɔ (Th)	//
return here,	with father & mother	& windscreen	& father.	

gʌm ki	lon hot	lon tok	//	ji' nɛh	mɛt look (Th)
Don't	mind fall,	mind drop off,		be such	your child.

This is the prayer for the baby girl three to seven days after birth. Please note that we have two slightly different words for father with very much the same meaning and often used at random: jyong "father" and yong "male, person, man (father)".

1987, 1b, 805, Kit (aged 44):

kuuk hmal muu	mɛ' cho	//	'oh gʌh	pen glang pen yong	'oh chuʌk lon
Spirit soul return mother (with baby)			I myself	being husband & father,	I tie mind &

chuʌk hmuul	di thɛh yɣm thɛh mɣk 'a bong yuk	//	ching dɣng ching ten
tie soul	get good stay & living; [sp.] have eat rice.		Boar watch out boar walking

wʌl yɣm	wʌl chuu	kap chak	kap chruʌt	//	gʌm ki cho'	ki gret
return stay,	return here	with body	with chest.		Don't [get] pain	not unhappy,

gʌm ki	dəkat ki tay (Th)	//	kuuk hmal muu	ji' nɛh
don't get	fever not die		Spirit soul return,	right here.

This is a repetition of the prayer for the mother who has had a baby, probably because her husband fears she might have caught puerperal (or child) fever, which kills many Mlabri. It is said that the soul of the mother is presented with an offering of rice, while the (muddy) boars, being believed to carry a deadly spirit (just as in the Mlabri Ml), are asked to return her soul.

2nd line: hmuul "soul" corresponding to Thai vinyan i.e. that part of the soul that is reincarnated. Note the connection to che.muul "vapour, mist". The Mlabri themselves agreed to the similarity between the soul and the not substantial water vapour seen as small clouds drifting upwards through damp mountain forests during late morning. ching dɣng ching ten means take care not to touch the muddy places where boars roam, since they may harbour bad spirits wɔk ruʌt wɔk tung.

1987, 5b, 992, Kit (aged 44):

'ɣh 'ah ray (Th)	ka dii	leh Not Li	'ɣh 'ah ray	ka dii leh	//	'ɣh 'oh lon
Do anything	good come	(two names)	do anything	good come		do my mind

'oh hmuul	Not 'e Li	chung thɛh chung mɣk	//	'ar 'mɛt	kuut bah	at bɛr tawin
my soul	(names)	please good living.		Had eyes	born You two	suns

lɔy	wʌl yɣm	wʌl chuu	kap 'uy kap yong	//	gʌm ki cho'	ki gret
ago;	return stay	return here	with mother and father;		don't pain	not unhappy [or]

160

keh	gʌm ki cho'	ki gret		gʌm ki dɔkat	ki tay	//	mɛh kɯt	'oh gʌh mʌc
break	don't pain	not unhappy,		don't [get] fever	not die.		You born,	myself seen

'at bɛr	tawin loy	bɛr tawin loy	//	yom thɛh	yom mʏk	//	wʌl yʏm
[but] two	suns ago	two suns ago;		stay well	good living.		Return stay

kap chɯ	kap yong	kap pɛl	//	kuuk hmal mɯ
straight	with father	& mother;		spirit soul return.

Kit said on this occasion that he would name the baby girl already three days after the birth ("two sunrises ago"). In the first line we find the name for the small child, Not.

2nd line: chung lit."high up" or "please". bɛr tawin "two suns" actually includes three nights and therefore corresponds to three days, as for example when working for the Hmong. loy (jrʌʌk) "swim" (Rischel 1995, p. 289), because the sun is considered to swim across the firmament.

5th line: yom "sit down, settle down", whereas yʏm "sit, stay", but both are used for "stay".

Marriage (M3)

1987, 3a, 950, Sak (aged 31):

kuuk hmal lon Gomla	//	'oh wʌl toc	wʌl yʏm	nɛng mɛh	gʌm ki lon hot
Spirit soul mind (name wife);		me return catch	return stay	with us.	Don't mind fall,

lon tok	ni wʌl	di mʏk	//	wʌl chuʌk	ma' blɛng ma' hnɛl	ni yʏm	thɛh
mind drop,	return	good living.		Return tie,	get arm & leg,	to stay	good

yʏm mʏk	gʌm ki cho'	ki gret Gomla	//	kuuk hmal	lon Gomla
living.	Don't [get] pain	not unhappy (name).		Spirit soul	& mind (name).

ya	hak	wʌl yʏm	to trl.dɯng
Wife	separately	return stay	body together.

2nd line: mʏk "good, suitable", while di mʏk or thɛh mʏk "good living".

Marriage is just as informal an affair as with the main group (Ml) and the prayer resembles those for an individual who is ill. However, Sak explained that during the short ceremony man and wife simultaneously tie the string to each other, and the new couple are asked to stay together. This also happens in Thailand and in India, where the ceremony probably originated.

4.6 Accidents and Illness

Some Mlabri, especially the younger ones, are well aware that accidents and some diseases may have natural causes, while the older generation still believed they are caused by the spirits. Over the years we have tried to obtain information on these matters, including the limited cures at the Mlabri's disposal. However, the Mlabri have not been all too happy to discuss such things. They fear that merely talking about these issues might provoke them to happen; very much the same applies when asking about dangerous animals. In the latter case, the Mlabri would utilize transliterations in order not to encounter such animals shortly afterwards. If someone becomes really ill, they believe that the soul is about to leave them. Similarly, when they dream they also think it is the soul that takes its leave and experiences the events they see in their dreams ('ɛm mac "sleep see" mʌc cɔnre "see (deceased's) spirits".

For everyday ailments such as cuts and burns, toothache and headache, they use special leaves or extracts of roots; for burns they may also apply squirrel's blood. For insect and snake bites, they have a few similar remedies. These now include the alkaline material from old batteries, used to destroy the poison. However, all the dangerous, rare and invisible diseases are still, to some extent, believed to be due to the malicious spirits, in which case they may put an offering into a leaf and fix it to their body with a string, whereupon they will go to pray to their parents, making a small altar in the forest.

The Mlabri take refuge in prayers and offerings, or they might consult the other hill tribes for help, whenever a situation approaches a real crisis (fig. 87). As we shall see, the prayers are, in some respects, similar to those dealt with in the preceding chapters. The Mlabri offer some roots, eggs, a bamboo rat or the like in the event of less serious diseases, whereas a pig is required in severe cases. The person who leads the prayer has to kill the pig himself. A boar is not safe to use, as it has a strong and perhaps vengeful spirit, or it might host the spirits of wet soil and water pools, wɔk ruʌt wɔk tong. Both spirits are considered responsible for causing illness, together with those of the sky and the earth. But also the spirits of the dead parents may inflict diseases if they do receive regular offerings. Accidents are often thought of as being caused by the spirits and any danger is in fact the very definitive quality of a particular spirit!

Previously, if someone was seriously ill further measures were taken in order to appeal to the spirits, including putting soot on the fingernails. He or she could also be asked to chew a yellow colour and to smear it on their face and body; if this was not possible, someone in the family could do it. To learn whether a sick person was able to survive, two beeswax candles were placed, one on each side of the head of the patient. If the candles burnt down, everything would be all right, but otherwise he or she might be unable to recover.

If a person is so ill that there are difficulties in moving on to the next camp, the Mlabri told us that they will try to ease the path by cutting a trail through the jungle, because they say that carrying such persons means bad luck. However, nowadays they leave some of the close family behind to take care of their relative. But in 1970 we heard from a Thai hill farmer who sometimes visited the Mlabri that in the case of a chronically sick or immobile old person the band would not or could not remain. Therefore, they put the person in a tree, where they made a nest of branches, tied together with vines, or in a large basket hanging in the tree. Here they left the unfortunate person with food and water. If the patient recovered, he or she would climb down to search for the band. Otherwise, the platform or the basket would serve as a sepulchre! The Mlabri themselves denied this former practice, probably because they did not wish to be considered 'uncivilized', but an old Mlabri said that previously a cave closed with a fence made of bamboo sticks had served the same purpose.

Mlabri Ml

1980, 1b, 830, Ajan (aged 35):

gɔk klar	gɔk bɛ'	hmal mɯ	cɔbut yong	katong	mɯ kɔmbɛr chingto
Spirit sky	spirit earth	soul return;	pig male	put up [altar]	return relatives

di hlon   di   hmal
mind   &   soul.

Ajan is not an expert on the prayers and this example is, therefore, only a short version. The prayer asks these two powerful spirits most responsible for diseases to bring back the soul of the sick while the offering is presented.

1st line: When repeating the prayer he instead said wɔk klar, therefore both are "spirit", gɔk and wɔk presumably having the same meaning. katong "jump (down)", but also means "to put down something", as when offering some roots or meat on a leaf or a stone put on the ground, such as the M3 Mlabri do (fig. 77), and the Ml Mlabri did beforehand, and as we saw Paeng do during a spear spirit ceremony in 1978. Even though the Ml group have placed their offerings on altars at least since 1975, they still use the old word katong for this action.

2nd line: Here it is easy to hear the marked aspirations both in: hlon "mind, soul" and hmal "soul". The M3 Mlabri also use both of these words, but in addition they have chɯr.mɯl "soul", while chə.mɯl "mist". There is a similar correspondence in Northern Thai: khwan "soul, smoke" as well as in many other languages of Eurasia.

1980, 6b, 446, Som (aged 28):

kuuk hmal   mɯ   roy ding //   cəbut   yong   katong   'oh   katong   bong   //
Call soul   return child   pig   male   offer (put down), I   put down   meat.

gʌm ki   jak long (Th)   chak   klaw   cho'   bɯl   cho' tay (Th)
[Soul] don't   get lost (lit. into)   unable   scrotum, pain   die   pain die;

kɔmbɛr lɛng chingto 'e nɔ'   'a chə 'al   nom (Th)   kə rɯm 'ɣh   rɣm bet   //
   relative   baby   have bad smell, milk   no have [for]   several days cry

pia 'dɛ   'i 'dɣ //   mʌc koc   mʌc hnɛl   gather   mʌc   gəchong
animals edible.   Find (see) bamboo rat   find rat, squirrel, find   land turtle.

The soul of the sick boy is asked to come back. Many of the Mlabri, and especially their children, starve during the dry season (February-April), when it is hard to find food.

1st line: cəbut "pig" from the farm, whereas ngay "boar" (seldom used for offerings).
   katong lit. "jump down, put down", i.e. the offering of food on a flat stone.
2nd line: long "get into" or "get lost"; compare long thang (Th) "lose one's way".
3rd line: Rischel 1995, p. 313 has (in Mlabri M3): mɛ' rɯm "it rains for several days" hence the translation rendered.

1982, 5a, 555, Gui (aged 37):

'ot   ɛw   di lon   'ot   ɛw   hik dəkat 'ot   'ɛ   gʌm jak hnguh kulkol   drol
My   child's mind (soul), my   child very ill;   my child don't go   stay   rolling very end

kulkol ruʌng di gɯn leh   'ot   'uy   'ot   yong   gʌh pɣ'   gʌh mi // gʌm ki
rolling river, return (him) my   mother my   father [sp], this want his have.   D'ont

jak   hnguh 'ac   cənre bɛ'   cənri pa tae (Th)   cənre' lam ding   lam dɣng
go   stay [with] bird [or] spirit earth, sp. former (dead people), spirit tree big,   tree watch,

cɔnre' kwʌr cɔnre' lam // 'ot 'ɛw hik dəkat ray (Th) // gʌm ki jak mo' wɣk
spirit stranger, spirit tree.   My child   very   ill,   fiercely,   don't go [away] stay stream

mo' nam (Th) // 'oh way (Th)   'ek cəbut   to 'ɛw ching   jak 'ɣh   bɔ' lon   bɔ' hmal
stay stream.   I rattan wicker take (put) pig,   small   pig; send carry [back] mind & soul.

The beginning and the end are very much like those of the other examples. But in the middle of the prayer it is said: "Don't go stay with bird", which means that the soul should not fly far away with a bird, a concept shared, for example, with the Orang Asli (Senoi) living around the Thai-Malaysian border. Moreover, it is requested that the soul should not stay with the earth spirit (spirit of disease and death), with dead people's spirits, the tree spirit (who likes to have some company!) or with any strangers. The Mlabri have explained that the more ill the person is, the larger the offering must be. The dismembered pig is put on the small "wicker-work (things made of)" made of rattan, way, wai (Th), leaning against an old tree, the latter is believed to be the abode of the spirits of the parents.

1982, 5a, 600, Gui (aged 37):

'e mɣm   'e ding   'e ta'   // klol   gɯn   jak 'ɣh   jak joy   khon   poh chuʌn   poh mɔn
[Sp.] father old uncle,   like   return   make   help   people   clearing   the land.

// 'oh klol   'ɣh   klol   chuʌk   di 'ɛw   di lon   di hmal   'ot 'ɛw   hik dəkat
I like   do   like   tie   child's   mind & soul,   my child [has]   much fewer

tɛk naw (Th) // sernan (Th?)   loh chɯ   loh ma'   bo' cəbut   bo' ching //
& cold [malaria]   Master   find buy,   find give,   [I] carry pig   carry [Hmong] pig.

kro'   kro'   to no (Th) 'oh   hɛk dəkat   lɛk   'oh gʌm blʌk   'oh nɔn //
(Night)   into [have]   little, I [am]   very   cold,   evening I   dont   into   [fall] asleep.

'ot myu' gʌh krɯl   'i yɛt // 'ot ta 'ot roy   loh 'ek   krum bro' no   roh (Th) mɔy
My wife here like sarong,   My relatives   find take   thick cuts small,   one piece each.

The first part of the prayer asks the deceased old people to come to help preparing the land to grow rice for the Hmong and to attend the ceremony. Gui relates that he likes to tie the soul to the body of the child and that we went to buy the pig for the offering (from the Hmong) and took the pig back. The last part tells the spirits that we had promised the Mlabri some textiles from the market, which we had bought for the women in the band, since the nights can be quite cold in the mountains during December and January.
1st line: klol "hearth, like". 3rd line: tɛk "cold" and in Thai: nawn.
5th line: bro' no' roh mɔy the Mlabri said was: "give one each", but bro "a cut", viz. in this case of the double sarongs we had bought for them, each to be cut into two pieces.

1982, 6b, 1060, Ta (aged 38):

kuuk hmal mɯ // 'i mɣ'   'i mɣm 'ɛw roy   'e ding   'e ta'   gʌm   ma pam
Call soul return [dead] mother father,   young & old relative, uncle, don't come tease,

ma loh   'oh klol   'oh hmal   gʌm ki   thet   ki pam   'oh yong   bun mla'
look for   my heart & my soul,   don't   cut   not tease;   I father   good deeds persons,

164

gʌh pɣ'	gʌh mi (Th)	gʌm ki	hnguh yak hnguh	kulkol	drol	kulkol	ruʌng
this want	this have,	don't	difficult stay on	rolling	very end	rolling	stream.

Ta was feeling weak because of an attack of malaria and therefore asked his deceased relatives to return his soul, but two years later he actually died from this disease.
3rd line: drol "whole", here in the meaning of "to the very end of" (the stream).

1987, 9a, 996, Paeng Noi (aged 42):

kuuk	hmal	mɯ //	mɛh rɣm	ki	to lon	to hmal	mɛh rɣm	ki jak	hnguh
Call	soul	return.	You follow	not	harm mind	& soul;	you follow	not go	stay

kulkol	drol	kulkol	ruʌng //	'oh pa 'ɣh	'ar chuʌk	'ar ma'
rolling	very end	rolling	river.	I make	have tied	have given,

man hnɔr	bun hnɔr	sɔng blɛng	sɔng gr.tʌl //	mɛh rɣm	kə jak hnguh
luck [tie] string	merits string	two arms	two elbows.	You follow	not go stay

kulkol	drol	kulkol	ruʌng	ning gec	jɛng pol	lam	jɛng ton //	mɛh
rolling	very end	rolling	stream	with spider	hole pangolin	tree hole	trunk.	You

di mɯ	di wʌl	'oh yong ta'	chaw nay	gʌh pɣ'	gʌh mi (Th) //	'oh gʌh mo'
return	back,	I (male) uncle	& official	this want	this have.	Myself keep

gʌh bling	gʌh mɛh	mɛh gʌm ki	jak hnguh	kulkol	drol	kulkol	ruʌng
alive	with you.	You don't	go stay	rolling	very end	rolling	stream.

mɛh rɣm	ki to lon	to hmʌl //	mɛh rɣm	ki jak 'ɣh	jak ngɔr	bɔ' wɣk
You follow	not harm mind	& soul.	You follow	not send	go footpath,	carry water

bɔ' nam	tan na chɣt //	to gʌh 'ɣh	'ar chuʌk	'ar hmal	bun hnɔr bun hnɔr
& stream,	get clogged very end.	Body here	have tied	have soul	merits strings (tied),

// sɔng blɛng	mɛh gr.tʌl	gʌm ki jɔra'	ki cɔrɔng //	mɛh	gʌm ki	dəkat
two arms	your elbows,	don't [get] hungry	not small.	You	don't [get]	fever

ki naw	gʌm ki	butbot	ki 'oh leh //	'oh pa 'ɣh	'ar chuʌk	'ar ma'
nor cold,	don't	tremble	not me come.	I made	have tied	have done.

On this occasion I specifically asked for the prayer to be said when somebody is very sick. The string is put around both wrists, and the prayer is repeated several times. Once again we note that the Mlabri are afraid that the soul is going far away (downstream towards the lowland) or hiding in a crab hole, a hole for a pangolin or a tree hole.
1st line: rɣm "together, follow".
5th line: chaw nay (Th) lit. "citizen master" was translated: "official".

1987, 1la, 226, Poa (aged 50)

'oh	wɔk klar	wɔk ki' //	'ek cəbut	mo' lon	'ot hmal //	gʌm ki	jak hnguh
Oh,	spirit sky	spirit sun,	take pig	stay mind	& my soul;	don't	go stay

ja' la	di dii	dəmɔy //	di mɯ	di wʌl	ta' roy //	'uy yong	bong pɣ'
go to	leave on	well alone	keep	returning	to relatives.	Mother & father	food have,

gʌh	bɔ pɣ'	gʌh mi (Th)	//	gʌm ki hak	jak hnguh	di dii	dəmɔy	//
here	indeed have	this have		don't separately	go staying	on well	alone;	

di gɯun leh	di bɔ' hnguh	//	gʌm	hak jak	'ɣh	jak tɛ	di to	di	ləbo'
return back	carry [soul] stay,		don't	separately	go,	go truly	with	one	another.

Poa demonstrates in this and the next prayer what he will say if a person is very sick, in which case he may even call the spirit of the sky and sun (the latter very seldom being referred to in the prayers). It is said that a pig has been sacrificed to bring back the soul of, in this example, a sick child.

2nd line: ja' "shall, will, going to (Th)" and: la "leave (Th)".

4th line: di to di ləbo', Rischel 1995, p. 286, has an unspecific classifier, also as a noun modifier, e.g. person. The Mlabri said "with one another (person)" or much the same.

1987, 1 la, 240, Poa (aged 50):

'oh gʌm ki	to lon	to hmal	ya to lon	to hmal	di ni chal	wɔk ruʌt
You don't	harm mind	& soul,	don't mind	& soul	send this stinky	spirit wet soil

wɔk tong	ki gʌh	gah dii	//	ja' la	wɔk bɛ'	wɔk pa tae (Th)	gʌm ki	ja' la
& pool	not here,	this is good.		Shall leave	spirit earth	sp. fixed (dead p.),	don't	leave

rɣ' mɛh	rɣ' mɯn	ki to lon to hmal	//	wɔk bɯul	to di wɔk	lam ding
waiting	You [us] to come,	not harm mind & soul,		spirit dead	& you spirit	tree big

lam dɣng	'uy yong	bong pɣ'	gʌm ki	jak 'ɣh	jak leh	ja' la	gʌm
tree watch,	[sp.] parents	food have,	don't	come	come	shall finish [us],	don't

kro' 'oh mʌr	kup	mʌr kum	jak 'ɣh	jak leh	'dɣ tang mla'	tang glɣ'
inside me crawl	spirit,	crawl, hold,	(caused) by	bringing	any stranger	different mind

di	haw	chaw haw nay (Th)	//	gʌm ki	ja' la	ma' 'ɣh	mo' pran	bɛr lɛng	chingto
of	master	official.		Don't	cease	giving	luck	[to]	relatives,

cənyʌk	ki thɛh
likewise	not good.

Almost all the most feared spirits are mentioned, including the spirits of the empty and the full pool, that of the earth, those of their deceased family members and their abodes (old and tall trees), asking these spirits not to send sickness to anyone in the band. During this first meeting with Poa's band I ("master official") was likewise asked not to bring visitors to the Mlabri who might carry bad luck. We were in fact told that before coming to stay with Poa he had asked the spirits beforehand not to be offended or to harm anyone.

5th line: kro' "darkness, night, inside" (also kr'ung "hole"), kup "cloud" syn. for "spirit", tang "different" (Th); therefore tang mla' "stranger" and tang glɣ' "different mind". Notice that the Mlabri are afraid that the spirits of the parents might enter their body.

Mlabri M3

1987, 1b, 1161, Kit (aged 44):

kuuk	hmal	muu	'e cho	gʌm ki	jak 'a	ta wɔk	to roay	gʌm ki	ta keh ma
Call	soul	return	baby,	don't go	[with]	Mr. spirit	[of] tiger,	don't	breaking come

ta wʌk	to roay	//	wʌl yɣm	wʌl chɯ	kap 'uɣ	kap yong	wʌl yɣm chɯ
Mr. spirit	tiger.		Return stay	straight	with mother	& father, return	stay straight

kap chak	kap chruʌt	kap 'uy	kap yong	pen glang	pen yong	'oh lon
with body	with chest,	with mother	& father,	have husband	have father;	my mind

'oh muul	di yɣm	thɛh yɣm mɣk	//	gʌm ki cho	ki gret	gʌm ki	thapul	tharac
my soul	stay good	stay healthy.		Don't pain	not ill,	don't bad	stomach	& bowels;

di wʌl	di wʌl	yɣm wʌl jɣng	kap chak	kap chruʌt	//	gʌm ki	dəkat	ki jay
return	return	keep return [on] foot	together	with body.		Don't [get]	ill	not die.

//	kuuk	hmʌl	muu
	Call	soul	return.

1st line: cho' "pain", while 'e cho is a newborn boy. Moreover mɛ cho is a "mother" just having had a baby, and 'i cho "small (or newborn) girl", and ba cho "small boy". We noted that when a mother was caressing her baby, she might say: "cho, cho, …" ta is a particle of unidentified meaning, but ta (taa) is also "Mr." used as a sort of honorific title previously as well as for the larger animals in order not to be attacked! to "body" of animals or humans (classifier for animals and persons).

2nd line: yɣm "stay", whereas: yum "sit down" but also used for "stay with" (compare Bernatzik's "Yumbri" lit. "stay forest").

3rd line: kap chak kap chruʌt lit. "with body with chest", meaning that body and soul should stay together. pen (Th) "be in existence, be able to do something".

4th line: (h) muul "soul". Kit said that muul is vinyan or "soul" in Thai. Both Ml and M3 also have: hmal for soul as well as lon "(feeble) mind or soul"; kuuk hmal muu (1st line) and gʌm ki cho' ki gret (4th line) are other examples of the close relationship between the two dialects. But while both groups have wɔk "spirit" only the Mlabri Ml also use cənre'.

1987, 8a, 630, Sak (aged 31):

kuuk hmal	lon Kit	//	gʌm ki	lon hot	lon tok (Th)	'a pen ding pen roy
Spirit soul	& mind (name);		don't	mind fall	mind fall off,	have old & young relatives

'ɛ	pen ding	'oh chuʌk	lon roy	di thɛh di mɣk	gʌm ki cho'	ki gret	'oh 'dut
yes,	have father,	I tie	child's mind	get good living.	Don't pain	not ill,	my back

pen tom	pen hit	thɛh di mɣk	Kit	//	gʌm kul	'oh ki	lon hot
hot have	infection,	good living	(name);		don't roll,	me not	soul fall (off)

lon tok	tə yɣm	wʌl 'uy	nɛh yong Kit	//	'a pen ding	pen phaw
soul fall off,	return stay	return (to)	mother here & (father).		Have old,	have father (Th)

'oh	toc	'ɛw	to lon	to hnguh	di thɛh	di mɣk	kuuk	hmal	lon	Kit
I	catch	child's	mind	body stay	get good	health.	Call	soul	mind	(name).

167

This prayer is for Kit's sick son who was also called Kit when he was a boy.

1st line: pen "be (existence), able to do, have life" (Th)

2nd line: 'dɯt "back (of body)".

3rd line: tom, was said to be "infection", but is actually "boil" which though is an understandable transliteration. hit "itchy" (Th).

4th line: phaw "father".

4.7 Burials

Even though we have lived with the various bands of the main group (Ml) for a total of more than a year, we have fortunately never experienced a death. We have, therefore, not seen the actual preparations, the ceremony and the burial itself. However, we have had all the proceedings explained to us and, much to our surprise, in 1987 they started to make a coffin, etc. to demonstrate what should be done (fig. 89). This would have been quite unthinkable in almost any other culture, but perhaps because the Mlabri are so close to life and death, they do not mind revealing such matters to us, who have known them since they were young.

The death ceremonies are in many ways the most important ones as they embody the most crucial transformation of body, mind and soul, thereby revealing many of the key points of Mlabri beliefs. However the death ceremonies themselves are not at all elaborate. In fact, we know that previously some Mlabri groups merely placed the corpse on a pile of branches. Then they knelt down and wept for a while before hurrying away for fear that the spirit of the dead should take someone else in the band. We have asked the Mlabri of the large group many times whether they once did something similar, but have received conflicting answers. Is is worth noting that the main group have no specific word for "bury", but rather use combinations of a few other words: jak dor "put away", jak bɛ' dor "earth put away", chuʌk dor "dig put away" and chuʌk bɛ' "dig earth" (M3 also have chuʌk tɯp "dig cover" a grave). Thus, including what has been said by the Mountain Thai and the Hmong, we realize that simple burial is not an old custom. But there were formerly various procedures for disposing of the dead depending on the status of the person concerned, and where and how he or she had died.

A generation ago, if someone died on a hunting expedition in a remote spot, his companions did very little and in much the same way as explained above. However, if death occurred in or near the camp, they sometimes laid the corpse on a pile of branches in a place with many termites, finally covering the body with twigs and leaves and only a thin layer of earth. A stick put down beside the body together with the termites then produced the characteristic termite heap (kɔm.puc). This enclosed the body and prevented it from being dug up by tigers or other animals. Men would have their weapons and a pipe with them in the grave, whereas women would have a pot or a bamboo container, while children would be given only some food. If the deceased had been an important person, the preparations and the funeral would be more elaborate, even including burial under large stones. However, if the dead man or woman was not particularly respected, he or she was sometimes just left in the jungle with almost no preparations, just as has been observed by the Hmong on several occasions. Naturally, the Mlabri themselves have not been too keen to reveal such facts, as they like to appear just as 'civilized' as their more prosperous neighbours, especially the Hmong, who undertake substantial preparations for a burial.

168

In areas with many tigers they would wrap the corpse in a bamboo mat and place it in a tree, sometimes making a sort of trap, so that tigers would be impaled if they tried to jump up at the corpse. Other deceased Mlabri were, at times, placed behind rocks and dead children were often put into holes in large trees, the hole being covered with pieces of wood. A person injured by a tiger was simply left sitting under a tree or tied to a large, forked branch up in a tree to delay the tigers (fig. 83). This was to prevent others in the band from being followed and attacked; the latter procedure took place for the last time around 1960.

By the end of the 1950s, some Mlabri began to make real graves. This was due to complaints, both from Thai and Hmong mountain farmers, about their traditional methods of disposing of their dead. Today they always bury them in a place not suitable for making fields and far away from streams. A grave is dug less than one metre deep. The floor and sides are lined with pieces of bark and split bamboo. Then the corpse is dressed in some old clothes and wrapped up in a mat before being buried. The grave is covered with a roof of wood to prevent the corpse from bending and animals from digging it up; it is covered with only about 50 cm of earth. The funeral ceremony takes place only after all preparations have been completed.

During our last visit in 1994, some members of the big group (Ml) told us that they put a lighted candle made of beeswax at each of the four corners of the grave. Then the head of the family carries another lighted candle around the grave while inclining his head towards that of the deceased. Finally, the family members kneel down and weep for a while, after which the band hurries away.

If somebody dies during the day, burial will take place the same day, but if death occurs in the evening or at night, they will wait until next morning to dispose of the corpse and perform the ceremony. In both cases nothing is eaten between the death of the person and time when the band has left the area. To prevent anybody from coming close to the grave, shrubs and branches are cut down and burned around the spot to indicate that this is a place of no entry.

1980, 8a, 1404 Som (aged 28) and Muang (aged 42):

mɛh gʌm	rɣm	pam	rɣm loh	'oh pa 'ɣh	'ar jom	'ar thɣng	'ar 'yh
You don't follow,	tease	search for [us].	I made [grave]	have covered,	we have	done,

'ar jom	wɔk bɛ'	wɔk bɛ'	// gʌm ma tit ma tae' (Th)	kɔmbɛr kɔmchingto
have covered	sp. earth	sp. earth;	don't come stick to touch	relatives

nak cərɔng	nak lɛng	gʌm rɣm rap	rɣm jak	hnguh di
very small	& smallest children;	don't chase	follow. (Muang interrupts:)	Stay on

di dii dəmɔy	mɛh hak	kə rɣm 'oh	rɣm hnguh	mɛh hak
well alone. (Som again :)	You departed,	not follow me	follow stay,	you departed

kə rɣm	hnguh	bi' chən bi' mɔn	'ek to ma	pia' 'dɛ 'i 'dɣ
not follow	stay	full [work in the] field. (Others:)	Take send	(noise) animals edible.

Som said that this would be the prayer just after having covered the deceased with earth. The spirit of the deceased is asked not to follow the band or to trouble anyone. Halfway through the prayer, the surrounding Mlabri became so eager that first Muang and then the other men joined Som. They believe that the spirit of the dead stays in or near the grave, but that it may come up to trouble the living Mlabri, especially if not offered to. They also believe that the deceased parents may help the living ones clearing the jungle.

1st rɤm "together" or as here in the meaning "follow", while loh "search for".

5th line: hak "separated". My Thai dictionary has hak "break, break apart", which is also close to "depart" or "leave". bi' chən bi' mɔn is literally: "full [work] field, full cotton", which was commented on by saying that the dead Mlabri also had to help cutting down the jungle and clear the land before the Hmong plant rice. mɔn "cotton" is possibly mentioned, due to their many winding fibres being a symbol of the tiresome work in the field!

1982, 6a, 629, Kham (aged 54):

'oo la cənre   di   dii   bi'   pacho'   bɯl cho' tay // bi' gʌm   ma tit
Oh leave sp. (dead), got well [until] full (old age) suffered death.   Old don't come stick to

ma thal   // 'oh pama' jom ma' dɔk   bn.hnɛ' tɛ   cənre pol cənre khɔng
follow.   I gave & buried   honorable person indeed   & spirits blanket sp. things,

cənre mla'   cənre glɤ' // gʌm ma 'ek   bɔ' ta'   bɔ' roy'   // jak di dii
sp. of person   sp. head.   Don't take carry away relatives (old & young),   leave good,

di ngam   //   'oh 'ar jok   'ar jom   mɛh gʌm pɯh gʌm dɔy //   mɛh pa hak
get well.   I have dug out, have covered. You don't wake up & rise,   you separately

cho' bɯl cho' tay   //   phun 'ur   phun pɤy   gret 'ɤh   pa 'a
    deceased,   [through magic]   many larvae eat,   suffered caused by [entering]

   prak phrɔng blʌk // mir pa thu' mʌc to   mɛt   wɔk bɛ'   wɔk pa tae //
mouth & stomach into, insect rotten find your body, spirit earth sp. former person

 mɛh hak jak   di dii dəmɔy   li' la (Th) //   'uy po' chu'   pok nak ki bə
You separated, be well alone departing.   Wife provide   cover heavy,   not

    bə ta'   bə roy // bə to   lung bɛr   lɛng ti' nak cərɔng   nak pɤ   //
[having other] relatives,   no   relatives, children very small & smallest.

   'oh hak dʌm   chɛw chi   dʌm pɯh   jak long dʌl // 'oh hak chakamruc
I must (go) onwards   take care (pain), [be] alert   go in front.   I must [also get] old,

  chak mʌ'   'a dor   gɯn jak gɯn wʌl // 'oh hak dok   gʌm bɯl   gʌm tay
disabled bent, get disposed of leave & return.   I alone buried, don't kill [or let me] die.

//   mɛh hak jak 'ar wʌl   // 'oh rɤm jak   lɔh pɔl gɔt //   wɔk cənre   cənre
    you separately left & returned   I follow   close by behind.   Dead's spirit, spirit

   pa tae   mɛt kim   ki pɯh ki toc   cən(re) 'ot yong   'ot lang (Th) di gʌ' //
former one, your grave, not wake up, not rise. Spirit my father   my coffin stay there.

As mentioned before, Kham is one of the oldest men and, not surprisingly, his prayers contain more interesting details, although his enunciation is somewhat unclear. In this example, also for a dead father, he explains that he has buried his father together with his personal belongings, which now hold his spirit. It is also explained how the spirit of earth (i.e. that of sickness and death) has sent a very deadly spirit insect into the mouth of the father. As he has no brothers or sisters remaining, Kham's wife had to provide a blanket for the deceased. Now he himself has to take over responsibility for all the family and "take the lead". This kind person adds that one day he too must die and return (be reincarnated). He apologizes for burying his father, whose spirit he fears might kill another in the band. The spirit of the father is asked to stay in the grave and "not to wake up", in which case he might harm the living members of the band.

2nd line: Kham says that he has buried his father together with his belongings, which now must remain with the spirit of the dead person (cənre mla' cənre' glɣ',

3rd line). Egerod & Rischel, 1987, p. 55, mention a personal spirit of the same name residing in the head of living people. However, the general idea is that living people have merely souls and minds, and they are said to be spirits only if they are very vicious. For a discussion of the beliefs on the interactions between souls and spirits among some of their neighbours, such as the Lahu Nyi and the Red Lahu, see Walker, 1992, p. 268. khɔng, from khawng "things" (Th).

6th line: prak phrɔng, which according to the Mlabri means "mouth & stomach", probably from Thai: pak "mouth" and phrong "hollow". I specifically asked Kham if he had seen this special insect, but he denied this. As the death was caused by magic (one Mlabri said: "put spell"), the deadly insect seems to have been a spirit animal, sent by the earth spirit, the one of death.

9th line: 'oh hak dʌm chɛw chi' "I must (go) onwards (in time) take care", while dʌm pɯh "brain awake" or "alert".

10th line: chak mʌ' "disabled bent" like rattan.

11th line: lɔh pɔl gɔt "close by behind", as Kham himself felt he was getting old. cənre wɔk is lit. "spirit spirit", but means here "the dead person's spirit", as cənre is preferably used for the spirit of a dead person.

Last line: lang "large box, crate" (from Th).

1987, 6b, 1048, Gui (aged 42):

mla' bri'   mla' tae krok grɣng   gɯn 'ar mɛh   hak   bɯl // mɛh hak
Mlabri persons former, relatives close returned back, you separately died.   You separately

dɣ jak   gʌm rɣm tit rɣm tae (Th)   jak 'ot kr.dɯl   kr.chuɛl   'ot ta' 'ot roy
went away, don't stick to   touch   come my back & heels [of] my older & younger rel.,

'ot 'ɛw   'ot nɔ'   'ot ma ding 'ot ta'   chakam.ruc chak mʌ' // mɛh bɛ' dɔk
my children & grandch., my elder brother & uncle   old body bent.   You buried

hak bɯl hak tay mɛh gʌm   'dɣ rɣm tit   rɣm tae jak   gɣn 'ar mɛh   rɣm tit
separately died;   you don't   any stick to,   follow touch,   returned you, follow stick to,

rɣm tae jak   'ot ta' 'ot roy   'ot 'ɛw   'ot mɛh bɯl   patok pathiɔng   //
follow touch   my old & young rel.,   my children, mine you kill   finish all of them.

mɛh chuh   hik ma   hɛk 'a chɛ'   'a nak (Th) //   gʌm nɔ'   rɣm tit rɣm tae jak
you deep much come, very have many, have much. Don't children follow stick to touch,

seum (Th) // gɯn   'ar   mɛh   hak   bɯl // 'uy yoh   gʌh yong   gɯn 'ar
absorp;   returned have you,   separately died. Mother lost this father, returned have [also]

ding 'e ta'   'e yar 'e roy   gɯn   'ar bɯl hnɛ'   hak   toc //ya to (Th) 'e ding
old uncle, aunt & younger, returned have dead, he [was] separately caught,   Don't   father,

171

'e ta	'e ya	'e roy	gʌm ngɔr	rɯm	se klay	jak krok	kr.dɯl	'ot kr.chuɛl
uncle,	aunt,	young,	don't trail	follow	shamefully,	come relatives	behind,	my heels

'oh krok kr.wen	krok kɔm'ɔm	krok 'ay	krok	kɔmbur	kɔm.chingto
my band's nephews:	band's children,	brothers,	bands	young men,	women,

'e bur	cha.kamruc	chak mʌ'	krok kɔmbɛr komti'	nak cɔrong nak pɣ'
boys,	old [persons]	body bent,	band's children,	very small & smallest.

Gui did not specify to whom this prayer would apply, but from its content and that of the next prayer we realize that it would be for the father who has died. But Gui did say that he would say the prayer only after all preparations had been carried out, i.e. when the leaves and earth had been put over the body and just before leaving the place of burial. The prayer starts by asking the spirit of the dead person to stay in or near the grave, and that it should not follow the living members of the band and kill more of them. Finally, he mentions all the band members who have died and that they should not haunt the living.

1st line: krok grɣng lit. "relative in the middle" being the father of Gui. gɯn or kheun (Th) "return, give back something to someone", i.e. here being to return the dead to the earth, perhaps to be reborn as many Mlabri believe.

3th line: chak mʌ' "body bent" (lit. like rattan).

9th line: se, see (Th) emphatic word.

10th line: kr.wen really means "side (line), direction" but was translated "nephews".

Last line: nak cɔrong nak pɣ' is lit: "very small very have" or "very small and smallest".

1987, 6b, 1066, Gui (aged 42):

krok	kɔmbɛr	kɔm.chingto kɔmbɛr	rih bɛr	nak cɔrong	nak pɣ'	gɯn 'ar
band's	men,	women & children	here two	very small	& smallest,	returned have

krok	'e ding	'e roy	lungguh	hnɛ' hak	krok	jak krok	'e roy 'e ding
band's	elder	& younger,	daughter	he left	band,	left band,	relatives &

lungguh //	gʌm lɔh	rɯm tit	ɣm tae	jak lɔh	song (Th) khɔt	tarɔc tareng
wife.	Don't near	stick to,	touch,	go near	tall spear	young men,

krok 'e nɔ' 'e roy	nak cɔrong	nak pɣ' //	gɯn	'ar	krok 'e ding	'e roy
band's children	very small	& smallest.	Returned	have	bands old	& young relatives,

gɯn 'ar	bɯl hnɛ'	bɯl	pajak	ni' jak	pa ka dii	jak 'ek dor //
returned	dead person,	dead	send away,	[we] flee,	(after) making well,	have taken & buried.

pa hnam rɯm hnam	dor thu'	dor tray	dor roay	dor krok dor pok
For many years	put away [from] rot,	larvae	& tigers,	put away from band & covered.

krok	'e roy ding	də jo'	də cho'	gʌh to gʌ'	də yet	də kre'	nɛh bɯl
Band's	relative's	knife &	digging impl.	this is there	& loin	(cover) beaten,	this deceased's

də khɔng //	gɯn 'ar	yong	ya də khɔt	ding to'	də jo'	way də khɔt
belongings.	Given back [to] father,	bring spear,	big knife,	knife,	put in place spear

ding naw	də chɔrɛ	sarong (Th)	də kɔk	də gam	gʌh to gʌ' //	gʌm ngɔr
big sword,	shirt	& sarong	pipe	with handle	this [is] there.	Don't footprints

rɣm tit rɣm tae'	jak krok	kɔmbɛr	kɔm.chingto	kum.ɔm
follow stick to, touch,	leave band's	men,	women	& children.

Although Gui was asked to repeat the previous prayer, this one is quite different. However, it begins in very much the same way and it is also the prayer for a dead father (his wife still being alive). Care is taken to cover the dead, so that the body will not be harmed by worms, tigers or relatives. The Mlabri told us that they select a lonely, secluded spot in the jungle and, among other things, cut and burn the smaller trees around so that no one will cross the grave by mistake. The prayer also mentions all the things they are leaving with the body – his knife, digging implement, bark dress and also his spear, sword (really a long knife) and a sarong. On another occasion we were told that, previously, the spear was placed standing upright besides the grave. Finally, Gui says that now they have to leave the dead.

1st line: krok, krɔk "group, band, relatives" the term is vague and denotes any group of Mlabri.

3th line: jak lɔh "go near", while the Mlabri said "search for", however, which is rather jak loh, rɣm loh or jak kwehl.

6th line: pa hnam rɣm hnam "years together years" or "for many years".

7th line: də yet "loin covers" made of beaten bast. Before 1970 these were still being used (fig. 18), especially when the Mlabri men had to visit a village to exchange their jungle products for iron, salt, etc.

8th line: way də khɔt "put in place spear", from Thai: way "put in place". gʌm ngɔr rɣm tit rɣm tae "don't footprints (trail) stick to". Apparently Gui asks the spirit of his dead father to stay in his grave and not to follow the footsteps of anyone of the band.

1987, 11a, 770, Poa (aged 50):

pahak toc wɔk	nɛh bɔ' kum	ma' dor	wɔk bɯl gʌh //	ma' jom	hon 'dɣ
Separated catch spirit,	here carry coffin	give away	sp. dead here.	make	cover now,

nɛh bɔ' gɯr	mo grɯng	ki bɔ' kru'ung	pia' 'dɛ	'i dɣ	krok mla'	kə rɣm thang
here carry dig	each plank	not inside [use]	any kind [of wood],	relatives	exposed [to]

glɣ' //	gʌm ki rɣm 'ɣh rɣm 'dɛ	ta roy	to 'i bɛ'	to 'i pang	to 'i to gʌh
dizziness.	Don't [sp.] follow together	relatives.	Bring earth,	bring bamboo,	bring person.

'oh 'ar jak	gʌm rɣm 'ɣh	jak leh	bɔ' ta' bɔ' roy //	hnguh to mɛh	krɣng di
I walked ahead	don't follow	come here	carry away relatives.	Stay by yourself	(but) join

chən di mɔn	dʌm nɔn	rɣm gʌ' to gʌh	gʌm rɣm blʌk	rɣm blɛr	tɛ rɣm
work the field;	onwards sleep	around here;	don't follow	share (?),	indeed stay

blʌk	gʌm rɣm	'bu'	labo' 'uy	labo' yong //	ma thang	la thang glɣ'
inside,	don't follow	close by	other women	other men;	[If] come place,	leave dizziness.

More details concerning the burial are revealed, among others that the wooden planks for covering the grave should be made properly (not using different kinds of wood), otherwise the burial party will become dizzy. It is also mentioned that the dead person, or rather his spirit, should help in the field but not follow the band, just as its members should not approach the grave subsequently or they will develop a headache.

173

1st line: kum "coffin".

2nd line: kru'ung, krung "hole", thang glɣ' lit. "direction (disturbed) head, dizziness".

3rd line: pang, the Mlabri said means a kind of bamboo and indeed they have more than thirty different species to choose from for all sorts of purposes.

4th line: di krɣng "in the middle" (Th), which is in accordance with: jak di krɣng "go between".

5th line: dʌm nɔn "onwards (in time) fall asleep", rɣm blɛr "share [life with us]".

6th line: rɣm blʌk "stay inside [the coffin]", rɣm 'bu' "follow slowly (close by)";

Mlabri M3

Burial practices seem to be very much the same as in the main group, but among this small number of people all ceremonies are naturally less elaborate. Previously they did not bury their dead but either left the body on the ground and covered it with twigs and leaves. Alternatively, they put the corpse into a roll of banana leaves or a bamboo mat and hung the roll horizontally between two trees, so high from the ground that tigers and other animals could not reach it. Yet another way to dispose of the dead was to leave the body inside the windscreen and tear down the roof, thereby also protecting the body from larger animals. Nowadays they carry the body, attached to a long wooden pole, about one hundred metres away to be buried. The old Mlabri, Oy, said that they still (in the late 1980s) put ashes in the eyes of the dead and left cooked roots, rice and betel leaves close to the body, together with the deceased's personal belongings. But if they wished to keep an item, for example the iron digging implement, it had to be thrown between two persons from one side of the body to the other, while reciting a short incantation.

1987, 1b. 905, Sak (aged 31):

mɣm	mɛh 'a bɯl	lay mɛh	'a bɯl	mɛh 'ar bong	dor yuk gʌh
Father	you have died,	many you	have died.	You given food,	put rice here,

bong yuk yɣm	dor yuk	gʌh nɛh	//	dor to yuk	dor pi'	gʌh jak nɛh	//
eat rice, stay,	put rice	this here.		Put rice,	husked rice,	this get here.	

'ar jak toc	jak mɛh	jak tɯp	jak dor	//	ni thɛh	di mɣk	mɛh gʌm
Left, caught,	brought you,	gone grave,	bury (put away).		This (is) good	get well,	you don't

rɣm tɛ rɣm loh	//	gʌm cho'	bong yuk	bong yar	bong 'ay	hmiʌng
follow search for [us].		Don't hungry,	eat rice,	&	tobacco, eat elder brother's	tea leaves,

bong dɔng	//	mɛh lɛt	toc jak	dəmɔy	dəmɔy	mɛh yum dəmɔy
eat betel leaves.		You little [ago got]	caught,	(go) alone	& return alone,	you stay alone.

wʌl tɯp	wʌl to mɛh	'a thɛh 'a mɣk	//	gʌm rɣm leh	tɛ loh
Return grave,	return yourself	have good existence;		don't follow	really search [for us].

This prayer, said after the dead father is buried, starts with an offering of some meat and rice. This group has so little that hardly anything except some food, tobacco and betel is left with the body. Kit said that they would also leave the clothes with the dead and one or two personal items such as a knife. Exactly as with the main group (Ml), they bury the body in a hurry and try to persuade the spirit of the dead to stay in or near the grave and not follow the band.

1st line: lay "many" (Th, Ml), bong "eat" (M3), but "eat meat" (Ml).

2nd line: pi' "husked rice", whereas the Mlabri just said "uncooked rice".

4th line: hmiʌng, where it was said fermented tea leaves were meant.

5th line: dɔng "betel leaves" according to Kit, however they are usually called thup pru'. toc "catch" i.e. by the spirit of death, wɔk buɪl.

Last line: gʌm rɣm leh tɛ loh lit. "don't follow really search [for us]".

1987, 5b, 928, Kit (aged 44):

'ɣh	mɣm wɔk	toc bong	met yuk	met pi' gʌh	//	'a met (Th) yuk
do	father spirit,	take eat	seeds rice,	seeds husked rice this;		have seeds rice &

met pi'	thʌc muɪy nuny (Th)	//	gʌm rɣm	neh tɛ pruk	meh jak dəmɔy
husked rice,	meat fat put on.		Don't follow	here really chase;	you go alone &

wʌl dəmɔy	//	nyɛk	mla' tɛk	ma pabuɪl	meh pa	ki buɪl	ki tay (Th)
return alone.		No other	people hit	come kill;	you cause	not kill	not kill,

mɣm wɔk	//	meh tɛ	dor yuk	gʌh bong	jok dor yuk	di jiʌy yuk	dor
father spirit.		You truly	give rice	this eat,	suck put rice	to chew rice,	put

pi' gʌh	tɛ dor yuk	gʌh pi'	//	gʌh jak lɔng	wʌl klɣng	gʌm 'oh
husked rice here,	truly put rice	this husked rice;		here go [into]	return behind,	don't me

gʌm lɔng	'oh krl.klol klɣng	//	mɣm wɔk	'oh gʌh	pen 'ɛw	pen ngwɛ'
don't meet [into],	I like place behind.		Father spirit,	myself	am child,	[his] own child,

'oh yuk	gʌh pi'	gʌm ki 'ɣh	cho' yuk	cho' bong	mɣm wɔk
I [give] rice,	husked rice,	don't cause	hungry rice	& meat	father spirit.

This last prayer by Kit was also said to be for the father, who had just died. The prayer mainly deals with the offering of food to the spirit of the dead, who in return should not harm the living members of the band either by trying to meet with the Mlabri or making them starve, perhaps – as the old people say – by causing the roots to disappear in the area where they reside.

1st line: toc "catch, drag, take"; met "seeds" (Th).

3nd line: nyɛk "no other" according to the Mlabri.

6th line: 'oh krl.klol klɣng "I like [you to go] behind" (klol "hearth"). jak di klɣng "go place behind" (also Ml phrase).

4.8 Deceased Parents and Others

Before presenting the prayers for the deceased members of the band, it would be appropriate to repeat some of the main points of the Mlabri belief in the afterlife relating to this chapter. Among the older generation, the general idea is that the spirits of the dead lead a bleak existence somewhere in the jungle. Preferably, they should remain in or near the grave and visit the living only when offered to or when asked to come and help in times of difficulty. If not offered to regularly they may cause all kinds of calamities – accidents, sickness and even death.

Fig. 90. A camp for 17 individuals with four windscreens near Ban Hui Hom (M1 80, 32). The windscreen in the centre is double, i.e. a hut! In order to describe fully the most important ceremony, that for the deceased parents and grandparents the following pages cover the procedures from two similar events, which supplement one another. The first one took place in and around the above-mentioned locality in 1980, the second event near Ban Baw Hoy (M1 77, 25) in 1982. As for the prayers, see examples in Chapter 4.8.

Fig. 91. The women collect water, wood and leaves, whereas the men make the altar, kill the animals, cut and share the meat and lead the prayers.

Fig. 92. Domesticated pigs are preferred for the big ceremonies, such as those for the deceased parents, as they are believed to have less vengeful spirits.

Fig. 93. The pig is killed either by cutting its throat with a knife or, as here, by hitting it on the head with a club.

177

Fig. 94. The blood is collected in a pot, cooked and eaten later.

Fig. 95. The skin is singed using burning wooden sticks. Hides are not used for any purpose at all!

178

Fig. 96. Remains of hair, etc. are removed by scraping and applying water to clean the meat.

Fig. 97. The offerings are cut up, while all the remaining parts are carefully divided, so that each family has similar pieces. Providing food for everyone and sharing in the band is regarded as the finest virtue among the Mlabri.

179

Fig. 98. Each of the men in turn holds one of the lumps of meat to be sacrificed while praying to the deceased parents.

Fig. 99. However, the women, standing close together with old Khamla in the centre, touch the same lump of meat while saying the prayer together.

Fig. 100. After calling the spirits of their deceased parents from the hill-top above the camp, the men returned to pray. Muang to the left while pressing the raw meat against the tree. However, three young men put the meat on the crude altar and prayed while folding their hands in the Thai fashion.

Fig. 101. Before being cooked, these offerings, consisting of the head, the breast and the tail of the pig – symbols of the father, the mother and their children – are put on a small platform in the centre of the camp.

181

Fig. 102. The lumps of meat being presented to the spirits are cooked separatedly by an elderly woman and are not to be eaten until two days later.

Fig. 103. All the other meat is cooked in a number of bamboo internodes and is to be eaten in the evening and on the next day.

182

Fig. 104. Pha putting the cooked offerings on a platform in the camp while repeating the prayer for the last time.

Fig. 105. Paeng making an altar from split bamboo, probably quite recently inspired by the other hill tribes.

However, after discussing the matter with almost all of the elder Mlabri men it has become evident, as already mentioned, that some individuals have different ideas about the afterlife, ranging from a kind of heaven to complete annihilation. Furthermore, it emerged during our last visit in 1994 that more individuals than we were previously aware of within the main group think that they are reborn either as animals or humans. There are also those who quite frankly say that they do not know. Pha from the main group, the first and one of the most intelligent of our informers, has the interesting idea that when the forest is cut down and their land is turned into arid wasteland with only grasses and small bushes, all the spirits of the jungle will be gone including those of the dead Mlabri. In other words, the existence of the living Mlabri, as well as that of the spirits of the dead, depends entirely on the forest, which is better thought of than might appear at first. The non-conformity of the beliefs in the afterlife once again shows that the individual has a high degree of spiritual freedom. This is due to the fact that there are no professional spiritual leaders and that nobody is forced to believe in anything in particular!

Prayers to deceased parents are the most important and have been so at least since the first decriptions of the Mlabri from the beginning of the 20th century. Dead grandparents, except the mythological ones, are seldom included. Often they have not even known these, but they say they offer to the parents, because they are the ones who have mostly cared for and protected them. As there seem to have been neither shamans nor strong band leaders, the parents are endowed with greater authority.

The spirits of dead people, including those of deceased parents, are said to be unable to fend for themselves. This is why their children must offer to them regularly. Previously they offered roots and a little meat on an almost daily basis and a large sacrifice of meat at certain intervals. Still, whenever the main group can work in order to acquire a pig from the other mountain peoples, they perform the ceremony, even though they are in constant need of other things. The ceremony, in which all the members of a band take part (if several bands are together, they may all take part), strengthens the bonds between the various families and consequently improves their otherwise fragile ability to survive. Each time we stayed with a band, we had to supply them with a pig or two. Consequently, the ceremony to the deceased parents is by far the one we have witnessed most frequently, perhaps just as much to give them protein, as there are so few animals left in the jungle.

The first five prayers are among the most complete and authentic ceremonies we have recorded (see figs. 90, 96, 100-103). We encountered the band of four couples with their children and two elderly single women, i.e. about 18 individuals, in January 1980, two hours' walk from the Hmong village of Ban Hui Hom. This is situated another five hours' walk to the east of the main road connecting Phrae and Nan, leaving it about 20 miles north of the junction point, Rongwan.

The headman from Ban Hui Horn had arranged our meeting with the band, and we had already stayed with the Mlabri for some days. However, they were reluctant to show us the ceremony for their deceased parents, as the Hmong headman, their employer, was nearby. So it was decided that the Mlabri should move their camp further up in the mountain jungle in order to escape from the Hmong long enough to perform the ceremony without being supervised (fig. 90). As usual, there had been long discussions as to how big the pig should be and where to obtain it, and as usual the Hmong had exploited the situation to the utmost. Two Mlabri left in the

184

early morning to find the pig, while the remaining members of the band started to make four new windscreens, one for each family. They were placed in a row only 4-8 m apart and all facing northeast. Small trees, shrubs and old leaves were removed to ease passage between the windscreens.

The pig was brought in at 3 p.m. While the women fetched water as well as palm fonds on which to put the meat, the men collected wood and erected a small altar raised one and a half metres above the ground in the middle of the camp. It took three men hardly more than five minutes to tie up and kill the pig, which they did by severing the jugular vein with a long knife, draining the blood into a pot (fig. 94). Muang, the oldest of the four men, started with the following prayer:

1980, 7b, 074, Muang (aged 42):

'o	wɔk 'uy	wɔk yong	wɔk bɛ'	wɔk tɛn wang (Th)	//	lam ding	lam dɣng
oh,	spirit mother &	father,	sp. earth	sp. jungle vacant land,	[sp]	tree big	tree watch

gʌm ki	ma hnguh	ma tae'	cinyʌk	ki thɛh	mɛh di duhn (Th)	di rɛ' di 'yɛ'
don't	come stay	touch,	likewise	not good.	You move	run far [away]

di kutwʌt	// nɯng khon caw	khon nay	di gʌh	gʌh dii	gʌh 'oh 'o
to mountain pass.	One official	master	came here,	this is good,	[give] me money (?)

mɛh caw 'o nay	//	bn.hnɛ'	chingto	lɔbo'	gʌm ki	luh	ki gret
you official master.		[sp. deceased] men,	women	& others	don't	scold	not pain;

'e	di jam (Th)	cinyʌk	ki thɛh
yes	remember	likewise	not good.

The spirits of the deceased parents, those of the earth, the grave and the big tree are asked not to stay long with the Mlabri. It is mentioned that we have provided Muang with money to buy the pig for the offering. Finally he asks the deceased's spirits not to scold the band because both the spirits and the members of the band had been informed before our arrival.

1st line: 'uy "woman" and yong "man"; however in this connection the meaning is "mother"and "father", wɔk tɛn wang "spirit jungle vacant (land)" (Th), possibly synonumous with the spirit of the grave, as dead people are buried in small clearings in the jungle away from fields, streams and trails.

2nd line: tae' (tawng) "touch" (Th). duhn "move, walk" (Th).

3rd line: nɯng, neung "one" (Th). khon "person" (Th), caw nay thee "official master", where nay "mister, chief", from nai (Th). 'o (closed vowel) was said to be "money".

4th line: bunhnɛ', bn.hnɛ' "elder sibling, man". lɔbo' vaguely for "others". luh "back pain" an old word according to Muang (M3: "scold").

5th line: jam, jahm "remember" (Th), also mʌc, mɔc "have seen, remember". gret "pain, sick, unhappy".

Muang then urged the other men also to say the prayer, which they did. The pig was cut into various large pieces, and the meat for the offering was placed on a small platform in the centre of the camp (sort of altar, fig. 101). It consisted of three parts. He explained: "We take the head to remind us of the father, who led us through the jungle, a piece of the breast to remind us of our mother, who fed us, and the tail to remind us of our dead sisters and brothers, who followed us." (Others may use the head, liver, gullet and gut.). Then he took a piece of the breast from the altar and, holding it in his hand, started to invoke the main prayer assisted by Som. All, including women and children, looked very attentive and serious:

1980, 7b, 140, Muang & Som (aged 42 and 28):

	'ek jok	nak hluak	///
Someone behind:	Take suck [the offering]	much full,	(Thereafter Muang and Som :)

'o mɣm mɣ'   roy buɪl   nom (Th) nah   pr.nah //   mɛh rɣm ki   ma tit
Oh, parents   young died   young long time   [ago].   You both not   stick to

ma thal   mɛh rɣm   ki ma   kɛl mat   kɛl mɔh //   'oh jak 'ɣh   jak bɛk   pa chuɛh
& follow, you both   not come block eyes & nose.   Me bring: bear,   moonrat,

bɔ' mʌ' bɔ' 'do'   bɔ' thri'   bɔ' bɛk   bɔ' mo   mɛh di dɔk   mɛh jak luang
carry: python, porcupine (two spec), bear &   boar,   you placed,   you went ahead

    pa jak plɛng (Th)   // mɛh rɣm   kə jak   guɣh   jak hnguh   chuɛh   mʌ' //
went changed (arranged). You both   not hide yourselves, stay [with] moonrat & python.

    mɛh rɣm   ki jak   ki leh   mɛh di hnguh   to bɔn   kr'ung thal 'ding //
You both [parents] not come here. You [spirits] stay with [body grave] hole long & big.

'oh buɪl ma   tɛk nak   rɔp.yu //   mɛh hak   kə jak guɣh jak hnguh 'e mɣ'
Me not meet cold & difficult jungle.   You separately (stay) not hiding come stay, mother

'e mɣm buɪl   nom (Th) nah pr.nah //   'e ding roh   ki ma tit   ma tae'
& father died   young long time [ago].   Yes elder relatives   not come stick to,   touch.

'oh cəbut jong   mɛh katong leh   chɛ' na' 'a   pia' 'dɣ 'i to   poh   ngay poh bɛk
  I pig male   you offering here, many please   animals edible   kill   wild boar, bear,

poh 'do'   poh thri' nɛh mɛh   dɔk   mɛh luang   pa jak plɛng // mɛh rɣm kɣ
porcupine (two kinds), this you give, you in advance gone & arranged.   You both not

    jak guɣh jak hnguh   ki thɛh   di rɔp.yu   gɛng gʌh   yɛng   pol //   'o
hide yourselves & stay   not good   jungle,   nest this [of] spider & pangolin. Oh [parents].

The spirits of the parents are asked to come and receive the offering, but not to stay on with the Mlabri, who are afraid that the spirits may enter them through their eyes and block their sight while hunting. Also the parents' spirits should not come to meet the Mlabri in the deep jungle, but rather remain in their graves. However, the spirits are requested to deceive the animals by making them move out into openings in the jungle where they can be hunted more easily. Thus, on the one hand the parents' spirits may be devious, but on the other hand this capacity is used to trap the animals, thereby also enabling the spirits to receive offerings later on.
1st line: nak "much" or "heavy, hard" (Th).
2nd line: roy "young"; nom "young man" (Th); rɣm "together, both".
3rd line: ma thal "come long" or "follow".
4th line: mɛh jak luang pa jak plɛng "you go ahead (in time, gone change (Th)";
    actually Gui agreed that the spirits can be asked to guide the animals out in the
    open, where they are easier to hunt.
9th line: katong "jump down, put down" as when making offerings previously a stone.

186

Now, in turn, each of the men recited very much the same prayer while holding the same piece of the pig's breast in front of him. Then it was handed over to the oldest women, whereupon all the women touched it while muttering the prayer. At some point, Muang divided the sacrificial meat into two pieces, and after putting one piece back on the altar took the other one and went up on the steep hill behind the windscreens followed by the other three men. As they went up they kept on praying, thereby inviting the spirits of the parents to come and receive the offering. The four men, taking slightly different directions, called loudly on the spirits. After a quarter of an hour, they returned to a tall tree just above the camp, where another crude altar had been constructed. They put the sacrificial meat on this altar and prayed again (fig. 101). Another sequence of the prayer recorded was as follows:

1980, 7b, 375, Som (aged 28):

'o wɔk 'uy wɔk yong   wɔk bɛ'   wɔk tae (Th)   ki   gʌh ///   'e mɣ'
Oh, spirit mother & father, sp. earth sp. former [person] not [come] here.   Yes, mother

'e mɣm yʌk bɯl kul.kol   drol   kul.kol   ruʌng   mɛh   di mɣk   di wʌl
father thus died,   [gone] rolling very end rolling stream. Good living   return,

gʌm ya   ki 'ɣh   ki jat   'oh pia' dɛ' 'i 'dɣ   cəbut jong   katong   ɣ'
don't bring bad   not very much. I [like] animals edible,   male pig offering eat rice

katong bong   mɛh di mɣk   di wʌl //   gʌm ki ma   kawak   ma jahm (Th)
offering eat meat; you good living return.   Don't come [to] cross [us] remember.

jak 'oh   jak gɯr   pa koc   pa hnɛl   katɛl   gʌh gəchong   tɛ mʌc   di prang
Make me   wish: bamboo rat,   rat,   squirrel, this land turtle;   truly   find luck.

// mɣ' mɣm   di ma   'ɣ'   ma bong   cəbut jong   katong   khɯn   katong
    Parents come eat rice   eat meat,   pig male   offering   [put] up   offering,

ma 'ɣ'   ma bong   ma dɣng ma'   dɛn (Th)   gʌh   yʌk
come eat rice   eat meat,   come see & give direction [place] this,   like that.

1st line: wɔk tae (kawn) was said to be: "spirit former [person]", as kawn (Th) "before, first" (before something else):

3rd line: ki 'ɣh was translated "ungrowing, bad", while ki jat (Th) "not very much". katong "jump, put (down)", but here meaning the act of presenting the offering on the altar, as mentioned above. Previously offerings were placed on a stone on the ground, hence the expression.

4th line: jahm "remember" (Th).

7th line: dɛn gʌh is "direction this" from Thai daen "land, place, locality". yʌk "that one, there, thus, like that".

As the four men were standing around the tall tree to which the altar was attached, we observed (fig. 100) that the three younger men somewhat clumsily tried to fold their hands in the Thai praying fashion, while the older, Muang, just put his right hand on the tree trunk while praying in the old way, an observation repeated on several other occasions.

Finally, Muang and Som divided all the meat from the pig very carefully, so that each of the four families had not only the same amount, but also exactly the same cuts, while the women, children and the dogs attentively watched the operation.

187

Each nuclear family packed its share into banana leaves, and the men said a short prayer while holding the parcel in front of their head, before returning to the wind-screen. We noticed that, while each of the younger women started cooking her family's part of the meat (fig. 103), the sacrificial meat for the parents' spirits was cooked separately over another fire by the oldest woman (fig. 102), the mother of one of the married women. I enquired whether people might eat the sacrificial meat to which they agreed, but only after two days had elapsed.

It was almost dark when the Mlabri returned to their windscreens, so I was only just able to see that before one of the men, Paeng Noi, put his family's share on a small shelf in the corner of his windscreen, he held his parcel above his head, mut-tering yet another prayer, now for the windscreen spirit, wok gɛng. The whole ceremony was over by about 5.30 p.m. everybody then feasted on the, for once, plentiful meat. They said that it had been quite a long time since they had performed the ceremony. Spirits were high, with a lot of talking and shouting, though little by little turning into a relaxed satiety. From our small bamboo hut we could still see the lights of their bonfires until 9.30 p.m., but then the distant human voices were replaced by those of myriads of frogs.

1982, 2b, 895, Paeng (aged 52):

'ɣh	mɣ'	mɣm	//	ma 'ɣ' ma bong		cəbut cəbut	gʌm ki	chak	hnguh luah
Do	[sp.]	parents		come eat rice & meat		pig [much];	don't	disable	stay forest

blʌk	long	bri	//	di mɣk di wʌl	//	gʌm ki	jak	hnguh	luah	long bri	//
enter	into	jungle,		good living return.		Don't	go	stay	forest	into jungle;	

ta mʌc	pia' dɛ 'i 'dɣ	//	ma' koc	ma' hnɛl	ma' chəro'	ma' dɛl	poc	//
find	animals edible,		give bamboo	rat & rat,	give bamboo	& hornbill	bird(s).	

gʌm ki	jak hnguh	luah blʌk	long bri	//	ma 'ɣ'	ma bong	to cin
Don't	go stay	forest enter	into jungle,		come eat rice	& meat,	meat

pia 'dɛ 'i 'dɣ	//	gʌm ki	jak	hnguh	luah blʌk	long bri	lam ding	lam dɣng
animals edible.		Don't	go	stay	jungle enter	into forest	tree big	tree see (visit).

gʌm ki	jak hnguh	cəboh chung	cəboh long lɔng	to mo' to wʌl	ta ma
Don't	go stay	mountain high	mountain low,	animals keep returning;	bring

to mʌ' to trak	to kr.wɛk	kr.'oh	mo la'	chəpa'	kah.ohm
python (female & male),	banana-eater	& small kind,	water turtle,	soft shell	& water turtle,

to koc	to hnɛl	to bɛk	to mo	cing gʌm	gʌh loh	gʌh yak	//	ma' də
bamboo rat,	rat,	bear	& pig;	also don't	search for	[us].		Give some

pia' 'dɛ 'i 'dɣ	di thɛh	di ngam	//	gʌm	hn'ɛp	hng.ke'
animal edible,	get very	best.		Don't [sp.]	pack up [things into]	fireplace,

tɛ gʌm ki	pol kol	gʌm ki	na hom (Th)	poh pol	poh khɔng (Th)
truly don't	blanket roll,	don't	much cover up [body]	split blanket	& things.

The spirits of the dead parents are called to come and eat of the offerings of rice and pig. It is said that they should not remain in the deep forest or in the mountains, but should rather come to help the living Mlabri find many kinds of animals. Finally the spirit of the fireplace is asked not to make the burning wood roll down on people or their belongings, which unfortunately happens quite often, when the Mlabri sleep too close to the fires on chilly nights.

6th line: ta is a preverbal particle, here probably changing ma "come" into "bring, send".

Last line: (kul)kol "roll". na hom "much cover [body]" according to Paeng, evidently from Thai: hom "to cover up the body with clothes, etc."

1982, 4b, 427, Pha (aged 47):

mɣ' mɣm	//	ma bong cin	cəbut	cin chɛng	//	'ɛw	mla' dok	ma yak
Parents [sp.]		come eat meat,	pig	meat black (pig).		Children	Mlabri poor,	got difficulties

pr.nah pr.nah	'ɛw	chɛ' pɣ'	//	'i mɣ'	'i mɣm	jak 'ek cəbut	'ek
long time [really],	children	many have.		(Hon.) mother &	father	take pig,	take

chɛng	ma' ɣh	ma pa 'ɣ'	pabong 'oh	//	gret gʌh	'oh 'a	hluak	'a ding
black [one],	give	give rice	& meat I.		Sorry now	I have	become grown	& old,

'a cɯ	'a jahm (Th)	//	jak 'ek	cəbut chɛng	'i mɣ	'i mɣm	'a bɯl	'ur lam
have known & remember.			Take	pig black,	mother &	father,	[who] died	both,

ma'	krɔ'	ma'	pan chop	pan gʌh	bong dor	tal gʌh	ta pa hnɛl
give	please	come,	when asked	now	meat give away,	to-day	bamboo rat,

katɛl	'ul 'ak	//	kan ta bɔ	'oh ma'	bong	ma(')
squirrel,	mousedeer.		When nothing,	I get	meat	get [from another].

Pha says that now he is the one to lead the ceremonies and to handle the sharing of meat with the others in the band. But when he has nothing, he will get some from the others. Having a strong personality, he has always been a sort of leader, and has been very active in providing tools, clothing and food, including pigs for the offerings, for his band.

4th line: cɯ "know", jahm (Th) "remember"; therefore: 'a cɯ 'a jam has (come) to know and remember".

1982, 5a, 575, Gui (aged 37):

'ay	mɣm	'e mɣ'	'oh bɔ	'ɣh bo	'ek cəbut	po ching	'oh di lon	di hmal
Hon.	father &	mother	me not	do bad;	take pig,	pig [for]	my mind	& soul.

'o cən.re	cən.raw	ma' ɣh	ma' bong	gʌm ki	dəkat	gʌm ki	'ɣh dəkat
Oh, spirits (dead persons)	give eat rice	& meat,	don't	[get] fever	don't	cause bad fever

'ɣh naw	//	'oh di rɛ'	di rang jang	di chring	//	cən.re bɛ'	cən.re	pa tae
cold.		You run	trail energetically	to mount. crest.		Sp. earth	& fixed	(former people)

cən.re	lam ding	lam dɣng	'oh pa 'ɣ'	'ar 'ɣ'	pa cəbut	pok ching	//
spirit	tree big	tree see,	I feed (spirits)	have already	pig	(put on) fleshy.	

'e ding	'e roy	bul	mla' chɛ'	mla' na	//	krok	khon	ma 'ɣh	ma jɔy
Honorable	relatives	died,	Mlabri many	Mlabri many.		Band's	people	come	[to] help

po chən	po mɔn	'oh hɛk	ying yeng (Th)	'ek	gʌh	kao (Th)	///
work [in] the field;		I very	much tired,	take	this	old [parents].	

189

jɛr mɛw	yom gʌh	hɛk jir mɯk (Th)	hɛk chən
[We] dislike Hmong	staying here,	very angry [due to]	very much work [in the] field.

The spirits of his deceased parents are offered some pig meat. In return they are asked not to make him ill and, furthermore, to come and help in the field, as the Mlabri said they believe they can. The dislike and even hatred towards some of the Hmong, who pay them so little for their work, is also mentioned. Three or four men usually have to work for a week to receive only one pig. On the other hand, one has to admit that the Mlabri receive very little help from elsewhere!

6th line: yin yeng, Gui said it means "tired", but in Thai it just means "very much".

Last line: yom "stay" (M3), just as in Yombri "stay forest", Bernatzik's name for the Mlabri. mɯk,muk (Th) "stupid, foolish"; I have jir mɯk "angry" (Ml), while jɛr, jir.mɯk (jr.mɯk) "angry, disgusted, dirty" (M3). chən "field" (chuʌn in M3)

1987, 11a, 035, Poa (aged 50):

'oh lon	'oh hmal	'oh lon	'uy lon yong	bɯl tay	nom nah pr.nah //
My spirit	my soul,	my soul	mother & father,	[who] died young	long time ago.

'ek cəbut mot (Th)	'ot ngɔr //	kuk hmal mɯ	ta' roy	'uy yong
Take pig finish [come]	my way.	Spirit soul return	elder & younger	female & men,

bun bɯl	'a bɯl pa tuk pa tiɔng	gʌm ki hak jak	hnguh	di dii dəmɔy //
deeds died	have died altogether,	don't separate	stay [with us]	[keep] on well alone.

cəbut jong katong leh	lah poh 'uy	lah poh yong jak 'ɣh jak hɔt	'a thm.pɯl
Pig male put down [killed]	for mother & father above;	bring, arrive, put down [share],	

'a chɛ' nang	ma 'ɣh ma pa dii //	gʌm ki jak 'ɣh haw chaw	to hmɛ' to hmɛ'
have many sitting	come get well (together).	Don't bring master	another [stranger],

di mo' di wʌl //	gʌm ki to lon	to hmal	jak to lon	to hmal tʌny yah
stay & return.	Don't (harm) mind	& soul;	make mind	& soul speak we

thang rang	thang ton //	wɔk bɛ'	wɔk pa tae	wɔk mɛh	wɔk mɔy
way [of]	straightness.	spirit earth	sp. former (person),	spirit you	sp. myself

kao jao	haw nay	haw kwʌr	haw nak (Th)	gʌm ki	ma 'ɣh	ma kawak
long time	deed master	deed stranger	deed much,	don't	come [to]	cross (interfere)

ma kham (Th)
come to cross.

Pig meat is offered to the spirits of the dead parents, who are asked not to stay on after the offering or to harm anyone. Poa asks me not to bring other strangers to his camp, which I had in fact done on this sole occasion. I am ("old friend official") finally requested not to interfere with the affairs of the Mlabri.

1st line: nom, noom "young, youthfull" from Thai, but mostly used for males.

4th line: katong "jump, get up or down", however the Mlabri said: presenting the offering on the altar, being put on a raised platform so that the dogs, etc., could not reach it. Formerly it was placed on a leaf or a stone, and hence the somewhat vague phrase. lah poh "up above split", the idea being that the parent's spirits should watch from above that they receive their piece of meat to be placed on the altar before being cooked separately and again put on the altar. thm.pɯl "put

190

down", i.e. spreading the meat on banana leaves on the ground, so that each household can receive their equal share to be cooked separately.

5th line: nang "sit" (Th). to hmɛh "body new" or "another".

6th-7th line: tʌny yah thang rang thang ton "speak we way of straightness (as the trunk of a tree)", which is another way of saying that everyone should be honest; where: thang, thang "way" (Th) and rang, rang "track" (Th).

8th line: kao', kao' "old" (for things, Th) or "long-standing" (as for friends), haw, haw "tower (high), deed", while nai (Th) "chief, master".

Mlabri M3

Among this small refugee group the ceremony for the deceased family members, mainly the parents, is not as elaborate as with the big group (Ml), but also here it is the most important. However, during the many times we have visited them since 1977, they have never asked us for a pig for the ceremony, because they wanted other things. But the sacrifice of pigs to their parents remains in their prayers. Now they use chickens for the offerings, probably because they are too poor to buy a pig. We were told that they would call the spirits of their parents in the same way as among the large group (Ml). Likewise, when they see some insects eating the offering, it could only be the spirits of their parents who had arrived.

They have not made altars as long as we have known them, but have only used leaves or a flat stone on which to put the offerings (see fig. 77 showing Oy from 1994). This is of some importance, for one might suspect that the large group has adopted the idea of making altars from the surrounding mountain peoples. But the members of the small group have other ideas with regard to the afterlife. Thus Kit related in 1994 that he believes that the spirit of dead persons will visit all the places enjoyed during life, but after two or three years will vanish.

1982, 16a, 1060, Oy (aged 44):

'ɣ wɔk 'uy   wɔk yong   wɔk 'uy wɔk yong   //   wɔk 'ding wɔk bo'   wɔk mɣ'
Oh, spirit mother sp. father, spirit mother & father,   spirits father & mother   spirit mother

wɔk mɣm   ma' bong   dor yuk   gʌh pi'   //   gʌm 'ɣh   gʌm mak nyayh   gʌm ki cho'
& father   give food   put rice   husked;   don't do bad   don't sin,   don't [get] ill

ki gret   gʌm ki   dəkat   ki tai (Th)   //   di thɛh di mɣk   di thɛh yɣm   kum mla'
not pain,   don't [get]   fever   not die.   Get good living,   good stay   protect all people

gʌh kam.pong   gʌm ki buɪl   ki tay   gʌm ki cho'   ki gret   di thɛh di mɣk
myself (this head),   don't die   not die,   don't illness   not pain,   get good living.

wɔk 'uy   wɔk yong   mɣ' mɣm   di ta dɣng   ta jɛl   //
sp. mother   sp. father,   parents   look (after)   (?)   (Thereafter mixed with Thai)

kum pawng (Th)   khang na   rak sa   chung rak sa   di kum   di twom   //
all protect   in future   care for,   much care for   support   in general.

gʌm li'   'an hai   'an khʌt   'ɛw bo huʼ   m' yak   'an hai   'an khʌt
Don't anything   [get] lost & lacking,   children no   difficulties,   anything lost & lacking,

pen yat pen yong   lai kha' dii   //   phor mɛ   rak chung   rak sa   kum   hnguh
have infection;   anything yes good.   Parents   much   care for.   Support   keep

khwam luk dao	//	yoo (Th) khang lang	khang na (Th)		ya'	h(ng)uh
spread to children star.		Remain behind &	in front (generationwise),		shall	keep

phor (Th) gɔy	lɔi lam	'ɛ jɛp	phoo may	hu' kai	kə' naw
father carefully	above trees [look after];	not hurt,	person burn,	no fever &	cold.

The above prayer and the next example caused some trouble until it emerged that only half of each is in Mlabri, resembling very much that of the main group (Ml), while the other half of each prayer is mixed with Khun Muang (Northern Thai). Kit explained in 1994 that this was done to make the prayer more powerful. The meaning of the phrases in these second halves is similar to those in Mlabri (both Ml and M3).

1st line: wɔk 'ding wɔk bo' is another transcription for the spirits of his father 'ding "big, elder, father" and mother bo' "breast".

2nd line: mak nyayh is lit. like to resent or detest (Rischel 1995, p. 300), but the Mlabri said that nyayh here means "to sin"; anyway the two meanings are related.

6th line: khang (na was probably missing) "in future, in front" as khang alone is "side, part of", which does not make sense (see 9th line). rak sa "care for" (Th); chung "high, much" from Thai soong. di twom "in general" (thua pai (Th)).

7th line: an "things" in general (Th), while hai "get lost, disappear" (Th), and khʌt, khat "be absent, lacking, missing" (Th).

8th line: pen yat pen yong (Th) was translated "infection' where pen "climbing" and yat "leak" and yong "swell" all of which have a connection with an infection.

9th line: khang lang "behind, before", and khang na "in front of, in the future". Also the Mlabri of the main group (Ml) have the idea that the generations follow one another, just as when they walk to a new campsite with the adults in front and their children behind them. By the way, two or three times our party has stumbled into a whole band walking to a new site – the men in front and the women and children behind, all carrying their few and shabby belongings – indeed a strange and moving sight, looking more dismal than when they inhabit their camps. dao "star" i.e. their beloved children.

Last line: phor gɔy lɔi lam "father carefully above tree [look after]" is their dead father looking after his children from above. The idea that the parents' spirits look down from above to supervise and to help the Mlabri is a belief shared by many Mlabri of the main group as well. phu, phoo "person" (Th).

1982, 16 b, 714, Oy (aged 42):

'ɣ mɛh leh	wɔk 'uy	wɔk yong	nɔ' loh 'uy	loh bong	pia' 'dɛ 'i 'dɣ
Oh, you come	sp. mother	sp. father,	child & wife	search for food	animals edible,

mɔk kaa'	mɔk gɛyh	//	gʌm ki cho'	ki gret	gʌm ki dəkat	ki tai
cooked fish	& crab.		Don't [get] pain	not unhappy,	don't [get] ill	not die;

gʌm ki	chi'	kam.pong	chi' dʌm	di thɛh di mɣk	gʌm ki chi' duut	chi' phrat	//
don't	pain	head,	pain brain,	good living,	don't pain back,	pain backbone.	

	'i 'ɣh khai (Th) la	khang lang	khang na	rak sa
(Thereafter mainly in Thai:)	Do fever leave,	behind &	[in] front	care for,

192

la phi' phor	phi' mɛ	hak	chung rak sa //	mo' kum	h(ng)uh khwam
leave sp. father	sp. mother	separately	much care for;	keep support	& (stay) spreading

lay ka di	ma khʌt	pinyʌt	phai pɤ' mi //	bo huʔ	jep may	phai naw
much good;	be absent	infection,	danger no have,	not hurt	& burn	& danger cold,

phor hnguh	goy	lɔi lam //	lay khaʔ dii	hnguh ngam	di ni pay na //
father stay	carefully	above trees.	Much yes good,	stay good	now & onwards,

pɤ' mi	'an hai	an khʌt	'an mʌt (?)	an man	phor	gɔy	lɔy lam
nothing get	lost,	things absent,	things bad	infection,	father	take care	above trees,

to	bun phor	bun mɛ	sa duʔ
you	good deeds father	& mother,	be so

2nd line: mɔk "steamed fish" by putting it into a banana leaf and roasting it. The Mlabri M3 hunt only small game like bamboo rats, but they especially like to collect various animals in streamlets.

3rd line: phrat "backbone" as well as "mountain ridge" due to their similar shapes.

4th line: khang lang khang hak sa "behind & in front separately care for", as when their band is walking in the dense and dangerous jungle, with the strongest in front and at the rear thereby protecting the children in between.

5th line: kum "hold, support" (Th).

6th line: may "burn" (Th); phay naw, phai nao (Th) "danger cold". khʌt, khat "miss, be absent (Th).

8th line: man could be "luck" as it is among the main group, but Oy said that man "is the blue due to an infection", pay na "onwards" according to: taw pai "continue".

9th line: sa duʔ "be so" is used to indicate the end of the prayer in the Buddhist fashion.

1987, 1b, 1010, Sak (aged 31):

'oh	pa bɯl	chɛng	'oh gʌh	pa bɯl	chɛng	ma mɤ'	ma mɤm	bong //
I	kill	black (pig),	myself	kill	black (pig);	come mother	come father	eat;

mɤ' mɤm gʌh	wʌl	bong	mɛh 'oh	wʌl toc	wʌl bong	dor chɛng
parents	here	return eating;	you [from] me	take back	return eating,	give away black

dor liʔ	gʌh jak //	gʌm rɤm leh	tɛ loh	nɯng (Th) to gʌh	ma duk
give boar	this give.	Don't follow	search for	another person here,	[we have] hard

ma yen //	mlaʔ briʔ mlaʔ tae	dəmɛh	mɛh paʔa bɯl	mɛh 'a toc
poor [life].	Mlabri people former (one),	yourself	you have died,	you have fetched

to cheng	to yuk	gʌh bong jak //	gʌm	rɤm taeʔ	gʌm	'oh cho'	'oh gret
black pig	& rice,	this eating give;	don't	follow touch,	don't	[give] me illness	& pain

mɤ' mɤm //	mɯ	wɔk mɤ'	wɔk mɤm	wʌl di bong	dor chɛng	dor liʔ gʌh //
parents.	return	spirit mother	sp. father,	return to eat,	give black	put pig here;

gʌm rɤm leh	tɛ pruk //	toc bong	jak to chɛng	to yuk to yuk	to piʔ
don't follow,	(just) come here,	take eating	give black (pig)	rice (much)	husked rice

gʌh	//	'ɛw	'ɛng ngwɛ'	gʌh ta	yom thɛh	yom mɤk	gʌm ki cho'	ki gret
here.		Child,	own child,	here	stay good	living,	don't [get] illness	not pain.

2nd line: chɛng "black" (old word) according to Sak, syn. for black pig from the Hmong.

3th line: Oy as well as the Mlabri Ml had li' "boar" being used for offerings previously, when they still were able to find and kill the boars themselves in the jungle.

4th line: mla' bri' mla' tae "people forest people former (ones)" here probably syn. for their dead, as it seems to be the case with the main group (Ml). tae and tae' (Th) has two related meanings according to the situation: tae kawn "formerly" and tae' tawng "touch", probably as it is thought that if a person is touched by the spirit of a dead person he or she might die.

6th line: pruk "come here", but jak pruk "chase"; otherwise both Ml and M3 have: rap "chase".

This last prayer follows the ordinary pattern and resembles very much those of the main group (see, for example prayer 1980, 8a, 1483, p. 68). As we have heard, they also loudly call their deceased father and mother, who reside in different places, and the parents appear as the first insects to eat of the offerings. As said in the prayer, the meat to be sacrificed is a pig. However, we have never seen these Mlabri able to afford this. They always preferred other things, perhaps indicating that once they were better off, when they were a larger group. Finally, the plea is repeated that the spirits of their deceased parents should not follow their children, thereby inflicting illness or even death.

APPENDIX 1

Supplementary Expedition Notes

While chapters 1-4 primarily summed up the results of our interviews with the Mlabri M1 and M3 based on tape recordings and various other investigations, including the anthropometrical recordings, this first appendix embodies the main results extracted from our written records and by interviewing all kinds of informants. So besides commenting on experiences and talks with the two mentioned Mlabri groups, this compendium focuses also on other groups or splinter groups of Mlabri, both those we were able to find and those we merely heard about from Khon Muang, Lao, Hmong, Yao and T'in villagers.

The following Appendices 2-7 deal with various specific and more delimited subjects: Mlabri camps (2), tools (3), animals (4), plants and trees (5), our psychotechnical tests (6) and, finally, the investigations of their teeth, not only of the Mlabri M1 and M3, but also those of other relevant mountain peoples of the area (7).

The notes below in this appendix are arranged chronologically, with information on where and from whom they were obtained. We have endeavoured to include information only from persons who have actually met the various groups of Mlabri, information which occasionally may seem too strange to be reliable. However, generally speaking, most of the mountain people are reliable witnesses, and it should be remembered that they have lived under circumstances very different from those of the modern world. As regards the Mlabri, the older ones can naturally tell us more about former times, while the younger men do not so easily feel the need to conceal some of the less pleasant aspects of their society.

It was our hope to find other groups of Mlabri, even though chances were considered to be slender. But we did trace two or three groups, who had not met westerners before, as well as representatives of various splinter groups, see also Conclusion pp. 232-243. Their scattered presence, albeit in small numbers, indicates that they were more plentiful a century ago, as also related by

older people in the area. Many have died from disease or have been killed, while those who have married the other mountain people have ceased to be ethnic Mlabri.

The first time a new location of the Mlabri is mentioned, the following parameters are indicated and italicised: name of location, the geographical co-ordinates (in degrees and minutes), the Mlabri group in question (M1-M7 see p. 234), and a reference number (1-80). In the maps at the very end of the book, also the year in which our contact or the year in which our informers said they met them is given. This has been done to make it easy for the reader to find the localities on the maps as well as to establish the migrations of the Mlabri during the 20th century).

As the region is familiar to most readers by now, I have omitted general descriptions of its geography, botany and wildlife. But it should be mentioned that, at least during the 20th century, the Mlabri have kept to the mountains, which generally stretch in a north-south direction, dividing the lowland into similarly oriented river valleys. With the arrival of all the other hill tribes, the Mlabri have retreated to the remotest and least accessible mountain tracts, often preferring localities where two provinces meet in order to avoid officials of any kind, which is also clearly demonstrated in the maps showing the distribution of the Mlabri.

Travels in Northern Thailand 1970

Being the first invited to stay at the field station in Lampang for the Nordic Institute of Asian Studies, we used the compound as an excellent base for our uninterrupted series of tours by jeep and by trekking to visit the various hill tribes up north during the next seven months. Our aim was originally to study papermaking among the many, highly diverse ethnic groups and the use of paper primarily for religious purposes, but with three months left, we decided to concentrate all our efforts on the jungle dwellers, of which we knew very little beforehand but now received more and more information about.

Ban Pa Miang Mae Prik, 99°36'E, 19°39'N, M1, ref. no. 01, mountain ranges 17 km southwest of Amphoe Mae Suai. Here the villagers had seen Mlabri men until 1955. They were naked, but when visiting the Hmong village they had put on old clothes and always carried their spears. They liked to exchange honey and gall bladders from bears for rice, chilli and pigs to be used in ceremonies for the spear spirit and their deceased parents. At some point they had learned to make rattan baskets, but it was noted that they were still not able to share any food given to them, the Hmong doing this for them. Had a man killed a big animal he could allegedly choose any woman in the band to stay with him until the meat was finished.

The Mlabri were said to be honest, but otherwise quite 'savage', taking revenge if offended. They did not use traps, but a sling and a hook, to climb tall trees. They were very shy when they came to the village, had long hair and no body decorations at all. If someone became very ill, they were put in a large basket and provided with food and water and hoisted up in a tree to protect them from wild animals. The villagers almost never saw women and children, because they had to make a noise before approaching the windscreens. If the villagers stumbled into their women and children, the Mlabri would threaten the villagers with their spears.

An old Hmong said that he had seen them about 25 years back (1945), near *Ampoe Wieng Pa Pao, 99°31'E, 19°21'N, M1, ref. no. 02,* 30 km further to the south. They shifted their campsite every four to seven days, but did not have a powerful leader, as their bands sometimes moved alone and sometimes two or more together. At some point they had been able to kill elephants, whose tusks were much in demand. They said they used to feast in places with salty earth also sought by animals. The Hmong considered the Mlabri women to be good-looking, which is why they were sometimes raped.

Yet another Hmong, Lao Lhu, told us that he had seen the Mlabri between *Amphoe Prao* and *Wieng Pa Pao, 99°22'E', 19°22'N, M1, ref. no. 03,* 15 years previously (1955). Their women had been told to cover their faces if they suddenly encountered the Hmong, the men saying that otherwise they would be eaten by a tiger. The women might also start biting, if there were no other means of escape. When climbing a tall tree trunk they would use one or two long bamboo sticks leaning against

the tree. The Hmong added that they had not seen any Mlabri more than 50 years of age.

In Ban Mai, 99°30' E, 19°35'N, our porter to and from Ban Huai Miang told us that he had seen the Mlabri above the river *Mae Laeng, 99°37'E, 19°35'N, M1, ref. no. 04,* only 3-4 years earlier (1967) walking on a mountain ridge, only the men came down to talk with him.

Several sources, including one from Ban Pa Miang, said that there had been Mlabri in Amphoe Mae Hongson as well as in the Tak province previously. Even though we have also trekked in westernmost Thailand, we have only two or three somewhat uncertain reports to this effect. Apart from an old source from more than 50 km north of Mae Hongson into Burma, the furthest west is from a *Karen village, Lekko, 98°15'E, 18°18'N; M1?, ref. no. 05,* about halfway between Amphoe Mae Sarieng and Amphoe Chom Thong, where the villagers had seen a stranger sneaking around at night 15 years before (1955). A few days later the headman had found footprints of very small length in the jungle nearby, but in a place where nobody used to go. Although this is not a satisfactorily documented case, the next one is only 40 km further east and from the same year.

This was about *12 km south-west of Amphoe Chom Thong, 98°35'E, 18°20'N; M1, ref. no. 06,* also around 1955. At an altitude of about 500 m on the 1,656 m high mountain the villagers had found a large stack of bamboo canes with a corpse on top. A Buddhist monk had been called to chase away the spirit of the dead person. As already mentioned, the Mlabri had previously disposed of their dead in like manner. It is of some interest to note that the closest point to our other references for the Mlabri is northeast of Chiang Mai, which was also known to have held Mlabri formerly, the distance to the above locality being less than 100 km as the crow flies.

Ban Mae Ta Lao, 99°36'E, 19°34'N, Hmong village east of Ban Mai, M1, ref. no. 07, 30 houses close to Mae Ta Maeo under Doi Pa Tung. The headman said that when the Hmong met the Mlabri in the jungle they were standing ready to defend themselves with their spears, but were otherwise friendly. Their band consisted of five men, while the number of women and children was unknown (probably a band of about 20 members). They were always accompanied by their dogs. It was said they came from *Huay Pong Men, 99°34'E, 19°25'N, ref. no. 08.*

When visiting the Hmong village, they always turned up, three men, to ask for rice, which the Hmong had to divide for them, the Mlabri never daring to take anything by themselves, since they believed that if they removed pumpkins or corn cobs the plants would die. The Mlabri smelled terrible (like oxen) because they smeared themselves with excrement from this animal they preferred to hunt. The headman had noticed that they ate a sort of mineral if they had nothing else to eat, but they knew how to fish, making nets from a vine fibre and also rattan boxes for the Hmong, from whom we purchased an example. It was added that the Mlabri boys were taught to hunt with shorter spears from the age of ten (see fig. 153, no. 31).

Ban Tha Ko, 99°28'E, 19°30'N, M1, ref. no. 09. Thai village on the main road connecting Amphoe Wieng Pa Pao and Amphoe Chiang Rai. A schoolteacher told us that 16 years previously (1954) the Mlabri had stolen a Khon Muang girl from Ban Tha Kho. After the villagers had searched for her in vain, the men had gone up into the mountains to see if she was there. They had instead met four Mlabri men, who had asked for one more girl! As the villagers were afraid of the Mlabri, they proposed that they should come down to the village Ban Pha Miang (tea plantation), where they could discuss the matter. Already next morning four armed Mlabri men turned up and soon started quarrelling with the villagers, who could naturally not respond to their wishes. During the following struggle one of the Mlabri was wounded in the face, but all escaped leaving one spear (see fig. 153, no. 30). The headman in Ban Pha Miang related the incident to the present headman in Ban Tha Kho, who made a report to the district officer in Ampho Mae Suai, 20 km further north.

Kraisri Nimmanahaeminda and Julian Hartland-Swann 1962, p. 173, refer to a similar hostile encounter between the Mlabri and the Thai living in the mountain valleys, having taken place in 1959 in Changwat Prae: "Thai villagers had raided their camp and burnt it to the ground together with their stocks of rattan", probably due to disagreements as regards payment for some work to be done.

Since the incident near Ban Tha Ko the people there had not seen the Mlabri. It should be added that not only the Mlabri but also the Hmong and even the Khon Muang have raped or stolen girls from other ethnic groups, which might be the reason for some interesting intermingling of the various hill-tribes' gene pools. In such regions where government authorities were far away, many criminal incidents took place until the middle of the 1970s, not to forget the fighting between the Communists and government forces in the area, which

sometimes took place in areas we passed uncomfortably close by.

On the other bank of the Mae Nam Lao River in Ban Tha Kho, we found an old hunter who confirmed many of the details given above. The Mlabri came to him to exchange their beeswax, plaited rattan boxes and baskets for rice, etc., always carrying their spears and tools for making these. From Ban Tha Kho, besides the above-mentioned spear, we bought another example, as well as a Mlabri knife (see fig. 153, no. 32), found near an abandoned Mlabri camp on the mountain to the east. The latter probably belonged to the Mlabri who fled the area in 1954 according to the above-mentioned incident near Ban Ta Ko.

After returning to our base in Lampang, we tried to search for the Mlabri further north by going to Amphoe Fang and taking a motorboat from Ta Ton eastwards towards Chieng Rai, but dropping off halfway to visit other tribal villages (Akha, Lahu and Hmong). Leaving the banks of the Kok River, we walked southwards, crossing the high mountain almost along the 99°34' longitude, passing the two peaks 1,778 and 1,714 m high and stayed the next night in the *Akha village Doi Pang, 99°41'E, 19°50'N, M1, ref. no. 10.* Here a man about 55 years old showed us an old Mlabri spear (see fig. 5), purchased about 20 years previously (in 1950), of which we were able to buy only the rattan cover.

West of Amphoe Pong, 100°09'E, 19°09'N, M1, ref. no. 11. According to a Khong Muang hunter, Mun, some of the Mlabri M1 had stayed in these quite empty and lower altitude mountain forests west of the small town until six years previous (1964), although they were seen by only a few hunters. He said that they still had long hair at that time, and when he met them he noticed their strong smell, caused by their putting extracts of bear testicles on their bodies, so the Mlabri could approach the animal without being noticed.

From Mun we obtained an iron lance (see fig. 153, no. 36) which he had found in a deserted windscreen. He had heard that such lances had been poisoned, and by hiding one with a leaf and placing it in a narrow passage in the jungle, where the animals had to pass, the Mlabri could chase even big animals to their death. He added that the iron lance was found 16 years before (1954). This information would turn out to be of major importance for our project, since it would soon lead us to the Mlabri group in Nan province. Furthermore, it gradually emerged that the area, together with Doi Pha Chik, had served as a sort of bridge for the Mlabri between the eastern and western part of Northern Thailand from about 1950-1968. However, we were unable to go directly eastwards, due to heavy fighting between the Communists and the government forces which took place so close to our quarters just outside Pong that we could hear the shooting uncomfortably nearby.

Ban Pak Pok, 99°48'E, 19°06'N, M1, ref. no. 12, Thai village. Here, south of the beautiful Pha Yao lake (see fig. 3), Mlabri men turned up quite often and always with their spears in the dry season in February-March until 12 years ago (1958). Sometimes they exchanged beeswax and bears gall bladders for rice, worn clothes and a pig. If given some alcohol they would sing and dance. Their hair was often 'pot-cut', and they would all smell bad from the oil extracted from the testicles of wild pigs, of which a villager still kept a strong-smelling small flask. The Mlabri had a hole in each ear lobe and striped tattoos on their arms and legs. They would always greet the villagers by saying in Thai: Chaw pinong "Hey cousin, give some rice". When their spears were planted outside the Thai house, nobody was allowed to touch them. Overnight, they stayed in their windscreen near a mountain crest not very far away on the eastern slopes of Doi Luang, 1697 m.

Ban Pak-0, Ngao District, (probably the map's Ban Pak Mao) *99°46'E, 19°01'N, M1, ref.no: 13.* The Hmong headman of this village repeated many of the characteristics of the Mlabri we had heard in Ban Pak Pok, but added that one of the men might have been a Khon Muang (or a Lahu) who had committed a murder about 15 years previously (1955), being called Jao and having elaborate tattoos. Staying with the Mlabri, he was almost out of reach of the police. The headman also mentioned a poison the Mlabri used for their spears when hunting boar and antelope, adding that bears were easy to hunt, especially when they had cubs. It was quite surprising to hear how the Mlabri had hunted elephants. They made wedges from the hard skin of a dead elephant, which were dried in the sun and then soaked in a poison just before the hunt. When a wild elephant was crossing a river and was crawling up the other bank, the Mlabri hammered down the two wedges, one into the foot sole of each foreleg of the animal. When it started walking, the wedges went further into the foot soles thereby spreading the poison into its body. After about an hour the elephant got weary, at which point it was killed with spears.

Once the headman had the opportunity to visit a Mlabri camp, where he saw many of the items we later collected, including the double bellows of bamboo to provide air for forging red-hot iron pieces into spears, knives, etc. When the Mlabri came to the village, they always inquired about the police, staying on if no strangers were around. The men never took any rice or other foodstuffs back to their families, in order to prevent the women and children from getting a taste for 'foreign' food. The fine spear (see fig. 153, no. 37) we purchased from the headman was originally given to his father, the headman in Ban Ton Puang then living in (another) *Ban Pa Miang, 99°46'E, 18°54'N, M1, reg. no. 14,* near Nam Mae Meo about 22 km south of Ban Pak Pok (99°48'E, 19°06'N).

Thai village Ban Pua at the edge of the jungle covering the high mountain to the west of Pha Yao, around 99°46'E, 19°07'N, M1, ref. no. 15. In the dense mountain jungle some Khon Muang hunters had found a badly scared, small Mlabri girl in 1967 who had lost track of her band. They took her down to the village to feed the thin and exhausted girl and to show her to the others. However, she had cried and hidden her face and would neither talk nor accept any food, so they had to release her after a few days, upon which she ran back to the jungle. She never returned to her group. Actually we heard more about this sad story, for we met her parents in Nan province some years later. This late report of the presence of a Mlabri in the Phayao area was supported by villagers living close to the main road going south from Phayao. In two places they had seen them crossing the road as they went eastwards, probably towards Pong and Nan province.

All this gave us some hope of finding the Mlabri further east, the very reason for searching for them in Nan province, since we did not yet know of the short visits by Khun Kraisri to Nan in 1962-63! So on the way back towards our base in Lampang I persuaded Birgit instead to turn off at Amphoe Ngao and to go eastwards to Song, even though she was not too happy about it. Moving on a brand new and broad, but dark and completely desolate (military) highway, we stopped at 9 a. m. at a house near the highest point of the road to get information. A woman there told us that she had seen the Mlabri walking westwards about 16 years before (1954) and again only a year previously (1969) near *Ban Kao Kleung, 100°07'E, 18°37'N, M1, ref. no. 16,* where she had seen about 30 Mlabri, now moving eastwards along the mountain crest above the road.

Staying in Amphoe Song overnight, we arrived at Rongwan the next day and Ban Pa Hung in Nan province the following day, where we found the Khon Muang villager Phu Jaka, who eventually led us to the Mlabri ten days later. At this point it is worth mentioning that we visited the area south of Phayao once again. Moving up from Lampang, we left the highway about 15 km before Ngao, turning northwest at Pan Pang Kho to reach a Hmong village at an altitude of about 800 m, *Ban Mae San, 99°46'E, 18°38'N, Ml, ref. no. 17.* Here the headman said that they had been visited by the Mlabri about 15 years previously (around 1955), the furthest southwest they have been seen in fairly recent times.

Ban Pa Hung, 100°31'E, 18°35'N, Ml, ref. no. 18. This is the village where we found Mr. Phu Jaka, who arranged our first contact with the Mlabri. In 1970, he was 61 years old, and being a hunter he knew the jungle very well, including the Mlabri, while almost none of the other villagers had seen them! Phu Jaka, being a very kind person, was regarded as a sort of uncle by the Mlabri, because he took their products to be sold in the market in exchange for iron, salt, clothing and tobacco and he also acted as their trusted advisor. Another villager, Mr. Nian, then only about 20 years old, was also to become of great help as he accompanied us during all our expeditions until 1987. It was a kind of relief to stay in his large and hospitable home, after the rather demanding stays with the hill tribes. Actually the family still called the Mlabri phi pa (lit. 'spirits forest' in Thai) because so few had seen them, apart from their abandoned windscreens.

Our first tantalising meeting with the Mlabri has already been described (see p. 13). It took place in a deserted village *Ban Kum, 100°28'E, 18°38'N, Ml, ref. no. 19,* where Phu Jaka, together with two other farmers, still used the old fields. However, at this point I shall try to concentrate on what was related by non-Mlabri sources. Yao-villagers, a few hours walk further to the west, had also had contact with the Mlabri, who previously provided the Yao with elephant tusks. However, relations had been far from good. Once the Mlabri had taken all the honey from a tall tree with many bees only the day before the Yao had planned to do so. In their rage the Yao had removed the two bamboo sticks the Mlabri had put together to enable them to climb the tall tree, so the two Mlabri finally had no other choice than to jump down, thereby being killed!

Phu Jaka also said that there were three bands in the area, or about 70 persons, and that some of the older ones were able to speak Khamu quite well, but now they had

started to split up further, as the wild animals were no longer so plentiful. The former headman Sun Pha Wang, in the now deserted village Ban Kum, was a hunter and the very first to stay up there. Therefore the Mlabri came to him to beg for rice and flints. A Mlabri girl was once wounded by a bear and Sun Pha Wang had treated her wounds, but also raped her! The Mlabri were furious and threatened to burn down his house, but after receiving a pig they had withdrawn to their camp and left the area the same night. Since then, and due to similar incidents, the Mlabri preferred to stay further away from any villages, until they began to be employed to cut down the jungle and prepare the slopes ready for planting from around 1980.

Until about 1960 the Mlabri placed their dead in a basket and hoisted them up in a tree, just as the other hill tribes have related. It was emphasised that the Mlabri took great care not to be seen, never using trails or mountain crests, but rather keeping to steep, difficult slopes when moving from one place to another. They had hitherto never asked for medicine to treat diseases, which they believed were caused by malicious spirits. They were quite often coughing, due to tuberculosis, probably derived from the incoming settlers – the mountain Thai (Khon Muang) and the Hmong.

Phu Jaka further said that the Mlabri used to treat especially their children nicely. He also confirmed that the Mlabri, generally speaking, were very honest, trying only to conceal their camps and movements. Most of the early sources on the Mlabri spear groups note that they had stripes on their legs and upper arms. However these stripes were not observed among the Mlabri Ml in 1962 (see for example Booles, 1963, p. 146). But after having studied the men more closely, including sometimes asking them to wash themselves, we have found traces of old tattooing, which lead us to think that the Mlabri kind of tattooing is not so deep and long-lasting as that performed by the other hill peoples. We shall return to this issue later on when discussing the origin of the Mlabri Ml and M7.

Incidentally, an Akha man we met said that there were Mlabri up north near Kengtung in Burma. They were rather aggressive, using both spears and poisoned arrows for their blowpipes, and that they had come down to find salty earth there. Possibly this could be the Mlabri group of the Wa-type referred to by Gordon Young (1962, p. 69-70), having been reported by Lahu hunters in the Kengtung area, perhaps even having trekked into northernmost Thailand.

The M2 and M3 Mlabri

Towards the end of our seven months' of travels we repeatedly heard rumours of another kind of Mlabri, we never expected to find, although this happened in the crowded refugee camp Nam Yao in 1977. Among the first to describe these Mlabri, M3, in some detail was Robert Weaver 1956, pp. 289-296, who found them near Dan Sai in Loei province. Our first source was obtained through our interpreter, Olan. He had met an 80-year-old gentleman Yok Boon Prassart from Ban Sob Pon, who had seen them about 5 *km NW of Chiang Khong, Chiang Rai province, 100°21'E, 20°19'N, M3, ref. no. 20*. Mr. Yok gave the following details, dating back to about 30 years earlier (around 1940):

The Ang Tha Kae or Phi Tha Noi (lit.: 'spirits people short') live in the lower mountains near many streams, where they collect fish, crabs, shells and shrimps, although they also dig for a number of different roots. They were only 130-140 cm tall and naked, had next to no tools, and ran away if they met other people. However, Mr. Yok claimed that they did not have any language, which may be due to the fact that they usually speak in a very low voice or rather prefer to say nothing if strangers are around. The old man had an additional, but important, observation which has also been noticed by most others villagers, and by ourselves. All adults carried a stick when walking in the jungle, since they had very weak knees, probably, as we think we have established, because they ate many different kinds of roots, some of which contain toxic substances causing arthritis.

Our guide Olan added that his father had seen them during the construction work on the road between *Fang and Chiang Dao, 99°10'E, 19°34'N, M3, ref. no. 21*, around 1945, and these were called Phi Tha Kae (lit. also 'spirit people short'), but now he had only heard (1970) that similar people stayed in Peung Phra Pa and Peung Phra Lai in Laos, towards Cambodia.

Our further source is the Khamu, Daeng, who was the efficient handyman at the Nordic Research Station in Lampang. He said he met the Phi Tha Kae four times five days' travel from Chieng Khong towards the south where the *Mae Khong river meets the Tha river, 100°05'E, 20°22'N, M3, ref. no. 22*, actually where Thailand, Burma and Thailand meet. Daeng, who was 32 years old, saw them when he was ten (1948). He gave the following description: They were very thin, had no tattooing and had thin soft hair. They had very small kneecaps and (again) all except their children walked with a stick. They lived in groups of four or five adults plus children, and often they did not take the trouble of making a shelter, sleeping under trees or using tree holes and caves in the event of heavy rain. They utilised salty earth from hollows in the ground. This source, like the first one, claims that they did not use fire, which is definitely wrong, but may stem from the circumstance that during the day, and when travelling, they often did not take the trouble of collecting wood and making fire but ate whatever raw food was at hand. Apart from a few misinterpretations, most of the related details would turn out to be true, even though they seemed almost incredible to us in 1970.

Towards the very end of our stay in Nan we were told by a police officer that, due to the fierce fighting around the border between Thailand and Laos, the border police had brought some jungle people down to the *police station in Sa, 100°45'E, 18°34'N, M2, ref. no. 23*. Here we found eight persons – two couples, a young man and three children in the basement of the police station all in good health (figs. 108-109). However, especially one of the women and her daughter were very shy. The three men were called Jan, Khamuang and Ngam, while the two women were called Mai and Juniga Teun, and the latter's small daughter was Chi. Nobody was able to communicate with them, but the police officer said they were Khon Pa ("people forest"). To cut a long story short, we have arrived at the conclusion that they were indeed Mlabri but from a different group coming from Laos. By the way, the boy was singing in Laotian. To avoid misunderstandings, they are designated M2. We would have liked to study this interesting small group further, but unfortunately we had to fly back to Denmark a few days later. When we returned to the police station to ask for more information in 1976, nobody knew where they had been relocated, but they may have been released and crossed the undemarcated border back into Laos.

The Expedition 1976-77

This was our first of seven expeditions in the years to come with the sole purpose of studying the Mlabri people and trying to gain an impression of their camps, kinship relations, daily life, beliefs and language, as well as their relations to the other hill tribes. The results are summarised in the main text. But in the following we will tell how and where we found them, at the same time giving the main points on what was said, in part to enable the reader to follow the substantial changes in their life and behaviour which took place from the middle of the 1980s.

Ban Na Ka, 100°27'E, 18°42'N, Ml, ref. no. 24 Hmong village. After having met Mr. Phu Jaka again, we stayed overnight in Ban Pa Hung and went next day by truck up to Ban Na Ka along an impossible road, where the Mlabri had stayed from March to September 1976. But they had now gone to Ban Baw Hoy, due to the following incident gradually being revealed. About a year previously a young Mlabri, Lat, had run away with a Hmong girl, daughter of Lao Yi, which had created so much trouble that the Mlabri band had to leave. We shall return to this sad story, hearing later on that the girl had been killed by her own Hmong family by eating porridge containing bamboo splinters or poison! It was therefore perhaps not so strange that the Mlabri did not like foreign food, because they feared it might be poisoned, all the more so as such things still did happen in far away places. Even though we were politely received by the mentioned Hmong family we also abstained from eating there, because we had enquired about what had happened to Lat and his Hmong wife!

Ban Bow Hoy, Hmong village, 100°27'E, 18°30'N, Ml, ref. no. 25. This stay also became a memorable event, as it was here we met the Mlabri women for the first time. Actually, when approaching the Mlabri camps about an hour's walk up above the Hmong village, our host Lao Toa pointed to their camps in the distance, revealing that the Mlabri women and children were naked, the first and last experience of that kind for Lao Toa as well as for us. When we actually met the women, now dressed in old Hmong rags, they were shaking from fear; two of the younger ones having put mud on their faces to look less attractive (see fig. 21). But the Mlabri relaxed when they saw that I had brought my wife and our eldest daughter Xenia, then four years old, with us. Actually, the physical condition of the Mlabri was not too bad, but it was evident that they had experienced somewhat of a culture shock, because it was only recently that they had started to work for the Hmong.

Lao Toa, who was to become our kindest and most reliable Hmong friends, said that a year before the majority of the 140 Mlabri Ml had stayed at Doi Sathan, but due to a mistake by a Thai hunter, a Mlabri was shot dead, after which they split into smaller groups, but probably just as much due to the growing difficulties of finding enough animals in the jungle. Phu Jaka still being with us, the person who had had the longest and most uninterrupted contact with them, said that almost 50 years ago when they came to Doi Sathan (around 1930), the Mlabri did not have close contact with anyone else. At that time most of the Hmong, now staying in the area, had not yet arrived.

When he first saw the Mlabri men, as a boy, nobody was able to approach them, since they were very afraid of any stranger. At that time the men had only knives and spears made of bamboo or strong wood. They were unable to do many of the things they can do now; some of the men can now speak Khon Muang, sing and play the flute. But the women had been left behind in more than one sense, as they were still not allowed to visit the other hill tribes. Phu Jaka also said that 20 years ago the Hmong and the Khon Muang tried to persuade the Mlabri to give up their old habit of putting their dead into trees, but to bury them instead. But up until about 1980 it still happened that their dead were just left in the jungle after virtually no preparation.

The Mlabri had great difficulty, for example, when trying to count to ten or naming their own Mlabri words for the main colours. But we felt strongly that especially the young Mlabri were eager to adjust to their new neighbours. Therefore my wife and I, together with our Thai interpreters, have endeavoured to teach them whatever we judged could be of value to them during this and our many subsequent stays, hoping it would help them to survive and not be misused or underpaid too much by their Hmong employers. What the Hmong might have lost in this way was well compensated for by the increasing sums we had to pay them. Meanwhile we did not mind as long as we did not waste too much time discussing payments. But I sometimes had difficulty keeping my temper when hearing that the Hmong had confiscated some of our best gifts to the Mlabri!

Lissu village Ban Mai, 99°30'E, 20°04'N, Ml?, ref. no. 26. After reaching Ta Ton and taking the motorboat down the Mae Kok river, we dropped off near Ban Muang Ngam and walked up to Ban Mai, situated only 3 km from the Burmese border. In this village we met a Lissu farmer about 50 years old, who had once been a soldier. He gave the following information:

It was quite some time since he had met the Mlabri – perhaps 15 years previously (1962). They had tried to avoid him in the jungle, but liked to come down to the villages in the evening to exchange horns from various animals for rice, but never stayed overnight. He had met them in *Muang Wa in Burma* about one month's (?) walk from Ban Mai, where there was still dense jungle. His description of these Mlabri indicates that they resemble our Mlabri Ml. When approaching their camps he had to make a noise, so that the men could hide their naked women. The men were small, and had a hole in each earlobe. They used banana leaves or a piece of tappa to cover their loins. It may be of some interest to note that all the way further north into Burma there are high mountains that may hold Mlabri-like groups, although not necessarily related to those in Thailand. The Lissu had a 50-year-old spear, 190 cm long, which had belonged to the grandfather of the Mlabri who had sold it to him. As he thought the spear would bring luck, he did not wish to sell it, but we were allowed to photograph it (fig. 6).

After returning to *Ban Bow Hoy* we received some interesting additional information from the Mlabri Ml with the assistance of Mr Lao Toa. Among other things it was agreed that the Mlabri had almost never used the crossbow, probably because the Hmong had not allowed them to use this dangerous weapon. But they did have traps, and until recently poisons as well, but due to some accidents with children and the poison, they did not use it anymore. They still killed and ate the big constrictor, but never approached the tiger or the cobra, the latter being so poisonous that nobody would get back to their camp to say that they had been bitten, according to Lao Toa'. He also said that on average, one Mlabri out of the 75 now living in the area was killed by a snake bite about every other year.

First Meeting with the Mlabri M3

Ban Nam Yao, 100°97'E, 19°00'N, M3, ref. no. 27. Having heard about the very small Mlabri, called Kha Thong Luang by the Thai, we had been trying hard to find them, asking the authorities whether any of the refugee camps, among others one near Chieng Kham, would have any Mlabri. We also asked in the refugee camp at Nam Yao, but here they were not sure, however allowing us to look for them ourselves. After searching for them carefully in the crowded camp for two hours, we succeeded in finding their group of 11 persons. They were in an absolutely appalling state, both physically and mentally (see figs. 110-111), very thin from starvation and nervous because of the multitude of tribal people of all kinds around them. Moreover, it soon turned out that they were addicted to opium. They had a sort of leader, a T'in man, who also served as our interpreter. Below, I have included the main points of the first information obtained.

They said they mainly lived from eating roots and bamboo shoots, as well as from collecting water animals and killing small game in the lower mountains where there were many streams. They did not have spears, at least not any longer, but knives and clubs, also using tiny traps, and climbing trees to collect honey. They knew perfectly well how to make fire, a necessity especially at night in the jungle to keep away all kinds of unpleasant animals and insects. Their T'in leader told us that they originally came from the Juba forest in Sayabouri province, Laos. 30-40 years ago there had been more than a hundred of them, in bands of 10-15 persons each, but already before their removal from the border areas towards Laos by the Thai border police in 1975 they had been split into more groups, of which some might still remain in Laos.

It was interesting to know that they had their earlobes pierced one generation back just as many of the main group still had, but it was strongly emphasised that they under no circumstances could marry members of that group and tried to avoid them. When giving birth to a child, the mother stayed within the windscreen, not outside, as among the Ml Mlabri. It was added that now they buried their dead, but previously did very much the same as the Mlabri Ml, either hoisting them up in a tree or leaving the body on the ground, half-covered with earth. To all who have met them, including the Thai, they and the Ml group are two separate groups. We shall return to discuss their relationship later on, at this point only referring to what many of the mountain people say, that the small Mlabri are the 'genuine' Kha Thong Luang, probably having mixed even less with the other hill tribes than those of the Ml Mlabri.

The Expedition 1978

During the third expedition we continued to gather anthropometrical measurements together with, among others, our Danish friends Bente and Ryon Sørensen, respectively a school teacher and a physician. We also made further sociological observations, now staying closer to, and even in, the Mlabri camps. Already at this point we heard that the altogether 19 families or about 140 Mlabri Ml were divided into two groups, those around *Doi Khun Sathan, 100° 29'E, 18°16'N, ref. no. 28,* and those belonging to the mountains further north (west of Ban Fang Min), we had already visited. The first bands arrived in the Doi Khun Sathan area around 1925-1930, according to our information. Actually, the families seem to have kept more or less to their original areas, but there have been many shifts and much intermarriage between the two areas, so we have not been able to trace any ethnographical differences.

Ban Bow Hoy, 100°27'E, 18°30'N, Ml, ref. no. 25. Here we met among others, Pha, Ajan, Gu, Gui and Paeng Noi. Pha said that when a woman is about to deliver, a small windscreen is made at some distance from the others. The afterbirth is buried at the place of the birth. After one and up to five weeks a ceremony takes place near an old tall tree or a big stone to fix the soul of the child to its body. But, surprisingly, no ceremony is undertaken when the child attains puberty or later gets married. But before going hunting, a little food is offered to the spear spirit and the spirit of the forest. For the first time, they agreed on their previous practice of putting their dead on a big pile of bamboo which was then covered with leaves.

Lao Toa, our Hmong host, explained that the Mlabri marry three times on average, and that they are not always sure who of the men is the 'true' father of a newborn baby! He also said that it was only during the last two years that the Hmong began to have some contacts with the Mlabri, using them to work in their fields for about one or two months each year.

This was the stay when we witnessed perhaps the most important Mlabri ceremony of all, and in full – the one for their parents' spirits, to be undertaken regularly, at least once a year. Otherwise these spirits, not capable of finding food by themselves, would get hungry and consequently inflict accidents or disease on their living kin to remind them of their obligations. While the ceremony and the prayers have been described in full (pp. 184-188), we have subsequently had the prayers repeated more completely. Towards the end of the ceremony, the Mlabri expressed good wishes, and we gave them the items agreed upon – meat and other foodstuffs, alcohol, iron, tobacco, sweets, etc., from the local market in Rongwan. Finally the sweaters, trousers and blankets – altogether more than 100 items, or 70 kg, brought from Denmark – were distributed. Similar procedures were repeated in almost every camp visited, the amounts being adjusted according to the length of the stay. Now, when the Mlabri were also receiving a payment according to the length of their assistance, our interpreter told them the value of the Bath paper notes to prevent them being cheated too much by the Hmong or in the local market.

Staying for quite some days in the Mlabri camp, we could not help noticing that the women were being pushed around by the men if the latter wanted something done. Whereas the teenagers overcame their shyness and came forward to study us with sweet curiosity, the small ones, terrified, took shelter in their mother's lap or under their dirty blankets. When we gave the women or children something they snapped it out of our hands. Pha, who was about 44 years old, said he had had been married twice, his present wife being only 22 years old, while Gui (Pang) still had two wives, sleeping one on each side of him in the windscreen. But this was somewhat unusual and not really approved of.

Some of the old men, like Patot and Paeng Taw ("old"), had large tattoos on their chest and back made by the Khon Muang. But the Mlabri had also made some crude ones themselves. I specifically asked them whether they had made stripes of dots on their arms and legs previously, this they denied. However, Lao Toa said with a smile that they had forgotten, adding that normally they do not have a long memory probably as they don't keep any kind of written records. As already mentioned, when studying them more carefully anthropometrically we found some crude tattooing, which they admitted to having made themselves, using sap from a tree, some soot and a needle. The tattooing was, though, seemingly not as deep and long-lasting as that made by the other hill peoples. The reason for going into these details we shall return to later, being related to the question of whether there was a substantial difference between the alleged two spear groups originally, the Ml and the M7 (the 'fierce' one).

One subject the Mlabri remembered only too well – that of their family and friends being lost through accidents, by falling down from trees or getting bitten by snakes, but especially those killed by the other hill peoples. Out of relatively many cases, the Mlabri mentioned two recent ones. Two Mlabri were killed by two Thai hunters while they were all pursuing the same animal. Old Suk and Ton were killed at Bow Keng by an explosion (a hand grenade) due to quarrels with the white Hmong there. The two Mlabri, after having received payment for making mats, etc., of rattan, had tried to run away without finishing their job. As we shall see, it has almost always been the Mlabri who have been on the receiving end and have suffered a violent death at the hands of the other hill peoples!

At this point we also really felt what the Mlabri were up against, even though we had already had some scary experiences with the Hmong during our long stay in 1970. After having almost finished our studies this time in Ban Bow Hoy, we had collected 5 ml samples of blood for examination, and for comparison we also wanted blood tests from the Hmong. As we paid each individual one day's wage, some Hmong boys and girls also wanted to participate in the program. However, when the Hmong men returned in the late afternoon all hell broke out, as they claimed that the boys had now lost some of their sexual potency!

During the night our house was surrounded by Hmong men firing their guns into the air to threaten our party. The next day one of the Hmong families turned up now asking us to put back the blood into the veins of the boys or else give the family a large sum as compensation, this we refused. Then they threatened us with a hand grenade and refused to let us leave. We were trapped in a deadlock, so in the evening I went to discuss the matter with the Hmong headman pretending to be calm while lighting my pipe. At 11 p.m. he accepted one third of the sum first requested, and Lao Toa advised us to leave immediately. Helped by the full moon, and in the silence of the night, he and his friends took us to Nan in their truck.

After Ban Bow Hoy our party went back once again to the area south of Amphoe Mae Suai, 99°32'E, 19°39'N, which would prove to be very useful, as we received some important imformation without which we might not have been able to clarify the Mlabri M1's connection to this area. Near Ban Pa Miang Mae Prik, ref. no. 01, an old Thai woman had seen three Mlabri men with long hair coming to exchange honey for a pig about 30 years ago (around 1950), but also asking for rice for their women.

From Ban Mai on the main road going south we walked up to a *Hmong village, Mae Ta La, south of Doi Pa Tung, 99°36'E, 19°33'N, Ml, ref. no. 29.* The 38-year-old headman said that he had seen the Mlabri already when he was about ten years old, around 1950, while he was hunting together with his father. They had met about ten naked men (corresponding to two bands each of 20 persons) carrying spears. Whenever they approached the Mlabri women and children, the men had raised their spears ready to protect them. Another Hmong added that only ten years before (1967), they had seen the Mlabri coming to ask for rice. They had said that they were on their way east, actually, as it turned out, going southeastwards back to Nan province.

It was also on Doi Pa Tung that the headman had found a Mlabri polishing stone in an abandoned wind-screen ten years back (see fig. 153, no. 18), adding that it was after the fight with the Khong Muang in 1954 that the Mlabri had been chased away (see p. 197). It was important to hear that the brother of the headman was from Ban Po Keng, one of the villages in Nan province, which the Mlabri M1 first came to. He even knew the 'scandal' of Lat (Ut's son) having married a Hmong girl only three months earlier. Probably some of the Mlabri had heard about the jungle-clad mountain chain behind the Phayao Lake from the brother of the mentioned Hmong or his family in Ban Po Keng already before 1950.

Mlabri M3

The second meeting with the Mlabri in the Nam Yao Refugee Camp, ref. no. 27, was more encouraging than the first. Above all, this was because conditions had improved substantially, although the Mlabri obviously still did not feel at ease among the multitude of hill tribes. Their former T'in employer again served as our interpreter and started by saying that they had come from the area of *Muang Piang, 101°26'E, 19°04'N, M3, ref. no. 30: Sayabouri province, Laos,* before entering Thailand nine days' walk from the camp.

They said that their parents had small spears of hardwood or bamboo and they also had fine tattooed lines on their arms and legs, but this has not been confirmed subsequently. As with the Ml Mlabri, an offering was made to the spear spirit both before and after hunting, the offering being placed on a big leaf or on a stone and the spear being held above it. Formerly they also used traps and nets to catch boars, antelopes and snakes, but now they lived mainly from collecting various kinds of slow game, water animals and a number of different roots and tubers. They also sometimes caught birds and climbed trees to get honey. Wild tobacco was collected to be dried on the roof of their windscreen, but they did not know more than a few medicinal plants. Bark from a special tree was utilised for washing, and a black sap from another tree to make their present tiny tattoos on their chests. Unlike the Mlabri Ml, they regularly smoked opium, which has evidently endangered their health and has contributed to keeping them by and large slaves of their Hmong employers!

The father will help the mother during giving birth, and the afterbirth is usually put in a bamboo internode. There is a small ceremony sometime after the birth to fix the spirit of the child to its body, but none at puberty or when getting married. I asked one of the men if they, like the M1-group, remarry 3-4 times in a lifetime. He said they strongly resented this, almost being scornful of my question. He compared infidelity with stealing or lying – both being considered unforgivable sins. We also discussed at some length whether they made designs on the bamboo containers in the same way as the M1 Mlabri. Not only did he agree on this point, but he also fetched a small one with a modest design (see fig. 148), but very much like those of the Mlabri M1.

Before returning to Denmark we went again to the Nam Yao Refugee Camp. Now the Mlabri said that in their parents' time they were real Khon Pa, but after staying with their T'in leader they had been taught several things and had changed a lot! Therefore, during the afternoon we continued to discuss their life with their parents. Among others they said that one of the most important spirits was that of all the forest, but they also made offerings to special tall trees and big stones. Contrary to what we had heard before, they claimed they never slept under big trees but sometimes had used caves if there were many days of heavy rain. However, already at this point everything indicated that the life and culture of the M1 and M3 Mlabri were quite different, which is also evident from the numerous early sources and the fact that the other hill tribes as well as themselves distinguish two separate groups, which under no circumstances can intermarry. Actually, on the rare occasions the two groups had met, both felt uneasy and tried to avoid each other.

Just before leaving the camp I asked to see its commander, because the Mlabri were evidently suffering more than anybody else from staying there, proposing that they might be allowed to stay in the jungle not far from the camp. He listened carefully and promised to look into the matter, with the result that shortly afterwards they were released and started once again to work for their Hmong employers.

Mr. Yen, a Laotian, told us in our hotel in Nan that while hunting near Champasak in southern Laos, and about a 100 km from the border to Cambodia, he had met some Kha Thong Luang (M3) men at a distance of 10-15 m during a hunt. They were very small, only about 140 cm tall, had very worn teeth and a piece of wood in each earlobe, wore loin cloths and carried spears of bamboo. They had just looked at him briefly before hurrying away.

The 1980 Expedition

During our fourth stay in Northern Thailand we did not perform as many surveys as earlier but rather stayed longer in each Mlabri camp to undertake the numerous supplementary anthropometrical measurements. These included making tooth imprints under the guidance of our friends, dental surgeon Carl Erik Andersen and his wife Inger, who is a dental technician. My wife took blood samples to be stored in a double-insulated box with ice. Furthermore, we continued to collect very much the same sort of material from the neighbouring hill tribes, the T'in, Khamu, Khong Muang and the Hmong, for comparison, in the hope of getting an idea of the anthropometrical distances relative to the Mlabri (see also Appendix 7).

Ban Na Ka, M1, ref. no. 24, Khon Muang-village. Among others, Paeng, Gu, Ajan and Suk came down from their camp higher up the mountain to meet us. Suk, 14 years old, said on this occasion that if someone was feeling very ill, they put some food into a banana leaf and fixed it around the stomach with a string. Then he or she would walk up to a big tree, where a simple altar had been made leaning against it, to pray to the forest spirit as well as to the parents' spirits for recovery. If someone dies far away from the camp, they carry the body to a suitable place nearby, make an altar, dig a shallow hole and put the body in the hole, but only covering it with about half a metre of earth. We were also told that if someone had died at one side of their territory, they would move in the opposite direction after the burial. Incidentally, asking young Suk often proved to be more reliable, for he did not try to improve on the descriptions of their difficult life.

Ajan explained the way of saying hello in Mlabri to someone of the same age: jak kwehl "go search" (for food), while to an elder man, they might say: mɣm cha.kamruc "father old" to show him respect, a quality much appreciated by the Mlabri. All agreed that those performing religious rituals were not allowed to produce knives at the same time (also an old Indian belief). Ajan said they should also avoid rivers and waterfalls, because they may host the spirit dəkat. If they felt threatened while staying in the jungle they might offer some roots to this spirit. It was also related that it was not permitted to kill the bird to dɛo "woodpecker", because it warns the Mlabri against dangers such as snakes and tells them if someone approaches their camp. He finally said that if they watched animals copulating, the spirits could make them lose their appetite!

Ajan now demonstrated how they would beat a large bamboo internode vigorously to make a violent thunder leave them. Incidentally, the Mlabri did not share the outside world's idea of being properly dressed, saying with a smile that until recently they put on clothing only when approaching the other people.

Hmong village Ban Po Keng, 100°30', 19°43'N, Ml, ref. no. 31, groups of about 25 Mlabri, among others: Patot, Kham, Gaeo, Gui and Mun. The oldest of all the Mlabri was Patot. He was born in Laos and came to Thailand around 1916, when he was about four years old. He was almost deaf by now, and therefore difficult to communicate with. Previously, the Mlabri had gone quite far away, for example to the plains, which held very few people at that time, but there were many birds, buffalo and elephant. Here Ai-Suk (deceased) and Gu had stabbed an elephant, but not sufficiently, so they had to run away. Before 1950 they had almost no contact with anyone (except Phu Jaka in Ban Kum), and had to get the iron for their spears by searching the fields of deserted Khon Muang villages. The iron was shaped into spearheads and knives by using a strong fire and beating the hot iron into shape with stones.

As regards taboos, we were told that eating cows' meat may cause lightning, and pregnant women were not allowed to eat, for example, barking deer, turtles and bear cats. Only parents could punish their children – not even grandparents were permitted to do this. The parents' spirits staying in the earth may punish bad behaviour by sending animals to kill the sinner, or making tree branches fall on them. In this connection we heard that the elder and now deceased Ai-Suk and his wife had lost their child in the jungle 13 years previously (1967) – indeed a strange coincidence, because it was the very same year we were told by the villagers at Ban Puat near Pha Yao that a Mlabri girl had lost trace of her band, to be found in the jungle by some hunters above the village, only 2-3 years before we arrived there in 1970 (see p. 37). The girl never returned to her family. After she had been released and hurried back to the jungle, she was probably killed by a snake, bear or tiger. The incident indeed links the Mlabri having lived near Pha Yao to those in Nan province.

The Mlabri women at Ban Po Keng had almost never seen westerners before, and they tried awkwardly to imitate many of our gestures, believing for instance that when we were taking a picture with the camera that it was a sort of greeting! When asking if we could photograph them, their husbands pushed them into place, to

which they responded reluctantly. Most of our gifts, e.g. thread, needles and scissors, they had never seen before, but the small mirrors we gave them produced their greatest surprise. It was only when my wife sat down beside them that they relaxed and started investigating and commenting on the items in their charming, high-pitched voices. Obviously they had never stayed for long in any Hmong village before, because at some point the women asked if they could return to their windscreen, as they felt uneasy in the presence of the Hmong, whom they feared. Especially the proud (Ai-) Som had a hard time concealing his anger, when the Hmong smiled at the Mlabri, not necessarily meant in a negative way, however.

Staying in their camps we observed that their small children tried to cut wood with big knives or play with burning wood from the fires, pretending to cook food, while the boys moved around on steep slopes or climbed trees nearby. But neither here nor later on did we see them quarrel or fight. When asking the young men whether any of them had problems with their mother-in-law, the answer was why? We have arrived at the conclusion that it is connected with the fact that a mother-in-law may only be a rather temporary connection, and anyway the couple stay mainly with the husband's family.

Ban Bow Hoy, ref. no. 25. Eighteen Mlabri in one camp of four windscreens. Ai-Lek, our old acquaintance from earlier visits, said that the reason why the Mlabri had left Laos around 1916 had also been the hostility of the Lao people. This might be correct, as we heard exactly the same in Ventiane in 1989 regarding the villagers' attitude towards the Mlabri even so many years later. This is in contrast to the tolerant Khong Muang in Thailand, who have generally treated them well. Lek also said that the remaining Mlabri, who we had not met during our present stay, were living in Ban Hui Huang near the Khon Muang village there. He added that no Mlabri stayed exclusively in the jungle anymore, apart from his own parents and his parents-in-law, who never came out to meet non-Mlabri. The reason for not making holes in their ears any more was that they did not like to be identified as Mlabri when visiting the maket below.

Lek claimed that he had never used the oil from boar's testicles to trick the boars while hunting them. Their only remedy against snakebite was soot from their huge pipes, which they scraped out and put into the wound. As regards tree burials, he said that a young man, Suk Noi, was killed by a tiger many years previously, and had been put in a tree, a trap being made for the tiger by placing eight sharpened stakes under the tree, so when it jumped at the dead boy, they both fell down and were stabbed by the stakes. Lek added that previously they had also put people who had died while hunting or fetching wood, in trees, while those who had died when looking for honey or roots or when trekking far from their camp were just covered with leaves. Only those dying in or near the camp were buried. But evidently practice had changed during the previous 30 years.

Finally, regardarding Lek's son, who was about 20 years old and seriously ill when we came to the camp. All his body was swollen, and after Birgit had looked at him we offered to take him to the hospital in Nan and pay all expenses. However, Lek said solemnly that he did not dare try this possibility. It was probably also too late, for the boy died only ten days later. The day we left the camp, we noticed that his sister had two big red spots, one on each cheek, perhaps an appeal to the sky spirit to spare her brother.

Hmong village Ban Huay Hom, 100°28'E, 18°14'N, Ml, ref. no.32. Mlabri camp half an hour away, 17 persons, among others Muang, Wai, Mun and Som. Our kind and intelligent host Lao Wang and employer of the Mlabri arranged our stay in all details, including housing us in his village, thereafter letting us occupy a small farmer's hut near the Mlabri camp. This was of great importance, as we were able to arrange performance of the most important ceremony – that for their deceased parents. We were able to photograph it and thoroughly tape record it without the interference of others (the ceremony and the prayers have already been described in detail, pp. 184-188, 203).

During the preparations, Lao Wang told us many things about the past. Among others he said that even his grandparents themselves had used bast or tree leaves for their dress. The Mlabri (Ml) had never used a bow and arrow, and perhaps after meeting the Hmong they were possibly not allowed to use their crossbow, which is a deadly weapon. When he first saw them, 35 years ago near the border to Laos (1945), they talked in a very low voice and anyway did not say very much. The Hmong called them Man Kro and said they were very honest. It was interesting to hear that at first they had long stripes on their legs, but short ones on their arms. The stripes consisted of dots resembling letters, but all looking alike. He had heard that some Khon Muang were afraid of the Mlabri and had shot two of them more than ten years earlier near Doi Thung, 7 km to the north. Lao Wang concluded that the Mlabri understood what was explained, but they seldom had their own ideas.

They were peaceful people now, who seldom got angry or started fighting with anyone.

Muang said that previosly they had had a sharper division of work, but it was still the men who hunted and the women who collected most of the roots. Once they had trees with many fruits or nuts, each belonging to specific families. Such trees were marked with their family symbols. It is the spirit of the sky who had not allowed them to grow anything. Asked about marriages with the Hmong, the Mlabri said it had happened, since twice a Mlabri boy had married a Hmong girl, and twice a Hmong boy had married a Mlabri girl. However, in both instances their children had gone to stay with their Hmong family! Poisons were not used anymore, but were previously made from the sap of the Yanong tree, the white marrow of the palm tree (daw), the head of the centipede and the head and tail of a venomous snake. Asked specifically about the bamboo containers, the Mlabri said they had always had them, which is of some importance as concerns the question of the very provenance of these people.

The Mlabri M3

Also during this visit we received quite a few early accounts of other groups resembling the M3 Mlabri. Thus in the Khon Muang village Pa Hung, ref. no. 18, the village of our helper Nian, a middle-aged couple said that there had been some Ang Tha Kae both near *Pa Hung* and to the southeast near their former village of *100°59'E, 18°23'N, M3, ref. no.33, Mae Saliem, Sa district,* in their early childhood, the latter place actually not being far from where the M3 group came to stay in the mid-1970s. Their parents had told them that they had seen three naked persons. Though looking like the Ml Mlabri, they were considerably smaller and thinner. Because of having quite weak knees, they were easy to catch, but in that event had started biting. It was added that they ate much of their food raw and sometimes stayed in caves.

This is almost the same description as many of our other sources give, including the Hmong Lao Toa in Ban Bow Hiew, ref. no. 25, who had heard his parents say that similar people had lived *in the deep clefts near Doi Phu Wae in northern Nan, 101°09'E, 19°19'N, M3, ref. no.34,* around 1945.

Near Hui Oiy, ref. no.38, even the Mlabri Ml said that their grandparents had told them about the Phi Pa ("spirit forest") living in Laos, saying that they were very small and thin, that they slept on the ground under big trees and had eaten raw meat. They had been difficult to approach, and even then they had only whispered, exactly as the M3 we know of, sometimes making it difficult to record their speech.

The expedition 1982

During our fourth expedition we stayed in six localities and 11 Mlabri camps as well as one M3 camp, when most of the anthropometrical measurements were almost completed, while still checking the anthropological data and collecting more prayers. At the end of the campaign my wife and I, together with our two daughters, took the plane to Pitsanolok and went by bus on to Loei province with the hope of finding traces of other Mlabri groups. Among others, we found one Mlabri boy from a group which, on the next expedition in 1987, would turn out to be from a Ml Mlabri band who had trekked all the way down to Loei province. Perhaps more significantly, we found one remaining Mlabri man from a local group, M5, not substantially different from the Ml Mlabri, and obtained old evidence of the M3 bands as well.

Ban Pa Hung, 100°32'E, 18°35'N, Ml, ref. no. 18. Back again in this Khon Muang village we were told of the following incident. Around 1935 the headman in Ban Kum was Saen Pa Wang, who received a sick Mlabri girl in his house. While recovering, she was out in the field with a cousin of the headman, who raped her. After having returned to her camp, the Mlabri had turned up and threatened Saen Pa Wang by saying they would burn his house to the ground. But by giving the Mlabri a pig he had got them to leave. Thereafter they avoided the villagers which, as a matter of fact, was still the case when we came to Pa Hung in 1970. Discussing the origin of the Mlabri, Mr. Siwai, a 58-year-old schoolteacher, said that to his knowledge the Mlabri here originally came from the Chieng Kham area up north and that in his opinion the Mlabri M1 in Phrae, Nan and Chieng Rai provinces all belong to one and the same larger group. He added that the walking distance to Pha Yao was ten days and estimated the population of the Mlabri (Ml) was 140 persons divided into 19 families.

Ban Na Ka, 100°27'E, 18°42'N, Ml, ref. no. 24, one band of nine Mlabri, among others Paeng Taw, Gu, Ajan and Pha. Having slept in the Khon Muang village, we went to stay in a Mlabri camp in the jungle at a bend of the river nearby for about a week. We all enjoyed the nice relaxed atmosphere, to which our two daughters contributed. It was only spoiled each time any Hmong were passing by. Then the Mlabri women would take their children on their backs and sit deep inside their windscreens, but we never learned whether this was their normal reaction or because of some incident. My wife, being an anaesthetic nurse, gave the women much practical advice also including how to use needle and thread, while 'uncle' Paeng Taw showed our children how to make fire with a piece of iron, a stone and some finely scraped bamboo.

Paeng related, among other things, that only previously, when most of the bands stayed together, did they have a sort of leader such as Nam Peung, who for instance decided when and where to move. Before, they had only occasional contacts with T'in and Khamu. When he himself was 20 years old, he had already killed five bears, five boars and about 10 deer, adding that it required 7-8 people to kill an elephant. Previously a young man had to come back to the camp with 3-5 different animals before he could ask the parents of the girl for permission to marry their daughter.

He said, moreover, that they dance the first time it rains at the end of the dry season (just like the Thai people do). But if the sky spirit is angry, there will be very dark clouds, thunder, hail or a rainbow, in which case they are not allowed to drink water, while Phi Pa is the spirit of the forest coming with the wind. Inquiring about why the rainbow spirit is asked to leave, Paeng said that it is because they believe that it may eat the body smell of persons, causing them to die. In the case of a murder, they believe that the earth is lifted up, so the sky comes down upon them. Finally, I asked Paeng about their sex habits. Obviously he did not like to go into any detail, but laughing he said: "Why do you try to make me angry"? However, from the young men I learned that we are more alike also in this respect than we have thought!

In the camp we had a thrilling experience. Our guide this time was Tee, a Lissu. At some point he asked us not to move and pointed to a big, green and yellow snake moving around in the trees surrounding the camp, causing all to be on the alert. Resolutely he took a stone and hit the snake on its head at a distance of 12 m. Our children would have liked to study the snake with its big triangle head in detail, but the Mlabri insisted on having it thrown out of the camp immediately, probably for fear of its bad spirit. In the event of snake bite the alkaline substance inside old batteries is used to break down the poison in combination with tourniquet of the limb.

Regarding medicine, they said the Hmong would help them when necessary, adding that they have worked for them since 1978.

Returning to an often asked question concerning silent trade, Paeng said they had not even dared to put some goods near the houses of the Hmong. When they first met them in the jungle, it had been decided to meet on a hilltop to barter, so that if they thought they were being cheated, they were still able to escape by running down to "their side" of the hill. As for the Mlabri songs, Paeng said at last that most of them derived from the Khon Muang and that they were not from Laos, as we had heard and believed they were.

The next days were used trying to trace other groups. First we went to visit the police stations in Amphoe Chieng Klang (100°53'E, 19°18'N) and Tung Chang, 15 km further north. In Pua, the soldiers said it would be all too risky to approach the border areas to Laos due to the fierce fighting going on right then. Finally, we went to the new settlement Pa Klang (Ban Pa Gang), which had replaced the now abandoned Nam Yao camp. In the Hmong quarters we found some interesting information on the Mlabri, and how to get to them. Obviously, the Hmong move more frequently than most Thai to trade or to visit their families, even going to faraway places, as a consequence they are very well informed on what is going on in the mountains.

Ban Megafai, 100°26'E, 18°31'N, Ml, ref. no. 35. Camp of 11 Mlabri, in four windscreens including Patot, Gaeo, Pha, Maiga with two children, Lat, Suk and Hramla (see pp. 258-259). Recording of prayers, hunting methods and psychotechnical tests. This time Birgit actually cured old Patot of *erysipelas*, causing him to recover within four days.

Ban Huay Yok, 100°30'E, 18°42'N, Ml, ref. no. 36. 26 Mlabri in three camps and near: Ban Po Keng, 100°30'E, 18°43'N; Ml, ref. no. 31. 32 Mlabri in two camps near this Hmong village. The three camps near Ban Huyak were situated, respectively, two hours' walk west of Po Keng (Thong's group), half an hour's walk south of Po Keng (Gui's group) and close to the Hmong village Po Keng (Seng's group). The Hmong Lao Toam was their employer and supervised their tree felling and clearing of the land to make it ready for planting with rice. Gui (Pang): The Mlabri quite preferred the Hmong to the Yao, finding the latter even more strict and difficult to work for. The Mlabri called the Hmong: Ma Hmong, the Thai: Ma Tao, and white people: kwar "outsiders, stranger".

Most of the Mlabri were too tired to be interviewed thoroughly, so we concentrated on their kinship relations and on surveying their camps. However, during the late afternoon we also obtained information from Ta: After a boy and girl are married (no ceremony), they go first to join the band of her parents. When a girl is going to give birth, water is boiled both to drink and to wash the baby and the mother, the birth now taking place only about ten metres from the windscreen. The umbilical cord is cut with a bamboo knife. The baby is given a preliminary name after three days, and after another three days or so a cotton string is put around its wrist, and its weak spirit is asked to stay with the body. Then the tongue, heart, liver and gall bladder of a small pig or of a chicken is sacrificed to support the soul of the new-born.

When asked about the prayer against thunder, Ta said that now they only take some rags and put them around a stone to show the thunder spirit that they are poor, "so please do not come to harm us". With regard to the rainbow spirit he claimed that they are afraid that it can make the mountains collapse. He insisted that only those killed by a tiger are put in a tree; all others are buried and have their belongings placed with them inside the grave, for it is believed that the deceased's spirit stays with the belongings. They do make an altar and leave the head of the sacrificed pig on top, as we have also seen when an offering was made to the parents' spirit.

Birgit's interview with Ta and his wife: The Mlabri list a number of animals that a pregnant women should not eat, but only beef is in fact totally prohibited, as it is for almost anyone now. Miscarriages do occur, and in such cases the woman is cleaned, and a blanket is tightly fastened around her to avoid her losing too much blood. However, from our interviews we know that many babies as well as women are lost, the latter being demonstrated by the fact that there are more elder men than women (see p. 50). As regards deformed babies, we were told that the mother is expected to kill the baby immediately after the birth and bury it, while if the mother dies during or after the birth her husband has to bury her.

Ta's wife said that they bring up their children mainly by supervising them rather than instructing them. It was earlier claimed that they refrained from sex one to two year after a birth to avoid producing more children than they could feed and carry from place to place. This might well have been the case earlier (see also Benjamin p. 249). But from what we know of the young Mlabri they do not wait that long anymore. She also said that she wakes up before the man, makes fire, cooks rice and washes the children – the last being rather superficial though. They do not know when the children can do various things, because they do not have any means of keeping check with months or years, which also means that most Mlabri have only a vague idea of the age of their family members, including themselves. However Ta's wife did say that some girls do marry before their first menstruation.

When trying to help women carry water from quite far away from the windscreens I observed that she and her children had many untreated sores on their arms and legs, as well as insect bites, including scabies, fleas and lice in myriads. When we returned to the camp my wife sat ready with our big box of plasters, iodine, penicillin, etc., to cure infections, including otorrhea. We could not help noticing that the middle-aged women were often completely worn out because of the hard work in the hot Hmong fields and the lack of proper care, such as the widow of Ai On. She was hardly more than 40 years old but looked 55. The Mlabri women in particular suffered from having too many obligations, and now they also had to work in the fields, besides as usual collecting roots, preparing food and moving their camp every 10-14 days with children and their belongings.

After Ban Po Keng we went on reconnaissance trips with local taxis to Amphoe Pua and to the northwest of Nan, passing deserted roads and guarded checkpoints, finally being turned back near *Doi Phu Wo, 100°38'E, 19°22'N, M1, ref. no. 37,* where the soldiers did not even dare to come out of their bunker due to the insecure circumstances! Up here we were told that they had seen the Mlabri only rarely and a long time back – perhaps 20 years previously, which was agreed upon later by the Mlabri themselves, saying that the area, Doi Dan Yao and northwards, did not belong to their basic one.

Ban Huai Oiy, 100°26'E, 18°13'N, M1, ref. no. 38. 16 Mlabri in one camp of three windscreens including Ut and Lat (Ut's son), Paeng Noi and Ajan. We stayed one week pursuing the investigations of family relations, anthropometrical measurement, drawings of wind-screens, etc.

Ban Pha Tong Silapet at Mae Uan, 101°01'E, 19°02'N, M3 & M4, ref. no. 39. The Hmong, Lao Ju, we had met at the Mae Charim refugee settlement, guided us up to his village, magnificently situated in virgin mountain forest at the southern end of the about 50 km long and up to 2000 m high north-south-oriented mountain range.

Here we met again the 11 Mlabri M3 who had been taken up there from the now abandoned Nam Yao refu-gee camp. Half an hour's walk brought us to their new home, where they had made a sort of double windscreen with a living room and sleeping quarters somewhat like a Hmong house, but much smaller, holding all of them (figs. 144-145). Around the meadow the Mlabri had cleared the land to grow rice for their somewhat strict employer.

It was said that in the Communist controlled east-oriented slopes of the *Doi Pho Ka mountain, 101°13'E, 19°11'N, M4, ref. no. 40,* there was allegedly a group of about 30 Mlabri living near *Ban Maeo Lao Leng Khun Kwang.* However, we were not able to visit, as the whole area was controlled by the Vietnamese Communists, mined in various places, and therefore too risky to approach. After having made drawings of the Mlabri M3 windscreen and trying to obtain further information on various subjects, we decided to ask Lao Ju if he could arrange a meeting with two members of the Mlabri further north, which he said he would try to do.

Early next morning we left our two daughters, Xenia and Sara, with our Khon Muang helper, Nian, in Ban Silapet and started climbing a steep trail up north together with our Hmong host, to what should turn out to be his opium fields at an altitude of about 1400 m. Here we were asked to wait in a small hut so he could bring back two Mlabri from a different qroup. As the day progressed we started wondering if we were going to sleep up here in the chilly wind. Not until around 4 p.m. did Lao Ju return very exhausted with two men, Gaeng and Toeng, respectively about 30 and 45 years of age, but looking somewhat different from the M1 and M3 Mlabri. Neither of them spoke Mlabri M1 or M3 but a strange, guttural and abrupt language, sounding like playing a tape recording backwards. They called them-selves mla' 'yng, and said that they worked for the Hmong and otherwise stayed in the mountain jungle. They showed us a spear and a cho', a small hand spade to dig for roots of the same kind as that of the Mlabri M1 and M3; however they did not wish to sell them (see fig. 118), since they had belonged to their parents. Lao Ju added that they also stayed in windscreens in the jungle. To us the two men resembled some sort of a mixture between T'in and Mlabri, exactly as our Hmong host had hinted and we have heard of before also staying in windscreens.

After having recorded their voices on the tape recorder we left their extremely flea-infested windscreen and descended the mountain in a hurry in the last light. However we still had a surprise in store. At 11 p.m. we woke up, because lights were flickering around the silent village. Our Hmong host told us to keep absolutely quiet, as it was probably the Communists coming to search for something – food or perhaps for us! They went from house to house, while we almost paralysed held our breath. But they seemingly avoided our house. I shall abstain from referring to what the border police officer in charge in Nan said when hearing that we had been staying in this very village for some days!

Back in the refugee camp *Ban Pa Gang, 100°55'E, 19°07'N, M4, ref. no. 41,* we met Lek from Gaeng and Toeng's group, who had been sold to a Hmong when he was a child. Actually, we interviewed him for four hours at our hotel in Nan, asking him about Mlabri words, and whether he could remember anything about his family. But it turned out he had forgotten almost everything, saying only that when he was small, he had visited some of his family members in their windscreens in the jungle a few times. In the end we made our anthropometrical tests, photographed him (see fig. 119), etc. Contrary to the Mlabri M3 also working for the Hmong, he was well-fed and not opium-addicted.

Travel to Loei Province, Northeastern Thailand

At the end of our stay in Thailand in 1982 we, including our two daughters, took the plane to Pitsanulok and the next day went by bus to Loei via Nakhon Tai and Dan Sai. Even though we asked about the Mlabri on our way, nothing concrete was obtained until we had passed Dan Sai to stop just before a big market at *Ban Kaeng Laeng, 101 °17'E, 17° 23'N, M1, ref. no. 42.* In the middle of the day and inside the bus it was very hot, our children were car sick and my wife slept. Then I saw a 13-year-old boy of a slightly darker complexion than the Thai entering the bus, thinking I heard some Thai women whispering "Phi Tong Luang". However, before I was able to wake up my family the bus had stopped, and the women and the boy alighted at the market. The bus started again – too soon for us to get out of the crowded bus with all our gear. Had it only been wishful thinking? Adding to my bewilderment, my family did not seem convinced of my story!

Similar incidents usually end like that. But five years later in 1987 we indeed found the same Mlabri boy and his band at Doi Khun Sathan, ref. no. 28, in Nan, where

Poa told us about his band's twelve-year-long trek (1972-84) down to Loei and their dramatic return to Doi Khun Satan, during which four members of the band had been killed. Even though five years had elapsed since I saw the boy – now a young man – he admitted being at the market in Ban Kaeng Laeng to buy a few things in the dry season, while his band was hiding in the jungle not too far away.

After a long sleep in Loei we hired a car to take us along the large, flat sandstone mountain, Phu Luang, 50 by 5 km and up to 1500 m above sea level. There are some old references to the Mlabri having stayed up there as well as at Phu Khio, another large sandstone mountain plateau 60 km further south (Seidenfaden 1919, pp. 49-50). The villagers at the foot of the mountain had indeed some strange tales to tell about the Phi Bang But (lit. "spirits unseen") who had lived in the caves somewhere up there. Unfortunately, those few who had actually seen them 10-20 years before had all died, but the Phi Bang But (Th) were said to be real and to look like Thai people! It was said that the caves had contained many valuables, and that bells were heard from up there every new and full moon! At that time the plateau was still covered with dense jungle, and sometimes hunters and others approaching the caves had disappeared, only to return sick or worn out many days later, allegedly also having been threatened with their lives if they told what they had seen. The only reasonable explanation for these stories I can think of is that the caves had been inhabited either by criminals or Communists, the latter being known to use these plateaus as their hideouts during the 1960-70s.

However, the villagers said that the Khon Pa had also lived on the plateau, but they had only seen the men coming down to exchange animals for rice and cloth. They were quite dark-skinned and dirty and only stayed overnight. A fine, 75-year-old Thai woman in *Ban Na Luang, 101°35'E, 17°19'N, M5, ref. no. 43,* calling them Kha Thong Luang, said that they had always carried a spear, never letting it out of their sight. She added that they were not particularly nice towards one another, for they never shared anything among themselves. Not being interested in the poor Mlabri, she had only observed that they had long hair, a hole in each earlobe and were very dirty. But another villager, a man, said that when he was 15 years old (1967), he had close contact with eight Mlabri men for about a year, when they came once or twice every week to exchange animals for rice, etc. He even remembered some of their names: Gaeo,

Hor, Lung, Kian, Keun and Mun. They could speak some Thai, but talked Mlabri among themselves; and they danced if given alcohol.

The Mlabri had said at some point they could no longer find enough wild food on the plateau, so they would move northwards, which they actually did. The Thai villager added that he had seen their windscreens but neither women nor children, who vanished whenever they were approached, and that the men did not have any tattoos, but made decorated bamboo containers.

As we went 50 km further south, we also came to *Ban Si Than, 101°52'E, 16°53'N, ref. no. 44, M5*, 5 km east of the National park *Doi Phu Kradung,* where several sources refer to the Mlabri there, but no one could render any additional information. Let us instead refer to Keer, 1924, pp. 142-144:

"The village of Sitan lies at the foot of a large sandstone mountain, Pu Kading, the top of which is a pine plateau, some 6 or 7 kilometres long by 2 broad, ... Some ten years ago a party of 30 men belonging to this tribe suddenly appeared at Ban Sitan. These men were naked with the exception of a flap of cloth hanging over the privates in front and a similar one behind. Two or three of them could speak a few words of Lao. They carried spears but no other weapons, ...; they were used both for thrusting and throwing and by their means they could kill such large and dangerous game as Kating. The Ka Tawng Luang brought honey with them and this they were anxious to exchange for maize, rice they refused. They also wanted to know where there was another high mountain, as they wished to leave Pu Kading; they were recommended to try Pu Luang, ... they were very black, their backs were bent, a great deal of the white of their eye was showing and their hair was curly (!)."

Actually we were told later on that they had alternated between Phu Luang and Doi Phu Kradung. From the above information it can be established that the Mlabri in question are the same as Lot's group, i.e. belonging to the M5 Mlabri (see below).

Ban Kok Ngam, 101°15'E, 17°22'N, M5, ref. no. 45. After returning to Loei, and as a result of asking for the Mlabri in practically every other village we passed through, we were told that in Kok Ngam they had a Mlabri, Lot, staying there with a Thai family. We hurried to the village, where our presence drew the attention of more than a hundred Thai coming to watch the strangers. We found a nice elderly lady who had adopted Lot, now 29 years old. However, he had gone alone to stay in the jungle as was still his wish now and then.

Luckily he returned in the evening. Already as a child he came regularly to see the Thai family, then staying under the famous Phu Kradung further to the south, which is 10 by 10 km and a sandstone mountain about 1100 m high. As he rather preferred to live in the village, he had been adopted by the Thai family at the age of 14, but he still went to visit his parents on the mountain. When his father died, his mother 'i buut also came down to Kok Ngam, where the Thai family had moved to, staying at some distance from the village, but coming to see her son regularly while working for various Thai farmers. Three years ago she too had died. Lot had not been accepted in the Thai school, being too old, then 16 years of age, to start in the primary class, and therefore the stepmother had tried to teach him Thai on her own but with little success. Still, he attended the services in the temple and took part in the social life of the village.

We were told that they had kept his father's spear, of which only the cover remained. I was naturally happy to buy it, especially as it was very similar one of those from the Mlabri Ml group (Lat's see fig. 155, M5, no. 31) in Nan province. When the villagers were shown our photographs of the Ml Mlabri they said that the Nan group did not differ substantially from Lot's. But from the language they said they could hear that Lot's group derived from Laos.

In the late afternoon we were allowed to take Lot to a hotel in Dan Sai, among other things with the hope of seeing whether he could remember some Mlabri words. But soon we realised that he could recognise only a few words like that for a "human" mla'. However, little by little, he gave quite a few details about his youth at Phu Kradung. He said they had more than a hundred Mlabri at the beginning, with 10-13 persons in each band, the only family members he remembered the name of being his cousin Gaeo and Ai Ond and Ai Wai. When he was small he had to remain in or near the windscreen collecting roots, honey, etc. At some point he claimed that his group had met some hostile Mlabri, but apart from saying they had to fight with them, he was not able to give further details. But as we shall see, it could perhaps have been the 'fierce' Mlabri M7 trying to find animals and probably having returned northwards to their base in the border areas between Laos and Nan province.

Being asked about their religion, he remembered having seen his father making an offering to the sky spirit (the supreme spirit of the Mlabri), and that they also made offerings of flowers at each new and full moon

We have no knowledge of this among the Ml Mlabri. He also said that they buried their dead, so that the tigers should not follow them, adding that he had only heard about tree burials.

However, the Mlabri on Phu Kradung, as well as on Phu Luang, suffered from diseases and many accidents due to tigers, snakes, falling trees and from falling down the steep slopes. Thus his sister and three smaller brothers had all died. When at last only 15 of their group had remained, they decided to move to *Ban San Thong*, while he stayed with his adopted Thai family. Due to the meticulous people who made my fine (military) map and sheer luck, I have been able to find the village a little away from other villages and roads, about 27 km west of Phu Kradung and situated at an altitude of about 400 m. On the map their small habitation is simply written *"Phi Thong Luang"*, 101°28'E, 16°55'N, M5, ref. no. 46, its closest neighbour being a T'in village 4 km away. I bought the map in 1982, which would make it likely that the data are from about 1975, while his group had probably already left by 1977, as verified by Lot.

Lot had tried to find members of his group again, but in vain, believing they had returned to Laos. In the evening we all had a substantial meal at the hotel, together with Lot and our efficient driver. Lot said next morning, before our driver took him back to Ban Kok Ngam, that he had slept nicely with the cool air-conditioning turned on, perhaps reminding him of his youth on Phu Kradung.

The Expedition 1987

The first week all four of our small family went up to northern Nan and visited several hidden mountain tracts. Already the week after we went back again to Loei, this time by jeep, trying to keep as close as possible to the Laotian border, without obtaining much information. However, down in Loei results were better. Back in Nan two more Mlabri M3 individuals were traced, one in each of two villages. During the remaining six weeks we stayed in four different camps of the M3 Mlabri, while the group of Ml Mlabri at Doi Khun Sathan was visited four times as well. We had already recorded many prayers from both groups, but now it became of major importance to consult the older Mlabri about the many problems attending their translation, while this was still possible. By replaying the prayers again and again, we could ask those Mlabri who had made the prayer for us previously about their proper interpreta-

tions, as far as the Mlabri themselves understood them.

Ban Pa Gang, M3, ref. no. 41. Revisited the refugee settlement near Pua, where the Hmong Fu Jo said that when he was young, a Hmong who was hunting had been threatened by a Mlabri. When he had tried to block his powder gun, the Hmong had killed him and gone home. After the Hmong had returned with a better gun, several Mlabri turned up, and when they accused him of having killed their friend, he had tried to escape. But as the Mlabri now pursued him with their spears, he killed another three of them. Thereafter they had all disappeared, the incident taking place 35 years before (around 1952, exact location unknown). One of their spears is now kept in the Tribal Research Centre in Nan.

At Ban Pa Gang we heard that the M3 group had split into two, with seven persons staying in *Ton Praiwan (101°07'E, 18°50'N, ref. no. 53,* and four in *Ban Maeo Lao Leng, 101° 05'E, 19°12'N, M3, ref. no. 75,* see p. 229). In Ban Pa Gang the Hmong Lao Ju said of Lek (M4), that when he was two years old, his mother had stolen some corn from a Hmong field. As she was caught, she was forced to hand over Lek to the Hmong for two pigs! When he was 20 years old, she ran away with a Hmong Communist, and a few years later she died. From our collection of fingerprints, not only including all the Mlabri we have met, but also T'in, Hmong and Khon Muang, I think I have ascertained that Lek belongs to the M4 group (Gaeng and Thoeng's group, see also p. 211).

Salai, 101°18'E, 19°04'N, M3, ref. no. 47. Accompanied by six young border gendarmes ready to shoot if we should be attacked, we hurried by car to this T'in village, 2 km east of the Hmong village Ban Dan and only 1 km from the border to Laos. The villagers said they had seen the Mlabri, probably M3, about 35 years previously, i.e. around 1950. They had noticed that they had eaten rotten wood and a special kind of soil ('ibn), when there was nothing else to eat, as we had also heard from Kit (M3). Their women and the old Mlabri were seldom seen, because they had no clothes.

The villagers obviously spoke a kind of dialect from which the Mlabri Ml and M3 had adopted many words such as biɯk "bear", roy "tiger", cin "boar" ("meat" in Ml), khɔt "spear" and lam "tree". However, other T'in words were quite different, such as blɔng "spirit" and 'yng "I, mine". The last word is of some interest, as it is the name, the alleged Mlabri, Gaeng and Toeng, we met above Ban Pa Tong Silarpet, called themselves probably having utilised T'in words while talking with the Hmong Lao Ju there.

One day tour went almost up the northernmost border towards Laos at Ban Sop Pin, 101°00'E, 19°36'N, where we were stopped at a checkpoint due to fighting further to the east. On our return towards Nan we turned to the east at Pua and then north again, passing Doi Khun Satun along the mountain ridge, reaching *Ban (Hmong) Pang Kae, 100°59'E, 19°24'N, Ml, ref. no. 48.* Here, Lao Saeng, 60 years old, said that when he was 15 (in 1942) he had seen about 400 Mlabri Ml near *Hui Sam Ngao* east of there. However, this large number really does not fit other evidence and that most of the Mlabri Ml had already arrived further to the south in Nan and Phrae provinces before 1940.

By car from Nan via Mae Charim to a T'in and Hmong village, *Ban Nam Sang, 101°18'E, 18°57'N, Ml, ref. no. 49.* Som, assistant headman, saw the Mlabri 30 years previously (1957), when usually two to five men came to ask for rice, tobacco and meat. He repeated most of the previously mentioned characteristics of the Mlabri Ml, including that at this time they could speak some of their neighbours' languages. They had stayed here near the Laotian border since his grandparents' time (two generations or 35 years earlier, from about 1922), which is in accordance with the other information that the Mlabri came to Thailand around 1916.

Near *Ban Maeo Kiu Na, 101°08'E, 18°46'N, Ml, ref. no. 50, in Ban Nam Sang,* 23 km southwest of here, Jan, a Khun Muang, saw many Mlabri when he was 15. Since he was now 55, this would have been around 1947. The Mlabri used poison from a tree to kill animals. They had crossbows, made clothes of tappa sheets and were able to kill elephants. They placed their dead in trees. This perhaps, except the crossbow, indicates Ml Mlabri; 10-20 of them were once seen in *Ban Tong, 101°02'E, 18°51'N, ref. no. 51,* as well as around *Nam Xong, just inside Laos, 101°20'E, 18°53'N, ref. no. 52.*

Ton Praiwan, 101°07'E, 18°50'N, M3, ref. no. 53. This was the first time out of many we stayed with Kit, Sak and their family, altogether nine persons, near this Hmong village, nicely situated on the banks of the River Mae Sa Na. Kit said that along the Nam Xong in Laos, being a river flowing approximately along the 18°53'N parallel, their group had originally contained about 20 families (approx. 120 persons). However, most of them were now dead.

When staying by themselves they preferred to live in the mountain forest, but at a lower altitude than the Ml Mlabri. They did not have spears, but a small digging spade (cho'), for which reason they called themselves mla' cho' ("people spade" in Mlabri), while the other Mlabri were called kha hok ("people spear" in Thai), which he said only Oy had seen, being 16 years older than Kit. He said that indeed they ate a special kind of 'ibn "soil" when they were starving, but that they did not eat rotten wood mixed with honey any longer. Like the Ml Mlabri, they mostly boil their food, the best food being turtles and their eggs. As we have seen ourselves, they also eat many kinds of roots and leaves.

Because of the lack of young men, Kit would probably give his daughters to a Hmong or a T'in man! At their informal weddings they have to use chicken, bamboo rats and whisky, while using eggs for offerings, if somebody becomes seriously ill. After a birth, which takes place inside the windscreen, the father will wash the baby. Now they bury their dead, no longer putting them in a tree. As they had next to no tools, they sometimes asked the Hmong to lend them their large knives.

Trek to Loei Province

Our second trip to Changwat Loei was made by jeep in order to find more information on what had happened to the Mlabri down there. From Sa we went southeast, trying to keep as close as possible to the Laotian border, passing very poor villages and Nam Pat and Chat Trakan before we arrived at Ampho Nakhon Thai, 100°51'E, 17°00'N. After two days we reached Amphoe Dan Sai (ref. no. 55, see below). Driving up to a village situated on a small mountain, we arrived in *Ban Huay Hia, 101°17'E, 17°19'N, M5, ref. no. 54,* where an old Thai farmer had seen a group of 15 Mlabri several times about 20 years before (1967), probably Lot's group (Mlabri M5).

Next day we proceeded eastwards to revisit Ban Kok Ngam, 101°15'E, 17°22'N, M5, ref. no. 45, where we had met the Mlabri, Lot, five years before. However, he had gone somewhere else, but a Khon Muang, Lung Beo, said that he himself had met three Mlabri – two men with loin cloths and one woman in a sarong – in the jungle 6 km from Ban Kok Ngam about two to three years previously (1984). As it turned out, they were probably from the band of Mlabri Ml from Nan, having trekked down to Loei 1972-84 and being on their way back, and not Lot's group, which had already gone back to Laos in about 1977.

Returning to Dan Sai, we went by car to the southwest via Ban Nam Yen to *Ban Pa Wai, 101°02'E, 17°00'N, M5, ref. no. 55*, at the northern end of the National Park and situated at the foot of the 1,746 m high mountain. Yet another old man said that having stayed here all his life he had seen the Mlabri regularly until ten years before (1977). There had been more than 30 persons, they had spears and were bad-smelling, and he said they had looked somewhat like the Ml Mlabri on our photographs. He even remembered a few of their names: Pae, Oe, Toe and Sua, probably belonging to Lot's group the M5 group (from Phu Kradung) for there are no Mlabri Ml of these names, adding that they had moved northwards towards Phu Sai Dao (map's Phu Soai Dao) near the border between Thailand and Laos.

Back again in *Dan Sai, 101°09'E, 17°17'N, Ml, ref. no. 56*, we were told that the Mlabri had been seen there about seven years back (1980), which was repeated all the way up to *Amphoi Nae Haeo at the pass to Laos, 101°04'E, 17°29'N, Ml or M5, ref. no. 57*.

Next day we went to Ban Na Faek, 100°53'E, 17°22'N, where the police said that there were no longer any Mlabri in the area, while in *Ban Na Klai, 100°52'E, 17°14'N, Ml, ref. no. 58*, they had seen the Mlabri ten years earlier (1977). They also related that a Thai hunter had stumbled into a Mlabri woman digging for roots. She had made a cry, and immediately ten Mlabri men had emerged to threaten him with their spears. However, after he fired his gun they had got down on their knees to beg for their lives. In all likelihood, this was Poa's group from Doi Sathan on their way down to Loei province. An elderly woman who had listened to our interrogations said that they had stripes on their upper arms. In the village they kept an old Mlabri (?) spearhead, 81 cm long, which we bought, but unfortunately nobody seems to know its provenance (but most likely from the M5 group) see fig. 155.

Returning once again to Dan Sai, we went to see the officer in charge at the district police station. He said that some years ago they had received a Mlabri man who had fallen from a tree. Not being able to communicate with him, they had to let him go. The officer added that the police had shot two Mlabri men in the jungle some years before, taking them to be Communists, adding that another Mlabri had been killed by a landmine. Actually four Mlabri were killed, not by accident, but by shots from the local forest police, because the villagers did not want them to destroy their own hunting of wild game. About four years previously (1983), their band (Poa's group the Ml from Nan) had left the area.

An old man living in Dan Sai said that a long time previously he had stumbled into a Kha Thae ("person short"), who did not have a spear. The Mlabri had tried to defend himself by biting. This story was corroborated when visiting an interesting Mon-Khmer village situated high above Dan Sai, near *Phu Nam Taen, 101°06'E, 17°18'N, M3, ref. no. 59*. Here we heard similar stories, adding that these people had been living in caves, had no clothing and ate uncooked food. They were said to be called Mo Ru, allegedly also meaning "people short". The last excursion took us up once again to Ban Na Haeo, ref. no. 54, to the pass leading into Laos, but this time we went northwest about 20 km along the border as far as Ban Bo Muang Noi. Here we could see the dark, dense jungle inside Laos which at least still seemed to be intact, in contrast to what had happened in Thailand. The journey back to Nan via Pitsanulok, Uttaradit and Prae in an air-conditioned car was pleasant – and uneventful.

Nan Province

Ton Praiwan, ref. no. 53. Back in Nan province we went to see Kit (M3), who received us with a string of rattan around his forehead to treat a headache. I asked him once again if their weak knees could be due to their diet of many different kinds of roots, some of which contained certain toxic substances. We knew from the Ml Mlabri that if such roots were not cooked for several hours they would prompt severe stomach troubles and with time also arthritis. However, Kit rather preferred to tell of one of their delicacies, the bamboo rat, which is cut into pieces and put into a bamboo internode with salt and chilli, finally to be put near a fire to be cooked. A python was first put in the fire, and after removing the scales and the intestines, the pieces were cooked until tender, causing him to add that the king cobra had killed several of the Mlabri in his father's time.

A young Hmong from the village said that, according to an uncle, a Mlabri group had been seen near the border to Laos more than 30 years earlier (around 1955) at *Ban Lum Kao, 101°14'E, 18°51'N, M3, ref. no. 60*. From the details he gave, they fit entirely the M3 Mlabri, and therefore could have been Oy and Kit's original group from Laos, an interesting piece of information being that some Hmong had killed three of them! Another Hmong,

Lao Kao, 38 years old, said that he knew perhaps some members of the same group also living near the border about three days' walk distant, with whom the Hmong had had contact only five years before (1982) and also looking like the M3 group. Eventually he and his friend proposed that they should take their powerful motorcycle to search for them. After returning three days later they said that they had been told by the Hmong living closer to the border, that one of the Mlabri in question had been injured by a landmine, causing their small group, seven or eight persons, to withdraw to Laos.

Huay Yok near Doi Luang, 100°34'E, 18°49'N, ref. no. 61 we met one M1 band of 18 persons. When we interviewed Pha it was confirmed what had been said previously that if they did not make a hole in each earlobe, twigs would start growing out of their ears. Now most of the younger generation had given up the tradition. But they still considered that dangerous places like caves, waterfalls and trees that had been rubbed by a muddy boar had spirits, adding that if the sunset is very red no one is allowed to go hunting.

Now we asked Pha if he had been trekking west of Nan province towards Phayao near the big lake there, and to our great surprise he said "Yes". He and some friends went to the area when he was young, perhaps about 21 years old, or about 1955. Here they met a Mlabri group speaking another language they did not understand, but as they were threatened with their lives, they had to leave the place.

At first we were a little sceptical about the story, since only a few of the elders seemed to remember it, but in the end two more Mlabri related similar stories about having met some hostile Mlabri west of Doi Pha Chik, reg. no. 65 see next page. Meanwhile, Gordon Young, 1962 (pp. 69-73) also talks about two groups – one in the Chieng Rai province, speaking a Wa language, and another one, the Mlabri in Nan province, speaking a Mon-Khmer language. Actually it might rather have been the so-called 'fierce' Mlabri M7, the Kheeo, living on the Laotian side of the border, having trekked from their base in Laos just east of Nan province sometime during the period 1950-1967. We have some evidence of this for they were seen twice in the Hmong village Khun Sathan for a few days when passing by during these two years.

Gui confirmed that previously men had to bury males and women their dead females. Those who had been injured by a tiger had to go up or be taken up into a tree, whereupon the outer bark around the trunk was removed. When the tigers returned and one of them climbed up the tree and attacked the unfortunate person, both would eventually fall down, because of the slippery inner bark, and onto eight sharpened bamboo sticks that had been stuck into the ground and placed in a circle around the trunk. Gui, like many of the elder generation, used his hands all the time to demonstrate the procedures (see fig. 84). He also said that when he was young he had killed four buffaloes and one tiger. If they were not able to catch any animals to eat, they would offer flowers to some of the old tall trees, believed to harbour their parents' spirits and helping to guide them to the animals.

Asked whether they sometimes beat their children he said "very seldom", adding wisely that the children should later on take care of their ageing parents! Gui also said that the children really belong to their father as he has provided the sperm, but when I said that this was not quite fair he laughingly admitted that his two wives would surely disagree about this interpretation! Concerning miscarriages, he said that they are not killed, but put in a tree hole and covered with bamboo like a coffin, so the foetus would eventually die from lack of air!

Don Praiwan, M3, ref. no. 53. Sak now explained that they came from Ban Gob to Ban Pa Wai (ref. no. 52) and thereafter to Ban Pa Tong Silapet, then went back to Laos, staying there for three months following their Hmong employers and returning to Silapet and finally to Don Praiwan. He told us about the weird fate of one of their group who had been killed by the 'fierce' Mlabri in his parents' time. His companion had escaped to tell the others that the dead had been dismembered to be eaten! It was added that these Mlabri had spots on their arms and legs. We shall later give some further details on these alleged cannibals, which may indicate that the story is perhaps not entirely incredible. As a matter of fact, cannibalism in various forms was known less than a hundred years ago in Southeast Asia. This time we were also told of one important point on which the M1 and the M3 group differ: the first has had dogs for many generations, while the latter has never had them, according to what they themselves believe.

In Ban How Hoy, M1, ref. no. 25, we met Gu and Paeng's families, eight persons. Paeng said that when he was ten years old (1938) he lived near Ban Kae, 101°17' E, 19°17'N, Ban Kok and Chung Pei, 101°10'E, 19°00'N. Lao Toa added that after passing Phu Wae they had crossed the Nam Wa, and then gone to Ban Kae, to Nam Pong, to Na Noi and to Dao Sathan. The Hmong said that even though Paeng's group had previously killed elephants, the striped or 'fierce' Mlabri, the M7 group, just across the Laotian border, would be a threat to the M1 group!

Suk was an intelligent boy with great spirits and he feared nothing. But he had trouble with his uncle Mun, who had adopted him after his father Ai Suk died. Mun had insisted on sending Suk away, even though he had cried a lot. Now he was very much on his own, which might explain his careless behaviour and violent death in 1988, in which the Hmong Gwa allegedly had taken part, because Lat had had an affair with a daughter of Gwa's relative. Incidentally, this man, whom we too did not feel comfortable with, told us that Paeng's parents had stripes of spots tattooed on their arms and legs, which is an important point when an attempt is made to trace the origins and developments of the two groups during the last century.

Gwa also said that, to his knowledge, the Mlabri M1 came from Laos via *Ban Kae, Chung Pai, Doi Pha Chik, ref. no. 65, to Ban Po Keng (ref. no. 31)* and here to Bow Hoy. With respect to the long absence of Poa's band between 1972 and 1984, he said it was caused by the disagreements between Paeng and Poa, who had taken Paeng's wife. More importantly, he said that some bands had also been missing during the years 1950-1967, probably when they had gone west towards the Phayao area in Chieng Rai province.

Paeng now returned to the time when the Mlabri entered Thailand around 1916, the only survivor being Patot (we saw him for the last time in 1982 when he was about 70 years old), who had told him: When staying near Ban Kae, the Mlabri had split when trying to cross the River Nam Wa (another source adding that it was due to fights with the Hmong on the Laotian side of the undemarcated border). The one group going southwards had lost 5-10 of its members while trying to cross the Nam Wa River. When Gu was asked about former times, he said that the Khamu and T'in were the first they had met, at a time when the Hmong were just about to move into the mountains of Northern Thailand, while the Thai still stayed mainly in the lowlands. He also said that his band had killed a tiger once near Ban Hui Yok, and that some black tigers had killed three dogs. Gu confirmed that the first to come to eat of the offerings are the parents' spirits – moths, bugs or other small insects harbouring these spirits.

Thai village Kio Ko, 100°58'E, 18°21'N, Gaeo M3, ref. no. 62. Driving southwards from Sa and as a result of asking for the Mlabri in every other village we passed by, we found quite unexpectedly here in the plains one more person of M3 type. This was indicated both by anthropometrical measurements as well as what he himself said. Originally, he and his two friends had come to Kio Ko from Ban Nam Pong, 101°11'E, 18°35'N, just across the border with Laos. In his childhood in Laos there had been more than a hundred of them, but he could not remember exactly how many or how many windscreens there had been. He left his family simply to get more rice, but he sometimes visited them again, the last time when he was 20, now (1987) being 50 years old. One of his two companions had died and the third, Ot, now stayed in Ban Na Luang about 15 km north of Nan city since 1975, being married to a Thai woman there.

Gaeo's father was Kham and mother Khami, elder brother 'e ma, younger brother 'e Lat and younger sister Kham Pae, who had eventually been killed by a tiger. Neither his father nor his grandfather had spears, but Gaeo himself had kept their iron 'digging spade' cho'. Their group had mostly lived on various roots, bamboo rats, mice and other small animals, and he demonstrated a tiny mouse trap he still used to catch mice to eat. He did not go out by himself in the jungle anymore, but he was an able climber when collecting honey. When speaking, he almost whispered. The villagers said that he would sing Mlabri songs, but only when drunk! The house owner for whom he worked said that twenty years back there was a dense jungle with many animals left here. By the way, Gaeo was 151 cm high, his feet were 22.3 cm long, hands 18.1 cm long, spinal iliaca ant. sup. 93.2 cm, and he was A rhesus negative.

Ban Na Luang about 10 km north of Nan city, 100°47', 18°51', M3, ref. no. 63. We found Ot with his Thai wife (figs. 115-116), living quite nicely in the northern suburbs of Nan. Later on we also saw their five children, fine-looking youngsters not much different from other Khon Muang of the area, which is worth remembering when discussing not only from where the Mlabri derive, but rather the Thai themselves in rural areas! Asked about Mlabri words, just like Gaeo he could recognise only a few, such as roay "tiger", but was at least able to count to ten in Mlabri. Eventually his son of about 18 years old told us a rather strange but explicable story. When he was a boy he had gone with his father to a small forest not far from their house to meet ten Mlabri, whom his father obviously had not liked or dared to take home. He had heard his father talking with them – in all likelihood the M3 Mlabri we found in 1977 in the Nam Yao camp, where they had arrived the year before.

Next day we returned to Ot's home. Like Gaeo and their deceased friend, he also said that the three of them had stayed near Doi Sam Sao in Laos in their early youth, from where they had moved to Ban Na Waen somewhere near the border with his parents. Being only 12 years old (1951), he had left his family with Gaeo to settle down in Kiu Ko (see above). He had returned to visit his parents a few years later, but since 1975 he had stayed in Nan, being 48 years old at the time of our interview. Returning to his childhood, he said that if someone was killed by a tiger, his body was put up in a tree, but if he was still alive he would be taken care of, contrary to the traditions of the Mlabri Ml. As we could not help seeing that Ot was suffering from serious TB, we took him to the hospital in Nan. Sadly he arrived there too late to be cured!

Ban Khun Sathan, Ml, ref. no. 28. While we were staying with the Hmong Lao Toa (not the one living in Ban Baw Hoy) in his spacious house, he told us about his long experience with the Mlabri. Concerning their disposal of their dead, he said that the Mlabri were not careful about these matters, sometimes leaving the dead after next to no preparation. Dead children were preferably put in tree holes, others under some rocks or on the platform of a big tree that had been cut down to about two metres above the ground. Only old people were properly buried. The first Mlabri came to Doi Sathan about 60-65 years before (around 1925), at a time when the Hmong and the Yao were on bad terms. Neither Lao Toa nor old Ut had heard about the Mlabri at Phayao, perhaps as those Mlabri living at Doi Sathan were staying the furthest away from Phayao. Paeng Noi, son of Ut, said that the older generation had told him about Doi Sam Sao in Laos, the very same area as that described by the M3 group as their place of origin and in accordance with the information that the latter had met the spear group there.

The second visit to Ban Khun Sathan, Ml, ref. no. 28. This time, and during the next two visits, we stayed in our own windscreen beside those of the Mlabri, situated in the jungle, but not far from the Hmong village. Poa confirmed his band's long trek down to Loei province and back again (1972-84), the group consisting of Pan, Muang, Pokay, Ond, Ta, Nyor and Poa himself with women and children, all together about 25 persons. Poa also said that he had not met the Tha lae, the 'striped' ones, himself, but had heard about them from his father ta prɛc.

When discussing various subjects with the women, they said that to make sure before marrying for the first time that the young couple will get on well, they stay together in the jungle for 4-7 days. They also said that they knew perfectly well that they might get deformed children from marrying close kin.

Trip to Chieng Kham, Phayao and Ban Luang for reconnaissance. Leaving Nan, my guide and I went northwest of Nan (route 1148) via Ban San Klang to Wang Pha and almost up to the northern border to Laos, *Ban Pang San, 100°42'E, 19°31'N, Ml, ref. no. 64,* where the villagers said they had only seen the Mlabri 15-20 years earlier (around 1960). From there continuing to Chieng Kham and 15 km further north, we stayed over-night in a Hmong village, where they had heard about the Mlabri only 20-30 years earlier. However, they claimed there were Mlabri in Tak province near a Hmong village called Jaediko. Next day we arrived at Phayao after dark.

The following day we revisited the area behind the great lake with Doi Luang to the west, where the villagers said they had seen the Mlabri 20-40 years ago (rather 1950-67). It was something of a chock to see how the once so beautiful jungle-clad mountains had turned into almost barren wasteland with very little forest left. Hurrying on and passing Amphoe Chun, we reached this large Hmong settlement Ban Hui Tong with *Doi Pha Chik, 100°28'E, 19°05'N, Ml, ref. no. 65,* seen far away in the last sunlight. In the evening the Hmong said they had met the Mlabri there until seven years before (1980).

Next day, proceeding southwards, we reached *Ban Luang, 100°18'E, 18°45'N, Ml, ref. no. 66,* where our pleasant and very co-operative driver, Vilar, lived. Also here we were told that the Mlabri came to the village until seven years earlier (1980). The 55-year-old house owner even had a fine old Mlabri spear from his father, who acquired it about 35 years previously (1955-60). At sundown we at last reached the *market at Song Kwer, 100°39'E, 18°50'N, 25 km north-west of Nan, Ml, ref. no. 67.* Here we found Maiga, the good-looking daughter of Pha, now about 26 years old. She had left her band in the jungle to live with an at present, 45-year-old Hmong, much to the regret of our old friend and most often employed informant Pha, whom we had known since 1977.

Mlabri camp near a small Yao village northwest of Nan, approx. 100°22'E, 18°51'N, Ml, ref. no. 68. Two young couples, Lat and Si with wives and children, in all eight persons. The two windscreens were situated on the narrow sandstone banks of a river that had cut its way through a steep and narrow mountain gorge, see also fig. 140. Si, son of Gu (no. 50 and Si, see p. 55), said that according to Patot and Ut, the 'ang thok "bamboo" people (probably the M3) once lived near Doi Pha Chik, ref. no. 65. They had no spears and lived near streams. He also related the story we had already heard from the Mlabri and the Hmong about the Tha lae (lai, Th), the 'striped' (or 'fierce') Mlabri, who had killed other Mlabri and stolen their women.

On this visit Lat and Si said that pregnant women should not eat ngay 'boar', do 'porcupine' and above all not phool "(the red) barking deer", the latter being some sort of sacred animal. Asked if they still went on long treks, they said only about ten days' walk in the rainy season, when there are more animals in the forest, avoiding the Pha Chik area, because of the many landmines that had been left there. Concerning their beliefs, both of the young men told us that the younger generations hardly believe in the spirits anymore, except for those of their deceased parents, Si at last saying that when one dies there is nothing more. As a matter of fact, we found that many of the young Mlabri were less superstitious now than most other peoples of the world! Obviously, the young men, like many of our own younger generation, were embarrassed by their parents' generation, which in many ways belonged mentally to another era!

The Yao, for whom the Mlabri worked, repeated many of the Hmong's observations including the one that the Mlabri worked only when in need of something special, but often rather preferred to be free and keep moving. In reality they still worked for the Hmong for only three to four months a year.

Si confirmed what we have only heard of once before, that they used to paint their bodies with an orange colour from the tree, sa-al (Th), for special occasions if someone was very ill, as an appeal to the spirits for recovery. He also repeated that those making iron tools cannot perform the ceremonies. When burying someone they now dug the grave about 70 cm deep, put leaves or sheets of bark on the bottom, then the corpse wrapped in a piece of cotton, then bamboo cane above, and finally leaves and soil. But if the deceased had been a very important person, they would also put stones on top of the grave. Traditionally they would also half-burn the trees around so as to blacken them, finally fixing a piece of red cloth on top to indicate that no one should disturb the grave. Then he added that the old and the young

disagree on various issues, the latter criticising the old for not having taught them enough to meet the many new challenges – "but don't tell them what I have said"!

Lat had been listening and agreed to what had been said. He continued by saying that they cannot marry their cousins, and a man should not marry a girl and thereafter her sister – or he will meet a snake. However, they said it quite often happens that two friends, like Si and himself, exchange wives for a few days! The most desired animal to eat is called blɔŋ (see p. 222), which has a strong smell and looks like a pig, but has an almost white colour and paws like a dog. But they are not allowed to kill the kro' "crocodile" and previously neither the to dɛo "woodpecker" nor the kalang "parrot". Parents usually tell their children how to get children when they are 12-13 years old. The newly married wait 10-30 days before getting their new family name. If the man dies, his widow has to return to her maiden name. In the event of divorce, the man takes the elder children, the mother the younger.

After this visit we also took Si and Lat with us back to our hotel in Nan, where they had a room besides ours, much to the concern of some of the hotel staff. However, they did very well and soon enjoyed the benefits there including the shower, the TV and the soft beds, without being bothered, they said, by the insects in their camps. During the days they worked with us and our tape recorder for about six hours without complaining too much.

Ban Nam Uan, 100°34'E, 18°32'N, M1, ref. no. 69. One band of 16 persons, among others: Ton, Gui, Tung, Wang and Gaeo. Here Gui said that in old times many things were more difficult, due to mosquitoes, little food, no clothes and no others to meet. Except when they had their big annual meeting, making it possible especially for the younger Mlabri to find a partner to marry. But due to TB, killings by other hill tribes and the difficult circumstances because of the fighting between the Communists and the government forces in the 1960-1970s, their population had been reduced. With divorces, Ton said that if a man wishes to divorce, the couple have to divide the children, but if the woman wants a divorce, he can take all of them, but will usually leave the infants with the mother. Most Mlabri marry about two or three times, a few men twice that number. He added that they should not have sex outside marriage and if a child comes of infidelity it will not get a good life – no luck, he explained.

Ban Khun Sathan, ref. no. 28, our third stay. Lao Toa said that if two couples are neighbours and the man from one marriage agrees with the woman from the other one to move together to a new windscreen, their former marriages would in fact be annulled. This was being planned by Paeng Taw's wife and Thong, who himself already had two wives. However, the Hmong, their employers, said: "Don't do it or we'll call the police". Since then Paeng left for Hui Hom, as he was afraid to face trouble. Now staying in the camp of the Mlabri Ml we could see that a few of the elder men had their family symbols tattooed on their upper arm, for example four squares, each with a circle in the middle, though already quite blurred. They said it was many years since they were made, using a needle to penetrate the skin, thereafter smearing a mixture of charcoal and the liquid inside a battery into the designs, adding that their parents had done very much the same.

One evening Poa gave some more details on his and his band's long trek down to Loei province, lasting from 1972 to 1984. The reason for leaving was not only the rivalry between Paeng and himself, but more decisively that there were too many Mlabri at Doi Sathan and too few animals left. In 1972 the Mlabri still had very little contact with the villagers, and this was also the case with the group of those 25 persons leaving Doi Sathan. Poa said that they had tried to avoid visiting any villages. Only when they met a hunter in the jungle had they asked for salt, tobacco, etc.

All went well until they met some village protectors – a sort of police – above Dan Sai, ref. no. 53, who asked them to help cut bamboo in exchange for some rice, but in the end creating discord. On the pretext that the Mlabri were Communists, but in reality because the mountain Thai did not like them to drain their forest of animals, they were shot at. Po Kay and Muang (the elder one) were killed. The next incident happened when they were roasting some roots, during which they were also shot at, causing the death of old Ai Si, while Ai Ond died later due to an infection from a bullet. As already mentioned, we discussed the incident with the chief of police in Dan Sai, and he finally agreed with us that it was probably the Mlabri's hunting in the jungle The was the heart of the matter.

After having received messages about the ill fate of the Mlabri, probably from the Hmong, who know better than anybody else what is going on in the mountains, Ut, Paeng Noi and Lat went out to trace them. Even though they went so far that they could see the railway to Uttaradit, they could not find them. Poa said that they had never met any Communists during their long trek, contrary to what was at first claimed by the police in Dan Sai. But this actually happened to Thong and Suk when visiting Doi Pha Chik, once a Communist stronghold, where they were given some food and tobacco, and were told that now they were indeed communists! The Mlabri did not want to join them and while trying to escape they were shot at, Suk (the elder) eventually died from infections caused by the bullet.

The many fatal incidents demonstrate how the Mlabri always have been the loosing part and have been decimated to the point of being annihilated or absorbed by the other mountain peoples. As regards the killing of Suk (Noi) by the Hmong in 1987, the case was not even investigated by the Thai police because, not being registered as citizens, the Mlabri were not protected by the law!

Tak and Mae Hongson provinces. We had repeatedly heard about the Mlabri in Mae Hongson and Tak from various sources, including the Thai, Hmong, Lissu and Akha, and now my Thai guide and I were heading for both areas by flying first to Chieng Mai and then to Tak. Next day we went 60 km by car, going southwards to Jaediko, as we had been advised to by a Hmong near Chieng Kham three weeks earlier. However, it was not surprising that nobody in this quite modern village had heard anything about the Mlabri. Returning to Chieng Mai, we went by small aircraft to Mae Hongson. In a Hmong village, Ban Mai Kwu Wait about 40 km from Mae Hongson and up in the mountains, an old man said he had seen the Mlabri 30 years previously but about 100 km further north on the Burmese side of the border. When given some clothes the Mlabri had undressed as soon as they got outside the village. Flying back to Chieng Mai, we noticed that the forest cover was very open, not leaving much chance of finding any Mlabri there.

Ban Khun Sathan, 4th stay. When we asked Lat (Mlabri M1) about myths (pho tak), he told us a small story in this interesting genre: "Previously, bamboo did not have internodes, so when carrying water one had to put a leaf under the bamboo cylinder. But the Mok Tok (legendary very small man-like spirits in the jungle) had magical powers, which they used to create the internodes". The story is interesting, since it shows that the Mlabri do not consider themselves to possess magical powers, whereas the Khamu, the Hmong and Yao do so extensively. The Mlabri have usually shunned people with such abilities, perhaps as they fear they will be used against them. One exception is the protective tattooing made by the Khamu and the Khon Muang, although the Mlabri claimed that it did not work as well as promised!

As already hinted at, they have a justified suspicion of the other hill tribes, who often try to take advantage of them or harm them. In this connection, let us return to Lat's rendering of an explanation for why the Mlabri almost never stay overnight in a Hmong house, saying they believe that the spirits of the Hmong and the Mlabri will start fighting with one another. On asking Lat why we were allowed to stay in their windscreens overnight, he answered: "You do not make us unhappy, while the Hmong humiliate us repeatedly". Indeed, to the Mlabri the spirits are primarily something that harms them!

The Mlabri main staple was until now numerous kinds of roots and tubers, some of which they said have to be cooked for several hours to be edible. They use honey to remove the bitter taste of some of the roots. Meat might be fried, but usually it is cooked together with salt, but never using pepper. For in-between meals, mainly various smaller roots are just roasted. Women should not hunt deer, bear and porcupines (especially those having long, pointed quills), as they are too dangerous, but they sometimes kill the small bamboo rat (dun) and the bigger one (hnɛl). Likewise, we have never heard a Mlabri woman making a prayer on her own, therefore concluding that this was entirely the job of the men. However, Lat said that Paeng Taw's mother, ya to, was very good at remembering the prayers. The only taboo Lat remembered now was that, while shaping spears and knives in the hot fire, the Mlabri were not allowed to take part in prayers, a common taboo in many parts of Asia.

Being asked about what happens if a child is retarded when born; Lat said they would try to feed it, also asking the spirit of the parents for their advice. But if a baby is born with say only one leg, the mother has to kill the baby. Repeating our question about what happens if a person continuously makes trouble – starts fighting, etc., Lat said that in his father's time such a person had been taken out on a simulated hunt together with a trusted person, who would club the troublemaker down from behind, just as related by young Suk in 1982.

During this stay we had noticed that the women seemed to be less oppressed by the men than previously, not to speak of when we first met them in 1976-77. Now they were sometimes arguing and even scolding the men. When we asked Lat which of the two sexes gets the last word, much to our surprise he said it was more and more often the women. Could this be because now the men no longer undertook long hunting expeditions, staying more together with the women and doing very much the same work?

The Expedition 1989

This 7th expedition went first to Ventiane in Laos. Actually we had visited a few villages just inside Laos already in 1970, but since then it had been difficult to enter the country, apart from some selected areas. Now we wished to give it another try, hoping somehow to get access to places where the Mlabri still lived in their traditional environment. But after long futile discussions with various authorities, it turned out that we could not get the necessary permits, probably due to the adverse conditions in remote places. However, we did get valuable information on various Mlabri-like groups living in several provinces of Laos. We had been told by some Italian missionaries in 1970 that there were about 800 Mlabri left, but now perhaps only 200. During the following five weeks in and around Nan province we visited three camps of Ml Mlabri and had one week with the M3 Mlabri, in between taking a number of Mlabri down to our hotel in Nan to clarify parts of the prayers and tying up some loose ends on other subjects.

Ventiane, Laos

Already in the airport in Ventiane we met a Japanese TV-journalist who said there were some Kha Thong Luang in Sayabouri province and even a few in the capital, including a boy and his sister staying in an orphanage. Our guide added that he knew of some in Pakse province dressed as Laotians, and some in the central parts of the country.

Next day we met the former Minister of Social Sciences, Mr. Sisana Sisané and members of the staff in the Ministry of Cultural Affairs. We were told that there were about 20 Mlabri in Sayaburi province, while those living to the south, who lived like the Mlabri and had windscreens, were not ethnically Mlabri! But an anthropologist in the office, Mr. Khampheng, who had actually met the Mlabri in the Boropha province east of Ventiane, gave us some interesting details. He said that previously the men used a turtle shell to cover their loins and that their most sacred animal, mo lyng, looks like a light-coloured pig but has paws like a dog, the very same animal as described by the Ml Mlabri but called blɔng. Mr. Khampheng said that they have various names, such as Raem, but call themselves kri', while the Vietnamese across the border call somewhat similar people Ruk. Frank Lebar, 1964, p. 128 says: "A small group of 189 persons, Ruc or Roc, in Vietnam".

Mr. Khampheng also gave us some examples of the kri' language: 'an jaw "to eat" lit. "things eat", 'an trak "things drink", phaw "father" (Th), mae "mother" (Th), klok "head" (old Viet.) in Mlabri klol, mang "brother", ji' "sister", 'ɛm "young", ta' "uncle" wɔk "grandfather" (theoretically very interesting as in Mlabri Ml and M3 it means "spirit"), thɛh ("good", M3), mi' "me", mat "eye", "nose" ("soft" Ml and M3) and kawat "tie", of which five of the words are the same as in Mlabri (Ml or M3). But from the word list I obtained from Mr. Khampheng, the connections between the two vocabularies are not overwhelmingly numerous, perhaps due to different inventories of more recent loanwords. But their habits seem to be rather similar to those of the Mlabri Ml in Thailand. They also put people in trees if they have been killed or just injured by a tiger, and if they have had a bad dream they likewise have to make an offering the next day. The most important prayer, that for the deceased parents, also takes place near an old, big tree. Khampheng said finally that they have windscreens, but he had heard that they also use caves in the local sandstone mountains, the same as we had been told about the Mlabri in Loei province.

Mr. Ananda, a very pleasant person half Laotian and half French, invited us to his home and gave us some details from his substantial files on anthropology, including places in Laos where Mlabri had been seen. Among others he has written an article dated 5th August 1985: "Relations êntre les Salang et les Kha Thong Luang de Po Kaeo, de Sayaburi, Sawanakhet, Kha Muang et Sarawan." From this article Ananda quoted the following, of which the three last paragraphs seem to be about the small Mlabri being called Kha Thong Luang (our designation M3) in contrast to the Kiew, Kheeo (our M7):

"In Sawanakhet in the villages Ga Daeb and Kham Pilang, district Muang Pin and Muang Sae Pon, there are two ethnic Hang and ethnic Kiew, who exchange goods with the Kha Thong Luang. And in the province of Sarawan in the villages of Hui Meun and Tung Pang in the mountain Phu Piang as far as the plateau Polo Waen." "Sayaburi 1978-79: In the villages Pun Sa-at, Na Moh and Nam Lae as far as the district Pak Lai: Took a Mlabri boy from there to the school. He talked in a low voice, climbed high up in trees and played the flute well. He had loin cover of bast. Found another Mlabri boy 12 years old but very small, and took him down to Ventiane." "1979: Found a young man about twenty years old in Pun Sa-at, Muang Piang. He had walked 70 km and came without clothes, very weak and ill. His group had sent him away, not being able to feed him any longer. He talked at a high pitch but in a low voice and was also taken down to Ventiane."

"Ban Na Moh, Nam Lae: Met three children and their mother, who had been raped by a former Lao soldier, which had caused the Laotian villagers to chase their family of four persons away! They came to beg for salt and matches."

Finally Mr. Ananda told a rather unusual tale about the Phi Nya Wai, who were said to have consumed blood from animals and humans. We heard very much the same story from the Hmong in Thailand, but due to lack of reliable sources and because it seems to be a sort of myth we have abstained from referring to it, although cannibalism has not been entirely unknown in South East Asia until quite recently. However, we shall return to the subject when referring to sources concerning a special case, namely that of the Mlabri M7 living in the westernmost part of the Sayaburi province in Laos.

Together with people from the Ministry of Social Science we went to visit one of the Mlabri staying within easy range of Ventiane. After 70 km by car due north and arriving at *the great lake in U-don District,* we went by boat to the opposite shore, *102°21'E, 18°49'N, M6, ref. no. 70.* Here we met a woman, 'i An, about 30 years old and pregnant. She was quite small, only 139 cm tall, but in good health. With limited time at our disposal we managed to make the 23 most important anthropometrical measurements. We also attempted some of the psychological tests, but, as anticipated, she had great difficulties even with the easy ones, such as the cube test. Evidently she was quite shy, as well as nervous, not being used to meet officials and foreigners. When we tried to find out whether she knew some of the basic Mlabri words, it turned out that she could recognise only a few. She had probably forgotten, not having used her mother tongue since her childhood.

From her general features we found that she resembled more the M3 Mlabri, and her intonation was also closer to that of those we knew in Nan province. She was somewhat childish but in a sweet way, using her hands a lot and sometimes even touching us. Having prepared a small bag for her with some clothes, food, sweets and money, we said goodbye to this charming person, while she surprised us by giving us an old photograph of her sister and herself together with their 'owner', a Laotian man of about 50 years of age, who seemingly treated her well (fig. 122).

In conclusion, one may say that the situation of the Mlabri in Laos has been much worse than in Thailand, due to many years of senseless wars that have impoverished the population as a whole and the Mlabri in particular, and especially due to guerrilla fighting in their jungles, which has driven them to the point of extinction. Undoubtedly, it is true what old people in both countries claim, that there were considerably more of them at the beginning of the 20th century.

Back in Nan Province

After having returned from Laos we went on a reconnaissance trip, once again to eastern Nan. We followed the river Nam Muap to Ban Tan Pong (100°56'E, 18°28'N) asking for information in almost all the villages we passed through, but still we did not obtain any results. We even lost our way, at last moving to the northeast to Ban Nam Lan and Ban Nam Pun (101°08'E, 18°41'N), 10 km from the Laotian border. No one wanted to tell us anything, probably as the villagers were controlled by the Thai only during the daytime, but by the Communists after dark.

Ban Nam Phang, 100°08'E, 18°35'N, M3, ref. no. 71. In this Hmong village 5 km from the border where the road ended, a police officer said that one generation back there had been quite a few Kha Thong Luang, all with long hair. Now they were villagers! However, young Hmong traders said there were still some Mlabri living in the jungle near the border, but we were advised to not even try to walk further due to landmines.

Ban Khun Sathan, 100°29'E, 18°16'N, M1, ref. no. 28. 11 Mlabri including Poa, Lat and Nyot. Just before going up to this quite large Hmong village we were told that the American missionary Mr. Long and his wife had taken 11 Mlabri down to work in Ban Hui Oiy (ref. no. 37). When we arrived at Ban Sathan we talked with our old friend the Hmong Lao Ju to find out how far the Mlabri had developed during the last years. Concerning Som, he said that he had two wives and altogether four older children and 10 smaller ones! Being now about 45 he had already married six times, causing

Lao Ju to say that the Mlabri were now becoming somewhat loose!

Furthermore, he confirmed that they still put their dead children in tree holes, while all others are buried, the most important Mlabri having stones covering their graves. Then he said that they also still did not distinguish between right and left, and he had therefore to direct them by saying that they should go up or down hill while walking with them in the jungle. The very first time the Mlabri had worked for the Hmong at Doi Sathan was 14-15 years earlier (1975), but further north they first started in 1978. Finally he claimed that the Mlabri usually have a good memory, but had difficulties learning to do practical work.

Next morning Som told me that when he was about 10 years old (in 1954), he saw the Mlabri (M3) without spears near Pua whom the Mlabri had called Lao mla' bri', probably because some of them could speak Laotian. But, incidentally, he suddenly started talking about the Mlabri on the long mountain chain behind the large Phayao Lake, which had intrigued me, because the Mlabri until now had expressed only vague ideas about this topic. He said that about 30 years previously (in 1962 when he was 16 years of age) he had gone west alone trying to find a girl to marry.

During this trek he passed Amphoe Pong, which he had known from previous treks going west, but had continued further northwestwards, coming close to the Phayao district, where he had twice met some "striped" Mlabri (M7). Somehow he must have heard about them before, since he also called them Lao Mlabri, which as we shall see, might turn out to be very true. He said they were very aggressive and unfriendly, but more importantly he could not understand their language. Already on this occasion it struck me that the Mlabri in question could be the Kiew, as we have heard about in Laos, or rather Kheeo, the green-striped and hostile Mlabri said to live just across the border inside Laos. Just like the Mlabri M1, they too might, from time to time, have made long treks into faraway territories in search of wild game.

Actually, we had heard both the Mlabri and the Hmong talking vaguely about the 'fierce' Mlabri. Indeed our host now said that they had passed by Ban Sathan around 1967. We shall return to the matter later, at this place only repeating that Gordon Young (1962, p. 169-73) talks about two different groups of Mlabri east and north of Amphoe Phayao, one speaking the kind of Mon-Khmer language spoken by the Mlabri in Nan province, the other one speaking a Wa-like language (also related to Mon-Khmer), as told by Lahu hunters in the Keng-tung area of Burma. Incidentally, some Wa tribes there were head-hunters until about 1935.

Together with Lao Ju and Som, we tried to solve some remaining questions. Som said that it was ten years since he had stayed in the dense jungle, which he said remained only in western Nan. However, it was danger-ous to move around there due to landmines, and perhaps the soldiers might take him to be a Communist hiding in the jungle and shoot at him. He also said that they do not use bamboo thickets to protect their camps anymore (like the M3 Mlabri do) but use only fires; neither do they stay in caves, which are too cold and harbour nox-ious animals. During continuous rains they cover their windscreens with three layers of bamboo leaves. Previ-ously they had an annual meeting where many families met one another, but now they were busy working for the Hmong in various villages, which made such meet-ings difficult to arrange. At last Som said: before it was nicer, for there were many Mlabri and few Hmong – now it was rather the opposite.

Lao Phu Yai To Saen Sung, another Hmong, said that he had seen the Mlabri Ml at Po Keng, 100°30'E, 19°43'N, ref. no. 31, when he was a boy (about 1945), but Mlabri women in their camp first as late as 1976-77, as a matter of fact together with my wife and me. The first westerners they had met were evidently Nimmanahae-minda Kraisri and Julian Hartland-Swann's group in 1961-62, see fig. 11. They had come by helicopter with a bodyguard of ten men, staying only a few days. Old Ai On had hurried away to hide in a cave, only to come out five days later when the strangers had already left. Finally, it was repeated that old Suk was beaten to death by the Hmong while sleeping in his windscreen, because after having received payment he had tried to run away before completing the job.

Ban Bow Hoy, ref. no. 25. One band of 17 Mlabri in one open-air camp. When Paeng Taw was 15 years old they made tattoos using a gall bladder from a constrictor and charcoal. He said he came from Hui Chu Mun. On this occasion Paeng claimed that his grandfather was a T'in. Even though we knew him very well, this was the first time we heard about this, but it is a possibility that cannot be completely ruled out. We have heard that T'in and Mlabri previously stayed near each other, and some T'in also lived in windscreens. By the way, both Paeng Taw and his son Ton were about 10 cm taller than the average Mlabri males.

The Mlabri camp faced east and was situated near a rough earth road made by the Hmong for their trucks to bring down the harvest of rice. We all slept under some moderately high trees with big leaves – actually the first time we had seen a camp without windscreens, probably because it was now the dry season. Just like the wind-screens, this camp occupied three separate areas, one for each of the families of Gui, Ton and Paeng Taw. The branches of the trees served as hangers for various tools, for cloth and for food. For the first time we saw that the dogs were fed. Sometimes, the adults pretended that they were about to beat the naughty children, but never did so. We noticed that one black male dog was called 'e pyang and a brown female dog 'e ta rut, somewhat similar to the temporary names of their small children.

The children seemed to be more relaxed now than before and often came over to us. They played tag, and 3-4 year olds pretended to make food, cut wood, etc. Our plastic bags were filled with water and air to be hurled up into the air. As we for once relaxed, I also started making various types of paper aeroplanes for the boys. While the adults claimed they never caress each other, they did caress their infants, while those who were 6-10 years old walked two boys or two girls close to-gether. The laziest ones were the young men, probably as they had a day off from the hard work in the field, now letting the older people do the work of collecting wood and fetching water.

Thobitoa, previously married to Gu, was now 55 years old and seemed to be a little sour and reserved, perhaps because she was pushed around by the younger Mlabri, only Paeng and old Khamla being really nice to her – the old and wrinkled aunt. When she talked, her face became very expressive in a grimace, and she used her hands as well to demonstrate what she meant. We felt she was really an old-timer Mlabri, and like the other members of the band we could not help falling for her special charm. Old Khamla, now a dignified and still good-looking woman, supervised the band, ensuring that the children did not hurt themselves while playing with over-large knives or pieces of burning wood.

It was striking how often the Mlabri relaxed when not working for the Hmong, after breakfast and lunch and in the afternoon as well. When everyone in the camp fell asleep, my wife and our children included, I used the opportunity to photograph everybody around – old and young alike. For a moment I felt that time went backwards thousands of years to the everyday life of our common prehistory. When everyone woke up, Khamla, the young women and two of the men hurried to finish the fine, multicoloured shoulder bag they had worked on for several days to give us.

Huay Nam Yu, 100°28'E, 18°29'N, M1, ref. no. 72. Three big windscreens with 27 Mlabri, among others: Pha, Muang, Ajan, Pat, Saeng, Si, Su Mung and En-jo with wives and children. Si said that in Ban Lum Kao, 101°14'E, 18°51'N, ref. no. 57, the Hmong had told him that across the border to Laos there was some very aggressive Mlabri (M7), who sometimes had even killed one another! A few years back they had entered Thailand, but they had been caught by the border police and sent back to Laos. Si had been asked by the chief of police in Amphoe Sa to join him on a trip to the border to investigate the matter and if necessary serve as his interpreter! On this occasion he had also heard that they had tattooed stripes, and that they had sometimes killed intruders into their own area. But it was only the Hmong in Ton Praivan who claimed that they had allegedly also killed their own old or decrepit people to eat them. Apart from Kit also staying in Ton Rraivan we have no other sources confirming these somewhat weird stories.

However, returning back to Nan city, we did obtain reliable information confirming the very existence of this kind of Mlabri M7 across the border, coming from a Thai border patrol captain, whom we had already met four years before. He told us that only one year earlier (1988), he had crossed the border and gone into Laos, and while moving unseen through the jungle he had spotted a heavily built Mlabri man sitting under a tree, at about 80 m distance. He was naked, but had a skin over his shoulders and a spear in his hand, probably guarding the entrance to their domain. He also made a drawing of the person to substantiate his interesting observation (see fig. 124). For security reasons he could not reveal the exact locality, but evidently it was east of Nan province and could have been close to Ban Na Haeo, 101°14'E, 18°51' N, ref. no. 57.

While discussing moral issues with Si, he said that a man should not have sex with another woman, when his wife was pregnant. Still it happened causing many complaints. Asked about what happens with twins and relating to what we had heard that previously the mother had to kill the weaker of the two, Si said he had heard this too, but did not know what would happen nowadays. However, in our recordings on marriages and kinship we have never come across a single instance of twins. The Mlabri M1 and M3 do consider the killing of others to be a great sin, but in the case of newborn babies they are not yet considered to have anything but a tiny soul, so perhaps the killing of seriously disabled babies or of one of the twins might be tolerable. Otherwise, killing of humans is thought to be punished by the sky spirit, for example by letting a branch fall down on the murderer, while lying is punished by the spirit of the forest, making the sinner loose his way in the jungle. But Si said that in case of doubt, as well as during crises, they would consult the spirits of their deceased parents.

Interview with Pha and Si at our hotel in Nan. Again we took two of our Mlabri informers to Nan to explain the prayers, thereby avoiding the distractions in their camp. When somebody gets seriously ill and the family wants to know the prospects of recovery, the person is put on a mat somewhere outside the windscreen. Then two candles are set on the ground above the head of the afflicted person, where also a split bamboo (in Thai: tung) is stuck into the ground. If the candles, made of beeswax and with a wick of rattan burn down, the person will recover; but if they burn only partly he or she will not (Pha). A few weeks after a birth, eggs are sacrificed in connection with the ceremony to strengthen the soul of the newborn. The eggs have to be cooked and should come from a domesticated bird, usually from the other hill tribes, because if eggs from a wild bird are used, the weak soul of the child might be carried away.

When asking the Mlabri about what their spirits look like, we mostly received rather vague answers, such as like smoke or small clouds of vapour. However, Pha related the following about one of their most important spirits, that of the old, tall trees harbouring the spirits of their deceased parents. The spirit of such trees (Thai: phi ton yay "spirit trunk big", Mlabri: wɔk lam) is situated beneath the trunk, where the roots spread out. This spirit is believed to be enclosed in a sphere 15-20 cm in diameter and inhabiting a honeycomb having the same texture. In this connection it should be noticed that bees are not to be bothered, for example when drinking from a stream, pointing to the fine web of rules once governing the Mlabri spiritual world.

Therefore, I now gave Pha a large sheet of paper and asked him to reproduce the shape of the shell, upon which he carefully made a ball of it (see fig. 85). He added that if the shell was broken, the spirit inside would shine like the sun which, however, would bring very bad luck. Therefore, the Mlabri should not cut down such big, old trees, but were compelled to do so now when clearing the jungle for the Hmong to grow rice. In this

225

connection, Pha added that the spirit of the jungle, who looks after the big trees, is angry now, which he said is why they cannot find the animals as before.

Back again in Ton Praiwan at Mae Sa Nan,101°07'E, 18°50'N, ref. no. 53. Seven Mlabri M3 near the Hmong village, but staying by themselves in a bamboo thicket. Some of the Hmong here said that the 'fierce' Mlabri were still living close to the border inside Laos, and that they, including their children, had tattooed stripes on arms and legs. They had been seen when coming to ask for a few necessities, adding that 30 of them stayed near Ban Nam Yin. They were naked, had spears and knives and would threaten people if they met them in their jungle. The Hmong moreover claimed that 20 years previously (before 1970) they sometimes killed and ate the sick or decrepit members of their band!

T'in and Lao village Ban Suman only one day's walk away, 101°16'E, 18°49'N, M7, ref. no. 73, a young Hmong said he had seen these Mlabri only three years earlier (1986). Furthermore, the Hmong had seen them at Phu Kha more than 30 years before (around 1960) and also at Pho Kleua, while another Hmong, Lao Toa, said that he had seen male 'fierce' Mlabri near Doi Phu Keng when he was 15 (in about 1955), now being 50 years of age.

During a second visit to Ton Prai Wan we asked Kit if he could remember all the places he had been to earlier in Laos. He listed the following: Nam Mim, Hui Chaeg, Hui Toeng, Hui Sawen and *Nam San (101°20'E, 19°17'N), M3, ref. no. 74.* The source of the Nam Xong (ref. no. 49), where he went with his father, and finally Nam Phiang where he lived when he was 14 years old (1964). Thus Kit seemed to have a better memory than most of the Ml group, which might also have something to do with the fact that he has stayed near other tribesmen including the Hmong for several years. Finally, he said that three members of their group died after coming to Thailand, three in Ban Nam Yao, and his wife here in Don Praiwan about a year previously (1988).

The 1994 Expedition

During this last stay in Northern Thailand we concentrated on the prayers, while still receiving important information on various other subjects. Now it became evident that especially the young Mlabri were rapidly changing their lifestyle by driving trucks, going to the market and buying radios, etc., but still preserving their dignity, charm and warm kindness. However, we had still a surprise in store when approaching the border to Laos at the very end of this last expedition.

Ban Bow Hoy, ref. no. 25. About 20 Mlabri in three windscreens, among others Pha, Gui, Ton, Nyuk. Here the high-spirited Gui started by saying that before, when they did not have spears of iron, they were made of the strong wood from a palm tree. Old Pan, their former and the only real leader of all the Mlabri, could also make tattoos (Mlabri: sat mut), using charcoal, snake liver and gall bladder. Gui himself had a fine, big boar tattooed on his back. This had, however, been executed by a Khon Muang.

Asked whether they identify animals by their scent, he said they rather trace them by their noise or their footprints. He claimed that he had never used the oil from boar's testicles to overwhelm their own smell, contrary to what we had heard about and seen extracts of in the Phayao district. Gui's employer added that the Mlabri came to exchange their jungle products for iron, cloth and rice about four times a year from about 1965, but it was only from around 1980 that all the Mlabri began to work for the Hmong for a few months each year.

Returning to the subject of the so-called 'fierce' Mlabri, Gui now remarked that Som met the striped Mlabri already near Doi Pa Chik, ref. no. 65, at the village of Sao Dam, about 70 km further north of here (Ban Bow Hoy), although Som had himself stated earlier that he first met them after having passed Doi Pa Chik and reaching the Phayao area. But it is important that Gui also said that old Ut and Kham had seen these Mlabri near Ban Nam Wa (close to the Laotian border) half a century back, pointing to the mutual origin of the two groups (M1 and M7) in Laos.

At the hotel in Nan. As it was difficult to work with the tape recorder in the noisy camp, we asked Gui and his son Nyuk to come down to stay with us in the hotel for a few days. Nyuk: When selecting a partner, girls will try to find a good provider, while boys will choose a good-looking and active girl. Had a boy obtained permission from the parents to marry their daughter, he had to give them roots, eggs, some smaller animals, but also blankets, etc., from the market. When giving birth to their first child, the wife had two women to help, the younger one making a special windscreen, fetching wood and water. Girls are allowed to follow the procedures from a distance of about 10 m – boys not at all. But Nyuk's child died after only three days, and was buried on a small, isolated hill top. The grave was dug about 80 cm deep and thorny branches put on top.

A baby is a spirit (some say spirit soul) until just after it is born. A few days later they will give some eggs to the spirit of the jungle during a small ceremony, when a string is tied around the wrist to strengthen its tiny, weak soul. As mentioned earlier, there has to be a fine balance between the spirits and souls in the world of the Mlabri, including both the living and the dead humans and animals. This is in agreement with the concepts of reincarnation, in which most of the people of the area believe, many of the Mlabri included, at least now. Gui said in this connection that they think that if a small boy dies he will become a squirrel, a girl a tortoise, a bigger boy a bamboo rat, a man a bear cat, a women a monkey, whereas an old man will become a deer and an old woman a small deer!

When asked about previous habits, Gui said that it is true that before 1950 if someone was very ill, they had sometimes put him or her into a cave together with some food and water, after which they had blocked the entrance with a fence of bamboo, but making it possible for the person to escape, after a possible recovery. Asked whether if someone has done something wrong there would be any consequences, he said that the spirits will punish the person, for example by sending the wind spirit, who will discuss the matter with the spirit of big trees (those of the deceased parents). Only if the two spirits agree, will the tree spirit send, for example, branches down on the person.

On this occasion we were also told that the first time the Mlabri women were about to see my wife and me in 1976-77, they had asked the Hmong beforehand if we were going to kill and eat them, perhaps a reflection of their fear of the 'fierce' Mlabri and of strangers in general! The Hmong had naturally answered no, and we had thought it was just a weird joke. However, we now learned that even after we had arrived, they were still afraid that I would instead take one of their women with me (fig. 121), because it was not unusual that the Hmong and Khon Muang had been responsible for such acts until as late as 1980, often with the result that the Mlabri had left the area for some years. Gui added that Paeng had lost his wife in this way, and even after looking for her for three years, he had not been able to find her.

Ban Hui Yok, ref. no. 61. among others Ut, Muang, Si, Seng, Yok and Noi. Now staying in our own windscreen in front of a 10 m long windscreen holding all the 17 members of old Ut's band (see fig. 137 and drawing fig. 138), we were able to observe their movements, among others noting how much time they spend enjoying one another's company. This kind of windscreen was incidentally of the same sort as those of the alleged 'fierce' Mlabri. Actually, the Mlabri did construct various kinds of windscreens; including a sort of simple long-house holding perhaps 40 persons.

Going through the family relations once again, for among other reasons to ensure that Ut and Kham are half siblings, as are Gui and Som. After a marriage the man stays with his wife's band for 1-2 months, whereupon the couple moves to stay more permanently with the husband's band. If a man leaves his wife, the children will stay with her, but if a woman wishes to divorce, their children often stay with their grandparents. Previously men decided what to do in such cases, but now the women have much more say. From our recordings we have established that there is still a surplus of men, because many women die in childbirth.

Muang said that if an offering is made to the spirits of the parents, and no animal comes to eat it, it means that the spirits are angry, and then the band has to decamp immediately. When burying their dead before 1975, they had sometimes put them near a termite heap, so that the corpse would finally be enclosed inside these characteristic structures. First they made a hole half a metre deep, then they put a 40 cm thick layer of tree leaves to be held down by four big bamboo canes beaten flat, then came the body and finally a heap of earth and branches on top. Muang, Noi and Yok said that they worked for the Hmong for only about three or four months every year, after which they would go west of Doi Phu Keng to stay in the jungle there. They also said that they are more often sick in the cold, dry season than in the rainy one, where it is easier to find all kinds of food.

Hereafter we discussed their ability to keep a check on time, during which it became evident that they do not reckon with full moons, being aware only of the cold, the rainy and the dry season for clearing the land for the Hmong. However, they said that they always asked Si when they wished to know the onset of the next season. In this connection I asked if they were aware of the nine months between conception and delivery of a baby. To our surprise the Mlabri said again that they did not know it took that long! The worst problem the Mlabri had faced in recent times was the periods of famine, the most critical being that of the cold and dry season, when the animals retreat to their hideouts and their children cry endlessly and especially the old people often get dizzy from lack of food.

Birgit interviewing Seng's wife 'e lian: Women started marrying after their first menstruation, during which they may also have sex, but should stop one month before delivery, when the husband takes a blanket and sleeps by himself, to recommence nowadays already a week after the baby is born. The umbilical cord is cut with a bamboo knife and is tied with the same sort of string as used to make the net bags; 'e lian adding that it quite often happens that women die during a birth, because of the baby getting stuck, but she said that she had never heard about the killing of twins.

On this occasion we heard of a Mlabri M1 band we had never encountered before, among others ta-ke, ta-ko and ta-le-ke. Besides the about 130 Mlabri M1 we have met, we reckon there are only ten, or at the most 20 we have not seen, their entire group being still no more than 140-150 persons. In the rainy season they prefer to make their camp near big trees on the lower parts of the mountain because, somewhat to our surprise, they said there are less mosquitoes there than further up.

Although the women appear to be soft and very feminine, they normally have great strength due to their continued activity all day long. We have mentioned earlier that they sometimes fetch water 10-15 minutes away in the difficult terrain, and they are able to fell and cut up quite big trees, then to be carried away on their shoulders or dragged to the fires of the windscreen. It was also related how a girl had rescued the boy 'en-ko, when he was bitten by a bear. She had resolutely grasped a big stone and crushed the back of the bear.

At last we obtained substantial evidence about what other Mlabri had denied previously viz. that they sometimes sleep in trees, which they call ɛm tul lam "sleep up tree", while the bed in the tree is called ləgʌh lam "up there tree". Even though the Mlabri are still excellent tree climbers, we needed more substance to this story. Now the Mlabri said they used to sleep in trees when moving alone in the jungle, so they would not so easily be surprised either by wild animals or by people, for the simple reason that they could hear somebody approaching them well before, from up in the tree. Also the widow, Tobitoa, (Mlabri name 'e bun), said that she had often made a nest up in the tree, where three or four branches depart from the stem and using small branches together with lianas of a creeper to produce a platform and finally to fix herself to the tree. She added that these procedures had been followed in order to prevent her from being approached by young men during the night!

We shall return in a while to the extraordinary ability of the Mlabri to climb fast and high up in giant trees. To me, this suggests that they are born jungle dwellers and not just some refugees from culture, as it has been claimed by some writers!

Ban Bow Hoy, 100°27'E, 18°30'N, Ml, ref. no. 25. 22 Mlabri in three, separately situated windscreens, among others Kham La, Gui, Gaeo, Ajan, Som, Lat (Sai Taw's son), Paeng Noi, Seng and Gaep. With respect to those Mlabri who had been to the Phayao area, Paeng Noi claimed that they had not used extracts from the testicles of a boar to get close to the animal, but instead had simply dipped themselves in muddy places where boars used to come. Lao Toa's father remarked that the Mlabri at this time were very dirty and never washed.

Gui (Pang) said that his band had moved from Doi Phu Kha to Doi Phu Keng when he was a child (before 1945). From there they had gone to Doi Pha Chik and finally to Doi Sathan, also having stayed near Song for some time. Paeng Noi now said that, according to old Patot, they had never mixed with the 'striped' Mlabri, and that Paeng Taw had been to the area around Phayao about 35 years earlier (before 1960). Furthermore, it was related that Som, Wai and Poa had been up north towards Chieng Kham, which confirms the information obtained during our own trip there in 1989, that the Mlabri had been seen in the area a few times until about 1965.

Back in Ban Hui Yok, 101°21'E, 19°46'N, Ml, ref. no. 61. 14 Mlabri among others: Ut, Lat, Noi, Yok, Seng and Thong. Noi being asked how long it takes to walk from place to place gave the following examples: from Ban Hui Yok: to Ban Pho Keng two days, to Ban Na Ka one day and to Ban Bow Hoy one day, while from Ban Bow Hiew to Doi Sathan one and a half days, and from there to Ban Hui Hom half a day.

Noi then wanted to relate the following incident: Five Hmong went out to hunt but were attacked by some bears, and one of them had to leave his gun to hurry away. The Hmong now promised the Mlabri three pigs if they could find the gun. They encountered the bears and Gu killed one of them and also found and brought back the gun, receiving five pigs instead of the three promised ones. Even though the Mlabri have constantly been complaining about the Hmong, and as we have seen often with good reason, one cannot help thinking that their employers, of which some are naturally nice people, have been almost the only ones who have taken care of them in times of crisis!

Birgit interviewing Noi's wife, ya krul pɛl: On the question of what sort of man she would choose she said: Handsome or not – never mind. He has to be sincere, skilful at work and really love her, and yes, could have sex before marriage. She had to tell her husband if she was menstruating, during which he would sleep by himself. Indeed they did not know about the nine months between conception and delivery. After the marriage they start by living in the band of her parents to be sure that he treats her well. Yes, they do sing for their children, and if these behave badly they may slap them gently on their laps. Yes, indeed the children get jealous of one another: gʌm 'oh gʌm bɛr: "don't friends". In the event of divorce the women usually get the infants. Earlier, the children belonged to their father, but now they manage to settle things more peacefully. Incidentally, it was on this occasion that the best-looking girl in the band said that she thought it would be rather dull to be married only once, like my wife and I! With a charming smile, she said she rather preferred to marry about three times, as is common among the Mlabri.

Once again talking about burials, Thong denied that they put their dead into trees, but then he admitted that one young man who had been wounded by a tiger long ago had to go up in the tree voluntarily. Thong also revealed that long ago they had often just put their dead on the ground and had covered the body with branches and leaves (as also the M3 Mlabri had once done).

Thong's father Patot coming from Laos had told him: "Don't ever return! The Kha Lai, the striped ones, are very fierce". He also said that if two Mlabri keep on quarrelling, the band finds somebody who is a friend of both parties. If one of them is found to be the wrong-doer, he has to leave the band for ten days, but on his return nobody is allowed to mention the case. Finally, Thong said it never happens that they will ask anybody to leave the band permanently, for they will rather choose to find another one themselves. Quarrelling is very unusual among the Mlabri, and we have only witnessed one instance when some of the younger men were having a serious argument, but before sunset they were smiling again.

During the next 14 days we went to visit the M3 Mlabri near Doi Pho Kha (ref. no. 40) as well as those in Ban Ton Praiwan near Pua (part A). In between, a number of villages were visited along the border towards Laos where we just heard about the various groups of Mlabri (part B). Therefore in order to present this hetero-geneous material in a feasible manner it has been divided into two parts, A and B:

A. Primary sources:

Hmong Kao Lao Leng, 101°05'E, 19°09'N, M3, ref. no. 75. Oy and two daughters. In his childhood he stayed with his parents around the large mountain range Phu Sam Sao, 1959 m, in northern Laos. Oy related at great length how rice was introduced to their group according to his parents: First one Mlabri went to visit the Lua and tasted the rice. When he came back again some weeks later, the Lua told him how to grow it. Then the Mlabri had to clear the land, the Lua helping them to remove tall trees, but still the area was quite irregular. Now they had to learn how to handle the rice plants, cutting and drying them, and remove the husks to get the seeds. Finally they watched how the rice was cooked using bamboo internodes. After several attempts, however, the Mlabri did not succeed, probably having neither the necessary skills nor the patience.

Oy did remember that they had stayed in one area more permanently (around the Doi Sam Sao range in the Sayabouri province in Laos), while the more mobile Ml and/or M7 Mlabri, with whom they were not on good terms at all, had been seen only occasionally. Originally there were 22 families, of which only three went to Thailand. Altogether, he judged there had been about 130 of them, when they were possibly forced away from their original habitat, moving southwards along the Nam Huang, then turning west along the Nam San along the 19°31' northern latitude.

Approaching the border to Thailand they had reached *Ban Nam Mim, 101°15'E, 19° 16'N, M3, ref. no. 76,* where they met the first westerner (Dr. Michel Ferlus, see Rischel, 1989, p. 60), together with whom his younger brother Jan went out on a one-day excursion in the jungle and received various gifts. Oy was then about 24 years old, and being now 55 (1994), the meeting had taken place around 1964. From there he later crossed the mountain range between Doi Phu Khe and Doi Lo (2074 and 2077 m high, respectively) to enter Nam Mae and the source of the Nam Wa river system in Thailand.

As the result of the Cold War and the increasing resistance to the French presence there, civil war started in Laos, building up tensions along the border to Thailand, which feared a Communist invasion. Therefore, in the early 1970s, the population of the border areas was evacuated, sending several thousands of hill-tribe peoples to various refugee camps at a safe distance from what should become almost a war zone. Within weeks, the M3 Mlabri were ordered to walk to Pua, together with Lua, T'in, Khamu, Yao and Hmong, during which many of the mountain people, young and old alike, died from disease, starvation and fatigue. The Mlabri having no belongings to carry, were employed by those who did, such as the Hmong.

The Mlabri ended up in a temporary camp near Pua in 1974, where they stayed for one year before being moved to the camp at Nam Yao, M3, reg. no. 27, holding about four thousand people at its peak. The Mlabri stayed here for two and a half years, where we found them in 1976-77 and again in 1978. It was also here that one of their women, Kaeb (Mlabri name 'e liang), had married a Khon Muang (Pha Noi).

Oy said that they still hunt or collect small game like bamboo rats, mice and fish, and collect a great number of different kinds of roots. Furthermore, they work for the T'in and Khon Muang, but primarily for the Hmong, called phaw liang "father feed" (Th). However, most of the time they now stay in the nearby jungle, close to the river. The Hmong seldom visit their windscreens, but only having a digging implement and a small knife, the Mlabri sometimes go to the Hmong to borrow their tools or to obtain medicine.

Oy lived alone in a small hut next to his Hmong employers, while his two daughters stayed near the stream quite far below the house of their father. The elder daughter had married a T'in, but they had not succeeded in having any children. When these matters were discussed, it turned out, just as with the Mlabri Ml that they did not know about the nine months from conception to delivery of a baby. As regards burials, he said that previously they rolled their dead into a rattan mat and hoisted them up between two trees in order not to attract tigers, but now they buried their dead family members. They did not make altars like the Ml group, having adopted them from the Hmong, but only placed offerings on a stone or some banana leaves. Also, unlike the Mlabri Ml, they did not think it was the parents' spirits who were the first animals coming to eat the offerings. However, like the Ml Mlabri, they did believe that if they dreamed of their dead family members, it was because these wanted offerings already next morning.

Indeed this was demonstrated during the last day, when Oy slept next to our own Hmong room. Early next morning before sunrise I heard him talking with some-

body, only to realise that it was to his deceased wife, even discussing with her. When I came outside the house I could see that he had made an offering of some of the food left over from the previous evening. Asking him, he confirmed that this was for his wife, adding that he missed her so much, which was quite understandable, since she was a very nice and mild person.

Ton Praiwan, 101°07'N, 18°50'N, ref. no. 53. Seven Mlabri M3 including Kit and Sak. Just as Oy had explained, Kit said the reason for leaving their main group was disagreement on how their supplies of food should be divided. Then he told the following interesting story related by his father. A Lua came to their camp and said: "Please come to our village, because some of your own kind want to trade honey and mats for clothes". When the Kha Lai (Thai: "people striped") arrived at the village they had made a lot of trouble, but when they saw Kit's father they vanished in horror! Nevertheless next evening they had returned to collect the cloth, also receiving some pork. But from the story it seems that it could not possibly have been the 'fierce' Mlabri, but more likely the Ml group – if the difference between the two spear groups was not negligible or originally non-existent!

Returning to their beliefs, Kit said that they are not allowed to kill butterflies, or the sky spirit will make lightning. Anyone playing with or killing an insect drinking water from the stream will be killed by lightning. Moreover, they thought that the sky spirit and those of their parents can send lightning or wild animals to punish them. And exactly as the Ml believe, if an eagle is killed, its spirit may carry away the soul of a sick person.

If someone dies in the camp, they carry the corpse about 100 m away hanging by the arms and feet under a heavy bamboo pole to be buried, or they tear down the windscreen over the corpse before hurrying away. Previously, they made a heap of branches, put the body on top and covered it with leaves. But they had to put ashes in the eyes of the corpse, leave the clothes, and place roots, betel leaves and some rice on a stone as an offering. If they wished to keep the dead person's most precious item, the iron digging implement, they had to ask the deceased's spirit first (see ceremony p. 136). Even though their most powerful spirit apart from the sky spirit, is tharago' (tharagɔ', Ml), who is believed to be their saviour, this spirit is not included in their prayers. As it appears, the differences between the faiths of the Ml and M3 group are not substantial, which suggests that the two groups may have a not very distant common origin – just as is the case with their languages.

Ban Pa Gang, ref. no. 41, a *refugee settlement near Pua*. Here we were told by the Hmong that Lek of the Mlabri M4 was sold by his mother to the Hmong Lao Ju, when he was five years old. Now Lek was married to a Hmong woman, but they were poor, having many children to provide for. Lao Ju confirmed that his family, just as Gaeng and Thoeng (M4), was from the Phu Wae area up north, 101°09'E, 19°18'N, ref. no. 39.

Ban Kao Lao Leng, 101°20'E, 19°12'N, M3, ref. no. 75, our second stay. Oy looked pleased to see us again, as he sometimes felt lonely without the company of his former wife. Returning to the various groups of Mlabri, he said about the 'fierce' one that they were known to be unable to divide food – even among themselves, or to take something back to their families. If one met them in the jungle, they could be dangerous. They put their windscreens in a long row (like the Ml sometimes also do). There had been about 150 of them, and they were experts at throwing the spear "almost using it as a gun". Oy characterised them by saying: Kha Hawk (Th), sat mʌc or lit. "people spear, spots see" in contrast to themselves Kha Thong Luang. He was asked whether he could acknowledge kha cho' 'people spatula' for themselves, to which he agreed. Very importantly he said his father had told him that the striped Mlabri and their own group had spoken the same language and they, too, had hoisted their dead up in a tree by their feet. At this point I asked Lao Thae Jao Sang Chung, if he could distinguish between the different types of the spear Mlabri, to which he replied there are only two different groups:

a) Magu laeng "Mlabri red" looking as in our photographs of the Ml, the men bearing small pieces of loincloth. He had seen three bigger and two smaller men about 15 years before (around 1980), adding that they were not aggressive.

b) Magu dam "Mlabri black" with long stripes of black dots on their arms and legs and a bad smell. They had stayed longer in their area, were fiercer, and had made rattan containers and mats to exchange for pigs like the other Mlabri. He had seen seven persons, of whom two were quite old, about ten years previously (1984).

At this point the unusual thing happened that Oy disagreed with his strict employer by saying that there were indeed three spear groups – the black, the red and the striped, being different only as regards their tattoos. We shall return to these somewhat contradictory statements, which are important for our final conclusions at the end of this appendix.

B. Secondary Evidence on the Various Groups of Mlabri from Hmong, T'in, etc.

In the Hmong village near Khao Lao Leng we met an almost 80 year old Hmong Lao Tung, who was born near *Nam Wa and Doi Phu Khe, 101°13'E, 19°J9'N, M7, ref. no. 77,* saying that the Mlabri he had met had green spots, small loincloths and carried spears. They had threatened even the Hmong. However, he had invited them to have rice. They had said they cooked their food in skins. He thought there were about 150 of these *Kheeo*, when he had left Laos at 15 years of age (1930), adding they were somewhat taller than the Mlabri Ml – all very important information.

In the village, we were taken to another Hmong, Lao Kheu, who had met some Mlabri between the two highest mountains *Phu Khe and Doi Lo, 101°14'E, 19°17'N, Ml, ref. no. 78,* on the border to Laos. Being 12 years old when he saw them and 68 now, this would have been around 1938. He said they had only used spears for hunting and looked very much like our Ml Mlabri and could speak Lua (T'in). Some had holes in their ears. He had seen them twice, the first time five men and the second time ten men, adding they were very peaceful people. Finally he showed us a spear which his father had bought from them.

One day's drive to Nam Kan area and *Ban Na Plaek, 101°12'E, 19°26'N, Mlabri?, ref. no. 79.* On 6th February we went up almost to the very northeastern corner of Thailand with Senator Khon Pensak Chagsucinda (who was married to the former Danish Ambassador to Thailand, Frantz Howitz) in order to obtain further information. But the villagers seemed to be unaccustomed to visitors and rather unwilling or perhaps afraid to answer our questions. However, two villagers did tell us that probably there were Kha Thong Luang on the other side of the border, but it was impossible to get any nearer than about one kilometre from the border itself, due to landmines, barbed wire, etc., separating the two countries. From seeing the results of the fierce fighting in the 1970s, with almost no forest and little other vegetation left, we sensed the suffering the whole area and its people had been through. With some relief we hurried southwards again, not to be trapped in this deserted area after dark.

Ban Nam Tuang, map's *Ban Maeo Laeo La, 101 °14'E, 18°53'N, M 7, ref. no. 80.* Early next morning I went with our local driver rather fast in a Landrover to Mae Charim. After some hours on very deserted but good roads we came into a nice valley, almost squeezed between several mountains, except to the west, having the border to Laos on the mountain crest to our right to the south. We had apparently chosen the right day, as it was the Chinese New Year, so there were no guards at the checkpoint where we had entered the valley, while the few other people on the road might have taken us to be technicians of some sort. At last we arrived at a modern compound, of the kind where the officials ruled during the day and the Communists might be around after dark.

In the compound we met a young Hmong, Han Yung Sib, who kindly listened to our requests, before telling us that the Mlabri lived just across the border. One had to walk for two hours to Ban San Wang and from there another two hours to the border, but this was somewhat tricky due to landmines. Sending somebody over to contact the Mlabri would probably lead to nothing, because they might have moved further away. Being asked when they had seen the Mlabri last time, Han Yung Sib now related the following: A Mlabri man, his wife and their son had come to the village seven years before (1987), being very much afraid and speaking with feeble voices. Probably due to the fighting here the following year (1988), the Mlabri had been scared away. The man had long stripes of dots on his legs and wore only a loincloth, while the woman had put on a sarong, only revealing similar stripes on her arms. Han Yung Sib even made a drawing of the man and woman including their tattoos, resembling other informants' indications of the M7.

While walking through the village nearby with Han Yung Sib, we stopped in front of a house where an old Hmong came out to meet us, bringing with him a small, crude spearhead and the digging implement which had been exchanged for food a long time back. Perhaps this time we were dealing with members of the alleged 'fierce' Mlabri called Kheeo also on the Laotian side of the border. Even though we had possibly been closer to these Mlabri than at any time before during our many expeditions, we still had not met them. However, we had now found reliable witnesses in many quarters and probably obtained two of their objects. In particular the observation by our reliable Thai informant, who had actually seen one of them (fig. 124), was a sort of proof of their very existence.

The Various Mlabri Groups

At the end of this appendix, an attempt has been made to distinguish between the various groups of Mlabri M 1-7 we have met or heard about, as related above on our travels 1970-94, in order to discuss their origin and migrations. Unfortunately, we have no very old references to help us in this. To follow each group in space and time during the 20th century, please also consult the two maps at the very end of the book.

The Mlabri probably belong to the oldest stratum of hunter-gatherers in mainland Southeast Asia. Even though they might have lived very isolated for long periods of time, they have nevertheless had contacts with other peoples, but so little as they have preserved their simple lifestyle as hunter-gatherers until recently. Their first encounters with anthropologists occurred only at the beginning of the 20th century, but from them, as well as from old Thai people, we heard in 1970 that the Mlabri were once found in almost every hilly part of northern and northeastern Thailand.

With the advent of the 20th century, hill tribes from Burma and Laos, as well as Thai farmers from the lowland, also began to invade the mountain forests, with the result that most of the Mlabri have subsequently been killed or absorbed by the other peoples, almost disappearing as ethnic groups. In spite of the fact that we have met and heard about various kinds of Mlabri in the area, including Burma and Laos as far south as Cambodia, it nevertheless seems that there are but two sub-groups plus groups thereof who have mixed with other peoples:

A. Those of the smallest physical height (men about 147 cm and women 135 cm) including, besides the M3 group, also the two members of the M6 group. They formerly lived primarily on various roots and small animals, preferring to stay in small bands in the lower mountains near many streams. The Hmong may be right when claiming that they are the 'true' Mlabri, since they do not seem to have mixed with the other hill tribes until quite recently, whereby their have preserved the oldest characteristics. There were not even 20 left in Thailand in 1994.

B. Those of somewhat greater physical height (about 10 cm taller for both sexes) comprising the M1, M2, M4, M5 and M7 Mlabri, who have mixed occasionally, but still rarely, with other ethnic groups. They are more muscular and have hunted even such large and dangerous animals as the wild ox (gaur) and the elephant. They have inhabited a wider range of altitudes and trekked further afield. By and large they have also better maintained their traditional life as regards being hunters and sticking to their previous social structure until about 1985. However, there were probably not more than 230 left altogether in 1994.

Although the two categories have basically the same language and religious beliefs pointing to a common origin, they have not intermarried, having avoided one another as far back as anyone can remember. Also included in sub-group B are the Mlabri M4, who have mixed with T'in.

Subgroup A

This kind of people, being the smallest of all the Mlabri, probably belongs to the oldest stratum because they have chosen the simplest strategy of survival viz. that of mainly being gatherers of roots and small animals near mountain streams at lower altitudes than those of the subgroup B. The Hmong, who know all the Mlabri best because the latter work for them, also said that according to their opinion, they are the 'genuine ones' as they have not mixed with the other hill tribes until very recently, contrary to the case with the Mlabri of subgroup B. There are so few left that they are tardy accessible for thorough investigations anymore.

M3: Oy related that his group of originally 130 persons previously inhabited the Doi Sam Sao mountain ranges in the Sayabouri province in Laos until the 1940s. Due to lack of food, 35 of his family and friends split off and drifted southwards, at some point going west to stay in the borderlands between Laos and Thailand. As tensions built up between the two countries around 1970, his reduced group was forced by the Thai authorities to move to a refugee camp near Pua in 1974 and a year later further on to the nearby refugee camp at Nam Yao, also in Nan province, where they stayed until 1978. Since then they have worked regularly for their Hmong employers, whom they followed all the way from Laos. Of the 35 persons of Oy's group who left their larger group in Laos, ten remained in 1994, now

there are only three (2006). Ot and Gaeo staying with villagers in two locations in Nan province are also M3, probably also belonging to their originally larger group of 130 individuals in the Sayabouri province in Laos.

Small bands of this kind of Mlabri have also been reported to have stayed in Northern Thailand as far away as Chieng Dao and up to the border towards Burma already before 1950, and Robert Weawer, June 1956, p. 289-95, 336, met a small band comprising six men, one woman and her boy northwest of Dan Sai, Loei province, in 1956. Obviously the latter very much resembled the M3 Mlabri, and when we visited the area last time in 1989, we were told that their kind had been seen just north of Dan Sai until 1950 (see map p. 324, location no. 56). Their group might also have originated from the same larger group of M3 Mlabri in the Doi Sam Sao ranges up north in the Sayabouri province, for the long mountain chain making up the border between Thailand and Laos connects the two areas in question, see at the very end of the book.

M6: In Laos we met a woman 'i An about 30 years of age, who had been taken down from the border area towards Thailand together with her sister to an orphanage near Ventiane in 1971. She had been adopted by a middle-aged Laotian man with whom she now stayed near the shores of the great lake in the Udon district about 60 km north of Ventiane. From her features (see figs. 121-122) and what she said, it emerged that she and her sister were also of the Mlabri M3 kind. She had no idea about where her group had lived. Incidentally, our further material from Laos is not included in this summary, since it was not collected on location, but there are said to be several places hosting M3-like small groups, albeit their remaining number seems to be much reduced.

Subgroup B

M1: Just like the M3 Mlabri, their old people said that they also inhabited the Doi Sam Sao mountain ranges in the Sayabouri province until the beginning of the 20th century, when they crossed the Mekong river and entered Thailand around 1916. According to the Hmong who had lived in the area, their number was considerably greater than it is today. They stayed for some years in the borderlands further north but inside Thailand around the Nam Wa river system to reappear southwest of Nan, where about half of them settled around

Doi Khun Sathan east of Phrae. The other half settled in western Nan from around 1930 using these two locations as their base for shorter or longer treks since then.

Thus some bands went westwards towards Chiang Rai and even Chiang Mai provinces within the period 1950-68, while briefer treks took them northwards to the border with Burma. The longest trek was undertaken by Poa's band of about 30 persons from Doi Sathan, while drifting all the way down to Loei province and back again 1972-84. The number of Mlabri Ml in Nan province has stabilised since then at about 140. Even though they have had a religious ban against mixing with others, a few individuals have done so from time to time.

M2: In the police station in Sa we found eight Mlabri M2 resembling the M1 (see figs. 108-109). They might have lived just on the other side of the border inside Laos, since one of the Mlabri boys was singing in Laotian. None of the personnel at the station understood their language and unfortunately we had only half a day to investigate them. Nobody seems to know what has happened to them, but most likely they returned to the border areas towards Laos.

M4: Met Gaeng and Toeng from an alleged mixed group of Mlabri and T'in living in windscreens on the southeastern slopes of Doi Pu Ka in northern Nan province (see fig. 118). Their Hmong employer did not know anything about their origin, but said they had lived there for many years, at present being about 30 persons. Lek, staying in Ban Ba Gang, also belongs to this group. Similar mixed groups are found in southern Laos.

M5: By asking as usual in every other village we passed through with our patient driver we found a 25-year-old Mlabri, Lot, in Ban Kok Ngam in Loei province in 1987. He related that his group of about 120 persons had stayed on the large sandstone mountain plateaus Phu Krading and Phu Luang. From him and his Thai adoptive mother I realised that the material and spiritual life of his group had not been much different from that of the Mlabri Ml since they, for example, had also been able to kill even large animals. However, they had followed slightly different religious practices. Due to disease, tigers, various accidents, etc., their group had been decimated to the point of comprising only 15 when they decided to return northwards towards Laos around 1980 after leaving Lot with his new Thai family.

Almost certainly his original group is the one described by Keer, 1924, p. 142-44. He writes that about 30 men (corresponding to about 120 persons in all) had turned up in Ban Sathan in 1924. They were able to hunt such dangerous animals as the mountain ox and the elephant, and a few of them could speak some Laotian. Everything indicated that they were originally of the Mlabri Ml type also having stayed in the Sayabouri area. Instead of drifting westwards into Nan province in Thailand they had probably trekked further south to arrive in Loei province already around 1915.

M7: The so-called 'fierce' Mlabri, the Kiew of westernmost Sayabouri province, also seem to be related somehow to the Mlabri Ml, perhaps only a few generations back. According to our Thai, Hmong and Mlabri informants, they were very able hunters, having even killed intruders and had allegedly also been occasional cannibals! One source relates that about a hundred of their group (although seemingly a somewhat exaggerated number) had crossed the border into Thailand around 1986, only to be chased back by the Thai border gendarmes. Due to the heavily militarised area on both sides of the border, their number has probably also been reduced.

While visiting a military compound on the Thai side of the border at the end of our last stay in Nan in 1994, we met a local Hmong who told us that he had met a couple and their child who came to ask for food and a few other necessities and had the alleged striped tattoos. In the nearby village we bought some old weapons looking like those of the Ml, but more crudely made. A more recent indication of the existence of the 'fierce' Mlabri came from our long-standing Thai friend, who had actually seen a man at some distance not far from the border inside Laos around 1989. He had been sitting naked but with a skin over his shoulders and holding a spear in his right hand, probably to guard the trail leading into their area, see drawing fig. 123.

The problem of the exact relations between the Mlabri M1 and M7 bothered us already during our third expedition, especially as we had the feeling that the Mlabri did not like to tell us everything about their relations with the other Mlabri groups. So when Pha was asked to make a drawing of a human and he made one of a seemingly dismembered person (see fig. 156), I asked him if something similar could also have happened to the M7 Mlabri on meeting his own group a long time ago – no reply!

Figs. 106-107. Hramla, no. 76, is a typical representative of the M1 group, here seen from the front and in profile. Her face is triangular with broad cheek-bones, a broad and very flat nose, heavy brow-ridges, a protuding mouth and a long occiput. She has a slightly Mongoloid eye configuration, but without the epicanthal eye-fold.

Figs. 108-109. At the very end of our stay in Nan in 1970 we found eight Mlabri M2, in Sa, south of Nan city, reg. no. 23: two couples, a young man and three children, who had been taken down by the border gendarmes to the police station due to the fighting with the Communists from Laos. They could speak Laotian, however, which nobody around was able to understand. In the two pictures are one couple with their child, as well as another woman. Their features resemble those of the M1 group, but our old friend Pujaga from Ban Kum said that they did not belong to any of the Mlabri M1. We have labelled them the M2 group.

236

Figs. 110-111. We traced twelve M3 Mlabri in the refugee camp Nam Yao in 1976, reference no. 27 (see map at the end of this book). The Hmong claimed that they are the real or most 'undiluted' kind of Mlabri. They were in an appaling state of starvation. In the upper photograph are Noan, Cha and Oy, in the lower one Han, Pra, Pat and the small boy Kit. Noan is the mother of Han, and as is apparent, they both have the same genetical malformation of the facial skeleton, dysostosis mandibulofacialis, due to inbreeding, see also the kinship diagram fig. 47.

Figs. 112-113. Oy, reg. no. 25, from the M3 group resembles in some ways Hramla from the M1 group. Even though the two groups regard one another as being seperate and cannot intermarry, their language is quite closely related. The M3 group is considered to be the oldest and less mixed group, at least according to he Hmong, the employers of both groups.

Figs. 114.-115 Gaeo (abowe) and Ot (below) also belong to the group of M3 Mlabri from eastern Nan province. Gaeo worked for a Thai farmer in the village Kio Ko, ref. no. 62. He had remained unmarried and was now (1987) about 50 years of at age. It turned out that they had left Laos together around 1951 due to lack of food.

Fig. 116. We found Ot (fig. 115), 48 years old, his Thai wife and their healthy looking children in Ban Na Luang about 10 km north of Nan city, reg.no. 63. Apparent from the photograph, Ot was not looking well and was coughing a lot. Therefore we took him to the hospital in Nan the next day. Unfortunately it turned out that he had an uncurable TB. Of the five children, only the boy on the left looks different from the Thai. In many places the rural Thai population definitely already contains earlier autochthonous admixtures!

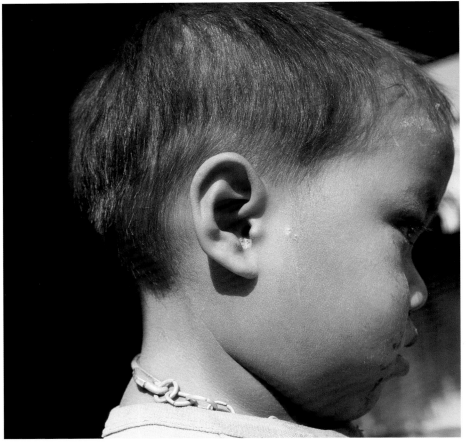

Fig. 117. The Ml-Mlabri Lat's son with a Hmong girl. As related on p. 204 his mother was allegedly killed by her Hmong family, with whom the boy now stays. As is apparent, his traits are an appropiate mixture of those of his father and mother. Lat is seen in fig. 139.

Fig. 118. The Hmong Lao Ju led our party up from his village Ban Nam Uan, ref.no. 39, along a steep trail northwards to what should turn out to be his poppy field at an altitude about 1300 m, where he left us at 11 a.m. He first returned in the late afternoon with the two men, Gaeng and Theung, whom he claimed to be Mlabri. However, they are probably rather of mixed Mlabri-T'in origin. He said that their group stayed further north-east and were said to live in windscreens in the jungle. They are labelled the M4 Mlabri. Gaeng and Theung showed us a typical Mlabri spearhead and the digging implement, but they refused to sell them, saying they had belonged to their parents.

Fig. 119. Lek, another acquaintance of Lao Ju, stayed not far from the refugee centre in Ban Pa Gang, ref. no. 41. Evidently Lek also belongs to the same group M4 as Gaeng and Theung, but resembles more the Mlabri M1.

Fig. 120. Lot, probably the last remaining Mlabri in Loi province. He was traced by us in 1982 in Ban Na Luang, ref.no. 48, and we have labelled his group the M5. It had lived on the two large sandstone mountain plateaus Phu Kradung and Phu Luang and had consisted of about a hundred persons, but had been decimated. The remaining small group, except Lot, had tried to make it back to Laos in 1977.

Fig. 121. 60 km north of Vientiane we met this 28- year old woman 'i An in 1989, labelled M6 Mlabri, but probably of the same kind as the Mlabri M3 living in Nan province. However, she had no knowledge about where she was born, but most likely towards the northwest closer to the border with Thailand.

242

Fig. 122 The girl on the right gave us this ten years old photograph of her 'owner', a Laotian farmer, together with her sister and herself. Evidently the sister has the same heritable, facial disconfiguration as met with already among quite a few of the other Mlabri groups, such as Gaeo and Mun's family (M1) in western Nan province as well as Noan and her mother Han of the M3 group, see figs. 110-111.

Fig. 123. Two Semangs (or more correctly Orang Asli) shown at the annual spring fair in Chieng Mai in 1970, were they demonstrated their various skills, as for example using their blow pipes. As is apparent, they both have curly hair and red-brown skin, but otherwise they have different facial features. The one to the left has heavy eyebrows, a depressed nose root, receding chin and a triangular face, similar to most of the Mlabri. They said that they derived from the border area between Thailand and Malaysia. Just like the Senoi and the Mlabri they are of mixed origin belonging to the autochthonous population of Indo-China.

Fig. 124. To our knowledge there are no photographs of the so-called 'fierce' Mlabri labelled M7. However, our aquaintance, a Thai border patrol captain, made this drawing of a Mlabri-like person close to the Thai-Laotian border southeast of Nan. Here he saw a man sitting under a tree, probably guarding the trail leading into their area. He made this drawing and we note the spear, that the man was heavily built and, in particular, that he had only a skin over his shoulder. The latter is a significant detail, as no other Mlabri we know of use skins for any purpose, but according to the Hmong this is exactly the pecularity of this group of Mlabri. The Thai authorities had some difficulties in chasing them back to Laos in the 1980s, when they entered the border land between Laos and Thailand.

Origins and Migrations

The Mlabri (Ml and M3) themselves have no idea of where they originally derived from, except that they came to Nan province in northeastern Thailand from Sayabouri province in Laos at the time of their grandparents. Therefore, we have to turn to what has been said by archaeologists and anthropologists about the other autochthonous peoples in Indo-China, as well as those who arrived later, in particular the Thai and the Hmong, to see how the Mlabri fit into the general population pattern. During our nine months travelling in Northern Thailand in 1970 we stayed with all the major hill tribes and especially the Hmong. In the still jungle-clad mountains they were all engaged in swidden farming on small fields near their villages while also being passionate hunters. When asking the old people it turned out that, at the beginning of the 20th century, there were much fewer people both on the plains and in the mountains, as the last big invasion of people from Burma, Laos and the Thai lowland had not yet taken place. Without further local information being available we have to turn to the more general information on the area.

G. Olivier, 1968, p. 34-45, divides the autochthonous people into three subgroups: the southern Proto-Indo-Chinese living mainly along the north-south orientated Annamite mountain chain through Thailand, Laos and Cambodia; the southwestern in Malaysia, Thailand, Laos and Cambodia; while the northwestern subgroup is found in Burma and India.

Out of the three subgroups, he already mentions the "Khas du Laos" or Kha Thong Luang in the first line under the heading: "Proto-Indochinois orientaux" and renders some of their main characteristics such as their oblong head, triangular face, protruding mouth and their apparent mixing with the Negritos, ending by saying: "Instead of having been mixed, these Proto-Indo-Chinese are rather more primitive and undifferentiated, because these representatives from the Indo-Chinese postglacial Mesolithicum hold in reality all the primitive Southeast Asiatic races: the Proto-Indo-Chinese, the Negritos and even the Veddas." Olivier concludes that their condition of life, their tribes, their isolation and their endogamy have retarded their evolution towards one of the major known races. However, he cautiously adds: "But that is still only a hypothesis."

In this connection it is curious to note the similarity between the Mlabri and the reconstructed head of the so-called Wadjak man, the first identified Homo sapiens in Southeast Asia, who lived sometime before 10,000 years BP in Jawa, see Coon, 1963, fig. 58C. Wadjak I. b. But as Coon writes, p. 405, Wadjak man might equally well have derived from the north, such as in Thailand or Indo-China. Some of the Mesolithic crania from Tam Pong in Laos, half as old as Wadjak man, represent less remote ancestors of the Mlabri in time and space. Their similar crania with a mixture of Negrito and Mongoloid features are voluminous, long and high, but with lower face and eye sockets, in short the so-called cranio-facial disharmony, traits which are still quite pronounced among some of the Proto-Indo-Chinese people including the Mlabri (see, for example, fig. 272). We shall return to this issue in a moment, which may show that the Mlabri in Laos are probably somewhat earlier than previously anticipated.

Gebhard Flatz in Kraisri Nimmanahaeminda, 1963, 161-177 gives valuable information on the Mlabri based on various examinations, especially of their health, diseases, blood, etc., the results of which he presents in an admirably transparent way. Under the heading "Racial classification", p. 172, he also enters into the question of their origin, arriving at the conclusion that the Mlabri, who Bernatzik and he himself met, are identical with those of the larger group, our Ml group. Moreover, he describes their ethnic affiliation by using the term of von Eickstedt, "palaeomongoloid", but rightly leaves out the additional qualification "race", as he says this term has not much scientific significance. But then he says, p. 174: "The somatic analysis leaves not doubt that the Mlabri are Mongoloids. No traces of Negrito characteristics are present. It seems doubtful that the Southeast Asian subcontinent ever harboured a Negrito population north of the Malayan peninsula. The area of the Mlabri must therefore be limited to the area of the Mongoloids."

However, these bold statements can all be questioned. First of all, the Mongoloid traits are usually not very pronounced, except that most Mlabri have the Mongoloid eye configuration, but without the epicanthal fold. It is a well-known fact that this is a dominant feature, still visible even after having been 'diluted' through quite a few generations. We have recorded a number of cases of sexual connections between the Mlabri and the mountain Thai, the Hmong, etc., which, as we shall see, are at least responsible for some recent Mongoloid influx.

When Flatz writes "No traces of Negrito characteristics are present", it is possibly because he did not study their fingerprints. They are, as we have seen, extraordinary and resemble those of the Senoi-Semang (Orang Asli) in Malaysia. The advantage of dermatoglyphs is that, just like the bones of the crania, they constitute a 'conservative' trait and therefore are not so easily changed by environmental factors. Finally, but without entering into a lengthy discussion, it should be mentioned that mainland Indo-China also north of Malaysia allegedly until quite recently held small groups of Negrito populations, but today only as mixtures with other peoples.

In fact, Flatz himself delivers yet another argument for our version of the origin of the Mlabri further south than their present home: "The flatness of the nose with a large nostril area is an indication of a domicile in the tropics for many generations", however, their present habitat in Northern Thailand has only a subtropical climate!

Evidence for the Isolation of the Mlabri

First of all I would like to emphasise that Mlabri men have probably always had some contact with the neighbouring hill tribes and rural Thai, bartering jungle materials for clothes, iron, etc. However, an important point is that until the 1980s they tried to hide their camps and asked others to stay away. Although the Mlabri's sexual connections with their ever-changing neighbours seem to have been very limited, due to the fact that everyone, the Mlabri included, has prohibited such links, we have nevertheless recorded quite a few such incidences between the Mlabri and the other Mon-Khmer speaking tribes as well at with the Thai and the Hmong, their main employers. However the resulting children from such 'mesalliances' have primarily remained with their non-Mlabri family and consequently have had less effect on the Mlabri's gene pool than on that of their neighbours.

This explains why the Mlabri have preserved some very ancient physiological traits – an important detail overlooked previously! Besides their low stature, especially as regards the M3 Mlabri, the most conspicuous traits are their low face, protruding mouth and parallel herewith the long occiput (back of the head). Out of 62 Ml individuals, with about an equal number of men and women, we obtained an average of 78 for their (meso-) cephalic index and almost the same as regards the M3 Mlabri. Furthermore, 22 anthropometric measures were obtained from each of the about a hundred Mlabri investigated besides those from the other mountain peoples; however these have not yet been published.

Every Mlabri, except babies, also had his or her fingerprints taken. All of them had a majority of whorls, the M3 Mlabri included. However, out of the 60 recorded, the Ml Mlabri men had: 84.7% whorl, 14.7% ulnar loop, 0.4% radial loop, and 0.2% arch, whereas the women had: 76.6% whorl, 22.6% ulnar loop, 0.4% radial loop, 0.4% arch and thus the highest number of whorls ever recorded for any ethnic group in the world. In all likelihood this has also been caused by their long isolation and the resulting genetic drift.

These results are important for our studies, since their small fingerprints, also with many fine dermatological lines, indicate negritoid admixture from Orang Asli sources which, together with the similarity of their material and spiritual life, strongly indicates a common origin south of their present home

All evidence suggests that the Mlabri have always been hunter-gatherers who shunned other peoples, except for brief contacts, as long as there were still uninhabited lower mountain tracts available. This, together with their extraordinary ability to move unnoticed from place to place, has enabled them to preserve their ancient lifestyle until as late as the 1970s. Our investigations show, for example, that they have trekked from Doi Sathan in Nan province far down into Loei province and back again, covering a distance of about 2 x 300 km, as the crow flies, in reality perhaps five times as much due to their continuous search for food through mountain jungles, within the period 1972-84. This, combined with the generally accepted view that similar autochthonous people were once more widespread in Indo-China, may explain why the Mlabri Ml, in particular, both physically and as regards their beliefs, resemble such distant jungle people as the Semai Senoi living south of Thailand's southern border with Malaysia about 1,500 km south of their present habitat.

While the two long ocean coastlines of Indo-China are believed to have been the main connections for the Mongoloid invasion down into Southeast Asia since postglacial times, it has been the north-south-oriented Annamite mountain ranges which have served as the connecting link for the southern proto-Indo-Chinese since Neolithic times. But we have no reliable records of the whereabouts of the Mlabri before the beginning of the 20th century. However, the similarity of, especially, the Ml Mlabri with the Semai Senoi suggests that they moved further northwards along the Annamite mountain ranges well after the end of the last glaciation, perhaps as late as between 2,000-4,000 BP. The smaller Mlabri M3, having inhabited lower altitudes, may represent an even older form, perhaps the very oldest type of all the existing Proto-Indo-Chinese people!

The Semang and Semai Senoi Hill Tribes of Malaysia as compared to the Mlabri

The Semang (fig. 123) traditionally occupy the lower, tropical rainforest, whereas the Senoi stay in the upper and steeper, jungle-clad mountain ranges extending up to 2,000 m. They have enjoyed long and friendly contact resulting in a multitude of mixtures of physical features, language and cultures. Semang have Negrito traits, are of very small stature, have a round head, low rounded forehead and only slightly prominent cheekbones. Their eyes are round, open and only slightly Mongoloid, while their hair is woolly, and their skin is of a reddish-brown colour. There are only about 2,500 persons left. According to Colin Nicholas in his article: "Organizing Orang Asli Identity" (2002, p. 119). This collective and less derogative term should rather be applied to the above two peoples, but before 1960 it did not exist. However, due to the many and often mixed subgroups of Orang Asli, it is also less descriptive.

The physically heterogeneous group Senoi (Sakai, etc.) are generally taller, have usually a long head with a flat forehead and very broad cheekbones (triangular face). Their eyes are rather more Mongoloid than those of the typical Semang, while their hair is long and often wavy. Skin colour varies from reddish-brown to yellowish brown. Altogether, the main anthropometrical features of the Northern Senoi are definitively closer to those of the Mlabri. Their population comprised about 20,000 a century ago, but there are now over 26,000 (Benjamin, 2002).

The linguistic position of the Semang language is uncertain. It might have belonged to a separate linguistic family (Credner 1935a, p. 250), but has gradually been submerged in Senoi, which is closely related to Mon-Khmer languages further north in Vietnam, (Laos) and Cambodia (Frank M. Lebar et al., 1964, p. 182). Most writers have assigned a greater antiquity to the Semang in Malaysia than to the Senoi, the former having arrived there at a very early date, perhaps from Indo-China, according to the latter source, p. 176.

While the Semang and the Senoi, just like the Mlabri, have traditionally been hunter-gatherers and have used windscreens or occasionally natural shelters, living in groups of 10-55; most Senoi now subsist mainly on swidden argriculture and live in groups of 50-200 more permanently in their settlements. The difference in economic life is reflected in other related ways; the Semang do not keep domestic animals, they have a simple way of trading and a division of labour according to sex. According to Schebesta, patrilocality and patrilineal affiliation prevail among the Semang. A typical extended family group or band is made up of three generations, and kinship terminology is not simply classificatory but includes age class, all of which resembles the Mlabri. Frank M. Lebar et al. 1964, p. 185-186, writes:

"The Semang do not conceive of their relations with the supernatural in terms of an organised religion. They have a large body of myths and legends, together with a belief in innumerable deities. Investigators have also found concepts which they describe as soul, heaven, and life after death … Schebesta (1957: 4 ff) comments on the extraordinary complexity of their religious beliefs and practices, many of which have been borrowed from neighbouring peoples."

Among the many other things we recognise from the Mlabri is, for example, the concept of a Thunder God who punishes humans, if they laugh at butterflies or copulate in the daytime, by sending thunderstorms or through animal messengers, such as tigers. The Semang also consider illness to be due to supernatural causes and previously they had the older and probably more honourable practice of putting their dead in trees. It is likewise believed that the soul leaves the body after death and the camp where the person dies is generally deserted. In the afterworld in the west, the deceased live a carefree, but shadowy existence.

But there are also similarities with the Senoi. It is said, p. 180-181: "As might be expected in a society where the individual is largely autonomous, religion is formless animism. Most living creatures have detachable 'souls'. There are two major categories of external spiritual agents, disease spirits and ghosts, but the distinction between the two classes is not hard and fast".

"Pregnancy is marked by an elaborate set of food taboos imposed on both parents, especially with their first or second child. There is a long postnatal taboo on sexual intercourse, the point of which, according to the eastern Semai, is to restrict family size so that the children will not suffer neglect. … Even though Senoi society is so undemanding that blind people, mental deficients, and old people can usually fill a production role, until recently those who became totally dependent on others were taken off to a hut in the jungle, given a week's supply of food, and abandoned … Despite the use of grave goods and a vague notion of flower scented world of the dead … most Senoi, even those who are terrified of ghosts, are extremely sceptical about the afterlife."

To demonstrate the many similarities that seem to exist, not only between the material cultures of Semai Senoi and the Mlabri, but also concerning their spiritual worlds, I have quoted below two articles by Robert K. Dentan, who has studied the Semai Senoi and related groups for almost half of century. Actually, he kindly send me some of his articles 25 years ago, but at a time I was not ready to grasp the importance of the connections between our findings.

Robert Knox Dentan (2002) writes p. 206: "This chapter deals with the construction of God by an Austroasiatic-speaking swiddening people, about 30,000 people known generically as Semai Senoi. They are now subjects of the dominant people of the Peninsula, the Malays, whose ruling class used them as despised slaves until the early part of this (19th) century. They are famous for their peaceability" (just as the Mlabri).

P. 207: In the first third of his suggestive article Robert Dentan describes the devastations the God of Thunder, God of the Dark, allegedly may inflict on the almost unprotected jungle dwellers, if they have violated the natural order: "by mixing immiscible things (foods) together; or of the social order, by disrespect or incest; or the personal order, by loss of self-control". Besides these 'sins', the Mlabri would also include not having made offerings to their deceased parent's spirits recently. In the vivid description of the horrors the Semai experience we recognise all what happens before and during a thunderstorm – the intense yellow-red evening sky the preceding evening – a warning that the spirits are angry, then the extreme black, heavy clouds building up over the treetops, the chilly awesome stillness, followed by the increasing rumbles and then suddenly – lightning exploding much too near, causing trees to tumble over during the following rainstorm. The jungle dwellers, now cold and wet, desperately plead with the Thunder God not to harm them further. This could cause floods, landslides and annihilation. It is mentioned that Shebesta said that, in order to make the Thunder God leave, the Semai would burn bits of roof thatch – the Mlabri use dirty rags!

P. 213: "(Semai' and related peoples') animism and naturalism stands to be the oldest religion known to human kind, with most indigenous communities throughout the world sharing this world view and morality, of the importance of establishing and maintaining balanced and harmonious relations with the natural order of plants and animals, based on mutual coexistence and respect. The religion dates back at least 25,000 years, the date linked to the oldest record of living human history."

P. 224-25: "Why do Semai portray so fearful a cosmos? I suspect it comes from living on the edge of a state based on slavery and a related notion of power unfamiliar to Westerners. In that conception power exists separately from the people who wield it (Anderson 1990a, p. 74) ... The Semai response to the slaver state and their general deference to Malay culture, for example, make sense in these terms. As long as penetration of the hills is only sporadic, for example by slave raids and kidnapping, a pervasive non-violence is reasonable: flight, not confrontation. For power is not subject to social control the traditional Semai notion of God exemplifies this amoral violent uncontrollable power."

"Elsewhere I've described how Semai tell horror stories to their children. ... They ready people for the uncontrollable fear of uncontrollable nature, for the horror of having one's children stolen for the convenience and prurient pleasure of powerful others. They protect them from facile stupid optimism."

In his article "Ambiguity, Synecdoche and affect in Semai Medicine" (1988) Robert K. Dentan further elaborates on the beliefs of the Semai Senoi, but is not so easily digested, because there are so many references and notes deserving to be read in full as they hold a wealth of thoughtful information. They also question the methods of collecting the data on these difficult subjects. I have chosen the following quotes for comparison with our material:

P. 857: Under "Abstract" concerning their beliefs: "Semai descriptions of their beliefs about health and disease vary from person to person. Moreover, at different times the same person expresses mutually incongruent beliefs. This amorphousness and fluidity merit analysis rather than neatening. This paper details Semai beliefs, loose ends and all, and suggests that their formal peculiarities are due to the prevalence of synecdoche in conceptual organisation. Their inconsistency and fluidity may stem from individualistic egalitarianism within Semai society and powerlessness in the face of non-Semai attack".

"The plasticity of Semai medical ideas seemed related to the cultural assignment of threat as a meaning to such commonplace phenomena as butterflies, dragonflies, and thunderstorms ... a generalised Semai conception of a dangerous and unpredictable world, a world which most ubiquitous and seemingly innocuous elements carry the potential for disaster and death."

"Anthropologists often neaten non-Western systems of thought, to make them comprehensible in linear parsimonious ways and to refute ethnocentric presumptions that non-Westerners are irrational and simple-minded. The tendentious claim that, like its supposed Western counterpart, non-Western thought was rational and well organised may be topsy-turvy. Probably all Westerners most of the time, and most Westerners all of the time, are not tidy-minded. Similarly, Semai medicine was not a crude facsimile of organised and written Western medicine but a lush jungle of conflicting ideas. How then to represent their reality?"

P. 859: "... Semai averred that no one could know what someone else thought or felt. Therefore, they said, trying to articulate one's own feelings or innermost thought was pointless. This code inhibited inflicting oneself on others." Yet another odd similarity with the Mlabri: "Semai rarely instructed children. ... Most people were reluctant to assert ideas. ... Knowledge therefore remained socially unchallenged and thus idiosyncratic." (Just like the Mlabri youngsters, who still complained of not having received proper instruction on anything including various technical skills in the 1980s).

On souls: "Timid head-souls, *ruwaay,* lived behind the centre of the forehead. They flitted away from the body during altered states of consciousness and diseases involving lassitude, notably forms of soul loss ... When a person died accidentally, however, the undevoured head-soul might survive as a bird, most likely a bird, which was also prey to supernaturals." Compare with the Mlabri's belief that an eagle, owl, etc, may carry the feeble soul of a child away causing it to die. ... "Other things had psyches or head souls. For instance, on every lofty Perak mountain the biggest commercially valuable calamus rattan had a psyche." The Mlabri would say that the creeper has a spirit, to which it is necessary to offer to avoid a disastrous headache.

P. 860: "Equating butterflies with head-souls supported East Semai notions that molesting butterflies or flashy dragonflies weakened natural order and thus risked cataclysmic upheavals like floods, thunder squalls and earthquakes."

Indeed, recent geological investigations have proven that such natural catastrophes have been much more frequent during the last thousand years than previously known in, especially, Indonesia. In the minds of both the Orang Asli and, interestingly, also the Mlabri they upheld a permanent worry and fear, which may be yet another indication of where the latter derived from at some point.

Some unusual phenomena cause anxiety both among Semai and Mlabri, e.g.:

P. 861: "Any unusual abnormal piercing was dangerous, e.g. a vine growing through a tree or a branch puncturing the surface or the earth." "An East Semai and Lengkok word, *turuuq*, affect by stabbing, referred to fallen trees made spongy by termites or to violation of species boundaries, e.g. intertwined trees of different species lying one atop the other (cf. mixing taboo below)."

P. 862: "Semai used the word 'ghost' almost interchangeable with 'rain spirit'. Still ghosts were peculiar. They originated from shadows of the dead". The Mlabri had similar stories about small families of spirits – father, mother and children, they said they had seen but briefly in the jungle.

Even though the Semai may have been swidden farmers for quite some time they also depend substantially on hunting and gathering, as the Mlabri did almost exclusively until the 1980s. Apparently their material and spiritual cultures have so many specific elements in common that they possibly derived from the same tropical area in or around Malaysia. This was before some of them went northwards, perhaps 2,000-4,000 years BP, the Mlabri after having mixed slightly with tribes possessing Mongoloid traits.

It can be stated that the Mlabri resemble the Semai Senoi physically more than the Semang, and Mlabri material life, descent, kinship groups and terminology also seem to have been very much the same as those of the Semai Senoi before they took up agriculture not long ago. With regard to the supernatural world, the Mlabri resemble the Semai Senoi in particular, and the latter resemble the Semang as they have been neighbours and have exchanged traditions and religious ideas since the remote past.

22 years ago, I wrote about a possible connection between Semang-Senoi and the Mlabri (ref: Trier, 1986), and I still consider that it is more likely that the Mlabri have always been hunter-gatherers who shunned other peoples except for brief contacts for bartering, as long as there were still uninhabited mountain tracts available. Together with their extraordinary ability to move unnoticed from place to place, it has enabled them to preserve their ancient lifestyle until as late as the 1980s. This, combined with the generally accepted view that similar autochthonous people were once more wide-spread in Indo-China, may explain why the Mlabri M1 in particular, both as regards their material as well as regards their spiritual world, resemble such distant jungle people as the Senoi living around the Thai-Malaysian border.

An article "On Being Tribal in the Malay world" by Geoffrey Benjamin, 2002, p. 36-37, describes the fine socio-anthropological balance existing in the Semang-Senoi-Malay culture complex which, astoundingly and down to even minor details, until recently corresponded with that of the Mlabri-Hmong-Thai culture complex. To this end I shall quote p. 36-37 from his well-written article: "On Being Tribal in the Malay World", however realizing that such cultural complexes are more wide-spread than first anticipated:

"How has the Semang pattern managed to be so persistent? Two main problems had to be solved. First, how to sustain an egalitarian low-density population over such a large territory, and segmentary right down to conjugal-family level? Second, how to retain their complementary distinctiveness from the more settled, farming-based ways of life espoused by their neighbours, The Senoi peoples and the Malays? I shall limit myself here to a bare sketch of the mechanisms they appear to have employed, which are founded on their distinctive kinship pattern (Benjamin 1985, 2001b)."

"As I have already suggested, the first problem – the maintenance of a low-density non-increasing population – was solved in two main ways. First, marriages usually had to be contracted over great distances. Second, they had children as infrequently as possible, through two mutually reinforcing mechanisms: (a) a ban on sexual intercourse for about two years after a woman had given birth, and (b) a preference for delaying weaning for two years. The latter practice suppresses ovulation through hormonal mechanisms, especially in women with low body fat (Bongarts 1980). Moreover, the affines meant that the husband could not easily find a substitute sexual partner at this time. The net result was a very slow, or perhaps flat, rate of population growth so long as the people remained nomadic. On settling down, however, the population growth rises spectacularly: the provision of alternative food supplies allows the mothers to wean their children earlier (onto grain-based porridge), and the people allow a concomitant relaxation of the post-partum coital taboo."

"Why should the Semang populations have bothered to organise their lives in this way? I suggest that they did so in order to maintain a lifeway that was distinctively complementary to that of their neighbours, the Senoi and the Malays. By so doing, they were able to reduce any competition that may have emerged between themselves and the other populations who shared their environment. But to achieve this end they had to positively maintain a commitment to nomadic foraging that was binding on a just sufficient number of people to maintain a viable self-producing population. Any attraction to the long-term sedentism espoused by their neighbours would have dissolved away this selective advantage. Differential kinship rules generated the demographic structure appropriate to each of the lifeway, and served to sustain an ideology that painted the other population's ways as inappropriate."

Now, if in what Geoffrey Benjamin has written above, the Semang are replaced by the Mlabri, the Senoi by the Hmong and the Malay by the Thai, there is an almost perfect match with the socio-anthropological situation of the Mlabri until about 1980 even down to all the minor details mentioned (cf. pp. 206-236 above).

Genetic study of the Palaeolithic and Neolithic Southeast Asians

In the following I shall refer to some of the main points of the recent discussions on the origin of the Mlabri, based on the promising genetic DNA analyses, by giving extracts from a few of the relevant communications on the Internet to see how this information may apply to our own results. The references and extracts are rendered chronologically:

Hum Biol. 2001 Apr; 73(2): 225-31. Oota H, Kurosaki K, Pookajorn S, Ishida T., Ueda S.

"DNA samples were extracted from six prehistoric human remains, found on the Malay Peninsula, dating to the Palaeolithic and the Neolithic periods. Nucleotide sequences of mitrochondial DNA were determined by the polymerase chain reaction – direct sequencing method. A phylogenetic tree between prehistoric and present humans was constructed based on the nucleotide sequence data. Mitochondrial DNA relationships and ethno-archaeological evidence suggest that there is continuity between the pre-Neolithic humans and the present Semang and that the Neolithic humans in this area might be an ancestral group of the Senoi."

Recent Origin and Cultural Reversion of a Hunter-Gatherer Group

The following are extracts from a longer report by Hiroki Oota et al. (2005):

P. 2. "The Mlabri have no mtDNA diversity, and the genetic diversity at Y-chromosome and autosomal loci are also extraordinarily reduced in the Mlabri. Genetic, linguistic, and cultural data all suggest that the Mlabri were recently founded, 500-800 years ago, from a very small number of individuals. Moreover, the Mlabri appear to have originated from an agricultural group and then adopted a hunter-gathering mode."

P. 3. "The Mlabri language seems lexically most closely related to Khmu and T'in, two languages of the Khmuic branch of the Mon-Khmer sub-family of Austro-Asiatic languages, both of which are spoken in agricultural highland villages. The grammar of Mlabri additionally has features that deviate markedly from typical Mon-Khmer, suggesting that Mlabri developed as a result of contact between speakers of a quite different language of unknown affiliation (Jørgen Rischel). The rationale for using genetic analyses to investigate this question is that previous work has shown that hunter-gatherer groups typically differ from their agricultural neighbours in having reduced genetic diversity and high frequencies of unique mtDNA types."

P. 4. "No other human population has been found to lack mtDBA HV1 variation, and mtDNA HV1 variation in six other hill tribes (all agricultural groups) from the same region of Thailand was significantly higher."

P. 5 "The Y-STR haplotype diversity in the Mlabri is again lower than that reported for any other human population."

P. 6 "Only the Mlabri exhibited a significant excess of observed for heterozygosity. Although more complicated scenarios are possible, the simplest explanation is that the Mlabri (but not the other hill tribes) have undergone a severe reduction in population size, as also indicated by the mtDNA and Y-STR haplotype data, and as also suggested by a previous study by Flatz of blood group variation."

P. 7. "Both the mtDNA and Y-STR data therefore indicate that the Mlabri underwent a substantial reduction in population size about 500-800 y ago (and not more than about 1,300 y ago, if the mtDNA and Y-chromosome data reflect the same event): There are two possible scenarios: (1) a bottleneck, in which the Mlabri were reduced from a formerly large population to a much smaller population size, which then increased to the current level of about 300 individuals; or (2) a founder event, in which the Mlabri began as a very small number of individuals, became isolated, and then increased over time to their present size."

P. 8. "Similar reductions in genetic diversity are predicted under either scenario, so the genetics cannot distinguish between these."

P. 9. "A critical assumption is the amount of genetic diversity present in the ancestral Mlabri population prior to the size reduction. Another assumption of this analysis is that the event that led to population size reduction completely eliminated the mtDNA diversity."

P. 10. Alternatively, some mtDNA diversity may have been present after the population size reduction, but was subsequently lost because of drift. Loss of mtDNA diversity due to subsequent drift is not likely, if there was a single event reducing the Mlabri population size that was followed by population growth, since mtDNA diversity is retained in growing populations. However, if the size reduction occurred more times over several generations, then it may not have been as dramatic a bottleneck as the resampling analysis implies."

As the last phrase seems to imply, the more plausible explanation remains that the Mlabri (M1), after having experienced a less dramatic bottleneck, also suffered several size reductions until recently. Instead of subscribing to some extraordinary founding event that the Mlabri are refugees from culture, they might have suffered a less pronounced bottleneck one or two thousand years BP. Thereafter a series of incidents during subsequent centuries, such as landslides, epidemics or killings by the other hill tribes, caused the extraordinary lack of mtDNA diversity and low Y-chomosome and autosomal loci.

Perhaps I am prejudiced in this matter, due to the fact that, contrary to what has been said by Hiroki Oota et al. above, the Mlabri leaders have constantly told us that they were always exclusively hunter-gatherers until the 1970s, when they gradually began to work as poor part-time workers in the fields of their Hmong employers. The fact that they were still professional hunter-gatherers was demonstrated continuously during our first three expeditions. When, for example, we walked with a band in the still intact mountain jungles and traversed steep slopes at an incredible speed. At some point I asked them

what they would do if they met with a pack of a species of small, but fierce and dangerous tigers. In ten seconds the band of about 10 people had taken to the trees, old and young, men and women alike with their babies on their backs. A strange, heartbreaking experience as it looked all too real. On subsequent occasions, young men insisted on demonstrating how to climb some giant trees and balanced on long lateral branches vertiginously high, 35m up, without support of any kind.

Finally, I would like to emphasise that the ubiquitous term "primitive", as so often attached to the Mlabri, should be questioned. Their culture could just as well be claimed to be highly specialised. These people have probably survived in their dangerous jungles for several thousands of years and have, therefore, developed formidable skills for extracting all kinds of material and foodstuffs, as well as avoiding hostilities from the other hill tribes. Even more surprisingly, from studying their beliefs, we realize that spiritually they have obtained a coherent view of their universe, including the animals, trees, plants and themselves. To us, this seems to be more sympathetic, tolerant, and in many ways, less superstitious than in most of the worlds dominant cultures. Also remembering that, to the Mlabri, spirit primarily refers to any effect that may influence them in an unwanted way.

Future Studies of the Mlabri and Other Hill Tribes of Southeast Asia

The fast dwindling number of Mlabri demonstrates the sad fact that ethnic groups, which have lived very isolated for long periods of time and only participated in the general gene exchange to a limited degree, become left behind. As their remaining number is now so small, these people will probably disappear as ethnic groups within the next few decades. This leads directly to the question, what is the most urgent work to be done scientifically as regards the Mlabri? I suggest it is to trace and investigate the last remains of other autochthonous splinter-groups in all of Indo-China and Indonesia. Furthermore, microbiological DNA studies of the various hill tribes of Southeast Asia should be undertaken. Together with other sophisticated analyses, this will surely reveal important evidence for comparison and further clarification of the ancient ethnical developments in this important quadrant of the world, all the more so, as the written records are few, and very old archaeological remains are even rarer.

The Mlabri M1 and M3 Camps

The following pages describe in more detail the location and construction of the Mlabri camps, especially those of the M1 Mlabri we visited between 1970 and 1994. We met the M3 Mlabri in their refugee camp in 1977 and in subsequent years, but it was not until 1987 that we managed to persuade them to build a traditional windscreen (see figs. 142-143), which they also used during our last visit in 1994.

Formerly, the Mlabri chose rather inaccessible locations for their camps in steep mountain jungles far away from and higher up than the villages and trails. They usually had the front of the windscreens directed downwards to see if anyone was approaching, so they were able to hide the women and children before strangers reached the camp. Apart from remoteness from others, they have the following preferences: dry firewood and above all good drinking water no more than 10 minutes' walk from the camp. Whereas they may prefer some higher altitude in the hot season, they move downwards during winter, sometimes having the front of the windscreens towards the east to catch the first sun on chilly mornings. However, little by little they have had to give up their splendid isolation, when most of the game disappeared and they were consequently compelled to work for the Hmong to obtain rice, etc., from about 1980. However, neither their camps nor the windscreens changed substantially until quite recently, because the Mlabri kept on living in the forest during the hot season and the monsoon, when the Hmong did not require their work.

A windscreen is basically a simple construction protecting against rain, strong wind and the sun. It usually consists of two or three poles of wood or bamboo carrying the upper horizontal beam, while the lower, inside beam almost touches the ground. Finally the screen is covered with banana leaves with up to three layers in case of prolonged rainfall. However, over the years we have realised that there are several variations such as windscreens with elevated floors (fig. 16), or a special kind consisting of one long windscreen for all members in the band (figs. 138-138). On one occasion we met 40 M1 Mlabri, staying in a 'long-house' consisting of two very long windscreens facing each other, and only having an opening at each end. Contrary to what both the M1 and M3 Mlabri had claimed previously, they sometimes just stay under some moderately high trees in the dry season, using the branches as hangers for their clothes as well as for food (fig. 141). Usually caves are avoided, except in Loei and Uttradite province and in Laos, for example where some of the Mlabri there have used the warmer and more comfortable sandstone caves as their dwellings. We have but one example of this kind, see fig. 140. However, let us not forget that the Mlabri have sometimes slept in trees, especially when only a few persons or couples are moving unseen in areas with other hill tribes.

The band leader stays with his elderly father or mother, with his wife and infant children, whereas a male friend may occupy another windscreen with his wife and their children. We may also find the band leader's son with wife and children and his unmarried daughter from a former marriage. Divorced single persons, such as an elderly aunt, often stay by themselves in a windscreen on one of the two flanks. Altogether there may be about 18 persons which, by the way, was the average number of a band before 1980, see example fig. 24. Among the Mlabri there is a high degree of flexibility which, for example, allows anybody, including youngsters, to join another band. But normally good friends stick together, some for life, and even a divorced couple may go on staying in the same band.

Mlabri use various materials to sleep on, such as grass, banana leaves and bark from the Yanong tree, which has to be beaten and washed because of its poisonous sap. An important ethnographical measure is the space required by each person. Actually, very little is necessary, since they sleep close to one another to keep warm during chilly nights. The windscreens are on average 180 cm deep from the foothold (to avoid sliding down into the fires just outside the windscreen) to the inner low wall at a level about 25 cm higher. This enables the Mlabri to get up in a hurry in case of danger, but it is also more convenient during the day. As the interior corner is occupied by clothes and a few personal belongings, there is only something like 150 by 60 cm for each adult person to sleep on. As the average height of Ml Mlabri men is about 155 cm and of women 145 cm, there is just enough space to sleep, a little curled up to one side. The smaller M3 Mlabri manage with even less space.

The Mlabri Ml's dingo-like dogs usually sleep outside the windscreens on the outer side of the fires. They eat whatever food is left, as well as human waste. Not until 1990 did we observe the Mlabri actually feed their dogs. The Mlabri are generally nice to them and even give them short names so they can call them individually. They are quite nice animals and only start barking and fighting if any animal or other unwelcome intruder shows up; if a bear or small leopard attacks the Mlabri they will fight them to the very end.

Looking around the windscreen, previously one could spot only a few items at first, since the Mlabri produced whatever necessary from wood, bamboo, leaves and bast. For many years the only foreign materials were a spear or knife of iron. Meat and vegetables are not kept longer than overnight and are hung high up on a pointed bamboo stick away from animals and insects. The only food stored for longer than this is uncooked rice, whereas salt and tobacco are put into bamboo containers.

When first visiting the Mlabri we were not allowed to – or particularly tempted to – stay overnight in their often disorderly, louse-infected camps. But their sanitary conditions gradually improved after we began to provide them with soap from the market to reduce their many infections. We had some joyful times when my wife Birgit washed and cut their hair, even persuading them to go down to take a bath in the stream below the camp.

At some point we also realised how pleasant it could be to live in a windscreen of our own next to those of the Mlabri. Apart from giving us much better opportunity to observe their activities at a discreet distance, it was also fascinating to watch the jungle, especially during the evening and early morning, with all its animals, noises and smells. Besides, one sleeps well in the open air guarded against stinging insects by the smoke from the fires around. But I still clearly remember a big hairy spider crawling over my sleeping bag, or the evening when myriads of ants marched into the camp and I spent half the night diverting them, using hot ashes to make them take another direction; we also had to clean all our belongings and burn the remaining ants. After this event, our youngest daughter feared them more than the big, green and yellow venomous snakes near the camp!

Apart from these minor inconveniences we have really enjoyed the natural kindness and tact of the Mlabri and in their own environment, rendering them the most pleasant and warm company we have experienced anywhere on our travels.

Fig.125. Above Ban Bow Hoey, January 1977 Mlabri M1 camp of 20 persons and five families: Gu's, Po's, Paeng's and Lek's with four more persons staying 50 m SW of the others: Po with his wife Lai, and Ajan with his wife 'i-bul. The camp was situated at an altitude of about 1,000 m and on a steep southern slope in the dense mountain jungle, which was rather chilly at this time of year.The camp could only be recognized when one was standing right inside it. As usual, all the married couples sleep with their infants. Notice that the strongest men occupy the flanks, while the noisy boys stayed by themselves on the slightly elevated bench (see drawing below) under which they had put embers to keep warm during chilly nights.

Fig. 126. Plan of the camp with four windscreens of which only the two on the right are seen in the photograph.

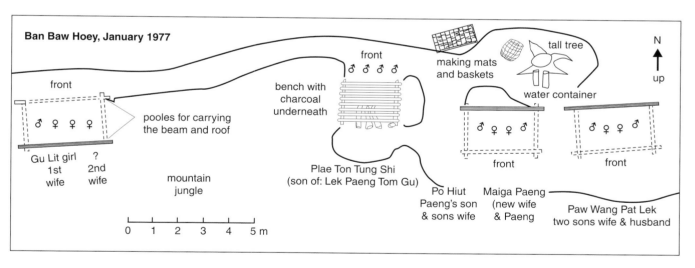

Ban Baw Hoey, January 1977

front

front

making mats
and baskets

tall tree

N

up

front

bench with
charcoal
underneath

water container

pooles for carrying
the beam and roof

Gu Lit girl
1st
wife

?
2nd
wife

mountain
jungle

Plae Ton Tung Shi
(son of: Lek Paeng Tom Gu)

front

front

Po Hiut
Paeng's son
& sons wife

Maiga Paeng
(new wife
& Paeng

Paw Wang Pat Lek
two sons wife & husband

0   1   2   3   4   5 m

Fig. 127. Ban Hui Hom, January 1980 Notice the position of the strong men to guard the windscreens, the exception being the divorced wife of Som staying on the left flank, which is often the case with single persons. No. 2 windscreen is a 'double' one, heavily covered with leaves – actually a hut. The camp was facing north, with a steep hill to the south (to the left in the photograph). It was here we witnessed the most complete ceremony – that for the deceased parents. The platform between windscreens nos. 1 and 2 to the left served as the altar for the offerings.

Fig. 127b. The four windscreens each holding a family. Note the altar in front of Phaeng Noi's hut.

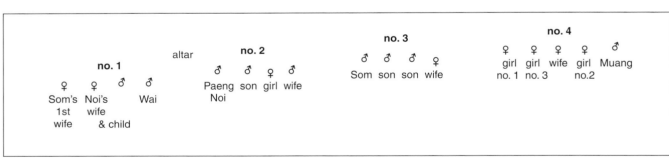

Fig. 128.-129. Ban Na Ka, January 1980, A band of only nine persons having two windscreens at a bend of a small river, with: l: Paeng, 2: his wife Maiga, 3 and 4: their two small boys, 5: Thobitoa, a single elderly woman, 6: Pinlanka, 7: her small girl and 8: Plae and 9: Gu a widower, his daughter married to Paeng's Paeng Noi (II). Here in the dry season bands of usually 15-20 persons often split into two, as food gets difficult to find, or, as in this case, the various Hmong employers only need smaller groups to clear their land to plant rice before the monsoon starts in June.

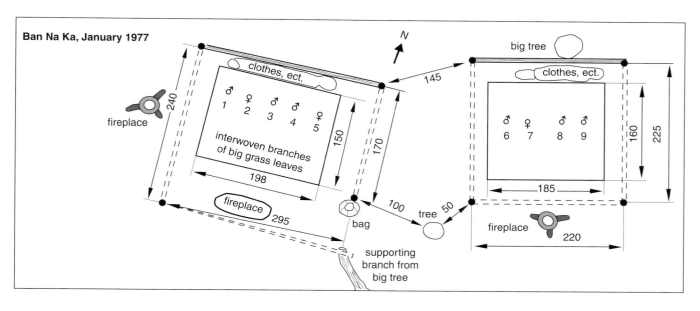

257

Fig. 130.

Fig. 131.

Fig. 132.

Fig. 133.

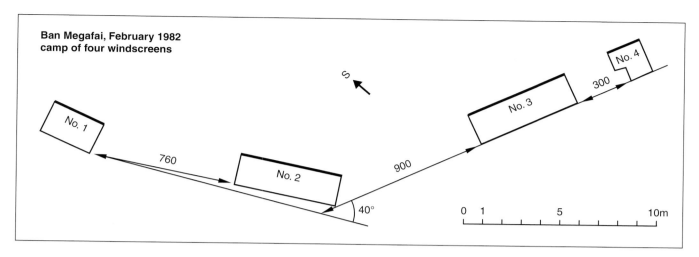

Fig. 134. Camp.

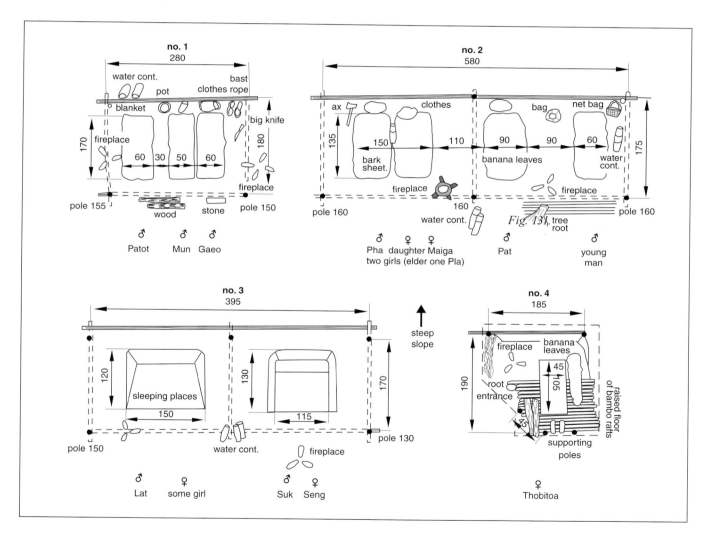

Fig. 135. Ban Megafai, February 1982 (see figs. 130-133) The 11-12 members of this band, except Patot and the infants, were all working in the fields of the Hmong. The four windscreens were facing northeast or north. In the first one lived old Patot (on the left flank) with his son Gaeo and his grandson Mun, who had lost his father. In the second were Pha with his wife Maiga and their small daughter, while Pat stayed with a friend in the other half of the windscreen, who meanwhile had gone to work elsewhere. In the third windscreen there were three teenage boys: Lat, Suk and Seng, while in the fourth one the widow Thobitoa stayed by herself in the less than four square metre windscreen.

259

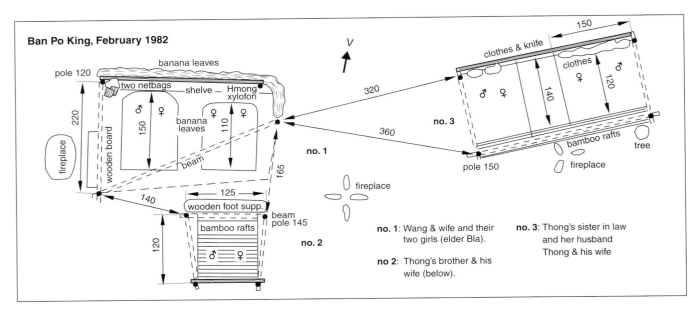

Fig. 136. As is apparent there are many types of camp and windscreen depending on the terrain, season, etc.

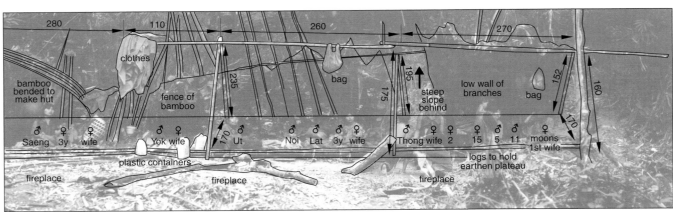

Fig. 137-138. Photograph, M1 Ban Hui Yok, February 1994. Drawing of position of each member, etc. Old Ut and sons with wives and children, plus Thong (Patot's son) with wife and two children, altogether 18 persons. They stayed in an about ten metre long windscreen, which is not common among the M1 Mlabri. The windscreen was facing north at this relatively low and warm altitude. The drawing below explains the photo taken from our own windscreen, with positions and names of the members of the band. As is apparent, each couple with children occupies one cell of about two metres in length, from which they can easily communicate with anyone else during the day, while still having some privacy after dark.

Fig. 139. Everyday life in the long windscreen preparing lunch, Lat and Si also looking after the infants, while Birgit and our Thai interpreter plan our own menu (to avoid an amoebic dysentery). 1994.

Fig. 140. Camp with Lat and Si, their wives and four children, northwest of Nan, M1, ref.no 68, 1987: The site of the two windscreens were cut into the walls of the river gorge of sandstone. This was the first of its kind we had seen in Thailand, but down in Loei province and in Laos we also heard of Mlabri camps being hollowed out in mountain walls of similar soft materials.

261

Fig. 141. In the dry, warm season before the monsoon a band may sleep under some trees using the branches as hangers. North of Ban Baw Hoey, 1989.

Fig. 142-143. Ban Ton Praiwan, M3, March 1987, photograph & drawing of traditional windscreen on the steep river bank on a northern slope at an altitude of only 500 m. The living space was only about 2.5 square metres for the six inhabitants.

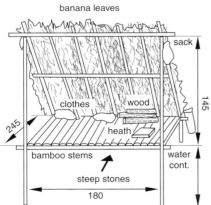

262

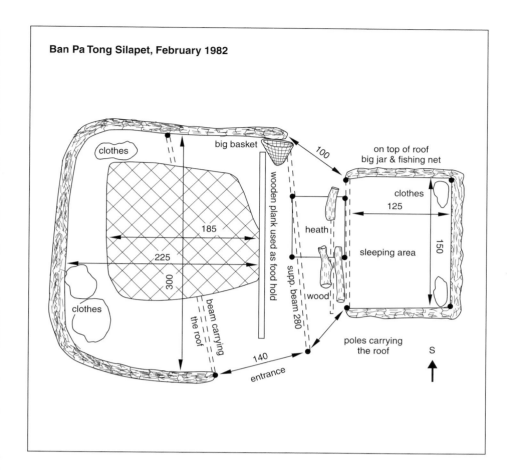

Ban Pa Tong Silapet, February 1982

clothes

big basket

100

on top of roof
big jar & fishing net

clothes
125

185

wooden plank used as food hold

heath

sleeping area

150

225

300

supp. beam 280

clothes

wood

beam carrying the roof

poles carrying
the roof

140

entrance

S

Fig. 144. Ban Pa Tong Silapet, Febr. 1982 While the above windscreen is of the traditional M3 type, this one to the left is for rather longer use. It has traits deriving from Hmong houses, having living quarters and a separate sleeping space for its 10 inhabitants. The hearth is inside, providing warmth for both areas, while the two entrances give fresh air in the hot season. The photograph below shows the windscreen seen from the entrance. During the rainy season the Mlabri M3 also leave to stay by themselves in the jungle, using the traditional simple windscreens.

Fig. 145. The Mlabri M3 still had only a few tools and other commodities. Among the traditional items they kept only the cho, the small hand-spade, of which two of them had belonged to their parents. They also had a small knife, some pots and each adult had a petrol lighter as well as platic containers for water, all from the market in the nearby Hmong village. For quite some time we thought they did not have any expressions of art, but they made some small bamboo containers bearing simple geometrical designs (and small tattos) similar to those of the Mlabri M1. Moreover they had a simple stringed instrument.

Tools and other Material Objects

Mlabri tools and other material objects can be divided into two main groups:

A. Objects made of bamboo, wood, fibres and other vegetable materials, see figs. 146-152.

B. Tools made of iron, see figs. 153-155.

While the items in group B are of more recent origin, probably not dating further back than to the 1930s, but modelled on far older objects, such as spears of wood, all the items in group A belong to the former traditional culture of the Mlabri. Actually, old M1 members like Ut, Paeng and Ai-Kham said they had seen their parents using bark dresses and wooden spears in their childhood, just as the Hmong related they had used similar ones further back in time.

Most typical of the Mlabri traditional items are the bamboo containers with their simple geometric and very decorative patterns. Strangely enough, they mainly depict plants and trees, and we have not a single example of animals and only one of people (see fig. 146, M1, no. 16, 1980). Probably there is a taboo against depicting animals and persons because they have souls, and all the larger animals were until quite recently mentioned only using epithets when moving through the jungle, such as 'the long-nosed' for elephants, or 'the striped one' for tigers, in order not to offend the souls of these animals, thereby preventing attack by them.

Some items of bamboo and rattan made by the Mlabri do not belong to their own culture, for example the specially elaborated rattan boxes, which the Hmong have taught some of them how to produce (see fig. 152, M4, no. 17, 1987). For carrying their bamboo containers, food and their few possessions, the Mlabri rather prefer their light but very strong and flexible nets.

Most objects are quite simple and need no further explanation as regards their construction. They are used for a limited period of time and then discarded, but especially the iron objects are handed down from father to son. Groups of items were absent in their traditional culture until quite recently (1975), such as jewellery and ritual objects. We have not collected Mlabri goods bought in the market, such as blankets, clothes, lighters, medicines – now even their first transistor radio. It has not been within the scope of our work to study in detail the transition of their material life from living almost entirely on their own products to gradually obtaining more and more things from the market, since the mid-1980s.

A. Objects of Vegetable Origin

Bamboo is by far the most widely used material of all for tools as well as for construction material, cf. the windscreens.

The bamboo containers (M1: truŋ hlek) are used for keeping salt, spices, tobacco and for small personal belongings, such as the fire steel. A division between two internodes serves as the bottom of the main body ('ding), while the upper part, the lid (M1: 'at glɣ', M3: tum 'urk) is taken from a slightly thicker internode. As the wall of the main body is often quite thin between the internodes, one or two ties (bok) of rattan are fixed around the rim to prevent it from breaking. The outer skin of the bamboo container is removed, except the part which is reserved for decorations (gutgit), either geometrical patterns or more complicated drawings representing plants and trees. The simplest designs are made with the tip of a knife. This is moved rapidly from side to side and at the same time slowly downwards (see, for example fig. 146, M1, no. 04, 1980), while the more elaborate designs are made with more continuous strokes. The designs strikingly resemble those of the Senoi (Orang Asli) living near the Thai-Malaysian border, with whom the Mlabri have much in common, both as regards their material and their spiritual culture.

Water containers (see fig. 151, M1, no. 11, 1982) are made from one complete internode, to be filled by submerging it in a stream, allowing water to enter through a hole about 15 mm wide. This is plugged afterwards with a leaf to prevent insects from getting inside. Women may carry about eight such containers, or about 25 litres, up from the stream, in all about 30 kg at a time (fig. 63). Bamboo internodes are also used for cooking rice, vegetables or meat (separately) by letting them stand 10-20 cm from the flames. After having been emptied of their contents, the half-burnt tubes are used for kindling the fires during the evening (fig. 103).

Moreover, bamboo is used for all kinds of utensils, such as scrapers and handles, as well as for sticks and clubs to kill small game. Also the chun (Ml), the knitting device for making the fine flexible net baskets, is made from a section of the wall of a bamboo internode (see fig. 148, no. 28-29, 1987). Formerly the Mlabri did not make altars, but from around 1980 the Ml Mlabri have copied them from the Hmong, including putting spirit traps and offerings of various foods wrapped in banana leaves on top of the altar (fig. 79).

Older Ml Mlabri still used a piece of iron and a quartz stone to make sparks for setting fire to finely shredded bamboo fibres in the 1970s, whereas the M3 Mlabri previously utilised a bamboo saw on bamboo to obtain the necessary heat through friction to produce fire, see fig. 151, M3, no. 03, 1987. However, we have not been able to see the alleged lamps with glowing charcoal being carried from one camp to the other during periods of incessant rain.

Specially selected thin-walled bamboo is used for making flutes (fig. 148, M1, no. 11, 1987) and a very simple stringed instrument (fig. 151, M3, no. 1982). Also the small tobacco pipes are made of bamboo, utilising the roots, which have thicker walls and useful bent forms. Hardwoods are employed only for specific purposes, being too heavy to carry from one camp to the next. But a special kind of almost black hardwood is necessary for spear and knife handles, to obtain the right weight as well as strength. Mortars to grind various foods and materials are made from species of wood which are less difficult to hollow out.

Fibres: Very fine fibres are obtained from the inner bark of small shrubs in the jungle, either *Brussonetia papyrifera* L. Vent with a distinct thin, black stem and small, white flowers with yellow petals, or from *Wikstroemia polyantha* Merr. The bark is soaked in water for two or three days, after which the dark outer bark is removed to reveal its fine white inner layer. The fibres are thereafter twisted by the women between one hand and their legs (fig. 64) into strong but very flexible strings. These are knotted using the turtle-shaped chun in a somewhat complicated manner (fig. 66) to produce their beautiful and extraordinarily durable bags (fig. 149, M1, no. 21, 1982; no. 27, 1987).

The Mlabri also find roots in the jungle to make yellow and brown coloured threads, whereas they obtain violet and black dyes from the Hmong. My wife and our two daughters have used such bags for about 20 years. They still show no signs of wear and tear, not even the somewhat crudely made carrying strap.

The more coarse rattan for the solid boxes (fig. 152, M4, no. 17, 1987), as well as for spear covers, is obtained from a special creeper in the jungle. The very strong fibres are prepared by scraping off the outer layer, after which they are soaked in water for about three days. Only then are they soft enough to be woven. But the Mlabri seldom use the big rattan objects themselves, since the items produced are rather heavy to be carried from place to place. These are made to be sold to the Hmong or in the market. Actually, the big boxes are also produced by the other mountain peoples and even by prisoners, as we were told, which accords with their former widespread distribution in Northern Thailand.

The thick resting- and sleeping mattresses made from the Yanong tree *(Antiaris toxicana)* derive from removing the outer bark from the inner and washing and beating it vigorously several times for two days in a stream to remove its very poisonous sap, after which the bast layer becomes softer and nice to sleep on.

I have included one 'modern' object, a child's toy made from an old matchbox and eight matches representing a Thai house on pillars (fig. 150, M1, no. 08, 1987). Mlabri children almost never had toys, but were excited to receive some from us, such as miniature cars and planes. Naturally they play among themselves, but seldom with their parents!

B. Weapons and Tools of Iron & a Flint Axe

Fig. 155, no. 02, 1970 shows an ancient flint axe which was probably produced by former hunters, perhaps some Lawa tribe. It was found by a mountain Thai farmer on the shores of a small lake near Chae Hom, north of Lampang, Phayao District around 1960. He said that the animals came here to drink the clear water, making it a very useful place for hunting, and where the Mlabri had also waited for the animals to come. However, they said that to their knowledge they had never used stone for weapons, apart from throwing big stones at dangerous animals if they were attacked by, for example, a bear.

At the beginning of the 20th century, when they had very little contact with any villagers, except perhaps the T'in and Khamu, but only rarely with the newly arrived Thai mountain settlers, the Mlabri obtained iron by searching abandoned villages for small broken pieces to be forged into small spearheads and fire steels. Later, when they came into contact with Thai and Hmong farmers in the 1950s and obtained iron through bartering, they produced a number of different objects such as the spear (khɔt), the knife (tɔ') and the pointed weapon (tul "pointed tip"), as well as the digging implement (cho). Especially the spears are often very fine and precisely made, being status symbols for their owners, who never lend them to anybody else since they are so vital for the survival of their family. As mentioned earlier, a spear was believed to harbour a spirit of its own, to which the hunter had to offer some meat both before and after hunting to ensure his continued luck.

The spears are of different kinds, from broad-bladed to knife-like, both having a point of hardwood or iron at the opposite end. Almost all the spears we have collected are fixed onto the conical, shaped shaft of hardwood, the one exception being an old and much heavier spearhead, fig. 153, M1, no. 37, 1970, weighing 585 g, in contrast to the others weighing only about half of this. It was bought in Ban Tong Muang near Tha Ko, (map no. 09), but came from Ban Pa Miang, 30 km further south. It was said to be 40 years old, corresponding to about 1930, and has a 14 cm long iron tang set very tightly into the shaft of black hardwood. The spear itself is very elegantly shaped and the steel is of fine quality. Probably the Mlabri obtained this spear from the Thai farmers, to provide the latter with valuable elephant tusks. The spears they themselves produced were not suitable for that kind of game, exactly as related by the villagers back in 1970.

The total length of the spears varies from about 165 cm (120 cm for boys) to 185 cm. When hunting, the Mlabri said they seldom threw the spears at the animals if they were dangerous, because if they missed their target they would then be defenceless. Especially if they were in the deep jungle, they might be circumvented and attacked from behind, in which case they only had to change their grip within a split second and use the pointed tip at the other end of the spear.

It is interesting to note that the spearheads of the Mlabri M1 differ from those obtained from the border areas towards Laos, the latter being smaller and more crudely made, see fig. 155, M7, no number, 1994, reflecting that we are dealing with the separate group M7.

On two occasions we have watched the Mlabri M1 producing spearheads and the digging implement, the cho'. In order to provide a high enough temperature the Mlabri use a double bellows made of two bamboo internodes. When one of the pistons inside the cylinder is raised the other is pressed down, producing a steady stream of air to be forced through the attached thin bamboo pipes onto the red-hot charcoal, thereby elevating the temperature so the iron becomes bright yellow. Each piston has a shaft ending in a tight ball made of banana leaves. When made wet, these provide a more steady pressure, fig. 152, M1, no. 30, 1982. Evidently the bellows have been modelled on the Hmong tea churners, in which milk and tea are thoroughly mixed, quite similar to the more widely known Tibetan ones.

Every ten minutes or so the iron is placed on a stone to be beaten vigorously. Previously this was with a stone, now an iron hammer is used, until the desired shape is arrived at. Starting in the early morning, four Mlabri men were able to produce a similar number of iron tools. Always lacking iron bars, they asked us to bring iron whenever we went to see them. On our last visit Noi gave us a digging implement, which we had seen him making on our previous visit two years before (fig. 154, M1, no number, 1989). All the items procured now belong to Moesgaard Museum, Aarhus, 8270 Højbjerg, Denmark.

Fig. 146.

M1, no. 04, 1980. Bamboo container, design depicting trees made with the point of a knife. The lid is decorated with two woven braids of 2.3 mm thick, split bamboo strips. Ban Naga, Nan province.

M1, no. 16, 1980. Bamboo container which has not been completed, and lacking the lid. Same decorations as no. 04. At the top it seems that the band's ten members are sitting in their windscreen. Made by Wai, son of old Ut. Ban Naga, locations see last page. Compare with the drawings in fig. 180.

M1, no. 02, 1980. Geometric drawings arranged in four sections depicting various plants and trees on the appropriate places of the designs: 1. ton mai, wild plants. 2. bai wai, rattan leaves. 3. glui pa, banana. 4. dok mak praw, coconut. 5. bai ko, chestnut leaves. 6. dok mai hom, thin roots, Amaranthus sp. 7. dok kau pood, maize, Zea mays L. 8. tan, palm leaves, Livistona speciosa Kurz. 9. dok kan yan. 10. bai daw, palm tree, Arenga westerhoutii Griff. 11. mai hia, wooden windscreen poles, Shorea sp. 12. bai mai hok, very thick bamboo for big jars. 13. bai sang, straight bamboo for bamboo containers.

M1, no. 14, 1980. The inner bark from the Sa tree, Broussonetia papyrifera, previously used for loin covers (fig. 18). Made by Som, Ban Hui Hom.

Fig. 147.

M1, no. 24, 1980. Muk with geometric decorations produced on a bamboo internode by Wai, who identified a few objects: gachoong "turtle" and mat "flower".

M1, no. 13, 1980. Container prior to completion by Som, who identified among others: banana plant with leaves and a rattan having a spirit! M1, no. 05, 1982. Bamboo container with unidentified patterns.

M1, no. 20, 1982. Bamboo container bearing the following species of roots and plants: du, hmaa', tom, wec, kung (Th daw), kətat and creg (species see Appendix 5).

M1, no. 26, 1980. Bamboo container made by Som, indicating chukut, pakalam (tok mai).

M1, no. 25, 1980. Bamboo container also made by Som, indicating the following species: wec, kuung, bay gui, tok mai and trut.

M1, no. 33, 1982. Small rattan box said to have been made by the Mlabri for the market.

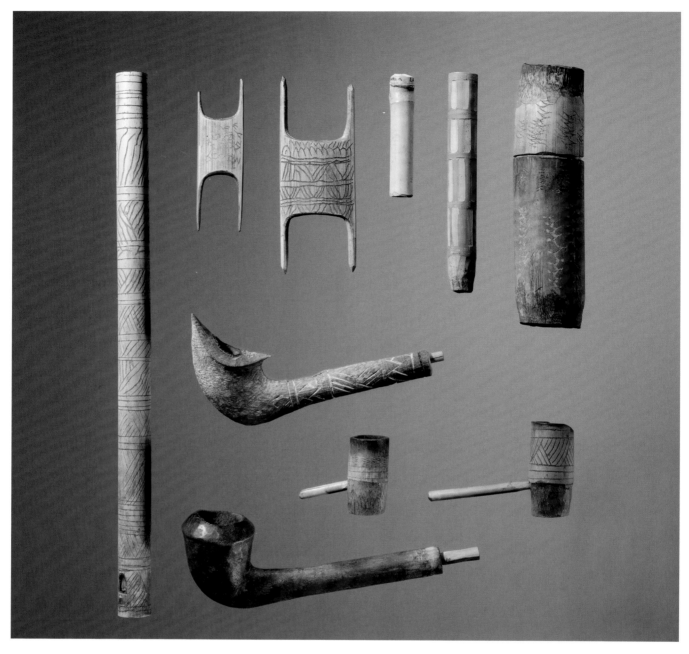

Fig. 148.

M1, no. 11, 1987. Flute with seven holes, made from thin walled bamboo. Belonged to Gu.

M1, no. 28, 1987. Small knitting device, chun, of bamboo for making the fine net bags, see fig. 149.

M1, no. 29, 1987. Larger chun for producing the larger and coarser net bags for men.

M1, no. 32, 1987. Bamboo whistle for an adult, which needs a lot of air and gives a sharp sound, Lat.

M1, no. 15, 1994. Bamboo whistle for a child, easy to blow but deep sound. Belonged to Muang's son.

M1, no. 10, 1978. Pipe of wood made by Ajan and of the old type.

M1, no. 06, 1994. Small bamboo pipe, belonged to the old woman Khamla, almost 70 years old.

M1, no. 10, 1982. Large heavy wooden pipe, also made by Ajan.

M3, no. 07, 1994. (extreme right): Bamboo container made by Kit, and below:

M3, no. 03, 1994. Designs resemble those of the M1 Mlabri.

Fig. 149.

M1, no. 21, 1982. Small net bag, 13x18 cm, for a nine-year-old girl of Paeng Noi, Ban Hui Hom.

M1, no. 27, 1987. New net bag (behind) 30x40 cm, made by Lat't wife, Ban Hui Yok. The net bags are made from Broussonetia papyrifera fibres, see sample to the right. The yellow colour is extracted from the red brown root just above the undyed fibres, while other dyes are from the market.

M1, no number, 1987. Two beads, one for a woman and one for a small girl, the wife and her child with Paeng Noi. The beads are dried grey-blue seeds from a plant. Doi Sathan.

M3, no. 04, 1987. Piece of a soft, reddish mineral ibn, eaten at times of starvation, Sak, Ban Nam Un.

M1, no. 13, 1987. Beeswax; the molten wax is poured into a bamboo internode and sold at the market or used for making the Mlabri's own candles.

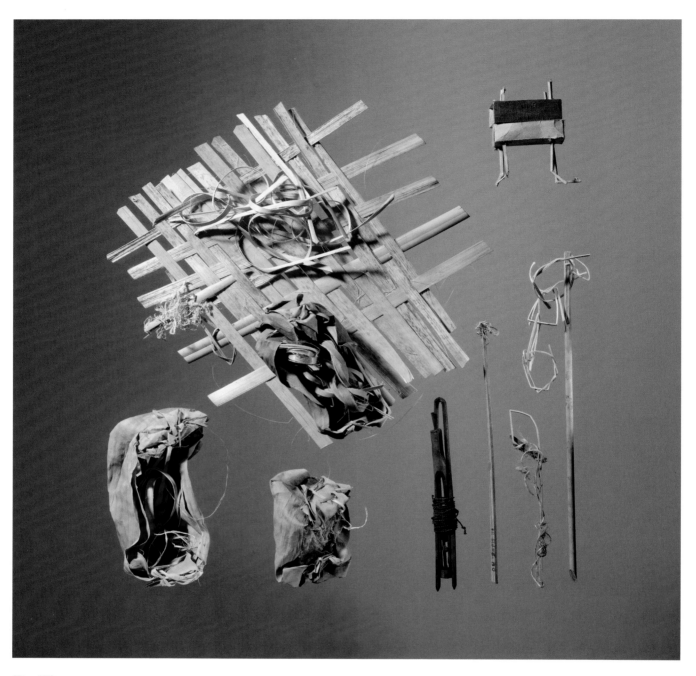

Fig. 150.

M1, no. 27, 1980. Altar for offerings of meat and "cups" of banana leaves with rice, alcohol and selected kinds of meat from the neck, heart and liver of a pig. The twisted, thin stripes of bamboo are spirit traps.

M1, no. 09, 1980. Trap of dark wood to catch small birds. Some food is placed in the hole, when touched the spring is released and breaks the neck of the bird. Finely executed, weight only four grams.

M1. no. 08, 1980. Thin bamboo stick with split fibres at one end to be impregnated with the sap of a poisonous plant, pipe soot or the alkaline contents of an old battery to immediately counteract snake bite.

M3, no. 20, 1994. Tiny mousetrap made by Oy. A string releases the spring of rattan, strangling the mouse.

M3, no. 19, 1994. Spirit trap (20 cm long) from Kit, to be put where a big branch has pierced the ground.

M1, no. 08, 1987. Toy Thai house on piles (top right), made from an old matchbox by a Mlabri boy.

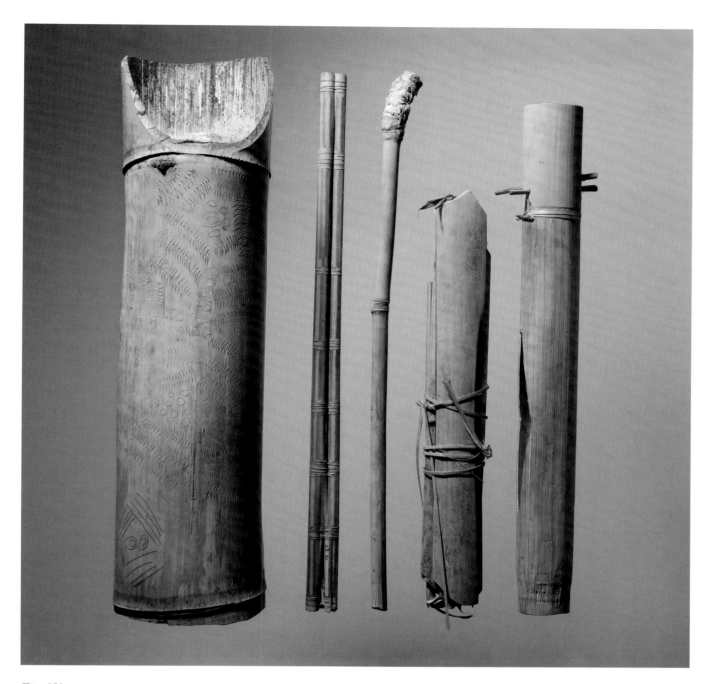

Fig. 151.

M1, no. 11, 1982. Water container, gurk, holding 3.5 litres. Belonged to Paeng, Ban Naka.

M1, no. 23, 1980. Bamboo club to kill bamboo rats and other rodents, Hui Hom.

M1, no. 18, 1980. Bamboo club to kill bamboo rats and other rodents, Hui Hom.

M3, no. 03, 1987. Package of dry leaves within two plates of bamboo to make fire, using the edge of the front plate (seen at the right side) as a saw perpendicular to the middle of the plate behind, see also the saw in operation, fig. 76. Belonged to Kit, Ban Doi Praiwan.

M3, no. 26, 1982. Musical instrument played by plucking two strings over the long slit (seen at the left side). Kit, Ban Pha Tong Silarpet.

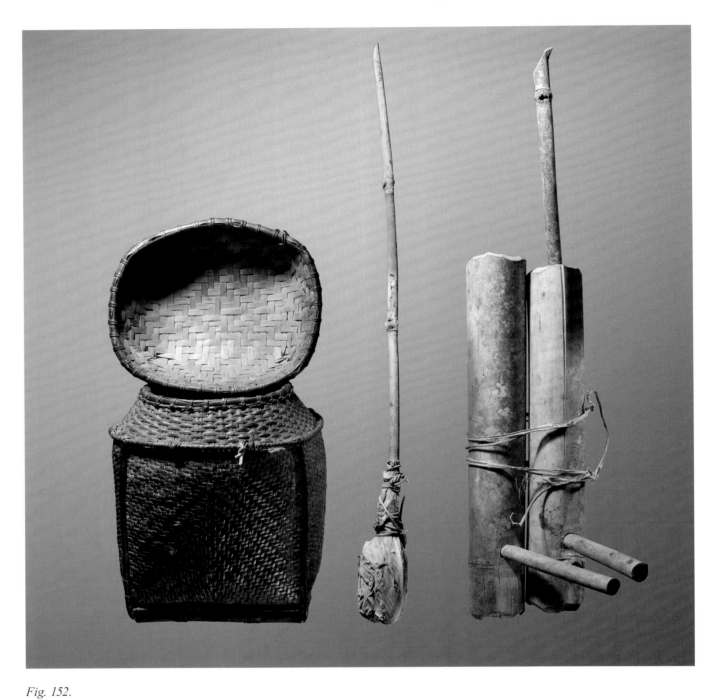

Fig. 152.

M4, no. 17, 1987. Strong and durable rattan box produced by the Mlabri M4, to be sold in the market by the Hmong. It has a wooden frame below to prevent it from overturning. This one belonged to Lek, who kept it because his deceased mother had made it in Ban Pa Gang, where he also stayed.

M1, no. 30, 1982. Double bellows from which the left piston has been removed to show how banana leaves have been fixed to a bamboo stick. When wet the head fits exactly the inside of the bamboo cylinder. By vigorously pressing the two pistons up and down the operator provides a steady stream of air from the two pipes to make the iron in the hearth in front hot enough to be hammered into shape.

Fig. 153.

M1, no. 30, 1970. Spearhead from Tha Ko, location map, reg.no. 09, Chieng Rai District, lost by the Mlabri during a struggle with Thai villagers in 1966, after which the Mlabri fled the area to return to Nan province.

M1, no. 31, 1970. Small spearhead for a teenage boy, also from the mountains east of Tha Ko.

M1, no. 32, 1970. Knife-like spearhead which is also mounted on a long lance of hardwood, Tha Ko area.

M1, no. 35, 1970. Spear cover of rattan bought by an old Akha man north of Wieng Pa Pao around 1950.

M1, no. 36, 1970. Spear point which has been poisoned to kill large animals, found east of Pong 1954.

M1, no. 37, 1970. Fine, old (Thai) spearhead from Pa Miang, bought in Ban Tong Muang near Tha Ko.

M1, no. 18, 1978. Whetstone for sharpening iron tools. Found by a Hmong on Doi Pa Tung about 1950, who confirmed that the Mlabri (M1) in the area had moved back to Ban Po Keng in 1966.

Fig. 154.

M1, no. 39, 1970. Spear bought from Paeng. Like the spear cover to the right, nicely made wickerwork.

M1, no. 01, 1977. Spear bought from Pa in Ban Naka, probably made before 1950.

M1, no. 02, 1977. Spear bought from Paeng, Ban Bow Hiew. As in the two ones above, blades are thin.

M1, no. 03a, 1977. Combined spear and knife, crudely executed, but an efficient weapon, and: 03b, 1977. The other end of the same spear just having a long thin point. Ban Na Ka, Nan.

M1, no. 40, 1970. Small hand spade, cho, besides the knife, the only iron tool also used by women.

M1, no number, 1989. Hand spade made by Poa on our previous visit in 1987, but now presented to us by Noi.

M1, no. 11, 1977. From Paeng, old fire steel, used together with the stone to ignite dry fibres.

Fig. 155.

M1(?), no. 12, 1982. Spearhead bought from four T'in men who visited our Mlabri camp, Megafai. They told us that they had found it northwest of Ban Song Kwer. It probably dates back to the 1950s.

M4, no. 29, 1982. Spearhead from a Hmong in Ban Pa Gang, who met two Mlabri in the jungle near Ban Pa Don Silarpet. They had said there were about 30 of their group on the eastern slopes of Doi Ya Wai.

M7, no number, 1994. Spearhead (a) and digging spade (b, below) obtained from an old Hmong in Ban Nam Tuang, ref.no. 80 (map Ban Maeo Lao La), who received them around 1970 from a Mlabri. M7 coming from the other side of the Laotian border, allegedly belonging to the so-called 'fierce' Mlabri (see p. 234).

M5?, no number, 1987. Mlabri spear probably from around 1950, bought in Ban Na Klai, Loi province.

M5, no. 31, 1982. Spear cover which belonged to Lot's father at Doi Phu Kradung, Loi province (p. 212).
Stone axe, no. 02, 1970, found by a lake near Chae Son, Amphoe Phrao, where wild animals came to drink. Probably belonged to Lawa hunters.

The Mlabri Animal Kingdom

In spite of the fact that the main staple of the Mlabri has probably been roots and tubers for many generations. These are available all year round, including the dry seasons when the animals retreat to their hideouts, it is animals who have received the greatest attention and for many reasons. For all, hunting has been almost their only way to obtain indispensable protein, while the need for minerals and calories, besides from roots and tubers, can be covered by vegetables, fruits, nuts and rice. The animal kingdom still commands much attention in the minds of, especially, the Mlabri Ml, because they have always lived in intimate contact with animals. Into the 1980s they still respected the larger animals to the extent that before or after going hunting they made excuses for killing them and made offerings to the spirit of the jungle, who supervises all living creatures. Various animals were not even permitted to be touched, such as some species of deer, since they are considered to be the property of the mightiest of all, the sky spirit wɔk klar.

Moreover, many Mlabri believe that they themselves might be reincarnated, preferably as the more graceful species such as a barking deer, squirrel or even a tortoise, which were said also to possess souls, as described in Chapter 2. Therefore, the deterioration of the wildlife has been especially painful to the jungle people. The first blow happened with the introduction of guns to the other hill tribes in the first half of the 20th century. This caused the bigger animals to retreat to the remaining jungles in faraway mountain tracts. The final blow came with the steady influx to the remaining jungles of people from Burma and Laos, as well as Khon Muang farmers from the lowland, because these people were also keen hunters. Above all, their slash and burn agriculture has left large areas devastated as half open, infertile bamboo thickets. Actually very little is left today of the once splendid mountain jungles of Northern Thailand – probably less than ten percent!

About one hundred species of wild game, as well as some dangerous or remarkable animals in other ways, are listed below with their names in Mlabri Ml and M3, together with the English name of species in question and a few other notes, including whether they are edible. Just as is the case with trees and plants, the Mlabri do not have any specific system of nomenclature. Probably the most important animals have old Mlabri names often imitating their sounds (onomatopoeic) such as rway "tiger", to dɛo (Ml) or pɔk (M3) "woodpecker" and 'u 'ʌk "toad". Whereas later acquisitions, such as the domesticated animals, for example horse and dog, have been taken from their Khamu or Thai equivalents. The names of small and less important animals are often characterised by a few specific traits such as their shape, specific qualities and frequently by their sounds, but remarkably seldom by their colours. By the way, some Mlabri men, such as Ajan (Ml), are still so familiar with the animals that they can imitate their sounds so effectively as to lure them out of their hideouts.

The lists in the next pages demonstrate two important features. About 70% of the glossary of Mlabri Ml and M3 is identical. Our interviews also demonstrate that especially the Ml Mlabri have kept their interest in being real hunters, while the few remaining M3 Mlabri know almost the same number of species, but their experience with the bigger animals is more remote and less intimate, because for the last thirty years they have depended more on help from their Hmong "owners".

Especially when going hunting in the jungle the Mlabri M1 had a great number of obligations both before, during and after the hunt. This was in order not to offend the spirits of the dangerous, precious animals or the mighty spirits of the jungle, wɔk bri, the guardian of all the animals. They also had to take care not to reveal their intentions regarding the animals to outsiders. Therefore, they had a secret naming system for the most wanted or feared animals.

Below I will cite a few quotations from an article by Robert Know Dentan: "The Mammalian Taxonomy of the Sen'oi Semai (1967), which again shows there are several similarities with the Sen'oi Semai or "Central Sakai" in Malaysia. Like the Mlabri, they also distinguish between the following kinds of meat "tree meat" and "land meat", the latter being further subdivided into those having a "hairy" and those a "furry" skin. P. 100 it is said:

"It is taboo (penalic) to eat a meal that contains both "hairy" and "furry" meat and even more taboo to mix "tree meat" with "land meat." Most taboo of all is to mix meat with foods from other categories of the same level of generality like fish (kaq, a category which in Ulu Telom includes testudinates and amphibians or "fungus" betiiŝ). "Within these categories animals have "names" (muh). These names are apparently assigned on the basis of gross anatomical similarity and may refer to anything from a variety or phase of a Linnean species to a family or two.

P. 101: "In situations which seem potentially dangerous the Semai use an argot called enrooq kerendei, "language making-not-to-know…(which) serves to keep strangers from understanding what the Semai are talking about." … "Speaking the animal's muḥ might lead to severe gastrointestinal disorders or even death, informants said".

Like the Mlabri, the Semai adress these animals "bah", which means "Mister" and in Mlabri the almost similar honorific "You" (plural). The reason I will not go further into this interesting issue is simply that, even though the Mlabri gave me some examples of names, especially of the dangerous animals, in this making-not-to-know language, I had the feeling that they did not like to reveal more details on this sensitive subject!

MI	M3	
thawa'	thawa'	Monkey species including macaque, specifically:
thɛng	thɛng, chɛng	Where M3 has thɛng white sp. and chɛng black sp., eat.
gɛng kwʌr	bun tok 'ding	Stump-tailed macaque, aggressive and clever animal.
jaw	thawa'	Gibbon, jaw is onomatopoeic; both spec. hunted (MI).
'ding	'ding	Lit. "huge", mountain ox, gaur (now extinct in Thailand).
pompoo or	chang (Th)	Elephant, hunted up to about 1950, also by some MI.
kleh	'ding	Water buffalo. Previously hunted.
ngay	ngay	Boar, hunted. Pig: chəbut, ching (M1, M3).
brang bri	mɔk mot	Wild dog; domesticated species choo' (MI and M3).
bɛk	biɯk, bɛk	Bear, hunted by MI only for its meat. Skins are not used.
rway 'ding	rway tr.nap	Big striped tiger, last seen in Nan province around 1950.
rway guh bung	rway chet	Leopard: "tiger skin spotted"(MI), resp."tiger small"(M3).
rway tokwɛk	rway chɛng	Black panther, lit. "tiger black".
mɛw, chi' phɛy	mɛw	Cat (or Hmong, an allusion to their slit eyes). Not eaten.
polh	polh	Barking deer, previously not to be killed due to red colour.
ciak	ciak	Sambur deer, now extinct in Northern Thailand.
twel, 'ul	twel	Mouse deer, previously not to be touched.
kɛh, thr.bɛ'	bɛ'	Mountain goat, also onomatopoeic. Eaten.
twer	twer	Rabbit, eaten.
puɛ'		Small-clawed otter; hunted.
pook		Yellow-throated marten, weasel-like.
dr'mɔ'	dr'mɔ'	Several kinds of civets ('i-hen (Th)), not to be eaten.
kr.wɛk	kr.wɛk	Bearcat. Slow animal, which can be shaken down from a tree. Has a strong smell. Can be eaten.
cac		Prevost, big squirrel, which MI have hunted with crossbow.

jur lɛl, kralh	kralh	Squirrels. Eaten (MI), but striped one (jur' lɛl) previously not to be touched, as it is said to belong to the sky spirit.
chak dʌl		Squirrel eating dʌl ("nuts and fruits"), hence the name.
proʌt	proʌt	Flying or rather gliding squirrel to lower levels. Eat (MI).
gather, gatɛl		Spotted squirrel. Eaten.
'do' kleh, trii'	'do', trii'	Long-spined porcupine with hard (kleh) quills. Eaten.
'do' 'ɔn	'do'	Best taste of the porcupines, 'ɔn "soft".
koc	koc hwɤk, thip	"Bamboo rat". Still plentiful, good taste.
klung klong	klung klong	Big rat. All kinds of rats and most other rodents are eaten.
jak	hwɤk yuk	Big rat, often found near rice fields, hence yuk "rice".
hnɛl cɛg	'pi loc, lɤ' kleb	Mouse, both groups also eat these small animals, including
hnɛl	tun	Very small mouse.
jook po'	jook po'	Nocturnal slow loris, sucks (jook) fruit from po' tree.
chu 'ɛh	pahul	Moonrat, hog-nosed badger, weasel-like, feeds on fish, eaten.
klul klɛk	klul, klɛkklɛk	Short-tailed mole, MI, eaten.
tək klɛk	birl	Flying fox, really a bat.
kuylua', bang	kuylua'	"Flying" lemur, escapes dangers by "gliding" kuy kwʌy, where the skin folds under its arms act as gliders.
'ying yɛng	'ying yɛng	Mongoose, kind of lemur, able to kill a snake.
'bor	'bor	Scaly anteater or pangolin *(Genus manis)*. When attacked this remarkable animal rolls itself into a ball. Eaten (MI).
trɤlang gung		Eagle, thought of as being able to carry human souls away.
galang	galang gung	Changeable hawk-eagle. These big birds are not hunted.
gi.kluiy	gi.kluiy	Owl, inedible.
ngol, gwɛng	trɤl	Peacock can be eaten; but due to bright colour should not be killed, since it belongs to the sky spirit (both MI, M3).
ya giang	dunring	Parrot should not be eaten, as it belongs to the sky spirit.
kokokdroy	kokokdroy	Pigeon species. (Rischel 1987, p. 63, has kokdroy "dove").
bok ji'rɔ'	bok	Rhinoceros hornbill bird, eaten (MI) or sold to villagers.
'i hurl	chɤhnɛl pɤɤl	Southern hornbill bird, eaten. Killed with crossbow, pɤɤl. 'i hurl onomatopoeic, as is the case with many birds.
sernoc		Large crow pheasant, eaten or sold at a good price.
ji.rum	ji.rum	Large racket-tailed drongo.
cher.gɛng	'ɛw 'yoc	Chicken, 'uy yoc "hen" 'uy yoong "cock", eaten,
kookdroy	kookdroy	Dove, pigeon sp., hunted.
	km.bo' lom	Pigeon, hunted.
to dɛo	to dɛo	Woodpecker, living close to the Mlabri. Warns against approaching dangers (snakes, etc.), hence not to be killed.
kap.wɤk	kap.ruʌng	Sandpiper, kap wɤk, and kap ruʌng "with (near) water".
chupchu	prung	Blue-breasted quail, pheasant-like, hunted.
pa.goy.wet	pa.goy.wet	Green-chested lizard. Can change its colour, and is therefore the property of the sky spirit. Must not be killed (M1).
pyee	pyee	Monitor, edible lizard.
kroc	kroc	Crocodile, extinct in Nan since about 1960.

gəchong	gəchong	Land- or mountain turtle. All turtles are much coveted.
chukklɣny		Soft-shelled turtle.
chappa	chappa	Soft-shelled water turtle, big.
(hng) gɯp		Water-turtle, big head and long tail.
kah 'ohm	(kah) 'ohm	River-turtle, small.
mʌ'	mʌ', pɛl	Constrictor, python, up to 6 m long and deadly. Fat used.
tom 'o'	tom 'o'	Venomous snakes, especially the king cobra and:
	chumroh	Bites can be deadly, none are hunted.
hmuk bok	hmuk bok	Scorpion, stings are painful, but usually not deadly.
kendep	kendep	Centipede, stings are very painful, but not deadly.
pom.pway	pom.pway	Spiders, eat only big species (roasted). Bites painful and
gɣnggɣng		just as in most other cultures, spiders are detested.
gec	gec, gɛyh	Crabs living in and around streams, eaten.
'u 'ak	'u 'ak	Toad, not to be eaten.
to.guk	to.guk	Frogs, many species are eaten (Ml).
		M3 Mlabri eat e.g.: lɔk, tik.tɛk, je'rɣng, rut, ɛng.ɣng.
kaa'	kaa'	Fish, several sp., caught by hand, in baskets or small nets.
dolkol	room.yong	Psammocharaid wasp, room yong "circling around".
tagul, kay	mɛng.pu'	Banded hornet, dangerous for children. There are many
pac	yɔh cing	other kinds of wasps, e.g. thread-waisted wasp yɔh cing "spit wood", which makes its nests by chewing soft wood.
baw		Carpenter bee, no honey.
'yek	'yek	Large Indian bee, honey yak yek, very good, waxes yellow.
lum ngol		Sting-less bee, honey good, but not plentiful, wax brown.
buk.luak		Grasshopper, big.
ta' rɛk	ta' rɛk	Grasshopper, small, both of these two species are eaten.
'bi'	'bi'	Caterpillar having bands of strong-coloured burning hairs.
rɣl.pɛp	rɣl.pɛp	Many strong-coloured butterflies. Property of the sky spirit,
'uʌ'	'uʌ'	and therefore children are asked not to play with them.
cin.brin	cin.brin	Cricket.
try	rɔy	Fly.
koh, thəpɯr truiny (flyings.)	thɯbɯr lɯng	Termite, with their characteristic heaps, km.puc; earlier used to enclose the body of dead persons. Not to be touched.
mut	mut, chʌiny	Mosquito.
mic mɛc	mic mɛc	Ants, many different species, including itchy one rɯmram.
mot	mot, 'a.nuny	Big species of ant.

Roots, Marrows, Leaves, Fruits & other Useful Plants and Wooden Materials

We have also made several lists of useful plants and wooden materials, with their names in Mlabri and Khon Muang. However, in spite of the many samples and photographs obtained, it has not been possible to identify more than some of the species in question; this would have required a separate project! Another problem has been that neither the Mlabri nor our interpreters were sure about the names of the plants and trees. Therefore our lists of plant materials have to be characterised as preliminary. The Ml and M3 groups hold about the same number of each of the following three categories: roots and tubers, marrows and leaves, and fruits and seeds. They are far from being equally important. Thus the roots and tubers are collected almost all year round, whereas the fruits and seeds are consumed only when the Mlabri happen to stumble on them. However, since the 1980s the ubiquitous rice among the other hill tribes has also become the main staple among the Mlabri.

With the introduction of sugar and sugarcane, the general health of the Mlabri deteriorated further and more so that of the Mlabri M3 because many of the latter are also opium addicts. This development can be evidenced when comparing the better condition of the Mlabri Ml around 1960, see Srisavasdi, B.C.: "The Hill Tribes of Siam" 1963, p. 188-194, Bamrung Press, Bangkok, and still when we visited them in the 1970s.

Surin Pookajorn and Staff, 1992, pp. 104-164, give lists of Mlabri Ml useful plants and trees with the names in Thai and in Mlabri, as well as some of their scientific names. These have helped us to furnish our lists with a few of the proper identifications. Included in the above-cited material are also some chemical analyses of their medicinal plants and herbs, showing that most of the medicinal plants have indeed the alleged properties. Concerning the nutrient values of the roots, it is said, p. 160: "The results showed that these roots provided fairly large amounts of vitamins and minerals, but were poor in protein and energy content". The latter property ranged from 20 to 115 calories / 100 g, which cannot, however, be said to be particularly low values, considering that potatoes have about 90 calories / 100 g.

At times both groups of Mlabri M1 and M3 have eaten less edible roots and tubers or they have not cooked them long enough to break down their toxic contents. While the Mlabri Ml are well aware of this difficulty, the M3 Mlabri do not seem to care too much. This is in line with what both locals and the first explorers have noticed, i.e. that the M3 Mlabri in particular have small weak kneecaps. As a consequence, the adults always carry a stick when on the move in the jungle. After having discussed the matter with Mrs. Eva Pike, toxicologist and dr. phil., Odense University Hospital, it has occurred to us that this has something to do with the less suitable roots not being cooked sufficiently which, together with Mlabri M3 malnutrition, may have caused this sort of arthritis.

In conclusion, we may state that the roots, tubers and also, to some extent, the variety of leaves consumed are characteristic of the Mlabri material culture, which incidentally also in this respect links them with the other autochthonous peoples in South East Asia. Finally some examples of useful plants and trees for other purposes than eating are given below.

Local name	Mlabri	MI roots and tubers
leuang	thrut	Roots up to 100 cm, middle part roast or cook, good taste.
khom	dam	Bitter roots, used only when there is nothing else to eat.
keb	hma'	3-4 cm thick, cooked or roasted, good taste (not sweet).
leum	wɛyh	Elephant roots 8-10 cm long, 4 cm thick, cooked or roasted.
'yak	kətat	From big tree, 100-200 cm, roasted; can cause diarrhoea ('yak).
mokadrul	cherɛk	Thick branches but thin roots, cooked for a long time or toxic.
taet	guyh cho'	Sweet potato.
sam-pa-rang	'e' lam	Varying sizes, can be dug up by hand, cooked briefly, sweet.
lai	guyh	Long roots, cooked for a long time, only then good.
hom	tu	Thin roots, up to 60 cm long, delicious.
kok	wec	Up to 100 cm, 5 cm thick, cut into pieces and cooked for a long time, regarded as the best one.
yan	lok	Thin, difficult to dig for, bitter.
wai	blet	Rattan species, 3-4 cm, roasted or cooked, bitter (*Calamus* sp.).
cong,man saw	kway	Taro, big, deep roots, cannot be roasted (*Discorea alata* L).

MI marrows and leaves

	kryng	Marrow eaten, bitter.
wai	thom	Marrow cooked with salt and chilli, fresh and a little bitter.
keung	daw	Palm tree, marrow cooked (*Arenga westerhoutii* Griff.).
	murca	Young shoots of tree, eaten fresh.
rai	mun tɛng	Bamboo shoots.
	bay khom	Leaves of a tree, eaten.
cha plu	whɛm	Leaves eaten with salt.
ta kut	kut, rɛt	Leaves cooked.

MI fruits and seeds

	yuk	Tree with big nuts.
ma pai		Fruit tree.
nam thua		Fruit tree.
ma kwang	chumpu	Fruit tree.
	Kr.to kr.tang	Fruits and leaves, fresh.
	lambo	Looks like wild ginger.
	glɯl	Fruits.
kui mo	dol	Wild banana, small and sweet. Marrow and flowers to cook.
	yol	Banana, fruit, flower and marrow eaten.
	ple' jao	Fruit, sour.
san	crɛg	Wild mango, very sour.
khing	pap	Ginger, *Cantimbirm malaccensis* Holt., eaten raw or cooked.
ma la kaw	ple' bo	Papaya plus other cultivated plants from the lowland such as:
ma phrao	praw	Coconut (*Cocos nucifera* L.)
som	chat	Orange.
ma muang	chrelh	Mango.

Local name	Mlabri	Ml roots and tubers
sapparot	gm.nat	Pineapple.
	jang	Gives stomach trouble if not cooked 2-3 hours.
	weyh	Elephant root, roasted or cooked for a long time.
	liuam	Small roots, bigger below, good.
leuang	thrut	Yellow root, upper ones thin – lower ones thick; the best one.
	plɛt, khɛt	Rattan species, roots roasted or cooked, bitter.
lay	tu	Thin roots going quite deep, delicious.
	khom	Various sizes, bitter, eaten if nothing else available.
	hma'	Roots 3-4 cm thick, cooked or roasted, good taste.
kok	wec	Roasted or cooked.
man saw	kway	Taro (*Discorea alata* L.).
	pip.plɛp	Soft and delicious.
	lok	Bitter tubers, have to be cooked.

		M3 marrows and leaves
nyae	kwing	Roasted or cooked, fresh.
bun	thom	Marrow fresh, also roasted or cooked.
daw	ta' 'o	Eaten raw or cooked.
no	kuung	Eaten raw or cooked.
hia	pɣy	Bamboo shoots to cook.
ka	kampong gechɛng	Spice.
cha	murl.cha	Leaves eaten raw, sour.
mei li	chumrum	Leaves eaten raw, sour.
chum gun	lumgu.cha	Leaves eaten raw or cooked.
hak	kuu'	Leaves eaten raw or cooked.
cha	mieng	Boil tea leaves, or packed in banana leaves with salt to chew.
nyuan	dongkap	Boil leaves, packed in banana leaves with salt to chew.
birk	thup pru'	Betel leaves, eaten fresh or after a special preparation.
pha kap lat	matul	Leaves eaten raw.
kut	kut	Leaves are fern-like, eaten raw or cooked.
pa kom wan	lam sang	Leaves used as spice.
pit	whem	Leaves, *Piper samentossum* Roxb.,cooked with salt.
kra lam plee,	lm.bah.	Various kinds of vegetables such as here "cabbage".

		M3 fruits and nuts
ma ku	lam boo', pap	Fruit *Catimbirm malaccensis* Holt. (make mats of its leaves).
mak kyapuang	mak kweng	Seeds are boiled or roasted.
mak komsat	ple' plung	Nuts eaten raw or roasted.
mak phrao	ple' braw	Coconut.
mak fai	ple' lamtal	Fruit and nuts.
	ple' mak	Areca nut.
mak ku.ling	ple' krel kambong tawa	Eat both fruits and nuts.
klui pa	ple' klui bri	Fruit and nuts + cultivated fruit plants, same as those of Ml.

Other useful plant & tree materials for various purposes, Ml

Malaria:
: The leaves of the plant sa'at, *Euodia roxburghiana* Benth., are rubbed on the body, or the leaves from a similar plant, *Clausena excavata* Burm.f., are crushed in a mortar, adding some hot water, after which the liquid is put on the head or the body. Or a decoction from the yellow root pap (*Cantimbirm malaccensis Holt.*) is poured over the head or swallowed in order to reduce the fever and the painful headaches caused by the disease. Its roots are perhaps the same red ones: haw dyao kao yen (Khon Muang) bartered with the Mlabri to be sold in the market.

Fever:
: Small leaves from the plant deb (Khon Muang) are heated over a fire and put on the loins; has a fresh smell like that of new-mown grass.

Pains:
: Leaves from the plant ya lam biel are cooked and the decoction applied to that part of the body giving pain, or the leaves from the plant ru' ma glum (only to be found in the deep jungle) are heated over a fire to be put on the stomach or other parts of the body; one may also use wild ginger.

Earache:
: A red fungus growing on tree bark is cooked and cooled; the liquid is poured into the ear.

Toothache:
: A special kind of tree bark is chewed.

Constipation:
: The leaves of lam bo, resembling wild ginger, are eaten. However, surprisingly, the Mlabri have no cures against intestinal worms, which are very common, especially in infants.

Bleedings:
: The sap of a plant: sap sua, gum bong, is used to stop bleeding, *Eupatorium odoratum* Linn.

Infections:
: The Mlabri said that in the event of infection of, for example, a wound, they can use the slime of a greyish-white snail they call: tum kan "infection (or heat) make leave", a typical Mlabri way of giving useful animals or plants names!

Bites from centipedes:
: The roots of a 1.4 m high bush, with long, sharp and pointed opposite leaves, probably *Scleria levis* Retz.; are collected to be rubbed on a stone and mixed with water; the liquid is applied to the wound.

Snake bites:
: The soot from the inside of a tobacco pipe is removed with a knife, or the alkaline material inside an old battery is applied to the wound. If nothing else is available, they may press a burning cigarette into the wound, causing the poison to disintegrate before it spreads to the more vital parts of the body.

Stings by the big hornet:
: The Mlabri said they apply the white pith from the palm tree daw, which somehow absorbs or reacts with the poison.

Poison for spearheads:
: The sap from the inner bark of the tree yanong (Khon Muang) is mixed with the marrow of the palm tree, daw, having a sticky, rubber-like quality, and with the fangs of centipedes, kn'dep, plus the head of a venomous snake; leave spearheads for several days in the mixture. As the poison stays in the animal killed in this way, the meat has to be properly cooked.

: Poison to facilitate the catching of fish in a stream using the plant: nam pla (Khon Muang) or lai (Ml), using about 20 kg for a stretch of 0.5 km.

: Poison made from the leaves of a plant: prym, previously and perhaps even now taken especially by elderly and disabled persons, who are no longer able to follow their band or who have unbearable pains.

Tattooing:
: Charcoal powder is mixed with the gall bladder of a snake. The design is made with a sharp pointed bamboo stick, after which the mixture is rubbed into the mutilated skin.

: Piercing of the earlobes is first made with thorns from the plant kr.duldul. After a small hole had been made it was previously widened with a piece of bamboo.

Textile
: Skirts and loin covers were previously made of the soft inner bark of Broussonetia papyrifera L.Vent. (Thai: Sa) or Wikstroemia polyantha Mers. (Ml luun).

Mattress, etc
: Underlays for resting and sleeping on, using layers of leaves of the plant bay kut, or the big leaves of the tree chu kut, or the small leaves of a fern-like plant kamdan (Th). A more permanent material is made of the inner bark of the above-mentioned yanong tree (Th). The inner bark of this tree is first beaten and thoroughly washed in a stream to free it of its poisonous sap, whereby it becomes soft and nice to sit or sleep on.

: Big baskets and mats are made in the traditional local fashion from a large rattan species (see fig. 152 M4. no. 17, 1987); primarily to be sold by their Hmong employers in the market.

Construction materials:

Khon Muang:	bung	hia, hiet	hok	sang	lam	krang
Mlabri:	tok	dəlaw	tr.luu	lal trang	mol lang	thrut
Use:	big bamboo support. beams	windscr. poles cooking pots	big bamboo for cooking	big bamboo containers	bamboo to cook rice in	spears of hardwood

(Roofs are covered with the big leaves of the banana palm or the bay ko tree)

While the Mlabri M3 use very much the same roots, tubers, leaves, etc., for food, they do not know or no longer use as many plants for medicinal and other purposes, because now they obtain medicine from their Hmong 'owners'. Previously they had a few peculiar specialities such as eating decayed wood mixed with honey, and a special kind of a mineral ibn, that they ate when starving, which gave them a sort of relief from hunger without harming the digestive system.

APPENDIX 6

Psychotechnical Tests and Rorschach Blots

Even after many periods staying with the Mlabri, important aspects of their psyche appeared to be inaccessible to us, leading to other approaches being considered. After advice from psychologists it was decided to try some simple psychotechnical tests and Rorschach blots. They were undertaken mainly in 1982 and 1987 but, whereas some of the female Mlabri Ml were none too happy with the former, we had no difficulties with the Rorschach blots. We were able to carry out combined tests with seven women and 24 men, of which three tests were repeated five years later to see if the results were consistent. For the results of the tests see fig. 156.

Tests undertaken

1. The road test. This test measures the ability to distinguish between turning right and left while moving along a zigzag path in a labyrinth. However, we immediately ran into difficulties, simply because the Mlabri seemingly do not have their own words for going right and left but rather say they for instance are going up the mountain or down to the river, going east or west. Some of the men knew the Thai terms, but then went astray while using them, or they tried with complicated explanations. In such cases we asked them to indicate the turns by using their hands, spending 20-30 minutes on each person.

Most men were able to distinguish between right and left as long as the turns moved away from themselves in the labyrinth. But when the turns were towards them they had an average of six faults during 14 turns or answers almost at random. Later, we experienced that they really do not use right and left when they are on their own. For example, when walking along a trail they will say go up or downhill instead of saying turn right or left. The results from the women's tests are too few to obtain proper averages, but it seems that they use Thai right-left terms even less.

A similar oddity concerns colours, for which the Mlabri have but a few fixed terms. For instance they seldom use colours to distinguish between the different animal species. But it is their sounds which make up part of their names, probably as they hear the animals long before they actually see them in the dense jungle. We tested about 60 Mlabri for their colour vision and not a single one had any deficiency of this kind. This is a highly unusual and important result, because in very old farming cultures something like 6% of the population have more or less pronounced colour vision deficiencies. Among the Mlabri it was probably eradicated from their gene pool as soon as it turned up, as their survival has entirely depended on avoiding all risks of not immediately identifying dangerous animals in the dense jungle.

2. The cube test Plastic cubes, each with two red and two white sides and the remaining two sides each having one red and one white triangle, have to be combined to produce simple patterns according to 10 different test cards in order to study the ability to reproduce patterns. The first five tests include four cubes, but the five last tests with nine cubes had to be left out due to lack of response.

We spent about half an hour with each person to assemble the five different patterns, each of the three first resulting in scores from 0 to 3, and the fourth and fifth taken together rendering also 0 to 3. It turned out that four of the men did not want to take the test, while six of them, even after receiving substantial help could not reproduce any of the five different patterns, while seven could reproduce one or two patterns. The remaining seven men were able to reproduce three or more patterns as well as repeat them almost without help. The women generally had somewhat less success with the patterns.

We had perhaps expected that the Mlabri would have done somewhat better, as most people find the simple cubes easy to handle. Their scores were also rather poorer than those of their neighbours, the mountain Thai

289

and the Hmong, some of whom are specialists in various, fine handicrafts. On the other hand it is surprising that most of the Mlabri tried the various tests and that some of them obtained fair results, considering that most of them had never had a pencil in their hands before. Moreover, the three men we tried again five years later (1989) then produced considerably better results!

3. Advanced Matrices 1 test. This test has 12 plates, each divided into two halves. Uppermost on each plate there are eight different, simple, geometrical figures plus one empty space. The latter is reserved for a missing figure, which logically fits in and has to be identified from eight similar figures on the page below, of which only one is right. Scores ranged from 0 to 2, nobody having 3 or 4.

As anticipated, this test was far too difficult for most of the Mlabri, who first saw photos and drawings from about 1980. Four men chose solutions at random, Seven did only a little better than that, while four men were able to grasp the principle and found the right figure, or one resembling it. The women had even more trouble with the test.

There was some agreement between the results of tests 2 and 3, pointing to large individual differences between the Mlabri themselves (see the tables next pages), as well as between them and the other mountain peoples.

The Rorschach Blots

This test has been utilised in the industrial world to investigate brain damage during World War I and subsequently, especially in people with mental problems. Experience with the test is based on literally millions of tests collected over the last 80 years. Results are not only dependent on the culture in question and the investigated social group, but also on the experience and background of the investigator. Already on this basis, it appears that the results of the tests carried out on ethnic minorities cannot be correlated with the above-mentioned huge body of evidence from the industrial world.

Nevertheless, the Rorschach blots test has been performed on various kinds of minorities and with exactly the same purpose as in our case, viz. to obtain an insight into psychological features which are difficult or impossible to obtain in other ways (see for example, Kihara, H.: "Peoples of Nepal Himalaya" Vol. III, 1957, on the mental implications of Lamaist religious symbols among the Sherpas).

1. The test performed Ten drawings, of which the final three are in colour, show abstract and almost left-right symmetrical shapes, which in part resemble various objects. The person being tested is asked whether he or she can identify humans, animals, plants, objects of any kind, landscapes, sequences of events, or whatever comes to mind. During the test, each identification is noted on the exact spot on a set of copies of the 10 cards with the drawings, together with the test person's own comments. The test reveals not only how an abstract picture is perceived but also says something about the vision, feelings and imagination of the investigated person. However, we restricted ourselves mainly to finding whether there were some trends linking the Mlabri men or women, or both together in relation to the other hill tribes investigated. As we had hoped for, some of the persons investigated provided further information of various kinds, sometimes on subjects the very existence of which we were unaware. When asked why, after almost twenty years, nobody had told us before, they apologised by saying: "You did not ask about the subject before, so therefore we did not tell you." However, during our last two visits in 1989 and 1994, some of the young Mlabri, in particular, did reveal information we had not recorded before.

Each test took 40-60 minutes, and only persons we knew well from previous visits were asked to participate. The following data were extracted, see table on next pages.
1) Number of tables with one or more identifications. If one or more table did not receive any response they were tried again after going through all the tables.
2) Symmetry in the Rorschach blots is estimated by counting the answers to the right and left side of each table and is rendered from very asymmetrical answers resulting in a score of 1 or else of up to 4.
3) Action. If no identification was connected with any movement or happening, the score was zero, while a score of 3 corresponds to three or more tables with happenings.
4) Variation of identified objects x/y was calculated from the number of different items x divided by the total number of identifications y.
5) Details (abbr. det.). Some Mlabri just stated the name of the identified object and only gave a few details rendering the score 1, while others giving many details in several identifications, leading to the score being 3.
6) Finally, imagination – a quality that cannot easily be accounted for. However, based on the five previous

performances, and for all the correspondence between identifications and further remarks, this test received scores from 1 to 4. As the results are, to some extent, based on judgement, the ratings are rather rough but otherwise reflect a considerable variation.

All the identified objects are put on top of the table next page and we have listed the number of identifications for each of the participants. Furthermore, the objects have been divided into four large groups according to their properties:

I: Large and often dangerous animals which have been hunted by the men.
II: Smaller and not dangerous animals that also the women might chase or collect.
III: Snakes, scorpions and spiders, as well as crabs, fish and insects (many having a spirit).
IV: Miscellaneous: Humans, trees, roots, plants, stones, tools, cars, the sky, etc.

Identifications id.no. name		Age years	Road test		Cube-tests				Adv. matr.	Plts. id.	Rorschach-blots					Drawings (humans)
			go	return	1	2	3	4-5			sym.	act.	variat.	det.	ima.	
001	Paeng	50	3/12	0/06	0	0	0	–	–	8	2	0	10/20	2	2	–
005	Pha	48	6/16	8/16	0	0	0	0	1	10	4	3	9/11	3	4	dismemb.
010	Seng1	14	6/14	2/06	0	0	0	0	0	7	3	2	5/09	1	1	realistic
020	Lat1	17	2/16	8/16	2	0	3	2	2	10	4	3	8/10	2	3	?
043	Suk	14	2/16	7/16	0	0	0	0	0	10	4	3	6/11	3	3	realistic
044	Ajan	35	0	0	1	0	1	0	1	8	4	2	8/10	2	3	squiggle
044	Seng 2	17	2/06	11/16	1	0	0	0	2	9	2	1	14/17	3	3	–
049	Gu	35	–	–	–	–	–	–	–	7	2	0	15/24	4	2	–
060	Gui	35	–	–	–	–	–	–	–	10	4	3	9/16	3	4	simple
061	Gaeo	33	alternating		0	0	0	0	1	5	3	1	6/07	1	1	squiggle
074	Mun	30	1/8		0	0	0	0	1	10	2	1	16/20	3	3	squiggle
075	Pat	30	2/12	5/06	2	0	2	2	2	9	4	3	0/09	2	2	simple
083	Ple	16	–	–	1	0	2	0	–	8	2	0	10/19	2	2	
091	Paeng N.	25	0	0	1	0	1	0	2	9	3	0	7/03	2	2	squiggle
207	Tong	30	good	faults	2	2	3	–	–	9	4	2	6/14	3	2	simple
210	Sai Taw	47	0	0	2	0	1	2	1	10	4	1	11/17	3	3	–
215	Paeng N.	20	1/13	6/08	0	0	0	0	–	10	4	2	7/16	3	3	–
218	Ta	30	2/14	3/08	2	2	2	–	1	10	4	2	8/10	3	3	squiggle
223	Lat 2	22	0	0	1	2	3	1	1	10	2	2	14/18	3	3	squiggle
316	Si	25	–	–	1	0	1	0	–	10	3	1	12/15	1	2	simple
334	Poa	45	–	–	–	–	–	–	–	10	3	3	16/19	3	4	–
351	Long	21	–	–	1	2	2	0	–	10	4	2	10/14	2	3	realistic
092	Noi	20	–	–	1	2	2	4	1	10	2	1	12/13	3	3	–
107	Wang	25	–	–	–	–	–	–	–	8	4	0	5/09	1	1	simple
083	Ple	21	–	–	2	1	3	0	–	9	2	0	11/13	2	2	–
020	Lat 1	22	–	–	1	0	3	2	1	10	3	1	10/17	2	3	realistic
223	Lat 2	27	–	–	2	0	3	2	–	10	2	1	9/10	2	4	realistic

Adv.: advanced. id.: identification. sym.: symmetri. act.: with action. det.: details. ima.: imagination

– test not attempted.
0 test unsuccessful.
Tests carried out in 1982
& repeated by three pers. 1987.

Drawings: see text and examples figs 160-187.
Dismembered: showing cut up body of human or animal.

Fig. 156. Results of the Psychotechnical and Rorschach tests together with the drawings, Ml Men.

	elephant	wild ox	cow	bear	tiger	deer	pig or boar	dog, domestic	monkey	other big anmals	porcupine	rat (mouse)	squirrel	bat	bird	chicken	oth. small animals	turtle	lizard	frog	snake	scorpion	spider	crab	fish	butterfly	insects	humans	tree	flower	roots	sky	various
001					2	4	5		1			2	1			2		1											1			1	
005	1	1			1		1	1							3	1													1			1	
010												1						5	1								1					1	
020					1		1					1			2			2									1	1					
043									1	1					1			6	1					1									
044									1			1	1		2	5													1			1	1
048	1				2	2	1	1							1		1	2	1		1			1	1				1		1		
049	1		2		1	2	2	2	2	2		2	1		2	1		2				1			1								
060					1		1								3			2						1	2				1		2		3
061					1			1	1						1		1	2															
074	1			1	2	1	1		2				1	2	1	1		1						1	1				2		1		
075					1										2			3											1			1	1
083			2	2	3	4	1	1						2	2	1													1				
091				2	2	1			2						3	2																	1
207									1						1											1	1		7	2	2		
210				1	1										1	1		3				2					1	2	2			2	2
215		1		1	3				1																		1	7	2				
218													1	1	1			2						1								1	
223	1				3	1									1		1	1	1		1			1	2			2		1		1	1
316	1					1			1	1					1	1	1	1		1							1	1	4				
334	1	1		2	2	1		1	1		1				1		1	1	1					1				1	2				
351					1	1									1		1	1	3	3	1						1	1					
092	1	1	1	1	1		1		1	1	1	2											1		1								
107					1													3					1					3	1				
	9	4	3	9	27	16	20	7	15	6	5	12	6	4	30	13	8	39	4	3	3	4	1	6	7	9	4	7	30	10	4	7	9

Fig. 157. Objects identified in the 10 Rorschach tables, M1 men.

Identification no./name	Age 1987 years	Road test		Cube–test				Adv.		Rorschach-test					Drawings (humans)
		go	return	1	2	3	4–5	matr.	no.	sym.	act.	variat.	detail	imag.	
071 Jaga	20	0	0	0	0	1	0	2	9	4	2	10/13	3	3	simple
072 Maiga	27	13/16	0	0	0	2	2	2	10	4	2	16/22	4	3	simple
204 ya king	23	0	0	0	0	0	0	0	10	4	2	20/24	3	3	dismemb.
335 Ying	35	–	–	0	0	0	0	–	10	4	1	9/12	2	2	–
355 Noi's w.	18	–	–	0	0	0	–	–	10	1	2	11/15	3	3	–
360 ya–yɛ	29	–	–	–	–	–	–	–	10	4	2	11/12	2	2	–
364 Dung	21	–	–	–	–	–	–	–	10	4	1	12/13	–	–	

Fig. 158. Results of Psychotechnical and Rorschach blots together with drawings, women.

	elephant	wild ox	cow	bear	tiger	deer	pig or boar	dog, domestic	monkey	other big animals	porcupine	rat (mouse)	squirrel	bat	bird	chicken	oth. small animals	lizard	frog	snake	scorpion	spider	crab	fish	butterfly	insects	humans	tree	flower	roots	sky	various
071	1			1	1	1	1			2				1			1	3									2					
072				3	1		1											1										6	1	7		1
204	1		1		3	1	1			1	1	2	1		1			2	1		1	1			1			1	1	4		
335			1						4	1	2	2						1														1
355		1	1		2	2				2	1	1						1			1				1			1				1
360									1			1	1	2	1			2				2						3			1	
364									1	1				2	4						1	1			1	1						
total	2	1	1	3	4	7	4	2	6	7	4	6	2	5	6		1	9	2		3	2			3	3	2	11	2	11	2	2

Fig. 159. Number of objects identified in the 10 Rorschach tables, women.

Comments on the Rorschach blots

Not quite unexpectedly, it turned out that the Mlabri did not find this test difficult perhaps because, generally speaking, they cherish people with fantasy and imagination, in contrast to cultures with very fixed and strict rules. The men found objects in nine out of 10 drawings, the women in almost all of them. The identifications by the men were somewhat more symmetrical than those of the women, and they had more happenings than the women. The latter was, however, probably a result of the women's greater shyness. The number of different objects out of all identifications (x/y) is on average 10/14 for men and 13/15 for the seven women. This difference is also seen in the fact that the women chose smaller objects and pointed out finer details.

When the number of identified objects is inspected it appears that men and women found almost the same percentage as regards the four main groups, but still taking into account that we have answers from only seven women:

	Big animals	Smaller animals	Creeping animals	All other objects
Men:	34%	23%	23%	20%
Women:	33%	21%	19%	27%

Men more often find elephants and tigers (dangerous on their hunting expeditions) and boars (much wanted), while women rather identify monkeys (might be aggressive and even dangerous towards women) and espe-cially roots, which they collect and which traditionally have been the Mlabri's main staple before rice attained that position. Some animals are almost absent, such as spiders, which nobody likes, and the women especially detest. We asked them why they did not identify them (obvious choices in plate 10), to which they answered that they did not like to, perhaps due to their belief that merely talking about such undesirable animals may provoke them to come.

Similarities between what the two sexes identify in the drawings are more pronounced than the differences. In spite of the fact that the two sexes exhibit pronounced sexual dimorphism and had, until recently, a clear division of duties, it seems to be more important that the dense and once impenetrable jungle has been their mutual world of experience – a very important result of the test. 80% of all identifications are of animals, of which 70% are edible. Even though rice has been the main staple of the Mlabri since about 1985, animals are still all-dominant in their minds, as the hunter-gatherers of food they themselves claim they have always been. Do the animals have a magical function? Probably once, but anyway no longer. However, the Mlabri know the animals in a far more intimate way and respect them much more than the other hill tribes. This is confirmed in various ways; it is not permitted to tease animals or to laugh at their behav-iour, and when an animal is hunted it is important to kill it quickly. Previously, some hunters even made excuses for the killings before going hunting. It is also to be noted that many Mlabri say that perhaps they themselves may be reincarnated as animals.

It is surprising how rarely humans are seen in the ten Rorschach drawings (nos. 2 and 3). Men and women find only 2% out of all identifications, which is less than one fifth of the usual average, even though humans were mentioned as a possibility to everyone being tested. I have no clear-cut explanations to offer, apart from the obvious one that the spirits may be offended. Objects like trees, plants and clouds are identified as on average, whereas clothing, tools and other manufactured goods amount only to about 1%, or once again under a fifth of what would be identified in the industrial world. As mentioned earlier, it is remarkable how little importance they have had in Mlabri society until recently when their very possession, except for the spear, did not afford the owner much higher prestige!

In conclusion, we may say that the Mlabri's ability to solve combinatory and three-dimensional tests is considerably less than that of the other mountain peoples. But their imagination and fantasy is often good, and their linquistic abilities are indeed extraordinary. The younger generation have shifted their interests to modern items and improved their technical skills since around 1990. This also applies to other fields of cultural manifestation from the outside world, although it does create some problems between the older and younger generation.

Drawings

As a further supplement to the Rorschach blots, we persuaded about 30 Ml Mlabri to make drawings of a man and a woman, which most of them said they had never tried before. Therefore it was not surprising that the drawings resemble our own children's productions from their early childhood, but with one interesting exception. Some of the first drawings from 1982 (e.g. Pha's fig. 160) pictured humans as they would appear, if the head, all the limbs and the organs had been dismembered exactly as done when cutting up a pig, just before sharing the meat among the families in the band. Incidentally, it has always been persons like Paeng and Pha who have been in charge of such demanding operations. Who knows, perhaps our friendly Ml Mlabri might occasionally have been cannibals some generations back, as it seems was the case with the Kiew, the 'fierce group', just across the Laotian border until as late as about 1970, see furthermore p. 223.

From the first drawings to the last obtained in 1994, there is a remarkable development from mere squiggles to more accomplished drawings, probably inspired by magazines and due to the contact with the American mission station in Ban Oij near Phrae, since about 1985.

Examples of the drawings are shown on figs. 160-180. These might be of some interest as they were obtained during the critical years when the Mlabri began to be forced to stay for long periods of time in one locality to work as part-time labourers especially for the Hmong. This was because first the animals disappeared and then the jungle itself. Among other things, we note that almost all the drawings by the men show the sex organs of both sexes, while none of the drawings by the women include them! Perhaps more remarkably, some of the men insisted that their drawing should contain all the members of their band (see examples figs. 162-179), showing the great importance of solidarity and feeling of unity among their kind.

Carved Designs on Various Wooden Utensils

The drawings do not stand alone. In fact Mlabri produce simple designs, especially on some of their bamboo containers. The designs are of two kinds: almost geometric ones and some with more rounded shapes. The first two examples of containers (fig. 146) have simple designs repeated all over, while the third container exhibits more details within the geometric design, of which we had many sub-areas identified through our Thai interpreter, indicating trees, leaves and roots. Fig. 147 shows more irregular designs. The tall container in the middle and the one to the right both depict various trees and roots, while the one below has rounded forms with regular patterns inside resembling turtles. J.J. Boeles in J.S.S., Vol. XX, plate 2, suggests that the Mlabri design on a bamboo container similar to ours fig. 147, M1, no. 20, 1982 represents the jungle below, above this the mountains and on top the sky. However, when asking the Mlabri they said, they never described such scenes, but merely pointed out the names of useful trees and roots.

The geometric designs are also to be found on other items, see fig. 148 showing a cup, a chun, used when making baskets and pipes of which the smallest is from the M3 group, linking the two groups! We saw similar patterns on various Semang objects of bamboo, for example on blowpipes, the use of which was demonstrated by five dark-skinned and curly-haired Semangs at the New Year Fair in Chieng Mai in 1970.

Psychological Tests from other Mlabri-like Groups

From the M3 group who came to Thailand proper around 1975, we obtained only two sets of tests, one from a man and one from a woman. Their performances were definitely more hesitant than those of the Ml group. One of them managed the "Road Test" well with the target moving away, the other one when the target was approaching the observer. But neither could perform the Cube or the Advanced Matrices test, and neither had more than a few identifications in the Rorschach blots and no happenings. In contrast to the M1 Mlabri, they had only a few identifications of big animals, which they told us they were afraid of, as they mostly hunt or collect small animals, roots, vegetables and fruits.

Incidentally, there was only one identification in group IV. However, the test does not necessarily reflect less inventive persons, as they were easier to understand when complicated matters were discussed. But their small number and their feelings of inferiority towards all other people – especially the Hmong – has definitely resulted in their sense of resignation, to which their long addiction to opium may have contributed.

We obtained test sets from two further Mlabri. One was from Lek (M4), a young man of about 30 years of age, who was sold to a Hmong family near Pua in Nan province, when he was about ten years old. The other one was Lot (M5), who was about the same age as Lek.

He had stayed with his Mlabri band at Phu Kradung down in Loei province, but had been adopted by a Thai family when he was 12 years old. While it turned out that Lek could not remember much about his Mlabri family, Lot could give more details about his childhood.

Lek had success with the road test, Lot did not. The Cube and A.M.I tests both gave better scores than for the Ml group in general, but considering that both had lived in a village for the last 20 years, the scores were not substantially better. As regards the Rorschach blots, the number of answers, etc., corresponds quite well with those of the Ml group, but we note that they had 50% identifications of animals in contrast to the Ml group having 80%.

In conclusion, concerning our evidence from the various psychological tests etc., it is evident that during their most important years of mental development, from about 0-5 years of age, none of the Mlabri we have met has received the intellectual stimulation necessary to live and work together with the other hill peoples. On the other hand, especially as regards Mlabri Ml having survived their childhood in the jungle, they might be better off than those from the splinter groups. From 1982 we started to take a few of our best Ml informants down to Nan city, the administrative centre of the province. It was really surprising to see how fast they adapted to the very different conditions – staying in the hotel, eating with a knife and fork, managing the TV in their room, etc., making us think that they stand a much better chance of surviving both physically and mentally than we had anticipated previously.

Drawings by members of the M1 group

All participants in the various tests were asked to make a drawing of a man and/or a woman, and we made sure that each one made their own independently of the other Mlabri.

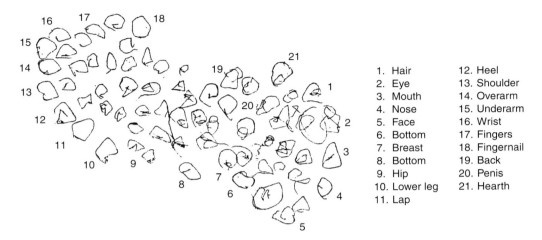

1. Hair
2. Eye
3. Mouth
4. Nose
5. Face
6. Bottom
7. Breast
8. Bottom
9. Hip
10. Lower leg
11. Lap
12. Heel
13. Shoulder
14. Overarm
15. Underarm
16. Wrist
17. Fingers
18. Fingernail
19. Back
20. Penis
21. Hearth

Fig. 160. Pha (no. 001), 45 years old in 1982: Dismembered body of an animal or perhaps a human, Scale 1:1. Each item of the drawing was pointed out by Pha with the outer parts around the rim and the inner organs in the middle (see list above).

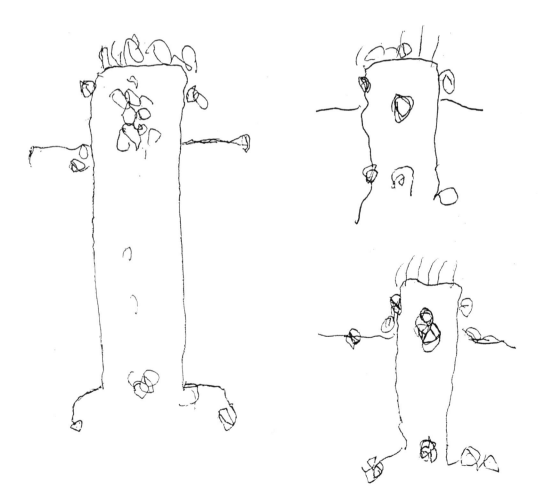

Fig. 161. Seng (010), Pha's son, 12 years old in 1982: Father mother and child. Genitals shown. Scale 1:1.

296

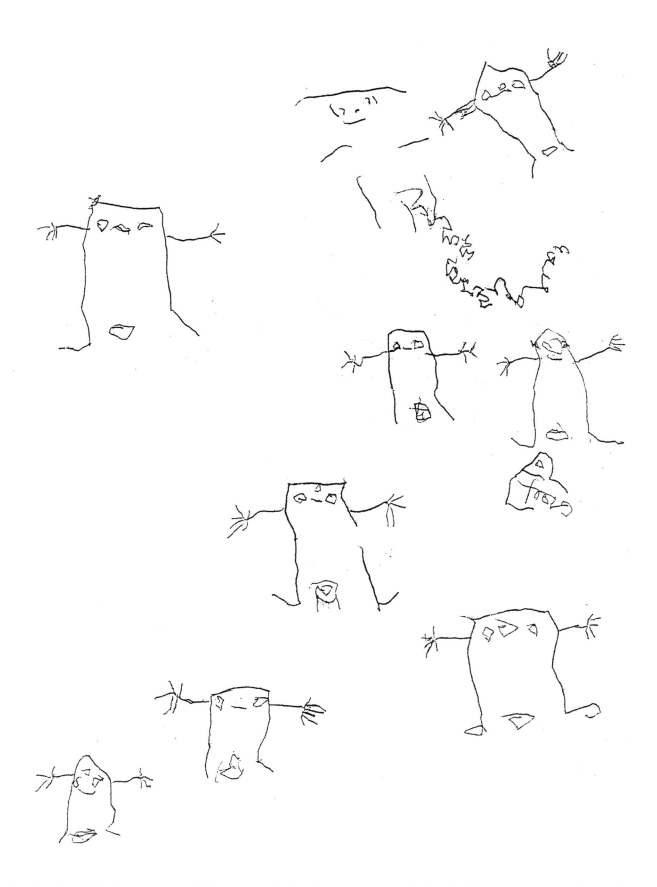

Fig. 162. Suk (049), 15 years old in 1982, staying with Pha. Suk insisted on including the following members of his band:
Above: Pha, Gaeo and Pat. In the middle: Patot, Suk, his friend and a dog.
Below: Thong, his wife and their child. Scale 1:1.

Fig. 163. Gu (060), 40 years old in 1982:
Man as seen in profile
(penis indicated)
and woman with breasts and skirt.
All drawings scale 1:1.

Fig. 164. Pat (076) 28 years old in 1982:
Child, father and mother.

Fig. 165. Upper right side: Ajan (044)
37 years old in 1982: man and woman
(breasts included).

Fig. 166. Below: Paeng Noi (241),
30 years old in 1987: Man and woman.

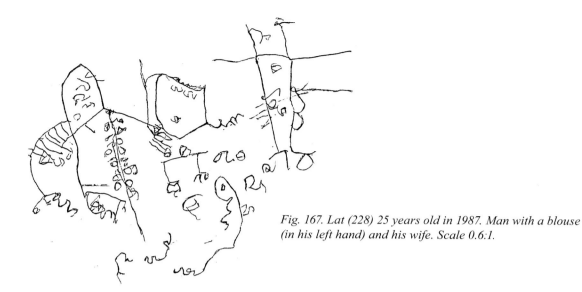

Fig. 167. Lat (228) 25 years old in 1987. Man with a blouse (in his left hand) and his wife. Scale 0.6:1.

Fig. 168. Thong (207), 32 years old in 1987: A man and a woman. Scale 1:1.

Fig. 169. Wang (214), 33 years old in 1987: A man and a woman. Scale 1:1.

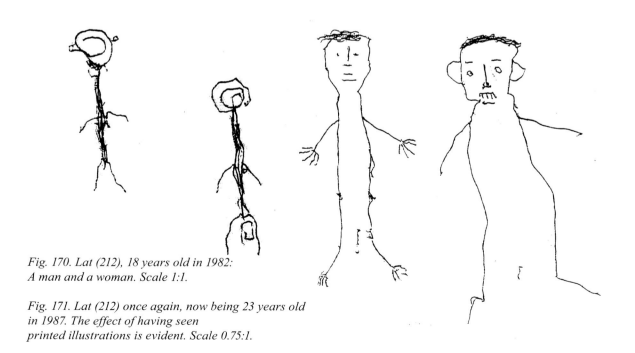

Fig. 170. Lat (212), 18 years old in 1982: A man and a woman. Scale 1:1.

Fig. 171. Lat (212) once again, now being 23 years old in 1987. The effect of having seen printed illustrations is evident. Scale 0.75:1.

299

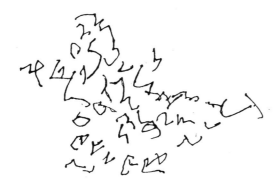

Fig. 172. 'e Sung (355), 28 years old in 1989. Scribble. Said she had never tried to make a drawing before. Scale 1:1.

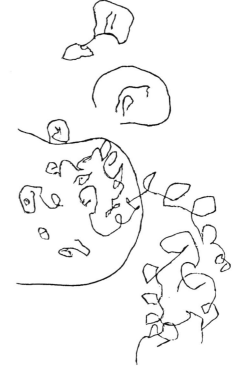

Fig. 173. Mun's wife ya king 27 years old in 1982 Disorganized drawing of three persons. Scale 0.85:1.

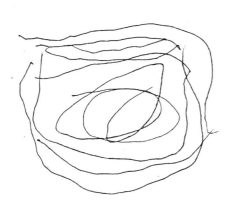

Fig. 174. Mai (072), Pha's daughter, 20 years old in 1982. Human 1:1.

Fig. 175. ya yɛ (360), 22 years old in 1982: Husband and wife. 1:1.

Fig. 176. Thobito (364), 47 years old in 1989: Head with hair, nose and mouth. Scale 0.85:1.

Fig. 177. Khamla (076), 40 years old in 1989: Unusual presentation of a human seen from above with the head in the center. Scale 0.75:1.

Fig. 178. Muang (094), 48 old years in 1989: An almost surrealistic drawing of a person. The structure to the wright could be the windscreen or just trees. Scale 0.82:1.

Fig. 179. Long (049), 30 years old in 1989: Woman (with breast) shown in profile, and a man seen from the front. Scale 0.82:1.

Fig. 180. Som (093), 32 years old in 1989: His windscreen with 11 persons, from left to right: Man, man, baby, woman, two girls, boy, woman, woman, woman, man: Mang, Si, i-Daeng, Jua, pung & i lai, i bai, Pui, i Pot (ja paeng), Pa Djom, Som. Their placing respecting both practical and psychological considerations; a mixture of Thai and Mlabri (the infants) names are affixed to each individual. Scale 0.75:1.

Fig. 181. Baw (341) Som's son, 16 years old: depicting the same persons as in Som's drawing above. Scale 0.75:1.

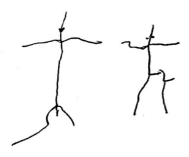

Fig. 182. Phan (022), M3, 30 years old in 1982, made these simple drawings of herself and her husband. 1:2.

Fig. 183. Oy (028), M3, 42 years, depicting himself and his wife and their daughters in 1982. Scale 1:2.

Fig. 184. Lek (235), M4, depicting himself and his Thai wife in 1987, when 30 years old. Scale 1:2.

Fig. 185 Lot (236), M5, made this drawing of himself in 1987, when he was 25 years old. Scale 1:1.

Fig. 186. Gen (237), M4, man and woman, 1982. Scale 1:2.

Fig. 187. Theung (238), M4, man and woman, 1982. Scale 1:2.

303

Mlabri Teeth Compared with those of other Ethnic Groups of Southeast Asia

by

Verner Alexandersen

The purpose of this study is to compare persons belonging to the Mlabri tribe in Northern Thailand with individuals from other selected hill tribes as well as with the Thai population in the area with respect to dental morphology and tooth size.

Dr. Jesper Trier and his wife made dental casts of Mlabri dentitions during their third expedition in 1978. More dental casts were added to the collection when Carl Erik Andersen and his wife, a Danish dentist and a dental technician respectively, participated in the expedition in 1980. For comparison, dental casts of individuals from other hill tribes and from the Thai population were gathered as well. Being a dentist myself, and also working for the Anthropological Institute at the University of Copenhagen with various prehistoric materials from all over the world, I was asked by Trier to study and evaluate the already existing material. With a grant from Kronprins Frederiks Fund, I furthermore went to Thailand in 1996 to collect more dental casts of the Mlabri, of persons from other hill tribes and of the Thai population.

Morphological traits of the tooth crown exhibit significant differences in frequency among the major geographic races. At the Arizona State University, Turner II and his co-workers have defined a large number of variable dental traits and studied their distribution in many populations (Turner *et al.* 1991). Based on the high frequency of certain dental traits in the Japanese population, Hanihara, 1969, introduced the term "Mongoloid dental complex". Studies by Turner resulted in a subdivision of this pattern into a North Asian Sinodont and a South Asian Sundadont dentition (Turner 1990). The Australoid dentition has recently been characterised using the same dental traits, and the Australoid teeth are similar to Sundadont teeth, although with a few important exceptions (Turner 1990; Townsend *et al.* 1990). Also the teeth of Southeast Asian Negritos have been studied and their teeth, too, belong to the Sundadont division of dentitions (Hanihara 1993).

The tribes in Northern Thailand are of great interest to science, because their history is not yet fully documented. In Northern Thailand there might still be groups who are descendants of the original Mesolithic population as well as descendants of the early farmers from the Neolithic period and newcomers from Southeast China and Burma. Each tribe (or population, as for example the Thai farmers) usually occupies a certain altitude interval within ranges right from the valleys to the highest elevations of the mountains and shows marked cultural differences.

Tooth size and dental morphology are genetically determined and therefore suited to assess population relationships and help to resolve micro-evolutionary problems. Differences in dental trait frequencies on key teeth in the dentition are considered to indicate the genetic distance between the samples. Several investigations have shown that there is a fair agreement between dental distances and those based on biochemical differences in blood groups. Furthermore, linguistic similarities have also been shown to be accompanied by morphological similarities.

The origin of the now vanishing small Mlabri groups with their modest material culture is not yet known. It has been hypothesised that they form an aboriginal relict group with links to the Semang and especially the Senoi (Orang Asli) living along the border between Malaysia and Thailand (Kerr 1924; Trier 1981). It is generally accepted that such people were among the first inhabitants of the once sparsely populated mountain jungles of Indo-China, who only occasionally came into closer contact with the larger populations of the Thai, Laotians and the hill tribes within the last hundred years.

1. Material

The Mlabri

Their number in all of Indo-China has decreased to only 300-400 (2000 A.D.), of which about half live in the Nan and Phrae provinces in Northern Thailand and the remaining part mainly in Laos and Vietnam (Trier, pp. 27-28). They used to live exclusively by hunting and gathering until about 1970, but now they occasionally work in the fields of others such as those of the Hmong and Thai. Their exact biological relation to the other inhabitants of the area is still not determined. According to the linguistic classification of hill tribes in Thailand by Matisoff, 1983, the Mlabri speak an Austro-Asiatic language related to the Mon-Khmer languages spoken by T'in, Lua and Khamu.

During the expedition to Nan province in 1997, headed by Dr. Nitisiri Parakat, Director of the Intercountry Centre of Oral Health in Changmai, it was possible to locate only 12 individuals belonging to the Mlabri group who were willing to have dental impressions taken. Seven persons were males and four were females. As already mentioned, Dr. Trier and the Danish dentist and his wife had already obtained dental casts of 28 Ml Mlabri as well as of maxillary teeth belonging to 8 M3 Mlabri. For comparative purposes dental impressions have been obtained from the following groups:

Hmong

The Hmong or Meo are Thailand's second largest hill-tribe group. Their origin is sought in south China. They migrated to Thailand during the last few centuries and are nowadays found in south China, Thailand, Laos and Vietnam. In Thailand they prefer high levels near mountain peaks or plateaus at about 1,000-2,500 m. Their language is considered to be an Austro-Thai language related to that of the Yao. Trier and his party collected dental casts of 10 Hmong and my party altogether 30 casts, all deriving from Nan province.

T'in

These people are also migratory swidden farmers and are primarily found along the northeastern Lao-Thai border. They appear to have lived in Thailand for a very long time. Dental casts were obtained from 11 persons in the village of Ban Pa Rai in the Nan province.

Lisu

The Lisu or Lisaw tribe originated in Tibet. They now live in Yunnan and in Thailand. Their language is Tibeto-Burman and belongs to the Sino-Tibetan group of languages, and their villages are situated at about 800-2,000 m. Dental casts were obtained from 11 persons.

Thai

Further comparative material was made available to me at the Dental School in Chienmai. Stone casts of 12 patients and of 84 orthodontic patients were studied and the morphology of their teeth recorded. Included are also the already mentioned dental casts of maxillary teeth from 10 persons obtained by Trier's party from a village in Nan province.

Population/tribe	Number	Males	Females
Mlabri Ml	41	24	17
Mlabri M	8	4	4
Thai	106	57	49
Hmong	40	27	13
Lisu	11	1	10
T'in	11	6	5

Table 1. Dental casts studied.

2. Methods and Results

Dental morphology

The ASU standards prepared by Turner and co-workers (Turner et al. 1991) were followed during the examination of the casts. The mesiodistal and faciolingual crown diameters were measured of unworn or slightly worn teeth that were accurately replicated on the dental casts. The mesiodistal diameters were measured between the mesial and distal contact points of teeth standing in their original positions in the jaw bones. The faciolingual diameters were measured in a plane at right-angles to that of the mesiodistal diameter.

Statistical analysis

The morphological variation was analysed using both univariate and multivariate statistics. Chi square tests were used to test for significant differences of the same dental traits in the various samples. Mean measures of divergence (MMD) were used to estimate the biological distance between the samples. The MMD was calculated according to the suggestions given by Sjøvold, 1973. Barlett's adjustment was used when the proportion of affected individuals was either 0 or 1, in which cases p=0 was replaced by p=1/(4 N) and p=1 was replaced by p=1-1/ (4 N), where N is the number of observations.

Each measure of divergence (x) for a given trait between two groups, 1 and 2, was calculated, using the equation: $x = (\theta_1-\theta_2)^2-(1/N_1 + 1/N_2)$, where θ = arcsin (1-2 p) the angular transformation of the fractional occurrence (p) of a trait. θ is in units of radians and N is the total number of observable trait sites.

The variance of x is given by the equation: var $x = 2$ $(1/N_1 + 1/N_2)^2$, and the standard deviation of x by: S.D. $x = (\text{var } x)^{1/2}$.

The overall distance between the groups may be described by the mean measure of divergence of its variants. The mean measure of divergence is given by: $x = 2 \, x/n$, where n = the number of traits and Z x = summation of the x-values (MD's) for the n contributing traits.

The variance of x is given by: var $x = 2/n^2 \, Z \, (1/N_1 + 1/N_2)^2$ and S.D.: $x = (\text{var } x)^{1/2}$. Both x and var x are normally distributed, and have expected values = 0. Hence significance levels of x and var x can be established by reference to normal probability tables. For example, if x or var x are greater than two standard deviations, it is 95% certain that two traits (or groups) are different (a significance level of. 05). Sellevold, 1977.

Winging

Definition: Rotation of the permanent maxillary central incisors. Classification:
1. Bilateral winging: Central incisors are rotated mesiolingually, giving a V-shaped appearance when viewed from the occlusal surface. When the angle formed is greater than 20 degrees, it is classed as 1 A; when less than 20 degrees, 1 B.
2. Unilateral winging: Only one of the incisors is rotated. The other is straight.
3. Straight: Both teeth form a straight labial surface, or follow the curvature of the dental arch.
4. Counter-winging: One or both teeth are rotated distolingually.

Population/tribe (sexes combined)	Group of winging					N	% affected
	1A	1B	2	3	4		
Mlabri, Ml	3	5	2	33	2	45	22
Mlabri, M3	3	2	0	3	0	8	50
Thai, rural	2	0	0	8	0	10	20
Thai, urban	1	12	1	69	1	84	17
Hmong	3	6	3	27	0	39	31
Lisu	1	3	2	6	0	39	50
T'in	2	0	3	0	4	9	5 0

Table 2. Winging of maxillary central incisors.

Discussion

Enoki and Dahlberg, 1963, considered winging a characteristic trait of Asian populations. They found winging in most cases to be independent of crowding, and Turner considers the trait a separate genetic system. There was no sexual dimorphism. In males the frequency of bilateral and unilateral winging was 45/203 = 26.6% and in females 54/197 = 27.41%.

Comparative data by Turner indicate that both Sinodont and Sundadont populations have winging of the central incisors with a frequency of 23%, which is very close to the results of the present investigation. There is a considerable variation among the small group, presumably due to family ties among the individuals studied. The Mlabri Ml group is phenotypically close to the Mlabri M3, so even taking them together will not make the frequency significantly different from that of the Thai. Mlabri and Yao (14/53 = 26%); urban and rural Thai (16/94 = 17%; 95% significance limits 10.17%-26.43%).

Shovelling of maxillary central incisors

Shovel-shape is characterised by prominent marginal ridges on the lingual surface of the tooth crown. The basal tubercle is, either weakly developed and more or less covered by the marginal ridges, or the tubercle is prominent. The prominence of the marginal ridges is evaluated in relation to the depth of the central fossa.

Classification
0. None
1. Faint
2. Trace
3-4. Semi-shovel
5. Shovel
6. Marked shovel

Population/tribe (sexes combined)	Grade	0	1	2	3	4	5	6	N	3-6/0-6 %
Mlabri Ml		6	4	5	17	5	1	0	38	60.5
Mlabri M3		0	0	0	6	3	0	0	9	100.0
Thai		0	13	39	29	11	1	0	93	44.1
Hmong		0	7	5	12	11	3	0	38	68.4
Lisu		0	2	3	4	2	0	0	11	54.6
T'in		0	1	5	3	0	0	0	9	33.3

Table 3. Shovelling of permanent maxillary central incisor.

Population/tribe (sexes combined)	Grade	0	1	2	3	4	5	6	N	2-6/0-6 %
Mlabri Ml		19	17	2	1	0	0	0	39	7.7
Thai		37	30	14	13	0	0	0	94	28.7
Hmong		9	7	3	1	0	0	0	20	20.0
Lisu		4	4	0	1	0	0	0	9	11.1
T'in		7	1	1	1	0	0	0	10	20.0

Table 4. Double shovel of permanent maxillary central incisor.

Shovel-shape frequency occurs in Asian populations, but rarely in European or African populations (Mizoguchi 1985). In the present study shovel-shape was scored in accordance with Turner's plaques. In table 3 the classes 3-6 are considered shovel-shape.

Among the larger samples the Mlabri Ml is intermediate between the Thai and the Hmong. The Thai sample falls within the range of Sundadont dentitions studied by Turner, who found a mean of 30.8% and a standard deviation of 15.8%, whereas the Hmong fall within the Sindodont range of variation.

Among individuals with Sinodont dentitions, the frequency of shovel is higher, with a mean of 71.1% and a standard deviation of 11.5% (Turner 1990). Both Mlabri groups are closer to the Hmong for this dental character. There are no significant differences between the Mlabri (Ml+M3) and the Hmong.

Double shovelling

Double-shovelling refers to the presence of marginal ridges on the facial surfaces of the maxillary incisors. Classification:

0. None: Facial surface is smooth.
1. Faint: Mesial and distal ridging can be seen in strong contrasting light. Distal ridge may be absent in this and stronger grades.
2. Trace: Ridging is more easily seen and palpated.
3. Semi-double-shovel: Ridging can be readily palpated.
4. Double-shovel: Ridging is pronounced on at least one half of the total crown height.
5. Pronounced double-shovel. Ridging is very prominent and may occur from the incisal edge to the crown-root junction.
6. Extreme double shovel.

The Mlabri group has a significantly lower frequency than the Thai (adjusted Chi square 7.30, p < 0.01). The difference between the Mlabri and the Hmong is not significant. Also the Lisu and T'in tend to have low frequencies of double-shovelling. Double-shovelling is characteristic for individuals with Sinodont dentitions.

Carabelli's structure on permanent maxillary first molars

The Carabelli's trait occurs on the lingual surface of the mesiolingual cusp of the maxillary molars.

Classification

0. The lingual aspect of the mesiolingual cusp is smooth;
1. A groove is present;
2. A pit is present;
3. A small Y-shaped depression is present;
4. A large Y-shaped depression is present;
5. A small cusp without a free apex occurs. The distal border of the cusp does not contact the lingual groove separating the two lingual cusps;
6. A medium-sized cusp with an attached apex making contact with the median lingual groove is present;
7. A large free cusp is present.

Population/tribe (sexes combined)	Grade	0	1	2	3	4	5	6	N	4-7/0-7 %
Mlabri Ml		18	4	6	2	0	4	2	36	16.7
Thai		18	5	4	3	0	3	0	35	14.3
Hmong		38	13	8	11	4	8	4	89	21.4
Lisu		5	0	0	0	4	1	0	11	54.6
T'in		6	0	0	0	2	0	0	9	33.3

Table 5. Carabelli's structure.

The Mlabri group is intermediate between the Hmong and the Thai, but no significant differences are found. Carabelli's structure is present but weakly developed in Asian populations, while it is more common and better developed in European dentitions. The small samples show a somewhat higher frequency of Carabelli's structure than in the larger groups.

Hypocone on maxillary second molars

The hypocone is the distolingual cusp. It varies in size and may even be absent.

Classification
0. No hypocone;
1. Faint ridging present at the site;
2. Faint cuspule present; 3. Small cusp present;
3.5. Moderate-sized cusp present.
4. Large cusp present;
5. Very large cusp present.

Population/tribe (sexes combined)	Grade	0	1	2	3	4	5	N	3-5/0-5 %
Mlabri Ml			4	1	8	13	13	0	39	66.7
Mlabri M3			2	0	0	1	2	0	5	60.0
Thai			4	6	9	31	29	3	82	76.8
Hmong			4	2	4	8	19	0	37	73.0
Lisu			0	0	0	8	2	1	11	100.0
T'in			0	0	0	4	6	0	10	100.0

Table 6. Presence of hypocone on permanent maxillary second molar.

Hypocone reduction or absence (grades 0, 1 and 2) is found less often in the Mlabri group Ml and M3 than in the other samples, but the difference is non-significant.

Seventh cusp on permanent mandibular first molars

This tubercle occurs in the lingual groove between the two lingual cusps of the mandibular molars, most commonly on the first molar.

Classification
0. Non-occurrence of the cusp 7;
1A. Faint groove is present, and two weak lingual grooves are present instead of one;

1B. A faint tipless cusp 7 occurs displaced as a bulge on the lingual surface of the metaconid;
2. Cusp 7 is small;
3. Cusp 7 is medium-sized;
4. Cusp 7 is large.

Population/tribe (sexes combined)	Grade 0	1A+1B	2	3	4	N	1-4/0-4 %
Mlabri Ml	36	0	0	0	0	36	0.0
Thai	69	8	3	3	1	84	17.9
Hmong	2	0	2	0	1	5	60.0
Lisu	11	0	0	0	0	11	0.0
T'in	9	1	1	0	0	11	18.2

Table 7. Seventh cusp on permanent mandibular first molars.

The seventh cusp is quite common in Asian populations. It is remarkable that the seventh cusp does not appear among the Mlabri.

Sixth cusp on permanent mandibular first molars

This tubercle is found on the distal marginal ridge lingual to the hypoconulid on mandibular molars. It is scored by size relative to the hypoconulid.

Classification
0. Cusp 6 is absent.
1. Cusp 6 is much smaller than the hypoconulid.
2. Cusp 6 is smaller than the hypoconulid.
3. Cusp 6 is equal in size to the hypoconulid.
4. Cusp 6 is larger than the hypoconulid.
5. Cusp 6 is much larger than the hypoconulid.

Population/tribe (sexes combined)	Grade	0	1	2	3	4	5	N	1-5/0-5 %
Mlabri Ml		12	0	2	1	1	0	36	16.7
Thai		25	1	11	7	0	0	35	14.3
Hmong		13	1	4	0	0	3	89	21.4
Lisu		7	0	1	0	0	0	11	54.6
T'in		1	0	0	1	0	1	9	33.3

Table 8. Sixth cusp on permanent mandibular first molars.

Cusp 6 is rare in Caucasians and Negroes, but more common in Asian and Melanesian populations (Bailit *et al.,* 1968; Mayhall *et al.* 1982). A high frequency has also been reported in Australian aboriginal groups (Townsend *et al.* 1990). The last mentioned authors found the sixth cusp on 61 % and mandibular first molars in aboriginals from Yuendumu in the Northern Territory of Australia (N:316 males and females combined). It is of interest here to point out that the group of Mlabri differs markedly from the Australian aboriginals, although high frequencies of the sixth cusp can be found in Northern Thailand today, as shown from the results presented in the table above.

Mandibular canine distal, accessory ridge

A small ridge occurs in the distolingual fossa between the cup and the distal marginal ridge.

Classification
The standards developed by Scott, 1993, and the reference plaque LC-ASU LC DAR were followed.
0. Deflecting wrinkle is absent. Medial ridge of cusp 2 is straight.
1. Cusp 2 medial ridge is straight, but shows a midpoint constriction.
2. Medial ridge is deflected distally, but does not make contact with cusp 4.
3. Medial ridge is deflected distally forming an L-shaped ridge. The medial contacts the fourth cusp.

Turner *et al.,* 1991 comment that a sex difference might be expected. Among the Mlabri four males and one female showed the d.acc.r. and among the Hmong, six males and four females showed this ridge. In the Thai sample there was no sex difference, and the results in table 9 are given for both sexes combined.

Populations/tribe (sexes combined)	Grade	1-5/0-5 %	2-5/0-5	%
Mlabri MI		43	3/37	18.9
Thai		54	21/89	23.6
Hmong		47	10/34	29.4
Lisu		89	2/9	22.2
T'in		91	4/11	36.4

Table 9. Distal accessory ridge on permanent mandibular canines.

This trait is impossible to score on severely worn teeth. On slightly worn teeth, only the marked grades can be recognised with certainty. The large variability among the samples, when all grades are used to calculate the frequency, is reduced considerably when only the more distinct forms of the accessory ridge are counted. The latter method is the more realistic for this material of dental casts. The results show no significant differences between the samples.

The number of lingual cusps on mandibular second premolars

Three lingual cusps of variable size can be observed on mandibular second premolars.

Classification
1. One lingual cusp
2. Two lingual cusps
3. Three lingual cusps

Populations/tribe (sexes combined)	Grade	2-3/1-3	%
Mlabri MI		11/30	36.7
Thai		31/88	35.2
Hmong		15/34	44.1
Lisu		4/11	36.4
T'in		4/10	40.0

Table 10. Lingual cusp variation on mandibular second premolars.

No teeth with three lingual cusps were found. The frequency of teeth with two lingual cusps was practically the same in all samples.

Deflecting wrinkle on permanent mandibular first molars

The first molar deflecting wrinkle is observed on the mesiolingual cusp.
0. Deflecting wrinkle is absent. Medial ridge of cusp 2 is straight.
1. Cusp 2 medial ridge is straight, but shows a midpoint constriction;
2. Medial ridge is deflected distally, but does not make contact with cusp 4;
3. Medial ridge is deflected distally forming an L-shaped ridge. The medial contacts the fourth cusp.

Populations/tribe (sexes combined	Grade 0	1	2	3	N	% affected 1-3/0-3
Mlabri M1	7	3	4	1	15	33.3
Thai	12	15	21	10	58	53.5
Hmong	4	3	6	3	16	56.3
Lisu	1	2	2	0	5	40.0
T'in	1	0	0	0	1	0.0

Table 11. Deflecting wrinkle.

The wrinkle tends to wear away, and the trait is most accurately studied in young individuals. If the molars are slightly worn, only the more distinct grades are still visible, and the frequencies shown in the table probably exaggerate the real frequencies of the higher grades.

Number of cusps on permanent mandibular second molars

The number of principal cusps varies between four and five. The variable cusp is the hypoconulid.

Classification
The frequency of 5-cusped LM2 is low in Europeans, higher in Sundadont dentitions and highest in Sinodont dentitions.

Populations/tribe (sexes combined)	Grade 5/4-5	%
Mlabri	20/30	66.7
Thai	61/84	72.6
Hmong	24/30	80.0
Lisu	7/9	77.8
T'in	6/8	75.0

Table 12. Number of cusps on permanent mandibular second molars.

When asymmetry was present, individuals with at least one five-cusped second molar were considered to belong to the group of five-cusped individuals. The results in table 12 show no significant differences among the samples. There is a tendency towards higher frequencies among tribes from northern regions, Hmong and Lisu, dropping to the Thai and T'in and finally to the Mlabri. In skeletal material from the Neolithic period of early Thailand and among living Negritos, the frequency of 5-cusped LM2 is also rather low, as shown in table 14.

Biological distances

In order to study the biological distances between the samples, the MMD were calculated between the Mlabri and the other groups. The distances were as follows:

Mlabri 1-Early Thai	0.04	Standard deviation	0.03
Mlabri 1-Negritos	0.10		0.03**
Mlabri 1-Hmong	0.10		0.03**
Mlabri 1-Thai	0.12		0.02**
Mlabri 1-Lisu	0.18		0.06**
Mlabri 1 – T'in	0.27		0.12**
Thai-Hmong	0.10		0.02**

Most of the distances were statistically significant and of the same magnitude for the three larger samples: the Mlabri, the Thai and the Hmong. Larger distances were observed between the Mlabri and the small samples Lisu and T'in.

It is of interest to point out that the distance between the Mlabri and the Neolithic Thai group is the only non-significant distance. The sample of early Thai is rather small but still suggests that the pattern of traits among the Mlabri is an old dental pattern. Also the similarity to the Philippine Negrito is remarkable. It can be concluded that the Mlabri possess the old Sundadont dental pattern. On the other hand, it cannot be concluded on the basis of this evidence alone that the Mlabri group has been an almost completely isolated group for 3-5,000 years (see further discussion p. 314). The similarity between the early Thai and the Mlabri could be coincidental, since the similarity among the samples is too uniform.

Data on Negritos and skulls from Early Thailand from T. Hanihara, 1992. The sample sizes are shown in parentheses. The Aeta tribe, Bataan Peninsula, Luzon, represent the Negritos. Early Thai skeletal material was excavated at the Ban Chieng site, Nong Han district of Udon Thani province in Northern Thailand. The material dates from the Metal Age (ca. 3000-6000 years B.P.).

Eleven dental traits are used for comparison of the Mlabri group with samples of Thai and Hmong. The Mlabri are similar to Thai in two traits, similar to Hmong in two traits and deviant from both in seven traits. The Mlabri group shows a number of reductions compared with the other samples.

Hanihara, 1991, has published dental data for Neolithic Thai and for Negritos. The early Thai individuals were excavated at Ban Chieng. Although the sample sizes are small, it is of interest to compare the Mlabri to such groups. The trait frequencies for the Mlabri have been made comparable to the data presented by Hanihara using a slightly different way of scoring the traits.

The comparison between the Mlabri and Early Thai indicates great similarity and so does the comparison with Negritos from the Philippines. The data taken at face value suggest that the Mlabri dentition is more

Dental trait	Scoring Technic	Mlabri 1		Percentage affected persons							
				Thai		Hmong		Lisu		T'in	
		N	%	N	%	N	%	N	%	N	%
Winging	1-2/0-4	45	22.2	94	17.0	39	30.8	12	50.0	9	30.8
Shovel	3-6/0-6	44	61.4	93	44.1	38	68.4	11	54.6	9	33.3
Db.shovelling UI1	2-6/0-6	39	17.7	94	28.7	20	25.0	9	11.1	10	20.0
Carabelli UM1	4-7/0-7	36	16.7	89	21.4	35	14.3	11	45.5	10	20.3
Hypocone UM2	3-5/0-5	39	66.7	82	76.8	37	73.0	11	100.0	10	100.0
Defl. wrinkle LM1	2-3/0-3	15	33.3	56	53.5	16	56.3	5	40.0	1	0.0
Seventh cusp LM1	1-4/0-4	36	0.0	84	17.9	22	4.6	11	0.0	11	11.8
Sixth cusp LM1	1-4/0-4	16	25.0	44	43.2	21	38.1	11	9.1	2	100.0
Fine cusps LM2	5/4-5	30	66.7	84	72.6	20	80.0	9	77.8	8	75.0
Lingual cusps LP2	2/1-3	30	36.7	88	35.2	43	44.1	11	36.4	10	40.0
Dist. acc. ridge LC	2-5/0-5	37	18.9	89	23.6	34	29.4	11	36.4	9	22.2

Table 13. Biological distances.

	Mlabri %	Negrittos %	Early Thai %
Shovel UI1 0.5-1.5 mm	7.7	66.6 (21)	73.1 (26)
Hypocone UM2 3+,4-,4	89.7	88.2 (17)	86.4 (44)
Carabelli UM1 5-7/0-7	17.0	25.0 (20)	18.6 (43)
Sixth cusp LM1	21.1	17.7 (17)	22.5 (40)
Seventh cusp LM1	0.0	11.8 (17)	0.0 (49)
Deflecting wrinkle LM1	33.3	17.7 (17)	42.9 (28)
Protostylid LM1	3.1	5.9 (17)	3.1 (32)
Four cusps LM2	33.3	58.8 (17)	57.1 (42)

Table 14. Comparison between Mlabri, Negritos and Early Thai.

similar to early Sundadont dentitions than to modern Sundadont dentitions. Even if this is true, it is not possible to say whether this is due to environmental conditions with influence on growth and development or to common genetic make-up.

Tooth size

The Mlabri teeth were compared with the tooth size in a Thai population from Chiengmai and a population of Australian aboriginals. The Mlabri teeth are rather small, and a few dimensions are significantly smaller than those of the Thai. Compared with the large-toothed Australian aboriginals, however, the Mlabri teeth are significantly smaller in most dimensions. The comparisons indicate once again that the Mlabri teeth belong to the Sundadont dentitions.

Maxilla Tooth	Males			Females		
	N	x	s.d.	N	x	s.d.
I1	15	8.3	0.54	9	7.86	0.39
I2	15	6.8	0.54	9	6.31	0.44
C	15	8.0	0.51	8	7.59	0.57
P1	16	7.2	0.55	9	7.04	0.60
P2	15	6.8	0.60	9	6.62	0.59
MI	16	10.4	0.52	9	10.09	0.56
M2	12	9.6	0.63	7	9.27	0.70
I1	18	5.34	0.37	7	5.06	0.36
I2	19	5.77	0.46	7	5.73	0.61
C	19	7.04	0.38	8	6.46	0.29
P1	20	6.95	0.32	8	6.95	0.48
P2	20	7.17	0.34	8	6.99	0.37
MI	17	11.82	0.57	7	11.11	0.71
M2	17	11.02	0.54	6	10.84	0.54

Table 15. Mesiodistal crown diameters of Mlabri (only teeth from the right side).

Tooth	Males (N= 35)		Females (N= 39)	
	x	s.d.	x	s.d.
I1	8.58	0.39	8.37	0.44
I2	7.08	0.48	7.02	0.46
C	8.03	0.45	7.70	0.36
P1	7.32	0.43	7.19	0.36
Maxilla P2	26.64	0.43	6.67	0.39
MI	10.46	0.54	10.34	0.50
I1	5.33	0.42	5.35	0.24
I2	6.03	0.54	5.92	0.26
Mandible C	7.11	0.45	6.75	0.34
PI	7.25	0.46	7.14	0.41
P2	7.16	0.46	7.08	0.39
MI	11.45	0.47	11.16	0.42

Table 16. Comparative odontometric data. Boondej and Sirinavin, 1990. Individuals of ethnic Northern Thai Origin.

Table 17. Mesiodistal crown diameters. Both sexes combined.

Tooth (Upper & Lower jaw)	Mlabri 1			Thai			Australian aborigines		
	N	x	s.d.	N	x	s.d.	N	x	s.d.
UI1	24	8.16	0.48	46	8.50	0.50	241	9.19	0.58
UI2	24	6.62	0.50	50	7.12	0.56	219	7.50	0.63
UC	23	7.86	0.53	52	7.84	0.48	164	7.62	0.49
UP1	25	7.14	0.57	52	7.35	0.40	184	7.62	0.44
UP2	24	6.73	0.60	50	6.75	0.35	179	7.11	0.44
UM1	25	10.29	0.53	54	10.38	0.52	224	11.14	0.51
UM2	19	9.48	0.66	53	9.68	0.60	161	10.51	0.60
LI1	25	5.26	0.37	46	5.49	0.29	253	5.78	0.42
LI2	26	5.76	0.50	46	6.13	0.41	242	6.49	0.42
LC	27	6.87	0.36	51	6.93	0.42	193	7.25	0.42
LP1	28	6.95	0.37	51	7.17	0.47	180	7.43	0.48
LP2	28	7.12	0.35	51	7.22	0.44	171	7.44	0.48
LM1	24	11.61	0.61	44	11.37	0.63	220	11.85	0.58
LM2	23	10.97	0.54	48	10.83	0.65	162	11.26	0.67

Tooth	Mlabri 1 – Thai	Mlabri 1 – Australian aboriginals
UI1	+ +	+++
UI2	+ +	+++
UC	—	+++
UP1	+	+++
UP2	—	+++
UM1	—	+++
UM2	—	+++
LU	+ +	+++
LI2	+++	+++
LC	—	+++
LP1	+	+++
LP2	—	+++
LM1	—	+
LM2	—	+

Table 18. - no significant difference, + significance on the 5% level, + + significance on the 1% level, and + + + significance level better than 0.1%.

F-tests were applied to the variances given in table 17. With one exception no differences were significant on the 1% level. The exceptions were found in the difference in variances between Mlabri and Thai for the upper second premolars. In this case there was no difference in the mean size, however, and no t-test was required.

3. The origin of the Mlabri based on odontological investigations

Some years ago Coon (1963) expressed the orthodox view that the Neolithic inhabitants of Southeast Asia were mainly a mixed group of Australoid and Mongoloid origin, with pockets of Negritos much more widespread than they are today. (Australoids according to Coon, p. 712: "One of the five subspecies of living man, including the native peoples of Australia, New Guinea, Melanesia; the Negroid dwarfs of Indonesia and South Asia; and certain aboriginal tribes of India"). More recent analyses of skeletal material from the Neolithic period have led to a modification of the hypothesis, i.e. Mongoloids rather than Austromelanesians were present in Southeast Asia during the Neolithic period and presumably much earlier (Turner 1990). Turner based his conclusions on dental trail analyses of 41 series of Sinodonts and Sundadonts plus a composite series of Australian aboriginals. His conclusions of interest also as regards the Mlabri are the following:

1. For at least 12,000 years both Sinodonts and Sundadonts have existed in East Asia. Sundadonts occupied mainland and island Southeast Asia and Sinodonts are hypothesized to have evolved out of the Sundadont condition, developing a more specialised and complex dental pattern in Northern China, Mongolia and Southeast Siberia.

2. Temporal changes in dental trait frequencies between early and later Malays, Thais and Laotians are, taken together, insubstantial and irregular. However, most temporal shifts that do occur are directional towards Sinodonty.

3. Australian aboriginals and Southeast Asians have remarkably similar frequencies for most of the eight traits used to distinguish between Sinodonts and Sundadonts. This similarity suggests that Sundadonts are an old group and evolved locally in South Asia.

4. Sundadonty is unlikely to be the product of admixture between an early Southeast Asian Australomelanesian population and southward migrating Mongoloids in Neolithic times. If this is so, Sundadonts represent the early Pleistocene stock from which many of the populations of East Asia, the Americas and Oceania evolved.

In other words, the older view is that Mongoloid invaders from the north mixed with the various populations in Southeast Asia. The more recent view is that Sunda-

donts evolved by local evolution in the Southeast Asian heartland (also called Sundaland). The autochthonous people in Southeast Asia, according to this view, probably had Sundadont dentitions rather than teeth resembling those of the Australian aborigines, and therefore mixtures between autochthone and newcomers from China and Burma would lead to a gradient in dental trait frequencies from South to North.

Negritos have, as far as is known, also Sundadont teeth (Hanihara 1991). There is evidence that Negritos were previously found also in regions of Thailand, Laos and Vietnam, that the Semangs just south of the Thai-Malaysian border are Negritos. This has also affected the Senoi – and therefore also the Mlabri. Comparison between the Mlabri teeth and those of Philippine Negritos show a fairly high degree of similarity. It is of the same or even shorter biological distance than the distances between Mlabri and the other hill tribes in Northern Thailand. Hanihara suggests that Negrito teeth are similar to the former Proto-Malay teeth out of which the Sundadont, the Australoid and the Sinodont dentitions evolved. The Mlabri teeth apparently look like 'primitive' Sundadont teeth.

The diversity among Mongoloid populations leading to the so-called Sinodont and Sundadont dentitions in Northern and Southeast Asia can be traced to the Neolithic period (Hanihara 1991 a.o.). The same dental traits are found in most human populations, but the frequencies vary. In Sinodont dentitions shovelling of the incisors is more frequent and more pronounced than in Sundadont dentitions. Other traits are also more common in Sinodont dentitions compared to Sundadont dentitions, and together they form a dental Sinodont morphological complex. A dental complex of the Australian aborigines can be defined which is related to, but still different from, the Sundadont and the Sinodont dental complexes.

Different opinions prevail as to the origin of the Mlabri. Most writers simply state that they are (predominantly) Mongoloid, and some suggest that they belong to remnants of autochtonous people (Boeles 1963). Gebhard Flatz, p. 171-175, in Kraisri Nimanahaeminda, 1963, having studied the matter more closely and referring to anthropometric measurements – blood tests, etc. – arrives at the conclusion that the Mlabri are Palaeomongolids of a human type found in Southeast Asia, which have not participated in adapting to the colder climates of inland Asia.

Trier on the whole agrees with these statements, but like Kerr 1924, p. 142-144, more specifically points to their similarities (see p. 246) with the Senoi, by some writers termed Proto-Malays, just south of the border between Thailand and Malaysia. He especially notices that, contrary to any of the other hill tribes in Northern Thailand, the Mlabri are the only people having been exclusively migrating hunter-gatherers until as late as the 1970s. Also their phenotype, material and social culture as well as their supernatural world are strikingly like those of the Senoi. Their transition to settling down (sedentism) and to undertaking other activities like farming, handicrafts, business, etc., is a major change for it implies planning and contacts with all kinds of people, in short a new kind of specialisation.

Dental traits are genetically determined, but depend, epigenetically, upon the activity of many gene products with influence on the timing and the velocity of growth in the developing tooth germ. In populations with a high frequency of the trait in its present state, it appears to be expressed in a dominant Mendelian gene with some variability of expression if the cusp varies in size. In other populations, where the trait is found with a lower frequency, the variability among families and among siblings might suggest that several genes with additive effect and environmental factors are involved. Experiments with animals have shown that the same dental trait can be caused by many different genetic and environmental factors.

Populations with a common history will show the same fluctuations and trends in tooth size and frequencies of dental traits through time. These can be explained only with reference to changes in the population structure (admixture, genetic drift) or major environmental changes.

Mlabri teeth are quite different from those of the Australian aborigines. Although both groups need strong and well functioning teeth, the fact is that the Mlabri teeth are of Sundadont size and significantly smaller and do not show a high frequency of supernumerary tubercles or cusps known to characterise the Australian aborigines.

Comparing the Mlabri to the Thai and Hmong presents a different problem. The multivariant analysis of the Mlabri teeth shows them to be significantly different from those of the present Sundadont Thai and Hmong. Studies of skeletal material from the Metal Age of Thailand have shown that Sundadont teeth existed here 3-4,000 years ago. In dental morphology, the Mlabri teeth are very similar to these early Thai dentitions. It means that the Mlabri tribe could very well be an autochthonous population. The few trait frequencies in Mlabri similar to the living Thai and Hmong could be due to gene flow by recent admixtures during the last few hundred years, since the mountain regions have been populated by agriculturalists.

Trier's comments:
First of all I would like to express my gratitude to Verner Alexandersen for his fine endeavours to collect and study relevant dental casts from many sources, including his own samples, as well as for his meticulous work in arriving at a comprehensible conclusion on what the dental material reveals.

In relation to what Alexandersen writes, above all at the very end of his report, that the dental similarities between the Mlabri and the Hmong, and especially the Thai, could be due to gene flow, I would like to draw attention to our findings on this important subject. Although the Mlabri's sexual links with their ever-changing neighbours seem to have been quite limited, we have nevertheless recorded quite a few such incidences between the Mlabri and the other hill tribes in Thailand and Laos, as well as with the Thai. Similar gene flows, albeit limited but crucial over time, might also have occurred much further back.

During our last three expeditions, my wife and I visited a number of lonely tracts along the border areas in easternmost Nan province towards the Laotian border. Here we were told that there had previously lived various groups of Mlabri who had intermarried with the local Thai population to the extent that they had now merged into their society, see also p. 223. Such large changes probably also occurred in other mountain tracts within recent centuries. These may explain why the observed differences in phenotypes are not more pronounced, especially between the Mlabri and rural Thai, but not including such specific old traits as those of the crania and, for example, the fingerprints. As mentioned above, it seems that there have been sexual connections between the various hill tribes and the Mlabri, but that the offspring of such liaisons have but rarely remained with the Mlabri.

Recent dental and genetic studies of Southeast Asian populations with relation to the Mlabri

My study of the Mlabri dental cast was completed in 1992. Since then a number of publications have discussed the origin of the Southeast Asian populations and the ongoing microevolutionary processes in the region. Studies of mt DNA, genes on the Y-chromosome and the autosomes have provided new information. According to Oota et. 2005:15, "the Mlabri, a present day group of hunters and gatherers, was founded recently and in all probability from an agricultural group". Besides this scenario, the genetic data also suggest that "the Mlabri were reduced from a formerly larger population to a much smaller population size, which then increased to the current level of about 300 individuals". Oota et al. prefer the first mentioned scenario, but admit that "the Mlabri are, indeed, quite different from the other Southeast Asian highland groups in that they never, in either their recorded or oral history, practised horticulture" (Stoneking et al. 2005). The bottleneck occurred, according to calculations by geneticists, some 500 to 1,000 years ago.

Recent dental studies using the same scoring techniques and analyses make it possible to place the results of my study of the Mlabri teeth in a larger context. The Mlabri group showed neither the Australoid dental pattern nor the proto-sundadont pattern, characterised by very large teeth, high frequencies of molars with maximum number of cusps and enamel folds.

On the contrary, Mlabri had sundadont teeth with greatest affinity to Turners' "Prehistoric Southeast Asia" group represented by samples dating mainly from the Neolithic Period (sites in Thailand, Kelantan, Tonkin, Malay Peninsula, Celebes and Java) Scott and Turner 1997), to recent Thai and Hmong (dental casts collected by Trier and Alexandersen). These MMD distances were practically the same. The closest affinity to early agriculturalists agrees with the hypothesis that the Mlabri, also in the past, had contact with populations with a culture involving horticulture.

The dental pattern cannot decide exactly when and how intimately the Mlabri had contact with horticulturalists. Besides focusing only on horticulturalists it seems relevant also to explore the close affinity to the Negritos.

It is worth mentioning that Turner, after scoring the dental traits in the Mlabri group during a visit to Copenhagen, placed the Mlabri sample in his large group of "Recent Southeast Asian" populations. Among the samples in this large group were Negritos and populations from the Southeast Mainland. "Dentally, the Negritos show closer affinity to other southeast Asian populations than to Australians and North Asians". The proto-Sundadont model (Turner, 1992, Hanihara, 1992) suggest-

ing a common thread underlying all Asian biological variation, is supported in its fundamental details by the genetic analysis of Nei and Roychoudhury (1993). By contrast, Cavalli-Sforza et al. 1994, support a genetic linkage between Southeast Asian and Australo-Melanesian population, but tie the North Asians more closely to Caucasoids. Such a relationship is contradicted by the dental evidence (Scott and Turner, 1997:285).

Close dental affinity between Negritos and other Southeast Asian populations suggests that the sundadont dentition is the original dental pattern in Southeast Asia in fact are modern survivors of ancient groups thus confirming the traditional view based on archaeology and physical anthropology (Macaulay et al. 2005).

An increasing number of researchers now agree that an early "southern route" of dispersal of Homo sapiens from the Horn of Africa took place 60,000 to 75,000 years ago along the tropical coast of the Indian Ocean to southeast Australasia. It has traditionally been suggested that a number of "relict" populations in northern India and southeast Asia and Australia are descendants of such an early dispersal. The inhabitants on the Andaman Islands undoubtedly belong to this old stratum. Matsumura, 2006, included a series of Andaman Islanders (N:69) in his study of dental variation among groups from the Neolithic Jomon period. MMD distances showed that the Andaman Islanders exhibited greatest affinities to Australo-Melanesians as well as to Prehistoric Southeast Asians. The large Prehistoric Southeast Asian group studied included samples from the Mainland and the Islands (Gua Cha, Guar Kepah, Middle Holocene Flores, Bac Son, Da But, Early Holocene Laos, Ban Kao (+Lue), Non Nok Tha and Khok Phanom Di). Several of these samples were also included in Turner's Prehistoric Southeast Asian samples with close affinity to the Mlabri.

Among the ancient groups are the aboriginal inhabitants of Malaysia, the Orang Asli. Their long history is confirmed by the study of mtDNA in 266 unrelated females by Macaulay et al. 2005. D. Bulbeck (Australian National University) and co-workers have studied tooth size and non-metric dental traits in three living Orang Asli populations: Semang, who until recently were nomadic hunter-gatherers, the Senoi, who are traditionally swidden agriculturalists, and Aboriginal Malays, who are horticulturalists and fishers. Especially the Semang are considered to be aboriginal inhabitants of the Malay Peninsula. As already suggested by Trier,

1988, both the Semang and Senoi are interesting groups to compare with the Mlabri.

It is necessary here to mention that agricultural techniques were introduced to Thailand and further south in 3,000-6,000 years BC and contact was established between agriculturalists and hunter-gatherers leading either to replacement or to transfer of new ideas to the latter. Matsumura and Hudson, 2004, used metric and non-metric dental data to test the "two-layer" or immigration hypothesis, whereby the early inhabitants underwent substantial genetic admixture with East Asian immigrants associated with the spread of agriculture from the Neolithic periods onwards. The immigration hypothesis was confirmed but the evidence was not always clear-cut. East Asian metric and/or non-metric traits are found in some prehistoric samples from Southeast Asia such as Ban Kao (Thailand) implying that immigration and contact between horticulturalists and hunter-gatherers probably began already in early Neolithic.

The changes in the dentitions of the original inhabitants could take many forms. The dental studies of the Orang Asli provide some examples. Rayner, 2000, studied the non-metric dental variation in groups of Semang, Senoi and Aboriginal Malays in the Malayan Peninsula. The frequencies of the non-metric dental traits differed between the three Orang Asli populations, but all were within the bounds of the sundadont dental pattern. The mandibular molars showed a simplified pattern in the Semang, while the mandibular molars showed an intensified pattern in the Senoi. The Aboriginal Malays conformed best to the early Thai (Mesolithic/Neolithic) and recent Thai groups studied by Turner and used for comparison by Rayner (Scott and Turner, 1977). The simplified molar pattern with fewer cusps and cusplets than expected for sundadonty showed similarity to the Mlabri and to the Philipine Aeta studied by Hanihara, 1992. The intensified molar pattern in the Senoi showed similarity to the pattern generally found in Australoid dentitions.

A multivariate discrimination analysis performed by Rayner demonstrated that in spite of the morphological differences between his three Malayan groups, it was not possible to place each individual in the right group by discrimination analysis. Only about 60% were assigned the right group.

Rayner, 2000, concludes that it is likely that Semang and Senoi are the descendent populations of two fairly distinct colonising events in the peninsula. This model is supported by Oota et al. 2005 based on comparison of genetic data from a few Mesolithic skeletons, recent Semang and Senoi. According to the genetic analysis the Semang could be representatives of the oldest stratum, the Senoi representatives of a later migration of people with Khmu language from the North, while a last migration is represented by the Malayans.

Tooth crown size in the hunter-foraging Semang was smaller than in the horticultural Senoi, while the largest teeth were found among the farming Aboriginal Malays (Bulbeck and Lauer, 2002). The Semang teeth corresponded almost exactly in size to the Mlabri teeth (both sexes combined). The only difference was the slightly larger molars in the Mlabri group. The Thai group in the present study by Alexandersen with relatively large teeth corresponding to those of the Aboriginal Malays. Hanihara and Ishida, 2005 studied the metric dental variation in 72 major human populations. They found that the Philipine Negritos had small teeth, and the Southeast Asians were intermediate in overall tooth size, while Australians and Melanesians had the largest teeth. The biological diversity among the recent Orang Asli groups makes sense because microevolutionary processes are at work from generation to generation. Migrations, admixture and genetic drift in small breeding populations modify the dental pattern and create diversity among recent populations as it did among ancient populations.

The dental studies cannot distinguish between the two possible origins of the Mlabri group: a founding event based on a horticultural population or a bottleneck in a population of hunter-gatherers. Microevolutionary forces are at work all the time and unexpected results might occur. This is evident from the fact that the Mlabri in at least one dental trait differ from the sundadont dental pattern and approach the sinodont pattern. The last few generations of Mlabri have been in contact with the Hmong and possibly other hill tribes. They are newcomers to the region and they have a dental pattern influenced by Chinese sinodonty. In shovel shape of permanent maxillary incisors the frequency in Mlabri is close to the frequency in the Hmong hill tribe, not to mention the few Yao individuals all with marked shovel shape (Alexandersen, table 3, this paper).

Manabe et al, 1997, also discussed the population history of hill tribes in Northern Thailand. They realised that the Thai tribe has lived in Northern Thailand longer than the Akha and the Yao tribes, which were the only hill tribes they studied. They assumed that sundadonty was distributed in early South China before the southward migration of the Thai tribe due to the pressure of the Chinese Yan dynasty. The Thai therefore show the sundadont dental pattern. The small amount of gene flow of sinodonty into the Akha, Yao and other hill tribes seemed to be later, more patchy and limited and, as we realise, detectable even in the Mlabri.

While the genetics estimated an origin of the present Mlabri M1 group to a founding event 500-1,000 years ago, we are almost certain that the Mlabri, as a hunter-gatherer population, have a longer history. The dental pattern cannot tell with certainty when it became established in Northern Thailand, but the dental similarity between the Mlabri and samples dating from Early Neolithic in the Southeast Asian region suggests that contacts with horticulturalists occurred from time to time over an extended period of time from the Early Neolithic.

Acknowlegements

Sincere thanks go to Dr. phil. Jesper Trier for stimulating my interest in the complicated population mosaic of Southeast Asia and in particular the elusive group of Mlabri.

Thanks to a grant from Kronprins Frederiks Fund a visit to Chiengmai was made possible for me in 1991. Contact was made with the WHO Intercounty Centre for Oral Health in Chiengmai. The Director at that time was Dr. Nitisiri Parakat, who organized the expedition to Nan province and helped collect the dental casts. Contact was also made with Dr. Sampan Srisuwan at the Dental Faculty of the Dental School of Chiengmai. Thanks to his great help I was given access to the collection of dental casts at the Department of Orthodontics, and Dr. Srisuwan also arranged for a visit to the Lisu tribe in Ban Chang in the Maitang district.

I also want to thank O. Carlsen, DDS, Head of the Department of Dental Morphology, at the University of Copenhagen, for valuable and stimulating discussions. For secretarial services I am greatly indebted to Birgit Holten.

References

Ahmad, Khamis. "In Search of the Mlabri." *Bangkok Post,* October 25, 1981.

Anderson, Edward F. *Plants and People of the Golden Triangle. Ethnobotany of the Hill Tribes of Northern Thailand.* Portland, Oregon: Dioscorides Press, 1993.

Bailit, H.L., DeWitt S.J. and R.A. Leigh "The size and morphology of the Nasioi dentition". *Amer.J.phys. Anthropol.* 28, 1968: 271-287.

Barrett, M.J.,T. Brown, and M.R. McDonald. "Dental Observations on Australian Aborigines: MD Crown Diameter of Permanent Teeth." *Australian Dental J* 8 (1963): 150-156.

Bell, Duran. "On the Nature of Sharing: Beyond the Range of Methodological Induvidualism." *Current Anthropology* 36, no. 5 (1995): 826-30.

Benjamin, G. and C. Chou, eds. *Tribal Communities in the Malay World.* Singapore: Institute of Southeast Asian Studies, 30 Heng Mui Keng Terrace: Pasir Panjang, 2002.

Benjamin, Geoffrey. "On being Tribal in the Malay World." In *Tribal Communities in the Malay World*, edited by Geoffrey Benjamin and Cynthia Chou, 7-77. P.O. Box 9515. 2300 RA Leiden: International Institute of Asian Studies, 2002.

Bernatzik, Hugo A. *Die Geister Der Gelben Blaetter.* München: Bruckmann, 1938. English translation: *The Spirit of the Yellow Leaves; with an Introduction, Linguistic Analysis of the Mlabi, and a Bibliography by Jørgen Rischel.* London: Robert Hale Ltd, 1951. French translation: *Les Esprits des feuilles jaunes.* Paris: Plon, 1955.

Birdsell, J.B. *Human Evolution.* 2. edit. Rand McNally, 1975.

Booles, J.J. "Second Expedition to the Mrabri of North Thailand (Khon Pa)." *Journal Siam Society* 51, no. 2 (1963): 133-160.

Boondy, A. and I. Sirinavin. "Permanent tooth size in Northern Thai with normal occlusion and soft tissue function". *Chieng Mai Dental J.* 11 (1990): 78-86.

Bourke-Borrowes, D. "Further Notes on the Phi Tong Lu'Ang." *Journal Siam Society* 20, no. 2 (1926): 167-196.

Bourke-Borrowes, D.: "Further Notes on the Phi Tong Lu'ang", *Journal Siam Society.* Vol. 20, pt. 2, (1926): 166-167.

Brace, C.L. Hinton. "Oceanic tooth-size variation as a reflection of biological and cultural mixing". *Current Anthropologi* 22 (1981): 549-569.

Brandt, John J. "The Negritto of Peninsular Thailand." *Journal Siam Society* 49, no. 2 (1961): 123-158.

Chou, Cynthia and Vivienne Wee. "Tribality and Globalization, the Orang Suku Laut and the Growth "Triangle" in a Contested Environment." In *Tribal Communities in the Malay World*, edited by Geoffrey Benjamin and Cynthia Chou, 7-77. P.O. Box 9515. 2300 RA Leiden: International Institute of Asian Studies, 2002.

Coon, Carleton S. with Edward E. Hunt, Jr. *The Living Races of Man.* New York: Alfred A. Knopf, 1965.

Coon, Carleton S. *The Origin of Races.* London: Jonathan Cape, 1962.

Cuisinier, Jeanne. *"Les Müöng". Gèographie humaine et Sociologie.* Travaux et mémoires de l'Institut d'Ethnologie / Université de Paris; 44. Paris, 1946.

Cummings, Joe. *Thailand, a Travel Survival Kit.* Hawthorn: Lonely Planet Publications, 1990.

Dentan, Robert K. "Ambiguity, Synecdoche and Affect in Semai Medicine." *Soc. Sci. Med.* 27, no. 8 (1988): 857-877.

Dentan, Robert K. "Band-Level Eden: A Mystifying Chimera." *Cultural Anthropology* (1988): 276-283.

Dentan, Robert K. "Lucidity, Sex, and Horror in Senoi Dreamwork." In *Conscious Mind, Sleeping Brain*, edited by Jayne Gackenbach and Stephen LaBerge, 37-63 Plenum Publ. Corp., 1988.

Dentan, Robert K. "The Mammalian Taxonomy of the Sen'oi Semai." *Malayan Nature Journal* 20 (1967).

Dowling, John H. "Individual Ownership and the Sharing of Game in Hunting Societies." *American Anthropologist* New Series 70, no. 3 (June 1970): 502-507.

Egerod, Søren and Jørgen Rischel. "A Mlabri-English Vocabulary." *Acta Orientalia* 48, (1987).

Endicott, Kirk Michail. *An Analysis of Malay Magic.* Oxford: Clarendon Press, 1970.

Enoki, K. and A.A. Dahlberg. "Rotated maxillary central incisors". *Orthodontic J. of Japan.* 17 (1958): 157-59.

Farland, Mac and B. George. *Thai-English Dictionary.* London, 1956.

Flatz, Gebhard. "Anthropometric, Genetic and Medical Examination." *Journal Siam Society* 51, no. 2 (1963): 161-177.

Fraisse, A. "Les Sauvages De La Nam-Om." *BSEI.* XXIV-1 (1949): 27-36.

Guignard, T. "Note sur une peuplade des montagnes du Quang-Binh: les Tac-Cui." *B.E.F.E.O.* (1911): 201-205.

Gurven, Michael, Kim Hill, and Hillard Kaplan. "From Forest to Reservation: Transisitions in Food-Sharing Behavior among the Ache of Paraguay." *Journal Siam Society* 58, no. 1 (2002): 93-112.

Hamilton, A. "Tribal People on the Southern Thai Border: Internal Colonialism, Minorities, and the State." *Malayan Nature Journal* 20, (1967).

Hanihara, K. "Racial characteristic in the dentition". *Journal of Dental Research.* Suppl.to No. 5 46 (1967): 923-926.

Hanihara, T. "Dental and cranial affinities among populations of East Asia and the Pacific: The basic populations in East Asia", *V. Amer.J.phys.Anthrop.* 88 (1992): 163-182.

Hanihara, T. "Negritos, Australian Aborigines, and the "Proto-Sundadont" dental pattern". The basic populations in East Asia. *V. Amer.J.phys.Anthrop.* 88 (1992): 183-196.

Hanihara, T. "Population prehistory of East Asia and the Pacific as viewed from craniofacial morphology: The basic populations in East Asia". *VII. Amer.J.phys.Anthrop.* 91 (1993): 173-187.

Heinze, Ruth-Inge. *Tham Khwan. How to Contain the Essence of Life. A Socio-Psychological Comparison of a Thai Custom.* Singapore University Press, 1982.

"The Hill Tribes of Thailand / by Technical Service Club, Tribal Research Institute." 1-52, 1989.

Keer, A.F.G. "The Ka Tawng Luang." *Journal Siam Society* 18 no. 2 (1924): 142-144, in Ethnological Notes.

King, Victor T. and W.D. Wilder. *The Modern Anthropology of South-East Asia: An Introduction.* London, New York: Routledge, 2003.

Lebar, Frank M., Gerald C. Hickey, and John K. Musgrave. *Ethnic Groups of Mainland Southeast Asia.* New Haven: Human Relations Area Files Press, 1964.

Lindell, Kristina, Jan Öjvind Swahn, and Damrong Tayanin. "Folk Tales from Kammu – III, Pears of Kammu Literature." *Monograph Series* 51 (1981).

Matisoff, J.A. In *Highlanders of Thailand*, edited by J. KcKinnon and B. Wanat, p. 65. Kuala Lumpur: Oxford University Press, 1983.

Mayhall, J.T., Saunders, S.R. and P.L. Belier. "The dental morphology of North American Whites. a reappraisal". In *Teeth, Form, Function and Evolution,* edited by B. Kúrten, pp. 245-58. Columbia University Press, 1982.

Mizoguchi Y. *Shovelling: A statistical analysis of its morphology.* University of Tokio, 1985.

Nimmanahaeminda, Kraisri. "The Mrabri Language." *Journal Siam Society* 50, no. 2 (1963): 179-183 with appendices.

Nimmanahaeminda, Kraisri and Julian Hartland-Swann. "Expedition to the Khon Pa (Or Phi Tong Luang)." *Journal Siam Society* 50, no. 2 (1962): 165-186.

O'Connor, J. D. *Phonetics.* London: Penguin Books, Hazell Watson & Viney Limited, 1973.

Olivier, Georges. "Anthropologie De l'Indochine." In *Rassengeschichte des Menschheit*, 25-108. München: R. Oldenbourg, 1968.

Oota, H., B. Pakendorf, G. Weiss, A. von Haesler, et al.: *Recent Origin and Cultural Reversion of a Hunter.Gatherer Group* (2005). http://biology.plosjournals.org/perlserv/?request=get-document&doi=10.1371/journal.pbio.0030071

Pookajorn, Surin and Staff. *The Phi Tong Luang (Mlabri): A Hunter-Gatherer Group in Thailand.* Bangkok: Odeon Store, 1992.

Rajadhon, Phya Anuman. *Essays on Thai Folklore.* Bangkok: The Social Science Association Press of Thailand, 1968.

Rischel, Jørgen. *Minor Mlabri, A Hunter-Gatherer Language of Northern Indochina.* Copenhagen: Museum Tusculanum Press, 1995.

Rischel, Jørgen. "Can the Khmuic Component in Mlabri (Phi Tong Luang) be Identified as Old T'in." *Acta Orientalia* 50 (1989a): 79-115.

Rischel, Jørgen. "Fifty Years of Research on the Mlabri Language. A Reappraisal of Old and Recent Fieldwork Data." *Acta Orientalia* 50 (1989a): 49-78.

Rischel, Jørgen and S. Egerod. "Yumbri (Phi Tong Luang) and Mlabri." *Acta Orientalia* 48 (1987): 19-33.

Schebesta, Poul. *Orang-Utan. Bei den Urwaldmenschen Malayas und Summatras.* Leipzig: F.A. Brochaus, 1928.

Seidenfaden, Erik. *The Thai Peoples.* Bangkok: The Siam Society, 1958.

Seidenfaden, Erik. "The Kha Tong Lu'Ang." *Journal Siam Society* 20, no. 1 (1926): 41-48.

Seidenfaden, Erik. "Further Notes about the Chaubun, etc." *Journal Siam Society* 13, no. 3 (1919): 49-51.

Service, Elman R. *The Hunters.* New Jersey, 1966.

Sjøvold, T. "The Occurrence of Minor Non-Metrical Variants in the Skeleton and their Quantitative Treatment of Population Comparisons." *Homo* 24, (1973): 294-233.

Skeat, Walter W. and Charles O. Blagden. *Pagan Races of the Malay Peninsula.* Vol. 2 London: Macmillan, 1906.

Smalley, William A. "Notes on Kraisri's Word Lists." *Journal Siam Society* 51, no. 2 (1963): 189-201.

Srisavasdi, Boon C. *The Hill Tribes of Siam.* Bangkok: Khun Aroon, 1963.

Suebsaeng, Nipatwet. "The Mlabri Family and Kinship System." In *The Phi Tong Luang (Mlabri): A Hunter-Gatherer Group in Thailand*, edited by Surin and Staff Pookajorn, 75-91. Bangkok: Odeon Store, 1992.

Thongkum, Theraphan L. "The Language of the Mlabri (Phi Tong Luang)." In *The Phi Tong Luang (Mlabri): A Hunter-Gatherer Group in Thailand*, edited by Surin Pookajorn, 43-65. Bangkok: Odeon Store, 1992.

Townsend, G.M.H. Yamada and P. Smith. "Expression of the entoconulid (sixth cusp) on mandibular molar teeth of an Australian aboriginel population." *Amer.J.phys.Anthrop.* 82 (1990): 267-74.

Turner II, C.G., C.R. Nichol and G.R. Scott. "Scoring procedures for key morphological traits of the permanent dentition: The Arizona State University dental anthropology system." In *Advances in Dental Anthropology. Wiley-Liss,* edited by M.A. Kelly and C. Spencer Larsen, 13-31. New York 1991.

Turner II, C.G. "Major features of Sundadonty and Sindodonty, including suggestions about East Asian microevolution, population history and Late Pleistocene relationships with Australian aboriginals". *Amer.J.phys. Anthrop.* 82 (1990): 295-317.

Turner H.C.G. "Late pleistocene and holocene population history of East Asia based on dental variation". *Amer. J.phys.Anthrop.* 73 (1987): 305-321.

Trier, J. "Article Revised: The Mlabri People: Social Organization and Supernatural Beliefs." In *The Highland Heritage, Collected Essays on Upland North Thailand*, edited by Anthony R. Walker, 225-265, 1992.

Trier, J. "The Mlabri People of Northern Thailand: Social Organization and Supernatural Beliefs." In *Contributions to Southeast Asian Ethnography*, edited by Anthony R. Walker. Vol. 5, 3-41, 1988.

Trier, J. "The Khon Pa of Northern Thailand." *Current Anthropology* 22, no. 3 (1981).

Weaver, Robert W. *Natural History* (June 1956): 289-296.

Winit Wanadorn, Phra. "Some Information Concerning the 'Phi Tawng Luang' obtained from a Few Residents of a Village in the Nam Wa District, East of Nan." *Journal Siam Society* 20, no. 2 (1926): 171-174.

Young, Gordon. *The Hill Tribes of Northern Thailand.* Bangkok: The Siam Society, 1962.

Index

candles in ceremony, 156, 163
cannibals, M7 allegedly once, 210
caries, seldom previously, fig. 40
carrying ill or destitute, cause bad luck, 156
caves, M1 avoid, 74
caves, M3 above Dan Sai, Loi province,
   said to have stayed in, 1950s, 87
celebrations, few among Mlabri, 37
charcoal, paint body ceremonies, 156
   trees burned around graves (M1), 163
chicken, vitality to newborn, 147
chiefs, institutional none, 25
climbing trees, figs. 51, 52, 55,
colour perception deficiency, none in Mlabri, fig. 43
colours in ceremonies, 156
colours little used in language, 94
communists fighting with Thai police, fig. 8
comparisons with Bernatzik's material on
   spiritual world, pointing to M1, 79-80
connections with hill tribes slight until 1980s, 21
contrapuntal songs, M1, figs. 32-34, 36
cotton string, tie volatile soul, 156
creepers of rattan, lianas creating headache
   various measures to avoid, 75, 127-128
crimes, no examples of, 25
crises, to counteract, 72-73
critically ill hoisted up into tree, 190
crocodile, connection with dragon spirit, 73
cultivating plants, Mlabri taboo, 49

day and jai, ancestral giants, 76
daily routine, M1, 48
daily routine, M3, 50
dəkat, "ghost", 79
dance, M1 first time it rains, 202
dancing and singing, M1 fig. 32-36

dangers, qualifying spirits, 70
dead persons, disposal of, 162-163
designs on utensils similar to those of
   Orang Asli northernmost Malaysia, 49
developments 20th century, M1, 50
diet, M1, 48
digging stick, M3, fig. 73,
ding-roy naming system, indicating
   person older or younger than speaker, 41
ding bɛr, roy bɛr or older and younger
   relative, relations through marriage, 41
disable, immobile taking poison, fig. 88
disagreements among M1, 25
division of work, M1, 49
division of work, M3 almost none, 50
divorce, M1, frequent, 38
domestic animals, none, 140-141,
   except: dogs M1 also having names, 42, 218
drawings by Mlabri, figs. 42, 160-187:
   M1, figs. 160-181; M3, figs. 182-183
   M4, figs. 184, 186-187; M5, fig. 185
dreams, meaning of, 69

eagles, may carry soul away, 77
earth spirit, causing illness, 76
eating leaves, M3, fig. 60,
economic life, daily routine, M1, 48-49
   hunting and gathering, M3, 50
eggs, in ceremonies for newborn, 147
elephants, hunted by M1 in 1950s, 70
ethical issues, 6
evidence of Mlabri isolation, 239
evil persons, 77

"fairy tales" pho tak, 214
falling trees, sign of spirits being angry, 109
families M1, number 19,
   kinship diagrams:
   M1: figs. 45, 46; M3: fig. 47
   M1 constitutes one interrelated family, 47
family of spirits, e.g. celestial bodies, 71
Ferlus, M3 meeting Oy 1964, 22, 223
fights, M1-farmers Ban Thako 1970, 191
   spear from incidents, fig. 313, no. 30,
fingerprints M1, 23, fig. 41;
fingerprints M3, 24
fire, making of, M1, fig. 58; M3, fig. 76
   its spirit, wɔk 'ohl, causing burns, 75
Flatz, G. in J.J. Booles, 1963:
   physical examination, M1, 239
flutes for signalling and music, fig. 60
food consumption, 1970-2000, M1, 51
forest spirit ordered Mlabri not to cultivate
   land or tame animals, except dogs, 74
forging iron, fig. 58; 48-49
formidable climbers, figs. 48, 51, 52, 55
fruit trees jungle, owner cut family symbol, 201

genetic studies, Palaeolithic and Neolithic
   Southeast Asians, mitochondrial DNA, 244

Maps

Group Year	No. Locality	Coordinates	Group Year	No. Locality	Coordinates
Expedition 1970:			**1982 (continued)**		
M1, 1950	01 B. Pa Miang Mae Prik	99°36'E, 19°39'N	M4, 1982	41 B. Pa Gang	100°55'E, 19°07'N
M1, 1945	02 Wiang Pa Pao	99°31'E, 19°21'N	M1, 1982	42 B. Kaeng Laeng,Loei prov.	101°17'E, 17°23'N
M1, 1955	03 B.Wiang Pa Pao & Prao	99°22'E, 19°22'N	M5, 1982	43 B. Na Luang, Loei prov.	101°35'E, 17°19'N
M1, 1967	04 Mae Laeng	99°37'E, 18°35'N	M5, 1924	44 B. Si Tan, Phu Kradung	101°52'E, 16°53'N
M1? 1955	05 Lekko	98°15'E, 18°18'N	M5, 1982	45 B. Kok Ngam, Loei prov.	101°15'E, 17°22'N
M1, 1955	06 15 km SW ChomTong	98°35'E, 18°20'N	M5, 1975	46 B. Phi. Thong Luang, –"–	101°28'E, 16°55'N
M1, 1950	07 B. Mae Ta Lao	99°36'E, 19°34'N	**Expedition 1987:**		
M1, 1950	08 Hui Pong Men	99°34'E, 19°25'N	M3, 1950	47 Salai, T'in village	101°18'E, 19°04'N
M1, 1954	09 B. Tha Ko	99°28'E, 19°30'N	M1, 1942	48 B. Pang Kae	100°59'E, 19°24'N
M1, 1950	10 B. Doi Pang	99°41'E, 19°50'N	M1, 1957	49 B. Nam Sang (Laos)	101°18'E, 18°57'N
M1, 1964	1 West of Amphur Pong	101°09'E, 19°09'N	M1, 1947	50 B. Maeo Kiu Na	101°08'E, 18°46'N
M1, 1958	12 B. Pak Pok	99°48'E, 19°06'N	M1, 1947	51 B. Tong	101°02'E, 18°51'N
M1, 1955	13 B. Pak Ma O	99°46'E, 19°01'N	M1, 1947	52 Nam Xong (Laos)	101°20'E, 18°53'N
M1, 1950	14 B. Pa Miang	99°46'E, 19°07'N	M3, 1987	53 B. Ton Praiwan	101°07'E, 18°50'N
M1, 1967	15 near B. Pua	99°46'E, 19°04'N	M5, 1967	54 B. Hui Hia, Loei prov.	101°17'E, 17°19'N
M1, 1954	16 near B. Kao Kleung	100°07'E, 18°37'N	M5, 1977	55 B. Pa Wai, Loei prov.	101°02'E, 17°00'N
M1, 1955	17 B. Mae San	99°46'E, 18°38'N	M1, 1980	56 Dan Sai, Loei prov.	101°09'E, 17°17'N
M1, 1970	18 B. Pa Hung	100°31'E, 18°35'N	M1, 5 1980	57 Amphoe Na Haeo,Loei	101°04'E, 17°29'N
M1, 1970	19 B. Kum	100°28'E, 18°34'N	M1, 1977	58 B. Na Klai, Loei prov.	101°52'E, 17°14'N
M3, 1940	20 B. N.W. Chiang Khong	100°21'E, 20°19'N	M3, 1970	59 Phu Nam Taen, Loei prov.	101°06'E, 17°18'N
M3, 1945	21 B. Chiang Dao & Fang	99°10'E, 19°34'N	M3, 1955	60 B. Lum Kao	101°14'E, 18°51'N
M3, 1948	22 Mae Kong meet Tha	100°05'E, 20°22'N	M1, 1987	61 B. Hui Yok at Doi Luang	100°34'E, 18°49'N
M2, 1970	23 Sa Police station	100°45'E, 18°34'N	M3, 1987	62 B. Kio Ko	100°58'E, 18°21'N
Expedition 1977:			M3, 1987	63 B. Na Luang	100°47'E, 18°51'N
M1, 1970	24 B. Na Ka	100°27'E, 18°42'N	M1, 1960	64 B. Pang San	100°42'E, 19°31'N
M1, 1977	25 B. Bow Hoi	100°27'E, 18°30'N	M1, 1980	65 Doi Pha Chik	100°28'E, 19°05'N
M1? 1962	26 B. Mai, Lissu	99°30'E, 20°04'N	M1, 1957	66 B. Luang	100°18'E, 18°45'N
M3, 1977	27 B. Nam Yao	100°97'E, 19°00'N	M1, 1987	67 B. Song Kwer	100°39'E, 18°50'N
Expedition 1978:			M1, 1987	68 near B.Yao N.W. of Nam	100°47'E, 18°51'N
M1, 1927	28 Doi Sathan	100°29'E, 18°16'N	M1, 1987	69 B. Nam Oun	100°34'E, 18°32'N
M7, 1955	28 Doi Sathan	100°29'E, 18°16'N	**Expedition 1989:**		
M1, 1950	29 Doi Pa Tung	98°36'E, 19°33'N	M6, 1989	70 big lake, Udon, Laos	102°21'E, 18°49'N
M3, 1950	30 Muang Piang, Sayabouri	100°97'E, 19°00'N	M3, 1965	71 B. Nam Phang	101°08'E, 18°35'N
Expedition 1980:			M1, 1989	72 Hui Nam Yu	100°28'E, 18°29'N
M1, 1980	31 B. Po Keng	100°30'E, 19°43'N	M7, 1986	73 east of B. Suman	101°16'E, 18°49'N
M1, 1980	32 B. Hui Hom	100°28'E, 18°14'N	M3, 1964	74 Nam San, Laos	101°29'E, 19°17'N
M3, 1940	33 B. Mae Salim	100°59'E, 18°23'N	**Expedition 1994:**		
M3, 1945	34 Doi Phu Wae	100°09'E, 19°19'N	M3, 1994	75 Kao Lao Leng	101°20'E, 19°12'N
Expedition 1982:			M3, 1964	76 B. Nam Mim (Laos)	101°15'E, 19°16'N
M1, 1982	35 B. Megafai	100°16'E, 18°31'N	M7, 1930	77 Nam Wa, Doi Phu Khe	101°13'E, 19°19'N
M1, 1982	36 B. Huyak	100°30'E, 18°42'N	M1, 1938	78 between Phu Khe & Doi Lo	101°14'E, 19°17'N
M1, 1962	37 Doi Pu Wo	100°38'E, 19°22'N	M?, 1993	79 B. Na Plaek	101°12'E, 19°26'N
M1, 1982	38 B. Huai Oiy	100°26'E, 18°13'N	M7, 1987	80 Maeo Laeo La, Nam Tuang	101°41'E, 18°53'N
M4, 1982	39 B. Nam Uan	101°01'E, 19°02'N			
M4, 1982	40 Doi Po Ka	101°13'E, 19°11'N	**Abbreviations**: B.: Ban; prov.: province		

Ban Hua Dong Ban Mae Suai Tai Ban Yang
Ban Ton San Ban Mae Sun Luang Ban Pratu Lo Mae La Ban Tha Sai 667
Ban Mae Ngon Khi Lek Ban Pa Sang M1 50, 10 Ban Yang
Ban Hua Fai Ban Musoe Ban Tha Ma O Ban Huai Sak Ban Ton Khuang
Ban Mae Khi Ban Pa Sak 422
Ban Mae Khi Ban Pong Sali Ban Cham Bon Thoeng
Nong Bia Ban Haen Ngum Mae Suai Ban Huai Muang Ban Pa Tung Nong Pet Ban Pa Yang
Lo Pa Han M3 45, 21 Ban Musoe Ban Huai Dok Un M1 50 -55, 01 Ban Hon
Ban Tham Klaeb Ban Thung Tom M1 67, 04 Phan PB
Ban Yang Ban Musoe M1 70, 07 TUNG Ban Pa Daeng Ban Mae Phung
ac Ping Khong M1 54, 09 M1 50, 29 1453
Ban Pang Tun Ban Rong Maet
Ban Pong Men Ban Pu Kaeng
Ban San Sai M1 50, 08 Ban Huai Ya
iang Dao Phrao Waing Pa Pao Ban Pha Wi Ban Khok Mu Ban Huai Kang Chun
Mae Na M1 55, 03 M1 45, 02 Ban Tha Ton Hat Ban Mae Wang Chang
Sop O Nok NB Ban Pa Chong Riang Ban Mae Wang Chang
i Tat Ban Buak Tao Ban Thung Pi Ban San Pa Sak
Man Ban Mae Hang Ban Rong Ha
ang Ban Mae Pang Ban Mae Khachan M1 67, 15 Phayao Dok Kham Tai M1 64, 11
ang Ban Mae Chedi M1 62, 13
842 Ban Thung Daeng M1 58, 12 Ban Wat Rong Khok
Si Ngam Ban Luang Ban Sop Pong
KHAO PHA DAENG Ban Huai Khian
Ban Khun Lao M1 ca. 1960 Ban Huai Kot 950 Ban Tha Fa Tai
Ban Pa Sak Ban Pang Haen
Ban Mae Song Tai
Rih Ban Thung Phung Ban Song Sop
Ban Sala Pang Sak Ban Ton Ngun Ban Yang (1) Ban Phaet
San Sai Ban Mai M1 50, 14 Ban Kho
Ban Kiu Ban Thung Hang Ban Rong
CHIANG MAI Ban Kuam Ban Thung Kha Ban Yang (2)
Ban On Luai Ban Mae Mae Ban Yang (3)
Ban On Noi Ban Du Ban Mai Ta Noi Ban On
Ban Thung San Ban Yangi Ngao
Chae Hom Ban Yao
Ban Thung Bom 975
Ban Tha Mon Ban Pa Ko Ban Huat M1 54/69, 16
Ban Mae Kong Pin M1, 53, 17 Ban Dok Kham Tai
1016 Ban Pang Kho
LAMPHUN Ban Dua 274 Ban Pu Choi Ban Pang La Ban Rat
Ban Huai Peng Ban Sop Khoi Ban Wang D
Ban Pang Kha Ban Sop Long Song
ROT FAI SAI Ban Long Kok Ban Cham Pui Ban Lu
THANG NORTHERN LINE Ban Sop Fuang Ban Tha Si Ban Tha Ban Huai Kho
622 Mae Tha Ban Cham Bon Ban Hat Ban Thun
Nam Mae 11 Ban Huai Hi Ban Huai Nam Khem Ban Ton Nu
NA Ban Mae Kong Nua Ban Pong Taen
Ban Kham 103
Mae Luang Ban Paen Ban Pong
859 Hang Chat Ban Pa Kho
Bang Yang Mae Liang LAMPANG 515
Ban Mae Phung Ko Kha Ban Mae Tha Ban Pha Maeo Ban Pha Mok Ban Suan Sak
Mae Kiap

Ban Houaychang
Ban Houayfuang
Ban Lao Choi
Ban Rangha
Ban Don Lom
Ban Yao
Muang Khop
Ban Lem
Ban Sontuang
Ban Pha Lat
Ban Cham Tong
Ban Maeo Chu Kua
Ban Maeo Long Hao
wang
Hae
Ban Dai Chi
Ban Lao Ri
Tong
Nong Bua
Ban San Kiang
Ban Huai Kwao
DOI KRATHING
Ban Sob Pua
Ban Hok
Ban Sob Khun
1955
Ban Huai Hai
Ban Ngun Pi
Ban Sen Louang
Ban Houaykhong
Menam Khong (Mekong)
Ban Khok Ek
Ban Houay Neo
Ban Khmou
Muang Hongsa
Ban Phalanc
Ban Kang
Ban Xianglom
Ban Khon
Ban Yao San Kiang
Ban Khing
Ban Xianghon
Ban Nam Sip
Ban Huai Kon
Kha-mu Ban Pon
Ban Pong Tom (Yao)
Ban Pop Ho
PHU SAM SAO
Ban Dong
Ban Yao Khun Ngop
QB
Ban La Sa
Ban Na So
M1 ca. 1915,
Ban Samet
Ban Huai Sa Lao
Ban Salung
M? 93, 79
M3 ca. 1940
Ban Song Khwae
Ban Dan
M1 42, 48 un Nam Nan
Nam Houng
Ban Lang
M1 62, 37
Ban Don Kaeo
M3 45, 34
Ban Si Udom
M7 30, 77
Ban Maeo Khun Nam Wa
Ban Nala
M1 38:78 Rai
Ban Thana
Ban Don Thaen
M3 64, 76
XAIGNABOURI (SAYABOURY)
Ban Pa Liu
Ban Maeo Huai Ti
M3 94, 75
Tiu
Pua
Rai Oi
Ban Khuang Thoi
M3 82, 41
Ban Khun Khwang
Ban Muang Lim
M4 82,40
Ban Tap
Muang Phiang
M3 77, 27
M3 50, 47
M3 50, 30
M1 80, 65
M3 82,39
Ban Houayhian
M3, 1945
Ban Huai Sine
Ban Na Kun
Ban Na Kok
Ban Hou Na
Ban Kok
M1 1938
Ban Na Khem
Ban Pang Phu Duang
M1 57;49
M1 87, 68
M1 87, 67
Ban Na Man
Ban Huai Pu
Ban Houay Louang
M1/M7 55 & 86, 52
Ban Muang Luang
M3 87, 63 uang Chang Tai
Ban Tong
M1 87, 61
Ban Mai
M1 47, 51
M7 87, 80
Ban Lao
Ban Si Niang
Ban Hua Wiang Nua
M3 87, 53
M7 86, 73
Ban Na Khou
Ban Pha
NAN
Ban Phae
Ban Na Mo
M1 88, 31
Ban Laeng
Ban Na Khoi
Ban M1 47, 50
Ban Na Ka
M1 82, 36
Ban Na Fang
Ban Na Kha
Ban Tiang Ling
M1 70,76, 24
Ban Na Dua
Ban Muang Fai
Ban Na Koua
QA
Ban Thung Phong
Ban Nam Phang Nua
Ban Namoun
Ban Khok Pha
M3 65, 71
Ban Nam Rong
Ban Nong
M2 70, 23
Ban Huai Ro
M7? 1980
QA
Muang Pa
Ban Kum
Sa
M1 70, 18 M1 87, 69
Ban Son Loi
Ban Nam Pu
Ban Pang Min
77, 25
Ban Khaem
M1 89, 72
i Tun
Ban Pha Hang
Ban Huai
Ban Sang Mai
Ban H Khuei
101
Ban Rong Proi
DOI KHON KAEN
Muang Thong
Ban Pauy Khou Lao
M3 40, 33
Ban Na Fai
Ban Kok
Na Noi
Ban Huai Lao
Ban Houaykha
M7 1955 & 67
Ban Nam Lom
M3 87, 62
Muang Va
M1 1927, 28
Ban Phun Noi
Ban Namxong
M1 80:32
Ban Hua Thung
R PHONH
Ban Mo
Ban Na Thanung
Ban Pha Nang
PAK-LAY
Ban Phouai

Invoking the Spirits

© Jesper Trier and Jutland Archaeological Society

ISBN 978-87-88415-47-6
ISSN 0107-2854

Jutland Archaeological Society Publications Vol. 60

Layout: Louise Hilmar
Cover: Louise Hilmar
English revision: Peter Crabb & Anne and David Robinson
Photographs: Jesper Trier
Drawings: Jesper Trier
Printed by Narayana Press
Paper: Hello Silk 130 g

Published by:
Jutland Archaeological Society
Moesgaard
DK-8270 Højbjerg

in association with
Moesgaard Museum

Distributed by:
Aarhus Univerity Press
Langelandsgade 177
DK-8200 Aarhus N

Published with financial support of:

DRONNING MARGRETHES OG PRINS HENRIKS FOND
HØJESTERETSSAGFØRER C.L. DAVIDS LEGAT FOR SLÆGT OG VENNER
LILLIAN OG DAN FINKS FOND
MINISTRY OF SCIENCE TECHNOLOGY AND INNOVATION
BODIL PEDERSEN FONDEN
VELUX FONDEN
ØK'S ALMENNYTTIGE FOND